W9-CNS-858

COMPARING THEORIES
OF CHILD DEVELOPMENT

R. Murray Thomas
University of California
Santa Barbara

Wadsworth Publishing Company, Inc.
Belmont, California

Library of Congress Cataloging in Publication
Data

Thomas, Robert Murray.
    Comparing theories of child development.

    Bibliography: p.
    Includes indexes.
    1. Child psychology. I. Title.
BF721.T456   155.4'01   78-9051
ISBN 0-534-00591-8

to Shirley

ACKNOWLEDGMENTS

We wish to thank the following for permission to use various excerpts and illustrations.

Alston, W. P. "Comments on Kohlberg's 'From Is to Ought' " in T. Mischel, *Cognitive Development and Epistemology*. New York: Academic, 1971. Used by permission of Academic Press. • Baldwin, A. L. *Theories of Child Development*. New York: Wiley, 1967. Used by permission of John Wiley & Sons, Inc. • Barker, R. G., J. S. Kounin, and H. F. Wright. *Child Behavior and Development*. New York: McGraw-Hill, 1943. Used by permission of McGraw-Hill, Inc. • Brown, R. *A First Language: The Early Stages*. Cambridge, Mass.: Harvard, 1973. Used by permission of Harvard University Press. • Freud, S. *An Outline of Psychoanalysis*. London: Hogarth, 1973. Used by permission of Hogarth Press Ltd. • Gesell, A. and F. L. Ilg. *Child Development: An Introduction to the Study of Human Growth*. Excerpts from Part I: "Infant and Child in the Culture of Today" copyright 1949 by Harper & Row, Publishers, Inc. Chart (list) from Part II: "The Child from Five to Ten" copyright 1946 by Arnold Gesell and Frances L. Ilg. Used by permission of Harper & Row, Publishers, Inc. and Hamish Hamilton Ltd. • Havighurst, R. J. *Human Development and Education*. Copyright © 1953 by Longman Inc. Previously published by David McKay Company, Inc. Used by permission of Longman Inc. • Hinde, R. A. *Biological Bases of Human Social Behavior*. New York: McGraw-Hill, 1974. Used by permission of McGraw-Hill, Inc. • Ilg, F. L. and L. B. Ames. *Child Behavior*. Copyright 1955 by Frances L. Ilg and Louise Bates Ames. Used by permission of Harper & Row, Publishers, Inc. and Hamish Hamilton Ltd. • Inhelder, B. and J. Piaget. *The Early Growth of Logic in the Child*. London: Routledge & Kegan Paul, 1964. Used by permission of Harper & Row, Publishers, Inc. and Routledge & Kegan Paul Ltd. • Kephart, N. C. *The Slow Learner in the Classroom*, 2d ed. Columbus, Ohio: Merrill, 1971. Used by permission of Charles E. Merrill Publishing Company. • Kohlberg, L. "From Is to Ought" in T. Mischel, *Cognitive Development and Epistemology*. New York: Academic, 1971. Used by permission of Academic Press. • Kohlberg, L. "Moral and Religious Education in the Public Schools: A Developmental View" in T. R. Sizer, *Religion and Public Education*. Copyright © 1967 by Hougton Mifflin Company. Used by permission of Houghton Mifflin Company. • Kohlberg, L. and R. Kramer. "Continuities in Childhood and Adult Moral

Development." *Human Development*, Vol. 12 (1969), pp. 93–120. Used by permission of S. Karger AG, Basel, Switzerland. ● Koppitz, E. M. *Psychological Evaluation of Children's Human Figure Drawings.* New York: Grune & Stratton, 1968. Used by permission of Grune & Stratton, Inc. and Elizabeth M. Koppitz. ● Lewin, K. "The Field Theory Approach to Adolescence." *American Journal of Sociology*, Vol. 44 (1939), pp. 868–896. Used by permission of The University of Chicago Press. ● Maslow, A. H. *The Farther Reaches of Human Nature.* Copyright © 1971 by Bertha G. Maslow. An Esalen Book, used by permission of The Viking Press. ● Maslow, A. H. *Toward a Psychology of Being.* © 1968 by Litton Educational Publishing, Inc. Used by permission of D. Van Nostrand Company. ● Peters, R. S. "Moral Development: A Plea for Pluralism" in T. Mischel, *Cognitive Development and Epistemology.* New York: Academic, 1971. Used by permission of Academic Press. ● Skinner, B. F. "Baby in a Box" in B. F. Skinner (ed.), *Cumulative Record: A Selection of Papers, 3d ed.* New York: Appleton-Century-Crofts, 1972. Used by permission of Prentice-Hall, Inc. ● Skinner, B. F. *Walden Two.* New York: Macmillan, 1948. Used by permission of Macmillan Publishing Co., Inc. ● Thomas, S. M. Drawings and Case Descriptions. Used by permission of Shirley M. Thomas. ● Tryon, C. and J. Lilienthal. "Developmental Tasks: I. The Concept and Its Importance" in *Fostering Mental Health in Our Schools.* Copyright © 1950 by the Association for Supervision and Curriculum Development. Used by permission of the Association for Supervision and Curriculum Development. ● Vygotsky, L. S. *Thought and Language.* Cambridge, Mass: Massachusetts Institute of Technology, 1962. Used by permission of MIT Press. ● Werner, H. and B. Kaplan. *Symbol Formation—An Organismic-Developmental Approach to Language and the Expression of Thought.* New York: Wiley, 1963. Used by permission of Bernard Kaplan.

CONTENTS

PART THREE: THE PEOPLE'S VIEW
OF A GROWING CHILD   89

A search for the underlying structure of commonsense ideas about development.

PART FOUR: DESCRIPTIONS
OF DEVELOPMENTAL MILESTONES   111

A search for typical steps of growth in many aspects of a child's life.

PART FIVE: MAJOR PATTERNS OF GROWTH   143

A search for general principles of development.

PART EIGHT: THE GROWTH
OF THOUGHT AND LANGUAGE   287

A search for patterns of development in children's cognitive and verbal skills, and for the mechanisms that bring these patterns about.

PART NINE: BEHAVIORIST APPROACHES TO DEVELOPMENT   383

A search for the way principles of learning explain development.

CHAPTER 17: SKINNER'S OPERANT CONDITIONING   385

CHAPTER 18: SOCIAL LEARNING THEORY: VERSIONS BY BANDURA, SEARS, AND THE KENDLERS   408

PART TEN: THE HUMANISTIC APPROACH   431

A search for the way the innermost self develops.

CHAPTER 19: THE HUMANISTIC PERSPECTIVES OF MASLOW AND BUHLER   432

PART ELEVEN: THEORIES FOR SPECIFIC EDUCATIONAL APPLICATIONS   451

A search for theoretical foundations on which to build instructional programs and evaluation practices.

CHAPTER 20: APPLIED THEORIES: MONTESSORI, DURKIN, KEPHART, AND KOPPITZ   453

PART TWELVE: SOURCES OF FURTHER THEORIES   475

PREFACE

Child development theorists are dissatisfied people. They are not content with existing explanations of how a child grows up, so they search for more adequate explanations. To guide their search, they set up goals at which to aim their efforts, goals that may be either stated or merely implied. This book's purpose is to identify the apparent goals and to describe the results achieved by more than two dozen theorists in their search.

This text has the same aim in the world of theories that a three-week guided European tour has in the world of travel. I do not pretend in this book to give a detailed, in-depth knowledge of any one territory. Instead, I propose to (1) suggest profitable ways to compare theories (Chapters 1-2) and (2) acquaint you with key aspects of a variety of the better known theories (Chapters 3-20). After reading these chapters, you should be able to study any of the theorists' original writings with greater ease and profit. You will be able to approach the theorists with an understanding of the chief features of their domains, and you will know how the features of each theory compare with those of others.

There are far more theories in the world than a single volume can accommodate. Therefore, it has been necessary to select those that are most suitable for our purpose. Each choice has been guided by three criteria, which can be stated as three sets of questions:

1. Has the theory been popular? That is, have many people subscribed to it or at least been acquainted with it?

2. Has the theory been influential? Has it affected people's treatment of children or influenced the beliefs of other theorists?

3. Is the theory representative of a class or family of theories? Theories often fall into groups, with the members of each group being similar in certain respects and dissimilar in others. Because it is not feasible to include all variants of a particular group, I have chosen only a few theories—in some cases only one—to represent each class. In making this selection I have been influenced not only by the representativeness of a theory but also by my own tastes and interests, including those theories that I feel are more interesting than others.

The eighteen chapters that describe individual theories are organized in ten parts. Each part reflects a key goal pursued by the theorists discussed within that part as they searched for descriptions or explanations of development more adequate than those found in existing theories. I have tried to suggest this key goal by placing under each part title a phrase identifying the sort of search that links together the theorists included in that section.

The final chapter of the book does not describe any theory in detail. Rather, it is an annotated bibliography that can guide you to sources of additional theories that you may find interesting to investigate.

If we inspect the origins of the theories in this volume, we discover that they display a geographical bias. All originate in the Western world. Their roots are in Western civilization, and they have been nurtured primarily in Europe and North America. In a future volume I intend to offer a similar compilation of theories arising from, and practiced in, the Orient.

A note of appreciation is due to both my students and my colleagues at the University of California, Santa Barbara. They have always been helpful in suggesting new sources of further theories and in offering those comments that force a teacher to improve the clarity and accuracy of what he says and writes. I also wish to thank those colleagues in other universities who read this book in manuscript form and offered valuable suggestions for improving its content: Andrew Collins, University of Minnesota; Bernard S. Gorman; Judy Todd; and Eleanor Willemson, Santa Clara University. In addition, I wish to express my appreciation for the wisdom and diligence applied to the production of the book by members of the Wadsworth staff: Kenneth King, Anne Kelly, and Nancy Benedict.

PART 1

STANDARDS OF COMPARISON

Since this book compares theories of child development, it is reasonable to ask at the outset: Compares theories against what standards? Or, compares them along what dimensions? The two chapters comprising Part 1 are designed to answer these questions.

Chapter 1 defines the way such terms as *facts*, *theory*, and *model* are used throughout the book. It also describes a variety of standards or criteria that people often use to distinguish "good theory" from "bad theory."

Chapter 2 looks at theories in a different way. It reviews a range of topics or questions on which a child development theory may focus. These questions are intended as guides to identifying the contents of a theory, that is, guides to the substantive focus of the theory.

Part 1, then, suggests viewpoints from which the theories surveyed in Chapters 3 through 20 can be analyzed at an introductory or basic level.

CHAPTER 1

THEORIES, MODELS, PARADIGMS, AND SUCH

Many people—parents, teachers, college students—say, "I don't want a lot of theorizing. I want to know what children are really like. It's the facts of child development I'm interested in."

For such people, "theorizing" means speculating about children in the quiet of a study, producing a kind of armchair philosophy that has little or nothing to do with the way children grow up in the real world. However, "facts," they feel, are practical and useful. Facts show how children really develop and why they behave as they do. For these people a book on child development theories is of no value.

The above distinction between "fact" and "theory" is not the one intended in this book. I see the relationship between the two in a different way. I consider facts or data to be either (1) discrete observations and measurements of children and their actions or (2) summaries of such observations and measurements. Here are three typical examples of discrete observations:

A first-grade teacher poured all of the water from a bowl into a tall drinking glass, then asked six-year-old Anne if the amount of water now in the glass was the same as the amount that had been in the bowl. Anne said there was now more in the glass.

The parents of thirteen-year-old Martin were upset because, they said, the boy acted "like a sissy." Martin did not like to play with other boys. He wore fancy rings and bracelets. His mother found him in her bedroom putting rouge on his lips and darkening his eyelids with her eye shadow. His father said, "Marty even walks like a girl."

Shortly after supper one evening, seventeen-year-old Linda received a telephone invitation to go to a movie, but she said, "Sorry,

Hank, I have to stay in all evening to study chemistry." A few moments later she answered another phone call with, "Okay, Larry, but only for a couple of hours. I'll study till eight o'clock. Then we can go out for a while."

Facts or data can also be in the form of summaries of observations or measurements: the average height of twelve-year-old girls, a list of the reactions of five-year-olds when they first enter kindergarten, the percentage of sixteen-year-olds who have smoked marijuana.

If these are facts, then what is theory? There is no easy, definitive answer to this question because many different meanings for theory are found in writings on philosophy and science. For the purposes of this book, however, I have simplified matters by adopting one definition broad enough to encompass all the different authors described. I define theory as *an explanation of how the facts fit together.* More precisely, I intend the process of theorizing to mean the act of proposing (1) which facts are most important for understanding children and (2) what sorts of relationships among facts are most significant for producing this understanding. Theory is what makes sense out of facts. Theory gives facts their meaning. Without theory, facts remain a clutter of disorganized specks on the canvas, unconnected spots that form no picture of how and why children grow up as they do.

Thus, a book on theories of child development can serve as a practical guide to understanding children, for it describes the underlying structure of different beliefs about what children are like and how they should be treated.

In this opening chapter we focus on four questions that people often ask when they first seriously consider theories of development: (1) What difference does it make which theory you adopt? (2) How does the term *theory* relate to such terms as *model, paradigm, analogue,* and the like? (3) What standards can be used to distinguish good theory from bad theory? (4) Why do scholars develop different theories rather than agree on an existing one?

THE DIFFERENCE YOUR CHOICE OF THEORY CAN MAKE

A theory can be likened to a lens through which we view children and their growth. The theory filters out certain facts and gives a particular pattern to those it lets in. To illustrate the way such filtering operates, we will briefly consider how the incidents of Anne, Martin, and Linda might be interpreted from the viewpoints of four theories presented later.

These interpretations will, of course, be much simplified since you have not yet had a chance to inspect any of the theories in detail. However, they still illustrate the point that the theory you choose for interpreting facts about children determines the meaning you assign to those facts. When you have read further, you will recognize the complexities the cases of Anne, Martin, and Linda would involve if they were interpreted more completely.

The four theorists whose lenses we peer through are Piaget, Freud, Lewin, and Skinner.

A Piagetian Viewpoint For more than fifty years a Swiss child psychologist, Jean Piaget, collected facts on how children of different ages solved reasoning problems, expressed their dreams, made moral judgments, and carried out other mental activities. He proposed that a child's modes of thought form a series of stages of intellectual growth common to all children in all cultures. We might reasonably propose then that Piagetians would interpret the cases of Anne, Martin, and Linda in terms of these stages.

For instance, we would expect an advocate of Piaget's theory to explain that Anne thought there was more water in the tall glass than in the shallow bowl because she had not yet reached the stage at which children understand the conservation of volume. By "conservation" we mean that Anne does not yet recognize that the quantity of water remains the same (is "conserved") even though the height and width of the two containers differ.

When we turn to Martin's effeminate behavior, we are on less secure ground in speculating about what a Piagetian would conclude because Piaget focused little if any attention on matters of socially "deviant" behavior. Piaget was more concerned with the thought processes of the typical or average child than with personal-social behavior which differed from a particular society's norms for sex-appropriate actions. However, Piaget did give a good deal of attention to children's moral judgments, to what children considered right and wrong and to how they supported such decisions. Piaget identified a series of stages through which children passed in the development of moral judgment, and we might use these stages for interpreting what Martin would say in defending the rightness of his wearing lip rouge and eye shadow. In other words, by posing moral-decision questions for Martin to answer, we could estimate the level of reasoning he uses to defend his actions.

When we use a Piagetian lens to view seventeen-year-old Linda's rejection of Hank in favor of Larry, we again receive little direct aid from Piaget since he did not theorize about sexual attraction and social interaction among adolescents. However, if we put the sexual-attraction question aside and limit ourselves to the intellectual-companionship aspect of Linda's choice, then we might find some aid in Piagetian theory. We could speculate that Linda may have preferred Larry because her stage of intelligence or mode of thought was more like Larry's than like Hank's. In other words, we would be estimating that youths of similar intellectual levels have a greater affinity for each other than youths of dissimilar levels.

We might also use Piagetian theory in another way to give meaning to the facts about Linda. Since Piaget identified stages of moral judgment that children pass through, we could ask Linda to explain why she thought it was right to reject Hank in favor of Larry. Then we could use her response to estimate her stage of moral judgment.

With this brief introduction to the use of Piaget's theory for interpreting discrete facts about children, let us turn next to a second theorist's perceptions of the same cases.

A Freudian Viewpoint   Toward the end of the nineteenth and the beginning of the twentieth centuries, Sigmund Freud devised a theory of child development based on the childhood recollections of adults that he treated for neuroses in his Vienna, Austria, psychiatric practice. Freud, like Piaget, proposed that children develop through a series of stages. However, instead of concerning himself with children's reasoning skills, Freud focused on *psychosexual* development. He identified steps in personality growth as influenced by children's ways of satisfying sexual drives from one period of childhood to another.

For example, Freud theorized that between the ages of 3 and 5, the typical child views the opposite-sex parent as a desirable love object that he or she wants to possess exclusively. In essence, the boy yearns to possess his mother and the girl her father. However, the child recognizes that he or she has been bested in this competition by the like-sexed parent. In other words, the boy's father has been the victor in the contest for the mother's sexual attention, and the girl's mother has been the victor in the competition for the father's love. To resolve this problem of yearning for the opposite-sex parent, the normal child in Freud's system seeks to acquire the characteristics of the victor. This means that the boy identifies with his father and seeks to adopt his father's traits, the traits of masculinity. In like fashion, the girl identifies with the mother and tries to behave in those feminine ways that apparently have made her mother successfully attractive. This process of identification, then, explains from a Freudian viewpoint why the normal boy develops the characteristics that his society considers masculine and the normal girl develops the characteristics considered feminine.

However, Freudians point out that sometimes the process of resolving the parental-love conflict goes awry. The boy may not identify with his father's traits. Instead, he identifies with his mother's characteristics, or perhaps some other twist occurs in the normal process. Consequently, the boy adopts feminine characteristics. From a Freudian perspective, we could reasonably assume that such a twist occurred in Martin's case. The boy apparently did not achieve a proper resolution of the conflict he faced in middle childhood, so that in early adolescence he is displaying sexually inappropriate behavior. To find out how this actually happened, Freudians would wish to gather information from the boy's unconscious mind—information collected by means of dream interpretation and by analyzing the free-flowing thoughts that Martin expresses while in a relaxed condition.

We can speculate that Freudians would see Anne's reactions also from a psychosexual viewpoint. Freudians—or at least some Freudians—would interpret Anne's reactions to the bowl and the tall glass in terms of sexual symbols. The meaning of the bowl-and-glass incident, they might say, lies in the girl's unconscious and relates to Anne's concerns about her own drives and the ways they are being satisfied or frustrated. In Freud's view, containers such as bowls and glasses symbolized female sex organs, whereas protruding, projectile-like objects symbolized the male. But exactly how such symbolization might fit into Anne's personality structure in the bowl-and-glass experiment would likely be unclear to psychoanalysts until they collected more information about the girl's feelings and thought processes. This information, intended to reveal the child's unconscious motives, might be gathered through the analyst's listening to Anne's verbalizations while she played with dolls or while she recounted her fantasies.

The case of the high school girl, Linda, might be analyzed in several ways from a Freudian viewpoint. Freudians might explain Linda's behavior in terms of how the characteristics of her two suitors, Hank and Larry, compared with the characteristics of other important males in her life, particularly her father. Did Linda select Larry because he reminded her of her father and was a substitute for him in the girl's affections? Or did Linda reject Hank because he reminded her of her father and she was symbolically striking back at her father whom she resents and wishes to harm? In effect, how is Linda's reaction to the two boys related to the manner in which she has sought to resolve the desire to possess her father—a desire that ostensibly began a decade earlier at the psychosexual stage known generally as the Oedipus stage or, for girls, the Electra stage or Electra conflict? The answer to such questions is not found in the facts of the Larry and Hank incident. Rather, the answer must be sought through the collection of far more information about the nature of Linda's unconscious motives and the manner in which she has interacted with her parents over the past years.

Thus, we see that the facts offered earlier about Martin, Anne, and Linda can assume quite different meanings when viewed through the lens of Freudian rather than Piagetian theory.

A Lewinian Viewpoint   A third theorist discussed in this book, Kurt Lewin, made his principal contributions to child development theory during the 1920s and 1930s, first in Germany and then in the United States. One of his favorite ways of viewing child behavior was to plot behavior visually as a map of the child's *life space*. By the term *life space* he meant all the different forces influencing the child's thought processes at the moment the child is making a decision about how to act. These forces are not simply the objects in the child's environment, such as the bowl and glass of water in the case of first grader Anne. Instead, they include pertinent memories of the past that the child brings to bear on this incident, the child's physical state at this time (such as degree of hunger or fatigue), and whatever the child is perceiving at the moment in the environment. Some of these forces push the child to act one way, and some push her to act another way. The child's final decision is the result of the stronger collection of forces winning out over the weaker collection.

In the incident of Anne and the water containers, a Lewinian would be expected to estimate which forces caused the girl to conclude that when the water from the bowl was poured into the tall glass, there was more water.

In the case of Linda, we might expect Lewinians to interpret Linda's choice of Larry over Hank in terms of the psychological forces bearing on the girl at the time of the decision. To illustrate Linda's apparent life space, Lewinians might draw a diagram like that in Figure 1.1. But they would need to gather additional data about Linda in order to determine which forces were influencing her decision at the moment. These factors would be included in the map of her life space at that moment. (For purposes of illustration, I have assumed that we have gathered some of this sort of information in preparing Figure 1.1.) As the diagram suggests, the forces are more favorable to Larry than to Hank.

As for Martin, followers of Lewin could be expected to map out the psychological forces that caused the boy to behave as his parents describe. However, in addition, Lewinians would likely interpret Martin's behavior as a sort of confused groping to understand this new stage of growth he is experiencing, the stage of early adolescence. According to Lewin, adolescence represents a time of movement from one stable period of life (late childhood) to another stable period (adulthood) as yet poorly understood by the youth. During the teenage years many puzzling body changes occur, and family and friends alter their expectations of how the boy or girl should behave socially. Lewin proposed that the adolescent feels new emotional tensions and may act in ways considered by parents, and by youths themselves, to be rather odd. So Martin, like adolescents described by Lewin, may be displaying, in his sexually inappropriate behavior, the confusion of a visitor entering a strange land, entering a poorly mapped domain whose terrain he only vaguely comprehends.

In effect, Lewinian theory casts the data about Anne, Martin, and Linda in a different light than either Piagetian theory or Freudian theory.

A Skinnerian Viewpoint   B. F. Skinner is a contemporary American psychologist who represents a school of thought known as *radical behaviorism*. He feels that it is more profitable to observe the factors in life that seem to influence people's behavior than it is to speculate about what might be in people's minds or personalities. The basic tenets of his system are quite simple. Every time someone acts, the action is followed by a consequence. The nature of this consequence determines whether the person will act in the same way in a similar situation in the future. If the consequence is pleasant and rewarding, then the person will tend to act in the same way in the future. If the consequence is not rewarding, the person will tend to act differently. In essence, according to Skinner, the behaviors we develop as we grow up depend on the consequences that followed those behaviors in the past.

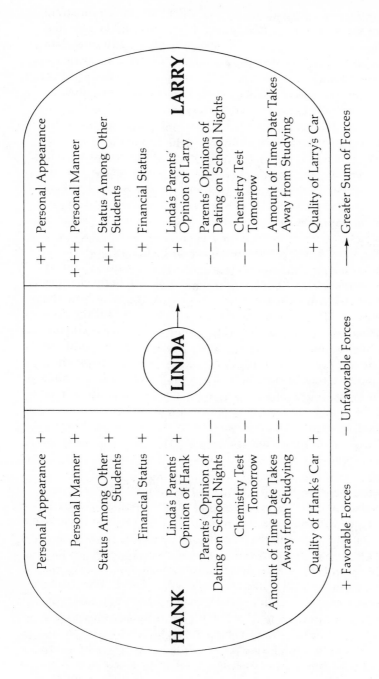

Figure 1.1   Lewinian Map of Life Space in Decision Making

Now let us speculate about how such a theory might enable us to interpret the incidents involving Anne, Martin, and Linda. We may assume that in the past Anne has been rewarded (behaviorists would call it *reinforced* instead of *rewarded*) for concluding that when something is taller, it is larger or bigger in general. Her own experience and other people's remarks have confirmed this conclusion for her. Thus, when she sees the water reach a greater height in the glass than it did in the bowl, she draws the same conclusion that has been reinforced in the past—that there is more of the substance when it is taller. If we wish to change Anne's misconception, we need to arrange the consequences of her behavior so they no longer reinforce her unsophisticated judgment. We will arrange experiments that force her to disconfirm her conclusion about the water containers, and we will also tell her when she is right and wrong. We may even wish to furnish some external reward, such as a toy or candy, for correct conclusions and withhold such reinforcers when she makes errors in judgment. Thus, according to Skinnerian theory, we influence Anne's intellectual development by manipulating the consequences of her behavior.

When we consider Martin's behavior from a Skinnerian viewpoint, we conclude that he currently displays feminine ways because when he has done so in the past the consequences have been more satisfying or reinforcing than the consequences following masculine actions he has attempted. Not only does he currently persist in retaining past feminine acts, but he can be expected to acquire even more of them in the future if the consequences of doing so are reinforced. The only way to alter his behavior pattern is to manipulate the consequences so that those following feminine acts are nonreinforcing and those following masculine acts are reinforcing or pleasurable.

In like manner we can interpret Linda's preference for Larry over Hank in terms of the consequences that have followed the girl's past contacts with the two boys. Apparently her relationship with Larry has been reinforced more strongly than her relationship with Hank. This greater reinforcement accounts for her preference to be with Larry.

So we see that when we view facts of child development through a Skinnerian lens, we achieve different meanings from those we achieved when we used Piagetian, Freudian, or Lewinian theories. Which theory we adopt makes a great difference in what we believe the facts mean and in how we treat children and youths as we seek to promote their optimum development.

Before leaving our four illustrative theorists, I should state explicitly that the interpretations I have offered of the data about Anne, Martin, and Linda are not the only ones that might be drawn from the four theoretical positions. Other interpreters might find other implications in the data. Thus, the conclusions I have presented are not supposed to be *the* correct or definitive analyses, but rather are simply illustrations of meanings that logically could be offered from the four perspectives. Furthermore, I obviously have given only a brief glimpse of each theory, just enough to suggest how data can assume quite different meanings when different theories are used for organizing the facts. A more complete examination of each theory is found in later chapters.

THE WORD "THEORY" AND OTHER TERMS

So far in our discussion we have stayed almost exclusively with the word *theory* in referring to authors' schemes for organizing data. However, in the literature on child development a variety of terms is used, and this is a problem for newcomers to child development theory. The problem is: How do such words as *theory*, *model*, *paradigm*, and *analogue* relate to each other? Solving the problem would be simple if all writers intended the same meaning for a given term, but such is not the case. One writer will use *theory* and *model* as synonyms; another will not. Before we move further into the analysis of theories, we will inspect a number of these common theoretical terms to see how they may be used by different theorists.

Of the many words we might consider, I have selected a dozen of the most common to discuss. The first six are used almost synonymously by many writers; they are *theory, model, paradigm, analogy, structure*, and *system*. The last six are typically used for identifying kinds of statements made within a theory; these are *assumption, axiom, postulate, hypothesis, principle*, and *law*.

When we read about "theories" of child development, we must be alert to the meaning the writer explicitly or implicitly assigns to the word *theory*. For us, a theory will be any statement describing (1) which facts are most important for understanding children and (2) what sorts of relationships among facts are most significant for producing this understanding. Other writers place more restrictions on the term. For example, *theory* can be defined as a "set of statements, including (a) general laws and principles that serve as axioms, (b) other laws, or theorems, that are deducible from the axioms, and (c) definitions of concepts" (Reese & Overton, 1970, p. 117). B. F. Skinner on occasion has denied that his explanation of behavior qualifies as theory; and if a very restricted definition of the term is applied, he would appear to be correct in his denial. However, in the broad sense of the word that we have adopted in these pages, Skinner's explanation does indeed qualify as theory (Skinner, 1950).

The word *model* has become increasingly popular in recent decades as a label for theoretical proposals. However, the term has caused some confusion because one writer will use it in a broad sense while another will limit its meaning. In its broad sense, *model* can mean any tentative ideational plan of relationships among variables. At this general level, a model can be a world view (Kuhn, 1962) or a world hypothesis (Pepper, 1942) that suggests something about the basic nature of man or of reality. For example, some child development theories are founded on a machine model in contrast to others founded on a dynamic organism model. That is, one camp of theorists pictures the growing child as a machine that reacts to things done to it by the environment: The child's behavior is primarily a product of the way the environment manipulates it. The other group pictures the child as an active, seeking organism who determines his or her own behavior by internally motivated desires. In a more limited sense writers have used the word *model* to mean, for example, an exclusively mathematical or graphic representation of the way something operates (Suppes, 1969, pp. 10–17). In child development literature, therefore, we should try to decide which of these meanings the writer intends. In the following chapters we will use *model* in the same broad sense as we are using *theory*—as any scheme intended to describe relationships among variables or facts of child development.

Another common term in child development literature is *paradigm* (rhymes with either "dim" or "dime"). Some people use *paradigm* to mean only a very general model (Kuhn, 1962), an overall viewpoint or description of relationships about reality or mankind. Others use it to mean either a broad, general picture or any more specific, more precise description of relationships among variables. In this sense, they equate *paradigm* with *model* and use the terms interchangeably. Again, it is well to determine the way an author intends the term to be used.

Theorists use the term *analogy* or *analogue* in comparing an aspect of child growth to something else in order to help explain that aspect of growth. For instance, theorists may say that the mind of the growing child is like an electronic computer, consisting of a finite amount of storage space for ideas and a system for retrieving the ideas when they are needed. Or the theorists can liken a highly mobile two-year-old to an inquisitive puppy that noses into everything without any notion of danger or responsibility. Analogies are thus kinds of models, in the sense of one thing representing qualities of something else. In this book, *analogy* or *analogue* will refer to a comparison between child development in a general sense and some other object or system; for example, an analogy would liken stages of growth to steps on a ladder which the child ascends as the years pass.

The words *structure* and *system* are considered together for they commonly carry the same meaning. Each identifies the elements that comprise something and describes the way these elements are interrelated. Therefore, a theorist's entire complex of beliefs and their interconnections can be called a "system." Likewise, one segment of an overall complex of beliefs can be singled out as a separate entity with its own constituent parts and be called a "system" or "subsystem" by itself. So we can speak of Piaget's complete set of ideas about child development as his system or theoretical structure, or we can pick one segment of this complex—such as Piaget's explanation of children's play—and view it as a subsystem with its own inner workings (Hall and Lindzey, 1970, pp. 317–318).

Next we turn to six words that refer to types of statements that may be included in a theory. They are *assumption, axiom, postulate, hypothesis, principle,* and *law.* Again, as with the words just discussed, not all writers assign identical meanings to these terms. However, we shall not take time to survey the various uses of each term. Instead, we will look at the most widely accepted meaning of each.

One useful way to approach the six terms is to think of their roles within a series of four phases a theorist may go through in creating and refining a model of child development (see Table 1.1). To begin, the theorist accepts certain concepts as true without testing them. These self-evident beliefs are frequently called *assumptions, axioms,* or *postulates.* An axiom or postulate is a formal statement of the conviction on which the theorist's model will be founded. In contrast, an assumption is either informally stated by the theorist or is not stated at all. Sometimes, theorists are unaware that they are making certain assumptions until critics point them out.

After establishing a foundation of assumptions and postulates, the theorist erects the superstructure of the model. Typically, the model, or at least certain aspects of it, is proposed in only a tentative form because the author is not sure that it represents an accurate picture of the way children develop. The author is saying, in effect, that "it seems likely that children grow up this way and for these reasons." However, he or she is not entirely sure. So to answer questions that are still puzzling about the theory's validity, the theorist can compose some "if-then" statements that derive logically from the model. These yet-to-be-proven statements are usually called *hypotheses*.

One popular way to state an hypothesis is in an if-then form. For example, in Chapter 7 we consider a developmental-task theory advocated by an American psychologist named Havighurst. The theory proposes that every few years as children grow up, they meet a new set of physical growth and social-psychological problems or *tasks* they must solve. The theory further contends that if children do not successfully solve a problem at one age level, they will have difficulty in solving tasks at higher age levels in the future. From this general proposal, we create hypotheses to test the validity of Havighurst's notion. As one illustration, we can take the area of emotional development called "giving and receiving affection." Within this area, the preadolescent child is said to face the task of "learning to give as much love as one receives." In early adolescence, the emotional-development task the child is to accomplish is that of "accepting one's self as a worthwhile person, really worthy of love." So we now have a pair of sequential tasks in hand and are thereby able to offer the following hypothesis:

> If, by the end of late childhood, a girl has not learned to give as much love as she receives, then in early adolescence she will not accept herself as a worthwhile person, really worthy of love.

As soon as we define the key terms in this statement (such terms as *late childhood, as much love, early adolescence, accept herself,* and *worthwhile person*), we are ready to set up an experiment or make observations of adolescents that will test the validity of

Table 1.1 Terms and Phases in Theory Building

	Phase 1	Phase 2	Phase 3	Phase 4
	Foundation Convictions	Model Descriptions	Logical Deductions	Conclusions
Products of the Phase:	Axioms Postulates Assumptions	Structure System	Hypotheses	Principles Laws
The Theorist's Behavior:	Accepts certain beliefs as being self-evident.	Defines the parts of the model and their interrelations.	Suggests relationships or outcomes that reasonably might be expected if the model accurately represents the aspect of development it is supposed to describe.	Draws generalizations from evidence collected to test or estimate the accuracy of the model.

(Although the process of theory building can thus be described as four sequential steps or phases, in practice a theorist frequently may not move systematically through the sequence. More often than not, theorists appear to shuttle back and forth among the phases, revising here and altering there, to produce a scheme they believe provides a convincing interpretation of the facts.)

the hypothesis. In effect, we observe children to decide whether this statement—and thus, one aspect of the theory—is true in real life.

An hypothesis or tentative estimate of the real state of affairs is not always in the form of an if-then statement. It can be a simple declarative sentence that only implies the if-then condition. For example, we could rephrase our hypothesis to read:

> A girl who has not learned to give as much love as she receives by the time she reaches the end of late childhood will not accept herself as a worthwhile person, really worthy of love, during her adolescent years.

Or, as another option, the hypothesis can be phrased as a question:

> Will a girl who has not learned to give as much love as she receives by the end of late childhood be able to accept herself as a worthwhile person, really worthy of love, when she is an early adolescent?

Despite the form in which a hypothetical relationship is cast, its status in theory building is the same. It functions as a reasonable, but as yet unproven, idea whose validity needs to be examined.

When the investigators have collected enough evidence to convince themselves that an hypothesized relationship is valid, they may then draw a generalization about it that they call a "principle." Thus, we are using the term *principle* to mean a generalization that is accepted as true—not because it seems self-evident, but because it is supported by what the theorists believe are sound data. Or if they regard the empirical data and logic behind it as irrefutable, the theorists can accord the generalization a higher status and term it a *law* or *law of nature*.

Finally, in our discussion of terminology, I feel it is useful to make a distinction between *evidence* and *proof*. Perhaps our most basic motive for comparing theories is to discover which of them is "true" or, at least, which parts of them are "valid." We might say that we are seeking proof of the theories. In this search I find it helpful to define the terms *evidence* and *proof* in the following way:

> *Evidence* is a public thing. It consists of the arguments, the logic, the patterns of reasoning, and the facts that bear upon what it treats.

This book is intended to present evidence about the theories it includes.

Proof, in contrast, is a personal, private thing. It is a conviction that something is true.

The significance of distinguishing between these two concepts is illustrated by arguments that arise over whether a generalization should be labeled an assumption, an hypothesis, or a principle. The arguments seem to arise because the people on the two sides of the debate either (1) have different kinds of evidence at hand or (2) are convinced by different kinds or amounts of evidence. The sort of evidence one person accepts as proof of a theory may not be the same sort that another accepts. A generalization about child growth which I now accept as a proven principle or law may be one that you still consider to be an hypothesis.

GOOD THEORY, BAD THEORY

Typically when we compare theories we are interested not only in learning how they are alike or different but also in judging whether one is better than another. To make this judgment, we need to decide what our standards of goodness will be. Indeed, not everyone prefers the same theory because not everyone uses the same standards for appraisal. Therefore, let's review some of the more common standards people use in differentiating good theory from bad.

We will consider nine popular standards of judgment. These are not necessarily ones you *should* adopt as your own; rather, they are ones you *might* adopt if they seem convincing and if they fit into your own set of values. Further, you will likely discover that they are not all of equal importance to you. You may wish to revise certain ones, eliminate others, and add a few of your own. In this way you will devise your own standards for judging child development theories.

At the beginning of this chapter the term *theory* was defined in a very broad manner. A theory, I proposed, is a description of (1) which facts are most important for understanding children and (2) what sorts of relationships among facts are most significant for producing this understanding. We noted later that some people use the term *theory* in a more restricted way. They usually restrict the term by adding the sort of criteria described by the nine standards that follow. For instance, some people are unwilling to call a collection of ideas a "theory" unless the collection is both internally consistent in structure and clearly provides for the generation of testable hypotheses. However, we will use these standards not for deciding what should be called a theory, but for deciding how worthwhile or how "good" a theory is.

Standard 1: A theory is better if it accurately reflects the facts of the real world of children.

Some theorists are criticized for producing a model of development that does not accurately represent children. We will consider three reasons why a mismatch may occur between a theory and the facts of child development.

First, a theorist may draw conclusions from a study of only a few children, then improperly apply these conclusions to many children—the error of generalizing beyond the data. This criticism does not apply to the common practice of studying a representative sample of children and then extending the resulting conclusions to the larger population of children accurately reflected by the sample. Indeed, such sampling is involved in virtually all research on development. But it is an error to apply conclusions about a small group to a larger population when there is good reason to believe that the conditions of the two groups are significantly different. For instance, Arnold Gesell (Chapter 6) has been criticized for improperly generalizing conclusions from a study of children who came to his clinic at Yale University. He apparently assumed that the group of children he observed and measured were accurate representatives of nearly all other children. But there is a serious question about whether his conclusions correctly describe child growth in other cultural settings.

Likewise, in the eighteenth century, Jean Jacques Rousseau (Chapter 4) wrote at length about the nature of children, founding his beliefs on three sorts of evidence: (1) his experience as a tutor for several sons of aristocratic European families, (2) some casual observations of French peasant children, and (3) hearsay impressions of the personalities of "noble savages" in primitive cultures. Critics of Rousseau have questioned whether his descriptions of child development, based on such limited data, actually matched the experience of all the children to whom he applied his conclusions (Boyd, 1963; Davidson, 1898).

A second reason why a theory may not describe children accurately is that a researcher who studies one facet of child growth may not be satisfied to limit conclusions to that facet. Instead, in an effort to discover general principles of growth that explain all sorts of behavior, the researcher applies the conclusions to explain other aspects of child growth as well. For example, he or she may measure trends in children's physical growth, and then seek to apply the pattern of increases and plateaus in physical growth to other areas of development, such as social or emotional or mental development. But principles governing one aspect of development may not be the same as those governing another, so risk may be involved.

A third cause of conflict between theory and fact is the researcher's faulty memory or inaccurate observation of children. Probably none of us can help being influenced by memories of our own childhood or by our casual impressions of children we have seen and talked with. Unless we are careful to use controlled observing, testing, and measuring of children, we risk allowing distorted observations from the past or from casual impressions to influence the schemes we devise for explaining development.

Standard 2: A theory is better if it is stated in a way that makes it clearly understandable to anyone who is reasonably competent ("reasonably competent" means having a suitable command of language, mathematics, and logical analysis).

More precisely, anyone with reasonable competence should be able to understand: (1) what facets or events in the real world are referred to by each part of the theory, (2) the meaning of terms used in the model, (3) key assumptions on which the model is founded, and (4) how the explanations and predictions about child development are logically derived from the definitions and assumptions.

This standard may appear simple and straightforward, but in practice it can be quite controversial. If we find that a theory lacks clarity, is it the theorist's fault for being obscure or confused, or is it our own fault for lacking the competence needed to understand the theorist? We usually have a higher regard for a theory whose elements we can readily comprehend.

Standard 3: A theory is better if it not only explains why past events occurred but also accurately predicts future events. Furthermore, it is better if it enables us to make accurate predictions about the specific behaviors of a particular child rather than only speculations about general growth patterns for a group of children.

People who seek to understand children are usually interested in both the past and the future. They look to the past to learn what forces in a child's life have caused the child to be the way he or she is today. They look to the future to estimate what the child will probably be like in coming years.

Many theories are better suited to explaining the past than to foretelling the future. And of those that say something of the future, most are better suited to predicting general characteristics of the typical child or of children in general than they are to predicting specific development characteristics of a particular child. However, those interested in child development—the researcher, parent, teacher, physician—value more highly a theory that produces specific predictions about a given child than one that foretells only general growth directions or yields only estimates of how the average child will turn out. For example, it is my own belief that a behaviorist of the social learning variety (Chapter 18) is better prepared to make predictions about a specific child's verbal development than is a person who founds his or her judgments solely on Werner's theory (Chapter 9).

Standard 4: A theory is better if it offers practical guidance in solving daily problems of child rearing to people responsible for the welfare of children—parents, teachers, camp counselors, pediatricians, clinical psychologists, juvenile court judges, and the like.

This standard, which is a practical extension of standard 3, is considered by many to be the most important, for they are interested in theory only to the extent that it improves their own skills in understanding and treating the children they meet daily. In contrast, some theorists, and readers of theory, are not particularly concerned with translating ideas into advice on child rearing. Rather, they are searching for basic principles of human growth and behavior; the question of whether these principles will enable people to treat children with greater skill is entirely incidental.

Standard 5: A theory is better if it is internally consistent.

The essence of a theory is its structure, a description of its elements and the way they interact. Theorists choose different ways to display this framework of their beliefs. For example, although all theorists explain their models of development verbally, some supplement their verbal descriptions with mathematical symbols that permit the theory's components to be manipulated according to rules of logic. By quantifying the components of his scheme, a theorist hopes to gain precision in analyzing and predicting child growth and behavior. Jean Piaget is an example of a theorist who has sought to enhance the clarity of his verbal explanations with the manipulation of symbols (Piaget, 1950).

Another way to supplement verbal description is through diagrams. For example, if a theory involves two main dimensions that interact (such as the relationship between chronological age and mental growth), then the relationship can be displayed as a simple graph, with age on one axis and mental growth on the other. As illustrated earlier, Lewin used a diagram—a kind of topological map—to show what he conceived to be the relationship among sectors of a child's life space.

Whatever the mode of presentation, however—words, mathematical symbols, or diagrams—the system, according to standard 5, should be internally consistent. A person seeking to understand the system should not have to disregard one segment of a model in order to comprehend another. The parts should all fit together logically.

Standard 6: A theory is better if it is economical in the sense that it is founded on as few unproven assumptions as possible and requires simple mechanisms to explain all the phenomena it encompasses.

This criterion is often referred to as the *law of parsimony, Occam's razor,* or *Morgan's canon,* the latter in recognition of a biologist, Lloyd Morgan, who proposed that if two explanations of a phenomenon fit the facts equally well, it is better in the long run to choose the simpler of the explanations. Note that the purpose of this standard is not to discourage theorists from formulating complex explanations of complex events—indeed, simpler explanations can prove to be inaccurate. Instead, it is intended to reduce the establishment of theories with elaborate, hypothesized internal mechanisms not well supported by evidence. Frequently, the more complicated the theory, the more difficult it is to test, and proponents are left to support it with argument and emotion.

Standard 7: A theory is better if it is falsifiable or disconfirmable.

In scientific circles a theory is generally conceived to be an estimate of the truth rather than a definite statement of the truth. Researchers must test the validity of hypotheses derived from the theory in order to determine to what extent it does indeed explain the facts satisfactorily. Thus, if a theory's hypotheses can be tested to determine whether they are true, then the reverse should also obtain—it should be possible to test that an hypothesis is false. In effect, many scientists feel that the validity of a theory should not only be confirmable through logic and the presentation of data, but it should also be falsifiable or disconfirmable.

Some theories of child development, however, do not appear to display this characteristic of falsifiability; that is, we cannot conceive of a research result which such a theory is unprepared to answer. The theory is built to explain the negative outcome of an experiment as well as the positive outcome.

We can illustrate the problem of falsifiability with the following example. Imagine that we create a theory of social development in which diet is the prime determinant of a child's social adjustment. We contend that a proper combination of B vitamins is particularly important. The proper combination produces a child who is socially constructive and amiable. The improper combination produces a child who is resentful and commits antisocial acts. Our hypothesis, in this form, becomes falsifiable when we have specified the proper and the improper B-vitamin combinations. Now we can create experiments to determine whether this aspect of the theory is valid or not. But let us add another element to our theory. We will call it the *counterpoise factor* and propose that when it is present, the B-vitamin combinations work in just the opposite way we would normally expect. By adding this factor, we have rendered our theory nonfalsifiable. If someone tries to test our theory and discovers that many children who eat the improper B-vitamin combination are socially well adjusted, we explain that in those children the counterpoise factor has been operating. Thus, the theory is nonfalsifiable—it is always "correct."

Many researchers are uncomfortable with a theory that is nonfalsifiable, so they include standard 7 among the criteria they apply for judging the worth of theories. Among the models reviewed in this book, those of Freud, humanistic psychologists, and the Puritans in particular can be criticized as nonfalsifiable.

Standard 8: A theory is better if it stimulates the creation of new research techniques and the discovery of new knowledge.

This can be called the *fertility criterion*. Some theories have been highly fertile, remarkable for the number of new vistas they have opened and the amount of research they have stimulated. As a review of child development journals will attest, a great proportion of published investigations in the 1960s and 1970s trace their origins to Piaget's writings (Wadsworth, 1971, p. 2). Likewise, Skinnerian behaviorists and social learning theorists have served as highly effective motivators of research in recent years. In contrast, the work of Havighurst and other developmental-task advocates has not generated much of a search for new knowledge.

Standard 9: A good theory is self-satisfying. It explains development in a way that we feel makes good sense.

This might be called the standard of *self-affirmation*. It is a sort of catchall that depends not only on the previous standards but also on emotional and intuitive factors that we cannot readily identify. The operation of these factors is reflected in our saying about a theory, "I just can't believe that's true" or "I can't believe that's the whole story" when we do not know exactly what it is we find dissatisfying about it. Or we may consider a theory valid because "I feel that's right" or "That rings true—it seems to be the way things are."

Among the theories described later in this book, the one type that appears to depend most heavily on self-affirmation factors is humanistic psychology, for it is based on the existentialist's belief that the individual's real world is the one he personally experiences. The feelings and inner experiences of the child are the most important, no matter what sorts of objective factors exist in the world around him. The development of the child's personally sensed *self* is what interests the humanistic psychologist, and this self is known only through introspection. The advocate of humanistic theory, therefore, can comfortably accept a theory because "it

feels right" and "makes intuitive sense" without requiring confirmation from outside, "objective" data. On the other hand, a
radical behaviorist, though she might informally say she "feels"
her theory is true, does not cite this feeling as validating evidence;
instead, she is compelled by her theoretical position to produce
observational or experimental evidence to support the theory.

In the final analysis, of course, all theories depend on self-
conviction for their acceptance. And this issue of what makes us
satisfied or dissatisfied with a theory brings us to our final question in this chapter.

WHY DO SCHOLARS DEVELOP
DIFFERENT THEORIES?

People who are new to investigating theories of development often wonder what influences theorists to propose new models. The
most obvious reason is that they are not satisfied with the answers existing theories offer for the questions they believe to be
important. Or they may feel that existing theories do not meet the
standards they use to judge the worth of a theory. But in addition
to these general reasons, we can identify several more specific
ones that cause theorists to generate new perspectives on children's growth.

All theorists are affected by the field of knowledge in which
they received their principal training. For example, a strong background in biological science can cause a scholar to focus more
attention on children's heredity than on their environment in explaining development. In contrast, a strong foundation in sociology may influence a theorist in the opposite direction. As
illustrations, the theories of Herbert Spencer and G. Stanley Hall
during the late nineteenth century were affected by their study of
biology, particularly by their study of Darwin's theory of evolution (Hall, 1904).

Not only do theorists' academic backgrounds influence their
explanations of development, but the problems they meet in daily
work also funnel their attention toward particular facts and their
possible relationships. In the late nineteenth century, the puzzling cases of neurotic patients that Freud met in his psychiatric

practice stimulated him to seek explanations that deviated markedly from the neurological theories popular in his day (Chapter 11). Early in this century, Piaget was working in a psychological testing center in France when he became curious about the thinking processes that caused children to give certain incorrect answers to test questions. This curiosity led him to a lifelong study of the growth of children's thought patterns and to a theory that organized the facts he discovered (Chapter 13).

The way investigators gather data also influences the conclusions they draw. Skinner distrusted the accuracy of people's reports of their own thought processes, so he chose to base his conclusions on objective observations of behavior by an outsider (Chapter 17). However, Charlotte Buhler, a humanistic psychologist, encouraged people to report their feelings, hopes, and ambitions (Chapter 19). Both Piaget and Kohlberg presented standard test questions to which children would respond (Chapters 13 and 16). But Roger Brown's investigations of children's language development involved recording long segments of natural speech rather than responses to a standard set of questions (Chapter 15). In effect, a researcher's sources of information favor his drawing certain types of conclusions and make it unlikely he will draw other types.

One of the most potent forces in giving direction to models devised by experimental psychologists is the appearance of surprising or puzzling results in research they conduct with children. When an experiment turns out in an unexpected way, researchers are faced with the possibility that the existing theory is inaccurate and that changes in it are called for. This sort of influence has been particularly prominent in the work of such behaviorists as Bandura, Sears, and the Kendlers (Chapter 18).

Finally, the personal, nonprofessional concerns of individuals also influence their proposals about development. Rousseau's atypical childhood in eighteenth-century Europe appears to have had a strong effect on the view of child growth he later proposed (Chapter 4). Maslow's dissatisfaction with the ways behaviorism and psychoanalysis explained his own personality and happenings in his own life played a part in the formulation of his version of humanistic psychology (Chapter 19).

In sum, a variety of factors interact to make theorists dissatisfied with existing explanations of development and stimulate them to formulate new models. As a result, there are a number of major theories and even more minimodels in existence today, and we can expect many more to appear in the years ahead.

CONCLUSION

Chapter 1 was designed to accomplish four purposes:

1. Give you an initial taste of several quite different theories and suggest how interpreting child behavior from each theory's point of view can result in very different conclusions.
2. Identify some general theoretical terms and the meanings that can be assigned to them.
3. Propose illustrative standards for judging the worth of a theory and suggest that you devise a list of your own that suits your pattern of values.
4. Note some of the factors that influence theorists to propose new schemes for interpreting child development.

The material in Chapter 1 should serve as a useful background for Chapter 2, which suggests a series of questions that can be asked about the contents of theories when different models of child development are being compared.

FOR FURTHER READING

The following publications are useful sources of information about theoretical terminology, criteria for judging the worth of theories, and illustrative appraisals of theories.

Baldwin, A. L. (1967) *Theories of Child Development*. New York: Wiley. Chaps. 1, 2, 19.

Brody, B. A. (1970) *Readings in the Philosophy of Science*. Englewood Cliffs, N.J.: Prentice-Hall. Pp. 252–267.

Developmental Psychology Today. (1975) New York: Random House. Chap. 2.

Hall, C. S. and G. Lindzey. (1970) *Theories of Personality*. 2d ed. New York: Wiley. Chap. 1.

Lerner, R. M. (1976) *Concepts and Theories of Human Development*. Reading, Mass.: Addison-Wesley. Chap. 1.

Marx, M. H. (ed.). (1965) *Theories in Contemporary Psychology.* New York: Macmillan.

Marx, M. H. and F. E. Goodson (eds.). (1976) *Theories in Contemporary Psychology.* New York: Macmillan. (This volume is sufficiently different from the 1965 Marx publication that both are worth inspecting.)

Reese, H. W. and W. F. Overton. (1970) "Models of Development and Theories of Development" in L. R. Goulet and Paul B. Baltes, *Life-Span Developmental Psychology.* New York: Academic Press. Pp. 115–145.

Skinner, B. F. (1972) *Cumulative Record: A Selection of Papers.* 3d ed. New York: Appleton-Century-Crofts. (See Skinner's questioning of the need for theory in the Part II selection, "Are Theories of Learning Necessary?")

CHAPTER 2

THE CONTENTS OF CHILD DEVELOPMENT THEORIES

In comparing theories, we need to consider not only the sorts of criteria described in Chapter 1, but also the content characteristics. By *content* I mean both the aspects of child development on which theorists focus attention and the key philosophical and methodological convictions that undergird the model they propose.

This second chapter introduces a variety of content categories often included in theories. One aim of the chapter is to alert you to questions that child development theories frequently try to answer, so you can decide which of these questions are the most important from your viewpoint. Another aim is to illustrate the fact that not all theorists seek to answer the same questions or accord the same significance to a given question. It is important to recognize this, because two theories that at first appear to be in conflict may, in fact, be merely directed at different aspects of child growth. Two ostensibly conflicting viewpoints could even, perhaps, be satisfactorily combined, as Dollard and Miller sought to do with behaviorist and psychoanalytic theories in their book *Personality and Psychotherapy* (1950).

In Chapter 2 a number of questions that identify either the content focus of theories or their philosophical and methodological understructure are presented. The questions are organized into thirteen clusters. The names of the clusters and an overall question that encompasses the subquestions in each are given in the following list:

1. *Scope or range.* What age levels, aspects of development, and human cultures are the objects of the theory?

2. *Nature and nurture.* How does heredity compare with environment as a contributor to development?

3. *Direction of development.* The infant grows from immaturity toward what sorts of maturity or what future condition?

4. *Continuous versus stepwise change.* Do children grow by imperceptibly small increments or do they periodically move up from one identifiable stage to another?

5. *Original moral condition.* Is the child born moral, immoral, or amoral?

6. *Personality structure.* What are the key components of human personality, and how are these related to each other?

7. *Motivation and the learning process.* What motivates development, and by what process does a child learn?

8. *Individual differences.* How does the theory account for differences in development among children of the same chronological age?

9. *Desirable-undesirable, normal-abnormal.* How does the theory distinguish desirable from undesirable development and normal from abnormal development?

10. *Philosophical origins and assumptions.* From what philosophical viewpoint has the theory arisen, and on what assumptions is it founded?

11. *Investigative methods.* What methods has the theorist used for gathering, analyzing, and validating his ideas, and how have these methods influenced the contents and structure of the theory?

12. *Appeal for acceptance.* On what sort of appeal does the theorist depend for convincing people of the theory's worth?

13. *Terminology.* What special terms are used in the theory, and how do they relate to similar concepts in other theories?

Before inspecting each of these topics in some detail, we should note three characteristics of this list. First, the topics are not mutually exclusive. They overlap and crisscross. For example, when we discuss Freud's proposed structure for personality development, we necessarily consider as well his growth stages, his idea of the child's original moral condition, and his special terminology. Thus, these questions are not separate entities but are simply different angles from which to view the integrated body of a theory.

Second, the list itself is not proposed as *the correct* list of topics for analyzing theories of development. It is just one possible listing, one I have found helpful for directing attention at significant aspects of theories. Other lists, different in content or organized in a different pattern, serve other people just as well.

Third, topics at the beginning of the list are more distinctly developmental than the rest. Within the broad field of psychology, practitioners are traditionally divided into several loosely defined groups: specialists in the clinical treatment of behavior disorders, psychologists who compare human behavior with that of animals, specialists in research on learning, and developmental psychologists. This last group is the one that interests us. Developmental psychologists have a dominant interest in questions about how and why people change with the passing of time or the advancement of age. In our list of thirteen topics, items 1 through 5 are most distinctly concerns of developmentalists. Items 6 through 13 are generally of equal or greater interest to practitioners in other psychological groups. Now let's turn to a more detailed explanation of the topics.

1. *Scope or range.* The term *scope* is used here to identify three aspects of a theory: (a) its *age range*—the way the theory marks the beginning and end of the development period; (b) its *variety of aspects*—the number and kinds of facets stressed or included by the theory; and (c) its *cultural range*—the variety of cultures the theory proposes to describe. To discover how a particular theorist treats these matters, we can be guided by the following set of questions:

1.1 How are the beginning and end of the child development period defined? What characteristics, such as age in years, particular changes in behavior, or changes in growth rate, define this period?

Some of the schemes discussed in later chapters are best labeled *theories of human development* since they propose structures and principles describing the entire life span, from conception to death. Others are more accurately called *theories of child development* because they focus exclusively, or primarily, on the first two decades or so of life. In this book we concern ourselves only with these initial two decades, regardless of whether the theory being considered extends into adulthood and old age.

Many theories use chronological age as the chief measure of the child development period, with either biological conception or birth marking the lower limit and age 18 or 21 marking the upper limit. Thus, the adolescent years are typically included within the span of the term *child development*, although some writers prefer to limit the word *childhood* to the years before puberty—age 12 or 14—and *adolescence* to the years between puberty and adulthood.

Other theorists find chronological age an unsatisfactory dimension in analyzing development (Wohlwill, 1976). They use some other characteristic, such as the attainment of adult height or the emergence of specified adult behaviors, as the indicator that childhood is over. Also their boundary lines for stages of growth throughout the childhood period are set by developmental signs other than years since birth.

Some authors focus their theories on the entire range of childhood and adolescence experiences, whereas others, such as Roger Brown and his theory of the young child's language development (Chapter 15), attend to only one segment of this range.

1.2 What aspects of growth or behavior does the theory include or emphasize?

Some models concentrate on a narrow range of behavior. For example, Kohlberg (Chapter 16) concerns himself solely with moral aspects and Koppitz (Chapter 20) only with children's drawing activities. Other theories are much broader in scope. Havighurst's scheme (Chapter 7) involves physical, emotional, moral, cognitive, and social aspects. Gesell (Chapter 6) also includes a wide range of behaviors and growth characteristics in his studies.

1.3 Does the theory propose to explain child development in all cultures or only in certain ones?

Most theorists want their model to apply to as many children as possible. In effect, they try to produce a universal theory. Their broad ranging statements imply that they are talking about children in all places and, seemingly, in all times. Such is true of Piaget, Freud, Lewin, Skinner, and many more. Other theorists state that their proposals are intended to describe development within defined cultural or geographic domains. For example,

Havighurst has said that his "tasks of development" are ones faced by mid-twentieth-century American boys and girls, particularly those from the middle and upper social classes.

These three facets of a theory's scope help delineate the territory the theorist is trying to map out.

2. *Nature and nurture.* Over the decades the most fundamental concern of child development theorists has been the heredity–environment issue. The terminology of the debate has varied from time to time—nature versus nurture, nativism versus cultural relativism, genetics versus social controls, maturation versus learning—but the basic issue has been the same: How do inborn factors compare with environmental factors in contributing to a child's development?

Through the years the form of the debate has also changed. It moved from the question of *which one* to that of *how much*, and now it has become *in what manner* (Anastasi, 1958). Let us inspect each of these in turn.

Which one? In past centuries philosophers seemed to be answering the question: Which causes developmental changes, a child's heredity *or* her environment? An example from the environmentalist side of the issue is the proposal of British philosopher John Locke (1632–1704) that at birth a child's mind is a void, an unmarked page or *tabula rasa* on which the contents of the mind are sketched by the child's experiences as she grows up. At the other extreme was Jean Jacques Rousseau (1712–1778), who considered the child's inherited "nature" to be the most influential force in determining his steps in development.

The which-one controversy can be simply illustrated as positions on either side of a fence (see Table 2.1). Traditionally the people on the heredity side have been divided into two groups: the *preformationists* and the *predeterminists.*

The distinction between preformationists and predeterminists chiefly concerns how powerful the theorist believes hereditary effects are. Preformationists believe that all of an individual's potentials—his personality, values, motives, mental abilities, and emotional makeup—exist completely formed within the infant at birth. As the child advances in age, these potentials unfold on a prearranged genetic schedule. Since all significant elements of development are preformed, the particular environment in which the child grows up has no role in determining development. Predeterminists, however, are not so willing to dismiss the influence of a child's physical and social surroundings. They believe envi-

Table 2.1   The "Which-One" Issue

	Hereditarians	
Environmentalists	Preformationists	Predeterminists
The child's experiences are preeminent in determining development.	Environment has no influence.	Environment has little influence.

ronment has some effect. But since they believe a child's genetic schedule is so important, they belong on the heredity side of the controversy along with the preformationists. Rousseau has been credited with formulating the "first definitive predeterministic theory of child development" (Ausubel and Sullivan, 1970, p. 2).

Actually, the issue of *which one*—heredity or environment— determines development is rather silly since even rudimentary reasoning will show that neither factor can exert influence or even exist without the other. A child's heredity cannot display itself in a condition of nothingness, that is, in a nonenvironment. Nor can a child be spontaneously generated without ancestors, as if springing in a puff of smoke out of nowhere to be influenced by an environment. Even the most radical environmentalists and hereditarians of the past recognized the necessary existence of both factors, nature and nurture. So the argument actually was not *which one* but *how much*.

How much? During the nineteenth century and through the first half of the twentieth, the nature–nurture issue centered primarily on the question of how much heredity contributed to development in comparison to environment. Graphically the issue can be pictured as a line, with the heredity component above and the environment component below (see Table 2.2). A given theorist's position on the issue can be identified at some point along the line. To illustrate, we cite the famous debate that attracted the attention of American psychologists in the 1920s and 1930s concerning which factor contributed more to a child's intellectual growth, heredity or environment. By statistical methods, Burks (1928) concluded that heredity deserved 83 percent of the credit for mental ability and environment only 17. Other investigators (Leahy, 1935; Shuttleworth, 1935) also concluded that heredity played the major role, though the proportions they derived were somewhat different. Still other researchers, based on a series of

Table 2.2 The "How-Much" Issue

	Extreme Hereditarians	Moderates	Extreme Environmentalists
Percentage of nature's contribution	95%	50%	5%
Percentage of nurture's contribution	5%	50%	95%

studies conducted in the midwestern United States, concluded that the opposite was true, that environment was the stronger factor in determining mental ability (Skeels, 1940; Skodak, 1939). This debate has never been settled, and the main reason may well be that the wrong question—or at least an unprofitable question—was being asked.

Investigations based on the how-much issue have led to conflicting conclusions about the same data and to interpretations of questionable usefulness. As a consequence, in recent decades there has been a strong movement among people interested in these matters to recast the key question from *how much* to *how* or *in what manner* the factors interact (Anastasi, 1958).

In what manner do nature and nurture interact? A basic tenet of this modern interactionist approach is that nature and nurture are two different dimensions, each operating 100 percent in its role. Although this approach does not entirely abandon concern with how much, its more important question by far is how does the interaction of heredity and environment take place in order to produce the observed development of the child. There are a variety of answers to the question, each depending on the point of view of the particular theorist being examined. Since it is our purpose in the present chapter only to outline issues that theories treat and to pose guide questions for use in comparing theories, we will not analyze a wide array of interpretations of interaction here. Rather, we will describe briefly only two views in order to illustrate the extent to which ideas about interaction can vary.

According to the first view, heredity defines the boundaries of potential development, and environment determines where, within these boundaries, a child's actual development is realized.

"Heredity determines what we can do, and environment what we do do" (Montagu, 1959). Furthermore, it is assumed that the boundaries differ for different characteristics. For certain traits, such as eye color, heredity sets very narrow limits within which environmental forces—such as nutrition—can operate. For other characteristics, such as the cognitive ability to analyze complex abstract relationships, the boundaries set by heredity appear to be wide, allowing considerable room for the operation of such environmental factors as nutrition, instruction, rewards for the child who practices such analysis, and many more.

Furthermore, this interactionist viewpoint assumes that the potential defined by heredity is manifested differently at different times in the child's life. For example, at puberty a genetically timed ripening occurs for the primary sex characteristics (maturing ova in girls, maturing sperm in boys, and equipment for delivering these cells) and such secondary sex characteristics as changes in body shape. Thus, puberty produces different potentials from those available when the child was age 2 or 4 or 6.

From this interactionist perspective, the question of how much nature contributes as compared to nurture is no longer of prime interest. Instead, we now seek to know (1) how wide are the boundaries set by heredity for various aspects of development— physical traits, cognitive abilities, frustration tolerance, and others; (2) what environmental forces influence the way these aspects will manifest themselves in the child's structure and behavior; and (3) how this interaction of inherited potential and environmental forces operates at different stages of the child's growth period.

Some idea of how the complex interrelations of this model differ from the interrelations of the which-one and how-much approaches can be shown in the simplified diagram in Figure 2.1. Three concepts are plotted here:

a. *Genetic influence over different developmental characteristics varies from one characteristic to another.* The three characteristics shown in Figure 2.1 are height, skill at analyzing abstract relationships, and emotional control under stress. The top and bottom of each box represent, respectively, the greatest and least genetic potential that is humanly possible for that characteristic (at a certain age level). The white space in each box represents one hypothetical child's genetic potential for that characteristic.

b. *Heredity establishes boundaries of potential for each char-*

SKILL AT ABSTRACT ANALYSIS

EMOTIONAL CONTROL UNDER STRESS

HEIGHT

Tallest

Greatest Skill

Greatest Control

F

U

F

F

U

U

Shortest

Least Skill

Least Control

•••• = hypothesized upper and lower boundaries of inherited potential

F = development in favorable environment

U = development in unfavorable environment

Figure 2.1   An Interactionist Viewpoint: In What Manner?

acteristic. In Figure 2.1 the hypothetical upper limit for development—for example, the tallest that child can grow—is the upper dotted line, and the lower limit—the shortest height the child can grow to—is the lower dotted line.

c. *Environmental influences determine where within the boundaries a child's development will manifest itself.* The range within which environment can affect development is shown as the white area between the dotted lines in each characteristic. The letter *F* signifies the level of development a child will exhibit if the environmental influences are very favorable (near the upper limit). The letter *U* signifies the level of development exhibited if environmental conditions are very unfavorable (near the lower limit).

Thus, in Figure 2.1 we hypothesize that there is more leeway for the influence of environmental factors in determining a child's emotional control than there is in determining either height or skill at abstract analysis. Whether such an hypothesis is true becomes a matter of empirical investigation.

To complete this first analysis of interaction, we need to explain which environmental factors are most potent in determining how genetic potential is realized and how these forces are interrelated. We also need to describe how the interaction may vary at different stages of the child's development.

Although this first interactionist approach does not tell us, as older how-much theories did, what proportion of development is due to heredity and what proportion is due to environment, it still enables us to differentiate between "environmentalists" and "hereditarians." In terms of Figure 2.1, theorists who picture the area between the inherited-potential boundaries as narrow are hereditarians, for they believe the child's genetically designed nature does not permit much manipulation by environmental factors. Theorists who picture the boundaries as widely separated are more environmentalist, for they think environmental influences greatly affect the way development characteristics are manifested.

Let's turn now to the second way of viewing the *in-what-manner* approach to interaction. Some writers consider interaction in terms of how directly heredity influences development (Anastasi, 1958; Lerner, 1976, pp. 48–83). To illustrate, let us consider three examples of mental development that range from very direct to very indirect hereditary influence.

At the very direct end of the scale is the case of a child suffering from phenylpyruvic amentia or amaurotic idiocy (Anastasi, 1958, p. 198). Both these mental defects result from hereditary metabolic dysfunctions that are not significantly improved by changes made in the child's environment. The affected child remains mentally defective.

Heredity has a less direct influence on mental development in cases of hereditary blindness or deafness. A blind or deaf child who is raised in an environment designed for children with normal sight and hearing will typically display symptoms of retarded mental growth. Although sight and hearing cannot be restored, changes can be made in the environment to compensate for the handicap. A blind child can be given audio-recordings of books and can be taught to read by the braille method; the deaf child can be taught sign language and lip reading. These compensatory measures enable mental development to proceed far more normally.

Our third example, from the very indirect end of the scale of hereditary influence, concerns social stereotypes. We recognize that genetic endowment has much influence in determining a child's skin color, height, weight, facial features, acuity of senses, and so forth. People within a given culture often associate certain intellectual or personality traits with such physical characteristics. In other words, people often hold social stereotypes. If a child's facial features and her movements are usually viewed in her society as typical of sweet, clever girls, then people will often treat this child as though she were sweet and bright. Since the way people treat a child influences the way that child comes to perceive herself, then we can conclude that the child's self-concept— her feeling of adequacy—is at least partially the result of social stereotypes associated with inherited physical characteristics. In effect, if the child perceives herself as clever rather than dull, she may be motivated to display more typical mental development than if she believed herself dull. Heredity, in this instance, has influenced mental development in a very indirect manner.

Earlier we said that although theorists who adopt one of these interactionist approaches emphasize the *in-what-manner* or *how* of nature–nurture interaction, they also have not entirely abandoned the question of *how much*. However, they phrase the question in new ways. For instance, when Anastasi (1958, p. 206) proposed that it is best to view nature–nurture in terms of a directness-indirectness scale, she added that the more indirectly heredity influences a behavior, "the wider will be the range of variation of possible outcomes." In other words, there is not much room for environment to influence a child's characteristics that most directly depend on genetic factors. Yet environment can very much influence those characteristics that are very indirectly linked to heredity. Thus, Anastasi is still posing a how-much question in terms of the amount of variability possible.

What can we say then about modern theorists' position on the heredity–environment issue? Today, most theorists consider themselves interactionists in that they think both nature and nurture are indispensable and work together to produce development. However, this does not mean that the debate has ended— theorists continue to disagree on the conditions of nature–nurture interaction. Indeed, one of the most incendiary social controversies in American educational circles in recent years centers on the question of whether the genetic endowment of certain racial groups limits their potential mental ability compared to that of other racial groups (Hebb, 1970; Hirsch, 1970; Jensen, 1969; Jensen, 1973; Layzer, 1974). Since the issues are complex and far from settled, arguments of this type can be expected to continue in the years ahead.

When we analyze theories of development, we can include such guide questions as the following:

2.1 Can the theorist be identified by such traditional labels as *preformationist, predeterminist, interactionist, hereditarian,* or *environmentalist?*

2.2 Does the theorist see some aspects of development more constrained by hereditary boundaries than others? For example: Are the inherited-potential boundaries narrower or the heredity connections more direct for skin color than those for oral language skills (if indeed two such different characteristics can be adequately compared in terms of amounts)?

2.3 Does the theorist see heredity as more constraining for certain growth characteristics at different periods of childhood? For example: Are the inherited-potential boundaries for the development of reading ability different at age 6 than they are at age 12?

2.4 Does the theorist describe the process by which the interaction of nature and nurture takes place?

3. *Direction of development.* The terms *growth* and *development** both imply change, and it has been one of the central concerns of theorists to identify the directions of this change.

A good example of a theory that gives central attention to directions of development is Werner's (Chapter 9). Werner identifies one direction of growth, for instance, as that from rigidity to flexibility. By this he means that an infant displays rigid behaviors suited specifically to given situations and does not readily alter these behaviors to suit new conditions. An adolescent's behaviors, however, are more flexible and adapt readily to changed conditions.

---

* *Growth* is often defined as change in size, *development* as change in the complexity and functions of the individual. However, both terms may be defined as change in both size and function. It is in this second, more inclusive manner that the terms are used in this book.

Perhaps the easiest way to discover the directions of development assumed within a theory is to ask: How does the child differ from the adult? In Rousseau's view of children, one important direction is from irrational to rational person. In the Puritan view, the proper direction is from naturally sinful person to consciously moral person.

In our search for the directions described or implied in a theory, we can ask:

3.1 What aspects of behavior or growth (for example, physical growth, cognitive development, social skills) are encompassed by a particular principle or statement of direction?

3.2 What interrelationships, if any, exist between the direction of change of one aspect and that of another? For example: Does attainment of physical maturity come before the attainment of intellectual maturity? Does the differentiation of behaviors in the young child proceed more rapidly than the integration of various individual actions into smoothly flowing systems of behavior?

4. *Continuous versus stepwise change.* Usually theories not only define directions of change, but they tell whether this change occurs gradually in small increments or dramatically in large periodic increments (steep advances) that are followed by periods of less apparent change (plateaus). Skinner's behaviorism is an example of a theory that pictures growth as occurring in imperceptibly small increments. In contrast, other theories picture growth as shifting from one major step or stage to another. Piaget proposed steps and substeps of cognitive development. Freud identified several major psychosexual stages of growth. Havighurst proposed that children at different points in their life are confronted with particular tasks of growing up and that these tasks form a series of stages in development. In effect, the essence of many theories is found in the sorts of stages they postulate and in the way they view the child's movement from one level to the next. The controversy about these matters among developmentalists has traditionally been known as the *continuity–discontinuity issue.*

Everyone agrees that development from one day to the next is gradual. No one claims that a twelve-year-old girl is a prepuberal child one week and a full-blown adolescent the next. In this sense, growth is continuous and occurs in small increments. The real question, then, is whether, during this process, the child's structure and behavior periodically display symptoms that warrant the label of a new stage of development. Behaviorists like Skinner answer no to this question; other theorists answer yes. Theorists who answer yes are then obligated to identify the traits of a stage so that, following their theories, we can recognize a new stage when we meet one.

Consequently, in analyzing a theorist's position on the continuity–discontinuity issue, we can first pose this question:

4.1 Does development of children proceed through a series of small, continuous increments without any dramatic changes or identifiable qualitative plateaus? Or do children develop from one recognizable stage to another?

If the answer to this first query is that the child does pass through stages, then we can profitably pose several more questions:

4.2 How does the theorist define *stage* or *step* or *period*?

4.3 How many stages does he identify in his system, and what are the names and distinguishing characteristics of each stage?

4.4 On what aspects of life or growth do the stages focus? In other words, what dimensions of development do the stages represent? For example: Are these stages of physical growth? of sexual development? of socialization? of moral judgment? of oral-language development?

4.5 Do the aspects or dimensions have the same importance at all times during childhood? For example: Are physical growth stages more prominent in the early years than they are later in childhood?

Further, the matter of whether children are growing up "normally" is of interest to many people—parents, teachers, pediatricians, and the children themselves. Therefore, it is useful to ask what a theory expects of developmental stages. To begin:

4.6 How are the levels or stages related to chronological age?

Of the proposals discussed in later chapters, that of Gesell's (Chapter 6) is the most specific in correlating age with growth characteristics. Gesell described in rather definite terms what the typical two-year-old is like and how her characteristics differ from those of the one-year-old and the three-year-old. The stages described by Piaget, Freud, and Havighurst are less closely tied to specific ages than Gesell's, and Maslow's levels of human needs (Chapter 19) are even less specifically correlated with chronological age than those of Piaget and Freud.

The question of age–stage correlation is not the only one pertinent to the task of judging the normality of a child's growth. For example, a number of questions arise about the universality and invariance of stages.

4.7 Are the stages universal, that is, true for all children in all cultures? Or do children in one culture pass through different stages from those in another? Within a culture, is it possible for a child to skip what has been described as a stage, or must everyone move through the stages in a single defined sequence? If a child can skip a stage or proceed by a different path than some of his peers, why does this deviation occur?

Many theorists consider the stages they describe to be universal—found among all children in all cultures—and their sequence invariant. *Invariant* means that not only are the stages found in all cultures for which we have reports, but the nature of development is such that no other sequence in the pattern of growth stages is possible. Such writers as Piaget (Chapter 13), Kohlberg (Chapter 16), and Erikson (Chapter 12) have assumed invariance although this position has been questioned recently by critics (Phillips and Kelly, 1975). Remember, therefore, not only to inquire about a theorist's position but also to consider whether the evidence or line of reasoning used to support that position is convincing.

Three other sets of questions can be asked about how growth rates, fixation at a stage, and regression to an earlier stage may be treated in a theory.

4.8 Does everyone go through the stages at the same pace? If not, why not?

The terms *retarded, normal, advanced,* and *gifted* have traditionally been used to describe children who are growing at particular rates compared to their age mates, regardless of whether growth is viewed as continuous or stepwise. Question 4.8 is directed at whether a theory recognizes such phenomena and, if so, how it accounts for them.

Another question related to the rate of passing through stages is:

4.9 Can a child display typical characteristics of more than one stage at the same time? If so, why does this occur?

Some theorists (Gesell, Havighurst) make little or no mention of this possibility; others accord it considerable attention (Erikson, Piaget, Kohlberg). An example of the simultaneous presence of multiple stages is found in Piaget's subtheory about children's ideas of causality. When Piaget studied what children believe causes certain physical events in the world, he concluded that a child who accounts for cloud movements by saying elves push the clouds is operating on a lower level of thought than a child who says that air currents (rising hot air, descending cool air) move the clouds. Piaget found, however, that while a child may use fantasy beings (elves) to account for certain physical events, the same child may give naturalistic explanations (air currents) to account for others. In effect, the child is operating on two stage levels at the same time (Piaget, 1930).

4.10 Can a child's progress through the stages become arrested or fixated at a particular stage? If sò, what causes the fixating? What can be done to release the fixation and stimulate progress to the next stage?

Theorists account for fixation in several ways. Gesell's system, which can be viewed as a predeterminist theory, views arrested development as caused by inadequate genetic endowment. Behaviorists feel it results from inadequate stimulus from the environment. Freud's psychoanalysis views it as seated in either too much satisfaction of needs at the present stage of development or far too little satisfaction.

4.11 Can a child return to an earlier stage after he has entered a more advanced one? If so, what causes this *regression* or *retrogression*? What can be done to help a child recover and move ahead once more?

Regression, like fixation, is of particular interest to therapists, whose task it is to assist children whose development seems to be going awry. The most popular explanation, by theorists who recognize the phenomenon of regression, is that a child slips back to an earlier stage of development when the adjustment skills he has developed at his present stage prove inadequate for coping with the current problems. However, some theorists, such as Kephart (Chapter 20), contend that there is no such thing as true regression. The child does not really slip back but just gives the appearance of regressing by adopting a segment of behavior from an earlier time. This appearance is not regression but illusion because in Kephart's view "development is irreversible" (Kephart, 1971, p. 40).

Our concern with retardation, fixation, regression, and uneven development can also lead logically to another question:

4.12 If a child experiences growth problems at one stage, how may these problems influence her success at subsequent levels? And how can we best deal with such problems?

For most theorists, problems that are not adequately resolved at one stage either will prevent the child from moving on to the next or will make it difficult for the child to adjust to subsequent levels. And most feel that therapy or retraining is required to correct or ameliorate the problems and thus enable the child to continue her development. However, not all theories see the issue in this same light. Theories like Gesell's, which see genetic factors as greatly restricting the range within which environmental factors can affect development, do not usually propose therapy or retraining. For instance, Gesell's model of development contains the concept of alternating "good" and "bad" years or phases of growth. This pattern of alternation is seen as a "natural" one, common to virtually all children. So problems at one level of growth are seen as instances of "going through a bad phase" that will naturally pass with time. Patience rather than therapy is needed to wait out the passing of the phase (Ilg and Ames, 1955, pp. 22–24).

In summary, twelve sets of questions have been proposed to guide our inquiry into the way a theorist handles the continuity–discontinuity issue. Although most of the questions are directed at theories that view growth as occurring in steps or stages, a number of them are also useful for understanding nonstage or continuous theories as well. For example, we can ask if a continuous growth model pictures all children as developing along the same route (4.7) and at the same pace (4.8). We can also ask if a child can become fixated (4.10) or can regress (4.11) and how growth problems can be ameliorated (4.12).

5. *Original moral condition.* An issue of greater interest in past centuries than it is today is that of the child's natural moral state. Some theorists either state outright or imply that the child at birth, and by natural inclination, is in a particular moral condition: good (moral), bad (immoral), or neutral (amoral). Rousseau considered children to be innately moral, and felt that if they are to remain good, they need to be protected throughout their growing years from the corruptions of an immoral society. The Puritans, in contrast, considered children to be innately immoral, and felt that they need a great deal of strict guidance if they are to be saved from the Devil. Freudians regard children as innately amoral—that is, without knowledge of right or wrong at birth— but with a capacity to internalize the morals of their social environment so that these values eventually become a part of their personalities, the *superego*. Maslow, as a humanistic psychologist,

viewed the child's sense of morals as being partly innate and partly learned.

Therefore, in comparing theories, we may wish to ask:

5.1 What is the original or genetically determined condition of the child: moral, immoral, or amoral? Can the newborn be some mixture of the three, depending on which aspect of development is under consideration?

6. *Personality structure*. Most theories of development assume that the child has a psychological system or a sort of mental machinery, which is known by such terms as *personality, mind, intervening variables*, or *cognitive structure*. Usually this system is assumed to contain elements or functions that interact to determine the child's behavior. Part of the task of understanding development, then, consists of identifying these components and the ways they interact over the first two decades of life. Freud's system includes three such key elements: the *id*, the *ego*, and the *superego*. Both the Puritans and Rousseau called the important elements of personality *mental faculties*. Thus, in analyzing a theory, we may wish to ask:

6.1 What are the components of personality or of behavior?

6.2 How do the components interact and change as the child grows up?

7. *Motivation and the learning process*. In the field of psychology, the topics of motivation and learning are often considered separately. However, motivation is typically seen as the fuel for learning, the director of the child's attention toward what he will seek to learn. Therefore, since motivation can be viewed as a beginning step or condition in the learning process, we will discuss them together.

Not all theorists use the same terms to identify motivating forces. However, the two most popular terms are *need* and *drive*. These terms are like two sides of a coin, two ways of looking at the same phenomenon. The word *need* implies intake, a void seeking to be filled. *Drive* implies output, pent-up energy searching for a place in which to invest or expend itself. So the need for food is the hunger drive, and the need for drink is the thirst drive. Although there is a tendency for some theorists to favor the term *need* (humanistic psychologists) and others to favor *drive* (behaviorists), in each case the intention is to identify a motivating force that energizes behavior (Hall and Lindzey, 1970, pp. 175–180, 425–436).

In some theories little or no attention is given to describing motivating forces (Gesell, Chapter 6; Kephart, Chapter 20; Kohlberg, Chapter 16). In others, however, motivating forces are at the center of the schemes (the Puritans, Chapter 3; Freud, Chapter 11; Maslow, Chapter 19).

Furthermore, some theorists conceive of a single general force that activates all behavior. In Freud's early model, he called this general force *libido,* an energy arising in a component of the personality called the *id* but utilized by other components of the personality as well to fuel their functions. Freud originally pictured libidinal energy as dominantly a sexual drive. However, in his later years he altered his beliefs and suggested that development and behavior are motivated by the interaction of two contrary drives, a life-promoting force (*eros*) that accounted for constructive events in the personality and a death-directed force (*thanatos*) that accounted for destructive ones (S. Freud, 1938, pp. 5–6).

Many theories of personality and development either explicitly or implicitly differentiate among levels of needs. For example, a commonly postulated basic need from the field of biology is that of self-preservation. But when we observe behavior, we can propose that this basic need is manifested through a variety of more specific needs, such as those for food, for oxygen, for sexual expression, and for succor (the need to be nursed, supported, and consoled) (Hall and Lindzey, 1970, pp. 174–180).

Theorists, then, differ in the number of motivating forces they identify or imply, as well as in the way they name and organize the proposed drives or needs. Therefore, we may wish to include in our guide questions the following:

7.1 Does the theorist identify or imply forces that motivate behavior? If so, what are these forces and what are their characteristics?

Not all theorists who propose the existence of various drives or needs agree as to the potency of each. For instance, Freud described his general force, libidinal energy, as being preeminently sexual. An early colleague of Freud's, Alfred Adler (1870–1937), disagreed that the prepotent human drive was sexual. Though he recognized sex as a significant drive, Adler contended that the truly overriding motive in human development was a *will to power,* a striving for superiority. He wrote that "whatever premises all our philosophers and psychologists dream of—self-preservation, pleasure principle, equalization—all these are but vague representations, attempts to express the great upward drive" (Adler, 1930, p. 398).

Maslow's system (Chapter 19) also recognizes differences in the potency of various motivating forces but pictures their operation in a manner different from Freud's or Adler's. Maslow suggested that a person's needs are arranged in a hierarchy, like steps on a ladder, with the lower-step needs requiring fulfillment before the upper-step needs. He relegated such survival needs as those for food, drink, and physical safety to the lower levels of the hierarchy and drives for creative expression and "self-actualization" to the upper levels.

Not only may theorists claim that some needs are more significant than others throughout life, but they may also propose that certain needs are more potent at one stage of development than at another. For instance, a need for physical protection and nurturance is often considered more important during infancy, while a need for sexual expression is considered more demanding following puberty. (See the developmental tasks of Chapter 7.)

From this discussion we can generate another set of guide questions:

7.2 If several motivating forces are identified in the theory, do all of them carry equal power and importance? If not, which are more significant and why? If they differ in potency, do their relative degrees of power change from one growth stage or one age level to another?

Most theorists agree that a child is not only motivated strongly or weakly, but is also motivated toward particular things in the environment. In other words, a motivating force not only has power but also direction. Theorists do not agree, however, about the source or cause of this direction. The question is essentially this:

7.3 Which source—the child's inner needs or the environment's stimuli—is more important in determining where the child directs his attention?

Such theorists as Piaget and Freud credit inner needs with the greater power to direct attention, while behaviorists consider environmental stimuli as the more important source of direction. To a substantial degree, this difference of opinion reflects the more basic disagreement about which model each camp of theorists believes best represents human behavior. In Chapter 1 we noted that some theories of development are founded on the analogy of the machine, while others are based on the analogy of an organism. A machine reacts to things done to it by outside forces. It is "motivated" by environmental stimuli. An organism contains internal driving forces that seek expression in the environment; it is motivated by inner needs that direct its attention to those things in the environment that will likely fulfill the needs.

We noted earlier that motivation or stimulation is commonly considered to be a beginning step in the learning process. Exactly what steps occur after this stimulation is a matter of dispute among theorists. A behaviorist like Skinner sketches one picture of the process, Piaget quite a different picture, and Lewin still another. Therefore, in analyzing theories, we can suitably ask:

7.4 In this theory, how does motivation fit into the overall picture of the learning process?

7.5 What are the conditions necessary for learning to occur? What elements or mechanisms comprise the learning process, and how do the elements interact?

8. *Individual differences.* It is obvious that children of a given age level are not all alike. They differ in many ways. Theories of child development also differ in how they treat this matter of variation among children. For example, some theorists—Gesell, for example—give little recognition to the issue of differences. They talk almost exclusively about the typical child, passing over the fact that nearly all children deviate to some degree from the average. Other theories, such as behaviorism and Lewin's topological viewpoint, account more adequately for differences among individuals. Hence, to guide our comparisons among theories, we can ask:

8.1 What sorts of individual differences among children are given attention in the theory?

8.2 How does the theory account for such differences? To what extent do the factors that cause differences arise from heredity or from environment, and how do the causal factors operate or develop?

9. *Desirable-undesirable, normal-abnormal.* One of the most common, practical questions asked by parents, teachers, and others who deal with children is whether a child's development is normal. Since not everyone defines the term *normal* in the same way, this question can be misleading. In one sense *normal* is used to mean "well adjusted" or "getting along very nicely." In another sense it means that the child's growth is about average for her age, or her behavior is common for her size or grade in school. We encounter problems of communication when these two meanings are mixed. For example, smoking cigarettes is very common among American youths in their upper teens and early twenties, so in this sense smoking is "normal"—that is, typical. But medical evidence suggests that smoking is not desirable, so in the sense of "getting along very nicely," smoking is not normal.

Another term that is often linked or confused with *normal* is *natural*. People usually think of *natural* as being what occurs if we do not consciously try to change things. It is letting Nature take her course. But not everyone agrees that natural growth is desirable or good. In the following chapters, the two theories that are most conspicuously on opposite sides in this debate are the Puritan and Rousseauistic views. The Puritans said that the child is naturally bad, so the task of parents is to combat these natural tendencies. Rousseau said that the child is naturally good and will develop into a paragon of wisdom and virtue if not corrupted by an evil environment.

Other theorists have not concerned themselves with the issues of either normal or natural development. Instead, they have either implied or specifically defined the characteristics of desirable or proper development. They have pointed out the desired goals or directions of growth, then assumed that deviations from the path toward the goals are undesirable.

To guide our efforts in sorting out these matters, we can ask:

9.1 Are normal or natural or desirable development defined, or at least implied? If two or more of these terms appear in the theory, are they used synonymously? If not, how are they different from each other?

9.2 Are such things as abnormal, unnatural, or undesirable development identified? If two or more of these terms appear in the theory, are they used synonymously? If not, how do they differ?

9.3 What causes abnormal, unnatural, or undesirable development? What, if anything, can be done to change such development into normal, natural, or desirable growth?

10. *Philosophical origins and assumptions.* No theory is an entirely new creation. Each has its philosophical progenitors, and our understanding of a theory is usually enhanced by our learning something of this ancestry. We can better comprehend Maria Montessori's view of the child (Chapter 20) if we know that she adopted convictions expressed by Rousseau. Our grasp of Maslow's brand of humanistic psychology (Chapter 19) is enriched by our knowing that his proposals, in part, represent his reaction against what he believed were the shortcomings of both psychoanalysis and behaviorism. Furthermore, we can profit from knowing that Erikson's ideas (Chapter 12) are founded primarily on Freud's teachings but have been influenced as well by methodology and concepts from cultural anthropology.

So we add another pair of queries to our list:

10.1 On what philosophical traditions, beliefs, and assumptions is the theory founded?

10.2 Against what beliefs is the theory reacting?

11. *Investigative methods.* There is something of a chicken-and-egg relationship between a theory and its investigative methods. We never know whether (a) the theory's structure has defined the methods it uses for gathering data or (b) the data-collecting methods have dictated the structure of the theory. In any event, models of child development are heavily influenced by the investigative techniques used in producing the data they treat.

For instance, Freud's main method of collecting information was listening to neurotic adults recall incidents from their childhood and from their current dreams. The particular recollections this method evoked clearly influenced the nature of the theory he proposed. The charge that his theory gives a gloomy, disturbed view of human development has been raised by critics who blame his choice of neurotic informants as the cause of the ostensibly pessimistic picture he paints of child growth (Stone and Church, 1973, p. 204). Likewise, his dependence on self-reports of memories and dreams as his source of data is compatible with his willingness to fashion an imaginary structure of the "mind" from which these memories and dreams are generated. In contrast, Skinner rejected introspective reports as sources of evidence and depended instead on descriptions of child behavior as recorded by an outside observer. This dedication to observable events is compatible with Skinner's unwillingness to speculate about such hypothetical elements as an unseeable "mind" or such mental components as Freud's id, ego, and superego.

Thus, in analyzing theories, we can ask:

11.1 What investigative methods are used by the theorist?

11.2 How have these methods influenced the form and content of the theory?

12. *Appeal for acceptance.* Typically, theorists want others to believe their proposals. To this end they seek to present the sorts of arguments they feel will appeal to the people they want to have accept their scheme. For instance, early Puritan writers appealed to their parishioners' faith in the word of God as found in the Bible and on a set of deductions about child rearing that pastors drew from church doctrine. Rousseau sought to convince his

readers by means of illustrative anecdotes drawn from his imagination or his experience as a tutor of children of aristocrats. Classical psychoanalysts propose that, in addition to the intuitive
good sense their theory makes, a person becomes convinced of its
validity by going through the process of psychoanalysis. Experimental psychologists describe their experiments in detail and cast
the results in statistical form, with the expectation that anyone
who questions the results can carry out the same experiments and
see for himself the validity of the conclusions.

Consequently, different theorists use different approaches in
appealing for acceptance of their schemes. Likewise, different
consumers of child development theories find some sorts of evidence more convincing than others. Whether you find a particular theory more useful or valid than another depends on how
well the theorist's mode of appeal matches the types of evidence
you consider most acceptable. Hence, we may ask:

12.1 On what sorts of evidence or on what types of appeal
does the theory depend to convince people of its worth?

13. *Terminology.* In the following chapters you will find many
terms created or adopted by theorists to describe their ideas of
personality structure, growth stages, and growth principles.
These include *id, orthogenetic principle, soul, growth gradients, topological maps, formal operations,* and many more. Often the essence of a theorist's position is contained in the terms he uses. If
you comprehend his terms, you understand the substance of his
beliefs.

If, in our investigation of a theory, we answer the twelve
clusters of questions already considered in this chapter, then we
will likely have learned the meaning of most or all the key terms
in the theory. But in case we have missed any, we can add two
final sets of queries:

13.1 Does the theory have a special terminology? If so, what
does each term mean?

13.2 Do the terms refer to concepts unique to this theory, or
do they identify things for which other theorists have used
different words?

CONCLUSION

In Chapter 2, a series of questions has been proposed that can be
asked about the contents and philosophical underpinnings of the-

ories we wish to analyze and compare. The list does not include all the questions that could be asked, but only ones I feel might be of general interest. You may wish to add others that focus on matters of particular importance to you.

In the following chapters separate theories are described. In organizing each chapter we have sought, as far as space permits, to answer the questions posed in Chapter 2. However, none of the chapters is designed as a sequential list of answers to these questions, with topic 1 presented first and topic 13 last. Such a catalogue pattern would make the chapters read too much like catechisms. Therefore, each chapter is presented in a form intended to give the essence of the theorist's approach in a logical and interesting fashion. In the process, as many of the Chapter 2 questions are answered as is feasible. Some chapters do not treat certain questions because the theorist or theorists did not answer such questions. In other instances, a topic plays such a small part in a particular theory that it was not worth discussing in this introductory level volume.

Now, with the perspectives of Chapters 1 and 2 in mind, we move to the theories themselves, beginning at a point several centuries in the past and then rushing quickly to modern times.

FOR FURTHER READING

You may wish to find additional topics and questions to supplement the list given in this chapter. If so, your most convenient source may be child development textbooks. Chapter titles and topic headings in such books often imply questions the textbook authors believe are important for theorists to answer. Thus an inspection of titles and headings can suggest additional guide questions. Furthermore, under such headings you often find concise answers to the questions as seen from various theorists' points of view.

To aid you in this search, the following list of representative sources is suggested:

Bernard, Harold W. (1975) *Human Development in Western Culture*. 4th ed. Boston: Allyn and Bacon.

Haimowitz, Morris L. and Natalie Reader Haimowitz. (1973) *Human Development: Selected Readings*. 3d ed. New York: Crowell.

Langer, Jonas. (1969) *Theories of Development.* New York: Holt, Rinehart, and Winston.

Medinnus, Gene R. and Ronald C. Johnson. (1975) *Child and Adolescent Psychology.* 2d ed. New York: Wiley.

Munsinger, Harry. (1975) *Fundamentals of Child Development.* 2d ed. New York: Holt, Rinehart, and Winston.

Mussen, Paul Henry, John Janeway Conger, and Jerome Kagan. (1974) *Child Development and Personality.* 4th ed. New York: Harper & Row.

Rogers, Dorothy. (1969) *Issues in Adolescent Psychology.* New York: Appleton-Century-Crofts.

Sutton-Smith, Brian. (1973) *Readings in Child Psychology.* New York: Appleton-Century-Crofts.

Travers, John F. (1977) *The Growing Child.* New York: Wiley.

Watson, Robert I. and Henry Clay Lindgren. (1973) *Psychology of the Child.* 3d ed. New York: Wiley.

PART 2

TRACES FROM THE PAST

A search for proper ways of reacting to the child's original nature.

Theories of child development are not unique to the twentieth century. People have always had beliefs about how children develop. Two sets of beliefs from the past are considered in Part 2. They illustrate contrasting patterns of belief that have exerted significant influence in Europe and North America in recent centuries. The first traces its origin to such Protestant writers as John Calvin (1509–1564) and John Knox (1505–1572). The second is based mainly on the writings of the Swiss fomentor of social protest, Jean Jacques Rousseau (1712–1778). Since vestiges of both viewpoints are found in modern society, an understanding of the basic elements of each is of interest and use today.

In the 1530s John Calvin, a Swiss theologian, followed Martin Luther's (1483–1546) lead and launched his own movement of protest against the church of Rome. The Protestant doctrines preached by Calvin and the Scotsman John Knox became the founding principles for Presbyterianism in Scotland and for Puritanism in England and in colonial America.

At the core of Calvin's doctrine was a conception of human nature that pictured the newborn child as a sinner, possessed of motives to do evil. The task of parents and teachers was to discover ways to dissuade the child from his naturally evil bent and make him worthy to enter heaven for his life after death. Thus, the Calvinist conception of child development represents a search for proper ways of reacting to the sinful and obstinate nature of children.

The Puritan view of the child was particularly strong in New England from the seventeenth to the nineteenth centuries. Then its popularity waned. However, Puritan concepts of child development did not entirely disappear. Elements of the doctrine can be found today in the words and deeds of many adults. As a result, the beliefs contained in Puritan theory are not just historical curiosities. Understanding them is useful for bringing to light the religious and cultural origins of the strict child-raising practices found today in some homes and schoolrooms. A Puritan view of child development is described in Chapter 3.

In 1762 the Swiss social philosopher Jean Jacques Rousseau published two books that made him famous. *The Social Contract* made him an idol among the instigators of the French Revolution, and *Emile* established him as a forebear of the nineteenth- and twentieth-century theorists who have written on early childhood education.

In contrast to the Puritans, Rousseau proposed in *Emile* that the child is born morally good. The child will naturally do the right thing unless misled by a corrupt social environment. So Rousseau's description of child development is the result of his search for ways of guiding children's growth so they remain true to their natural inclinations. Elements of Rousseau's beliefs are found today in the writings of such theorists as Piaget (Chapter 13) and Montessori (Chapter 20) and in books on "discovery methods" in teaching science. Rousseau's picture of child development is summarized in Chapter 4.

CHAPTER 3

THE PURITANS' SINFUL AND OBSTINATE CHILD

No Puritan author apparently ever collected early Protestant thoughts about child nature and organized them into a systematic description of the Puritan child development theory found in colonial America. Hence, we have to search through the writings of Protestant leaders to extract from them the Puritan picture of the child.*

The picture offered in the following pages is composed primarily of gleanings from a variety of seventeenth- and eighteenth-century Protestant writings, including those of such prominent theologians as Jonathan Edwards, John Cotton, Cotton Mather, Samuel Sewall, and Benjamin Wadsworth. But perhaps the most interesting of the sources is *The New England Primer*, a tiny volume hardly longer or broader than a young child's hand. The *Primer*, between 1687 and the mid-1800s, is estimated to have sold six million copies, or an average of 40,000 a year in a then sparsely settled America (Morison, 1936, p. 79). During the 1700s it was *the* schoolbook for children of Protestant families, and during the 1800s was still widely used in conjunction with other texts (Ford, 1962, p. 19). It is unlikely that parents, pastors, and schoolmasters would have permitted such heavy dependence on a textbook if it did not represent their idea of the truth. So it seems safe to assume

---

* The terms *Puritan, Calvinist,* and *Protestant* are used interchangeably throughout Chapter 3, with the understanding that *Calvinism* is intended to mean "Calvinism of colonial times" and *Protestant* refers to "an early Calvinist form of Protestant belief." I recognize that modern Calvinists would not necessarily hold all the beliefs reviewed in Chapter 3, and that all forms of Protestantism, today or in the past, would not include all the views described in this chapter.

that the view of child nature reflected in the *Primer* is a fair representation of the beliefs held by a major segment of the population.

In reviewing the Puritan model of the child, we will first consider some basic assumptions about child nature and the purpose of life. Then we will discuss the structure and functions of the human personality, stages of development, and the role of instruction and learning. Finally, we will make a brief appraisal from the perspective of the late twentieth century.

BASIC PREMISES AND THEIR CONSEQUENCES

Three key assumptions undergirded the Puritan view: (1) the child is born evil, bound to sin if not guided away from her natural state; (2) the child is born without knowledge, meaning that she is not sufficiently aware of sinfulness or of how to lead a good life; and (3) the child is born with a capacity to learn. The first of these assumptions was founded on religious doctrine, the second and third apparently on common sense.

The role of education in the home, church, and school was to redirect the child from her natural inclinations so she might be saved from an eternity in hell after death. Salvation was not guaranteed to the person who learned to live the good life, because salvation was a gift of God, not earned by humans through good works in the world. But Puritans believed that striving to lead the kind of life that would please God could open the channel to salvation. Leading a good life improved one's chances of receiving God's grace.

Most crucial to the Puritan doctrine was the idea that the sin of disobedience to God that Adam and Eve committed when they ate the forbidden fruit in the Garden of Eden was a sin carried down through all generations. The newborn child was the recipient of this original sin and would be condemned to hell after death if not redeemed. *The New England Primer* introduced children to the first letter of the alphabet with a verse that made this premise clear (1836, p. 11):

A = In *Adam's* fall we sinned all.

The result of this innate sin was that the child's natural motivation was to behave in evil ways that would please the devil.

The child would naturally frolic "and take delight among young folk who spend their days in joy and mirth" (*Primer*, 1836, p. 57). He would pass his time in idleness, disobey his parents and others in authority, lie and curse and steal, ignore his studies and play truant from school, hate others, fight with his brothers and sisters and schoolmates, refuse to pray or attend church, not read the Bible, fail to abide by the Ten Commandments, and refuse to accept or follow Christ (*Primer*, 1836, pp. 10–64). Such behavior as this signified to the Puritan the expected, natural course of development.

Thus, the child was urged not to follow his natural inclinations but instead to prepare himself properly for "life after death." In Calvinism, as in so many other denominations, the years between earthly birth and death are only a trial period. They are a time of testing and of preparation for eternal life in the "great beyond." To avoid an afterlife of eternal misery in hell, he needs to adopt the goals of the good child. The good child is one who keeps himself engaged in profitable tasks and does not idle away his time, obeys his superiors, does not lie or swear or steal, studies hard in school, forgives his enemies, speaks well of others and treats them with kindness, reads the Bible and prays regularly, attends church, abides by the Ten Commandments, loves Christ, and accepts Christ as his redeemer from sin. In this way, the Puritans defined the desired course of child development.

THE HUMAN PERSONALITY— STRUCTURE AND FUNCTION

The Calvinists did not invent the theory of human intellect to which they subscribed. Rather, they inherited it from medieval theologians Albertus Magnus and Thomas Aquinas and the philosopher–psychologists of the Renaissance who refined the theory. It was altered slightly to accommodate certain Protestant beliefs, but in the main it was the *faculty psychology* of the day as taught in books on physics and physiology. Puritan sermons abounded in allusions to this model of the mind, thus attesting to the general understanding of it on the part of both the theologians and their parishioners (Miller, 1963, pp. 242–244). Although it is here oversimplified, this model was accepted as obvious truth by the followers of Luther, Calvin, and Knox.

We can best explain the nature of the *mind* or *soul* from the faculty psychologist's point of view if we consider what occurs in a child's mental apparatus as she encounters a barking dog. The first part of the child's thought-and-action system that is activated is the set of *external senses,* the five senses Aristotle identified: sight, hearing, touch, taste, and smell. The noisy dog produces on the eye and ear a replica or image of the animal's visage and sound. Each image, the *phantasm* or *species* of the observed object, is then picked up from the eye and ear by *animal spirits,* the powers that convey information through the nerves from one organ to another (see Figure 3.1). The animal spirits deliver the dog phantasms to a chamber in the center of the brain labeled the *common sense;* this is the place in which phantasms from all the senses are collected,

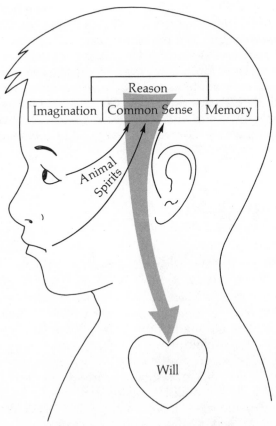

Figure 3.1   Faculties of the Mind

apprehended, and distinguished from one another. The common sense is an *internal sense* or *faculty*—"faculty" meaning a power, capacity, or function of the mind.

Within the common sense, the phantasms of sight and sound are identified as belonging to the species dog, specifically a barking dog that is showing its teeth and not wagging its tail. The common sense passes the results of its interpretation to a forward chamber of the brain where the faculty of *imagination* (sometimes called the *fancy* or *phantasy*) judges and compares phantasms with each other, retains them when the object (the dog in this instance) is no longer present, and renders them more vivid. The imagination compares the dog image with remembered images from the past and judges it to be unfriendly and perhaps dangerous. This judgment by the imagination is next relayed to the faculty of *memory* at the rear of the brain to be stored for future reference.

At the same time, somewhere above the common sense, the faculty of *reason* or *understanding* calls before it phantasms either from imagination or from memory. Reason judges whether the phantasms are true or false, desirable or undesirable, good or evil. Phantasms of past dogs (drawn from memory) and the present dog (drawn from imagination) are analyzed by reason, which concludes that the present animal might attack, particularly if the child should run as if afraid. Reason determines that the wisest behavior is to walk past the dog cautiously, without a show of fear, while keeping a wary eye on the beast.

This conclusion about wise action is conveyed from reason by animal spirits along the nerves to the faculty of the *will*, which resides in the heart. The role of the will is to accept the images of wise behavior from reason and to command suitable emotions (usually called *affections* or *passions*) in the heart to activate appropriate muscles to carry out reason's decision. This entire process, from the instant the child first sees the dog until her will orders her feet to walk, requires just a moment or two, and we see her hesitate only briefly when she meets the dog, before she walks by the animal as if not afraid, all the time willing her emotion of fear to be tempered with courage and caution (Miller, 1963, pp. 240–242).

This system of human thought and action was called the *soul* by both Renaissance philosophers and Calvinists. The soul, in contrast to the body, is not transmitted through heredity. Rather, it is individually "created by God of nothing, immediately infused into the body (at birth) as the proper form thereof, by which man is, liveth, is sensible, moveth, understandeth, willeth, and is affected" (John Norton in Miller, 1963, p. 240). The human soul is a unitary object; but like God himself, it forms a trinity consisting of a *vegetative* soul, a *sensible* soul, and a *rational* soul. The vegetative soul has the powers of nourishing and propagating, two characteristics that people share with the earth's plant life. The sensible soul has not only powers of nourishing and propagating but also additional equipment possessed by animals—external senses and animal spirits, as well as the interior senses of common sense, imagination, memory, the passions or emotions, and the musculature (*sinews*) that makes motion possible. But it is the rational soul, the highest in the trinity, that distinguishes humans from the earth's other living things. The rational soul contains all the powers of the other two, plus the faculties of reason and will.

It was the fate of this rational soul that sorely concerned parents in their child-rearing practices, for the soul was immortal and continued after death through eternity, condemned to misery in hell or blessed with happiness in heaven. As in life, the soul after death was a sensitive being. Jonathan Edwards told his parishioners, "An unbodied spirit may be as capable of love and hatred, joy and sorrow, hope or fear, or other affections, as one that is united to a body" (Simonson, 1970, p. 163).

This doctrine of the human mind or personality had many other aspects as well. For instance, an important additional faculty was the *conscience*, defined as the awareness of distinctions between good and evil, between right and wrong. Puritans held that conscience was inborn, so the young child—even though he lacked much experience in the world—could not excuse his misdemeanors by saying he did not know any better. As Edwards pointed out (Smith, 1959, p. 207):

> Conscience naturally gives men an apprehension of right and wrong, and suggests the relation there is between right and wrong and retribution; the Spirit of God assists men's consciences to do this in a greater degree, helps conscience against the stupefying influence of worldly objects and their lusts.

In the case of conscience, as in many other matters, Puritan thinkers struggled with the nature–nurture issue. How much of the child's character and faculties is innate or God-given, and how much is due to instruction and experience? It was agreed that the child normally was born with all his faculties, or mental chambers. But the contents of the chambers, such as imagination and memory, were not filled until the child had experiences or instruction.

The activation and development of faculties depended on two factors as the child grew to maturity: (1) God's grace in endowing him with a particular level of different faculties or abilities—a child might have a special "bent" that could be developed—and (2) influences in his daily life at home, in school and church, and in the community. Although the conscience or knowledge of right from wrong was considered to be innate, Puritans did not hesitate to nourish it with threats, moralizing, and the whip.

Another faculty, *intuition,* apparently did not depend on instruction for its development. A person searched for this inner "sixth sense" through meditation, prayer, and introspection. Edwards regarded intuition as the instigator of the "great awakening" of religious conversion that Puritans so valued. He preached that conversion did not consist of a person's acting in a pious manner or even in doing good works but rather it was an overwhelming and immediate sense of God's reality (Simonson, 1970, p. 13). From an early age, children were urged to seek out this sense.

These, then, are the general outlines of the structure and function of the human soul or mind in Puritan times, although as Samuel Willard in his colonial period volume the *Compleat Body* admitted: "Our knowledge of the nature of our own Souls, is very shallow and confused" (Miller, 1963, p. 244).

STAGES OF DEVELOPMENT

Puritan writers did not leave us a well-defined description of the levels of development through which they believed children grew. However, by considering the ways children and youths were treated at different age levels and by analyzing the expectations held for them, we can propose four stages that seem to represent generally accepted development periods.

Infancy: Birth to Age 1½ or 2   This was the time when babies were completely dependent on adults to meet their physical needs. The period ended with the child's being able to walk alone and say a few meaningful words in communicating with others. Early in this stage, the parents had the infant baptized; the child was officially named and blessed by the church and was pledged to a Christian life by his or her parents. This pledge by the infant's guardians was necessary because a baby's faculties of reason and of will were obviously not yet developed enough for the infant to make such a decision.

Early Childhood: Age 2 to Age 5–7   During these years the child became increasingly mobile and learned to communicate in a basic manner. Young children were expected, as John Cotton wrote, to "spend much time in pastime and play, for their bodyes are too weak to labour, and their minds to study are too shallow . . . even the first seven years are spent in pastime, and God looks not much at it" (Morgan, 1956, pp. 28–29). Though Cotton chose seven years as the upper limit for this stage of idleness, in many households children were put to useful work, at least part-time, at ages 5 or 6.

During these years, children were to begin their indoctrination into Christian duty and the dangers of a sinful life. Learning at this early age was expected to be rote, with little or no comprehension of subtle meanings of interpretations, since the faculty of reason was as yet undeveloped. Martin Luther had suggested that it is all right to deal with the complexities of ideas when preaching to "scholars or wise men," but "with the young, keep always to one form, and teach them first of all these articles, namely, the Ten Commandments, the Belief, the Lord's Prayer, etc., according to the text, word for word, so that they may repeat them and learn them by heart" (Eby, 1971, p. 89).

Later Childhood: Age 5–7 to Age 11–14   At this stage children were to engage in useful work around the home and to attend school, if one was available. The most essential skill was that of reading, with computation and writing close behind. Mothers would begin their daughters on sewing, cooking, and housekeeping early in this period. Fathers or older brothers would supervise boys in masculine pursuits around the farm, shop, or home. Boys also changed their long dresses, called "coats," for pants that fastened just under the knees. At least once a week parents were expected to assess each child's progress in Biblical learning and make new assignments.

The two chief purposes behind all this activity were apparently to ensure that children had constructive tasks to keep them from devilry and to establish early the habit of diligence. As John Cotton warned in the early 1700s, "Idleness in youth is scarcely healed without a scar in age" (Morgan, 1956, p. 29).

During these years the faculties of common sense and imagination were quickened, memory was being filled, and reason and will were maturing.

Youth: Age 11–14 to Age 18–21 or Economic Independence   This was often called the "age of reason," for the faculties of understanding and will were now thought to be relatively mature, at least mature enough for the teenager to be considered a rational, responsible being. It was at this time that the youth typically joined the church, consciously fulfilling the baptismal pledge parents had expressed at infancy.

At the outset of this stage, the youth was expected to heed his or her calling. A *calling* in colonial times was of several types. First, the youth accepted God's call to a Christian life, as evidenced by achieving membership in the church. *Calling* also meant that the adolescent identified the vocation for which he or she was fitted by God. On the basis of this identification, a boy accepted an apprenticeship or, for a chosen few, an opportunity to attend Latin grammar school and enroll at Harvard or Yale, usually to become a minister. Even though a girl's calling was always to be a housekeeper, she, like her brothers, might be sent at puberty to service in someone else's home. Apprentices always lived with their masters and typically served in the master's home and shop for seven to ten years, until the boy reached age 21 and the girl age 18. Morgan, a modern writer on Puritan times, suggests that (1956, p. 38):

> Psychologically this separation of parents and children may have had a sound foundation. The child left home just at the time when parental discipline caused increasing friction, just at the time when a child begins to assert his independence. By allowing a strange master to take over the disciplinary function, the parent could meet the child upon a plane of affection and friendliness. At the same time the child would be taught good behavior by someone who would not forgive him any mischief out of affection for his person.

Since the faculties of the soul by this age were well developed, the youth was expected to go beyond the rote memorization of theological material. Now he should be able to argue subtleties of meaning and identify the best reasoned among several interpretations. He was also expected to display a strong will, to act on what his reason told him was right. When all this had occurred, childhood was past.

THE IMPORTANCE OF INSTRUCTION

Since, in the Puritan view, children's fates depended so heavily on their being taught to combat their innate wickedness, it was important that those who cared about them should get about the business of providing suitable instruction as soon as possible. Puritans believed that both evil and ignorance could be overcome through education. To combat Satan's influence over the infant, parents were urged to begin instructing infants as soon as they were able to understand anything. But, assuming that young children had but limited capacities for learning, Puritan leaders suggested that instruction should, like putting a liquid into a narrow-mouthed container, be poured into them "but by drops" (Morgan, 1956, p. 53). In the early years, this instruction was to be casual and informal, with the parent "often speaking to them of good things, now a little and then a little, line upon line, precept upon precept, little and often, as they are able to receive" (Cotton Mather in Morgan, 1956, pp. 53–54).

The sort of learning that would lead to salvation was the mastery of truths about God's plan as revealed in the Bible. In their earliest years children were expected to memorize these truths as told to them by their parents or siblings. But as their capacities increased, they were to learn to read the Bible by themselves so that, in keeping with Protestant doctrine, they might be their own priest and communicate directly with the Lord and the Lord's written word. In 1647 this conviction that every child should learn to read was used to support a law compelling every sizable community to establish a school so as to foil the scheme of "that old deluder, Satan, to keep men from the knowledge of the scriptures" (Vaughn, 1972, p. 237).

To enable children to combat their natural evil inclinations, it was necessary for parents and teachers to generate in them a strong motivation to pursue disciplined, constructive lives. Important tools for generating such motivation were threats of dire consequences, moderated somewhat by expressions of love. Puritan children were not so much enticed into good behavior by promises of rewards, now or in the hereafter, as they were frightened out of bad behavior by prospects of the fires of hell. In the *Primer* and in such sermons as Jonathan Edwards's "Sinners in the Hands of an Angry God," the child and youth met far more threats of death and misery than promises of happiness and heaven. In the list of phrases intended to drill children on the letters of the alphabet, the *Primer* included these illustrations of the use of *L* and *U* (1836, pp. 15–16).

L = *L*iars will have their part in the lake which burns with fire and brimstone.

U = *U*pon the wicked, God will rain a horrible tempest.

Martin Luther had written that "children should be educated not only to fear their parents, but to feel that God will be angry with them if they do *not* fear their parents" (Eby, 1971, pp. 25–27).

Always in conflict with the picture of the innately wicked child who deserved harsh treatment was the Puritan parents' feelings of love and affection for their children. Parents' fear of letting their hearts overrule their reason was apparently a prime motivator of the common practice in New England of sending children out at age 8 or 12 or 14 to be raised in someone else's home, "even when there was no apparent educational or economic advantage involved. . . . I suggest that Puritan parents did not trust themselves with their own children, that they were afraid of spoiling them with too great affection" (Peter Laslett in Rutman, 1970, p. 44).

When direct instruction, admonition, and threats of dire consequences failed to keep a child on the path of righteousness, Puritans turned to corporal punishment. Luther, in an essay deploring the general use of harsh teaching methods in schools, admitted, "Nevertheless, the child needs the discipline of the rod; but it must be tempered with admonition, and directed to his improvement; for without this, he will never come to any good, but will be ruined, soul and body" (Eby, 1971, p. 32).

These sentiments, first voiced in Europe, were later echoed in the American colonies by such Calvinists as Cotton Mather, who entitled one of his sermons "Better Whipt, than Damn'd" (Morgan, 1956, p. 58). Though the rod appeared often in both homes and schoolrooms, it was generally applied as a last resort. Morgan, in his modern monograph on the Puritan family, concluded that the ministers who wrote and spoke on the subject of instruction "almost always counselled their readers and listeners to win children to holiness by kindness rather than to force them to it by severity" (Morgan, 1956, p. 58).

In sum, the purpose of instruction was to direct children away from their evil inclinations and toward God's way. Instruction consisted of giving information and advice, of relating fables and verses containing moral lessons, and of teaching children to read so they might derive truth directly from the Bible. Motivation to pursue this learning was encouraged by threats of an eternity in hell, by promises that the best chance for salvation came from leading a Christian life, and ultimately by a sound whipping with a birch rod.

THE PURITAN VIEW: AN ASSESSMENT

Although the Puritan period has passed, there are still vestiges of the Puritans' conception of child development in European and American societies, Catholic as well as Protestant. Some Christian denominations continue to subscribe to many of their tenets. Far more people accept only certain of the beliefs, such as that the child tends to be innately bad, that idleness in later childhood is dangerous, and that children are incapable of rational thought and behavior until after puberty. People still try to "scare the devil out" of children and attribute a youth's irresponsible behavior to his "losing his faculties."

Nevertheless, the Puritan view has greatly decreased in popularity over the past centuries. This decrease is the result of several forces. One is the advancement of science, which has produced new theories of human nature and new standards for the kind of evidence needed to establish a proposal as "truth." Darwin's theory of evolution struck a blow at the concept of the rational soul by proposing that humans were not so distinctly different from animals as church doctrine had supposed. Freud struck a further blow at the concept of the importance of reasoning powers in the governance of behavior by postulating that much of our behavior is motivated by unconscious forces. The growth of experimental psychology, with its rules of evidence adopted from the field of physics, has stimulated more and more people to doubt the validity of a model of child nature based on such sources of data as divine revelation and on "blind faith" in the word of theologians of a given sect.

The Puritans' view of the child, in addition to suffering attacks from the scientific community, also lost adherents during the eighteenth and nineteenth centuries to the rising humanist movement. The humanists or humanitarians objected to what they considered the harsh treatment of children, treatment defended on the grounds of Protestant doctrine.

People who wish to defend Puritan theory and practice can marshal arguments on their side also. Some students of colonial times suggest that in most Puritan homes kindness prevailed, and fear was used as a child control device only to protect children from harm, either in this world or in the one beyond (Martin Luther in Eby, 1971, pp. 33, 153; Morgan, 1956, p. 58). Furthermore, defenders of the Puritan position can point to the increasing rates of delinquency and a supposed lack of socially acceptable goals among today's adolescent population, and can ask whether these modern social problems are perhaps a result of the abandonment of Puritan views of child raising. Also, when the faculty-psychology conception of mental operations is criticized as naive or unscientific, defenders may ask whether modern theorists have not simply renamed the faculties without offering any better evidence of their nature—renaming them with such terms as *id* and *ego* (as did Freud) or *intervening variables* (as have certain behaviorists). Thus, arguments about the Puritan position are not yet settled to everyone's satisfaction.

To complete this brief assessment of Puritan theory, we will recall the nine appraisal standards from Chapter 1 and use them to judge the worth of Puritan views. As we make this appraisal, you should recognize immediately that it is not simply a matter of applying the criteria and arriving at an objective judgment with which everyone will agree. Rather, this sort of assessment involves a large measure of personal opinion. It is not a revelation of universal truth but simply an estimate on the part of the one doing the judging. In this case it is my own estimate, reflecting the kind of evidence I think bears on each standard and the kind of values I use to weight each piece of evidence. Consequently, the following appraisal is for your consideration, not necessarily for your acceptance. Which of the conclusions you accept, which you wish to revise, and which you choose to reject completely depends on your own values, on the evidence you think bears on the issues, and on the weights you apply to the evidence.

The standards are displayed in the form of nine rating scales. Such a system is easily read but oversimplified. To solve the problem of oversimplification would require several pages of detail on the line of reasoning and the evidence that led to the conclusions. But since space limitations do not permit a detailed clarification for every theory in this book, the explanation for each rating is

PURITAN THEORY

How well do I think the theory meets the standards?

The Standards	Very Well	Moderately Well	Very Poorly
1. Reflects the real world of children		X	
2. Is clearly understandable		X	
3. Explains the past and predicts the future	X	X	
4. Guides child rearing	X		
5. Is internally consistent		X	
6. Is economical		X	
7. Is falsifiable			X
8. Stimulates new discoveries			X
9. Is self-satisfying			X

limited to a few comments. You may find it useful to prepare a rating sheet of your own and list the reasons you would cite to support your judgments.

On each of the accompanying scales, the X indicates where, in my opinion, Puritan theory should be rated for each particular standard.

Puritan theory is rated highest on item 4 because the theory does indeed give clear advice to parents on how to raise children. However, if this standard read "Gives proper guidance for child rearing," I would have rated it low, because I disagree with the basic tenet that children are naturally evil. This brings us to the relatively low rating on item 1. I think the evidence supporting the concept of children's innate sinful strivings is not convincing. It consists of a few biblical passages and "divine revelations" reported by clerics of past centuries. However, I believe that some of the assumptions about children found in the Puritans' ideas of stages of development are accurate, so I marked item 1 overall as slightly below "moderately well."

The moderate ratings for items 2 and 5 are based on my impression that, while the main lines of Puritan theory are clear and consistent, there remain significant areas of confusion elsewhere. Such confusion seems inevitable when a model of child nature and development is founded on so many assumptions whose validity cannot be checked empirically but must be accepted on the word of an authority or on doctrine divinely revealed to a select few. An example of such an area of confusion is the issue of whether God, in choosing which people will go to heaven, will really include in his considerations whether a child has lived a good Christian life or not on earth. Another is the issue of what happens to the infant that dies before having had a chance to live much of a life at all, good or bad. Such clouded issues and inconsistencies in Puritan doctrine did, however, furnish ministers with a seemingly endless source of topics for their sermons.

Items 7 and 8 have very low markings because so much of Puritan theory is founded on "revealed truths" whose validity cannot be tested. The theory is essentially nonfalsifiable and does not stimulate the generation of testable hypotheses that might result in new discoveries. Furthermore, the theory is not very economical—it offers some rather complex explanations—as in its structure of the soul—to account for phenomena that might be explained with fewer untested assumptions. Of course, it can be argued from another viewpoint that the theory is quite simple in that when we ask why certain types of child growth take place, a Puritan cleric could respond, "It's God's will" or "It is the Lord's plan."

Item 3 gets both a high and a low mark. The high mark indicates that if you accept Puritan assumptions about innate sin and life after death, then the theory does explain accurately what has happened in the child's past (she has inherited Adam and Eve's sin) and does predict fairly well what will occur in the future (she will go either to heaven or to hell, depending on whether she receives God's grace). But if you do not accept these assumptions, then you mark item 3 at the low point, for the theory does not explain the past development of a child or predict her future development, except along the rather general growth lines suggested by the development stages.

This brings us to item 9. Because of the reservations I have expressed about Puritan theory, plus my intuitive sense of children's basic natures, I do not find the Puritan view self-satisfying. Other people who seriously study children's growth would probably rank Puritan theory equally low, as suggested by the fact that Puritan doctrine is no longer in the mainstream of theories of child development. Nevertheless, certain elements of the Puritan view are still very much alive, particularly in the commonsense psychology we will meet in Chapter 5. Understanding Puritan beliefs helps explain some of the roots of current theories and some of the beliefs against which other theorists have reacted.

FOR FURTHER READING

Greven, Philip. (1977) *The Protestant Temperament: Patterns of Child Rearing, Religious Experience, and the Self in Early America.* New York: Knopf.

Miller, Perry. (1963) *The New England Mind: The Seventeenth Century.* Cambridge, Mass.: Harvard University Press.

Morgan, Edmund S. (1956) *The Puritan Family.* Boston: Trustees of the Public Library.

The New England Primer. (Any edition.) This beginning reader for children of colonial times reflects Puritan views of child nature, the goals of desirable development, and ways of directing children's behavior.

CHAPTER 4

ROUSSEAU'S MORAL AND CURIOUS CHILD

To an eighteenth-century Europe that widely believed children were innately bad, Jean Jacques Rousseau declared, "All things are good as they come out of the hands of their Creator, but everything degenerates in the hands of man" (Rousseau, 1773, vol.1, p. 1).

This statement opened the novel *Emile*, published in France in 1762 when Rousseau, at age 50, was already widely known for his essays on social philosophy and for his recent, highly popular novel, *The New Héloise*. As noted earlier, *Emile* appeared the same year as *The Social Contract*, an antimonarchy volume that would later make the author a favorite among the activists of the French Revolution.

Emile, though in the form of a novel, was actually what its subtitle explained: "A Treatise of Education." In the treatise, Rousseau described the chief elements of a proper education for the sons of economically well-to-do European families. But his advice appears to have been intended for parents of children in other strata of European society as well. The description of the rearing of Emile from birth to adulthood implies a theory of child development, a theory that has exerted significant influence on generations of authors, educators, and parents in diverse parts of the world.

Rousseau's novel did not dwell exclusively on the education of boys. In the closing sections he discussed as well the proper training for the model girl, Sophia, who "must be endowed with every qualification suitable to her species and sex in order to act her part in the natural and moral system" (Rousseau, 1773, vol.1, p. 6).

Although the major part of Rousseau's conception of child growth was presented in *Emile*, he produced a number of other works that extended—and in minor ways conflicted with—the picture of children given in *Emile*. The view of Rousseau's theory offered here is drawn from these works.*

Over the two centuries since the publication of *Emile*, readers of Rousseau have debated the question of whether the ideas the book espouses were really new. Critics have claimed that most of Rousseau's key concepts are found in the writings of authors from Plato to Locke (Patterson, 1971, pp. 12–13). Rousseau's supporters, however, have held that most of the ideas were actually his own, and certainly the pattern they formed in his hands was new. But whether or not he originated the ideas, his supporters and critics alike agree that his writings strongly influenced people's views of children.

In surveying Rousseau's theory, we will begin by tracing the four stages of development he described in *Emile*. Then we will consider his beliefs about individual differences among children and differences between the sexes. Finally, we will look at likely sources of Rousseau's ideas and an assessment of his theory.

STAGES OF GROWTH

In Rousseau's system, children grew along four dimensions: physical, intellectual, social, and moral. The period of childhood and adolescence extended from birth to age 25 and was divided into four stages: infancy (birth to age 2), childhood (age 2–12), pubescence (age 12–15), and adolescence (age 15–25). The five sections or "books" that comprise the long treatise of *Emile* trace the ideal boy's progress through the four stages. Although much of the advice in *Emile* was intended to improve parents' child-rearing methods, the boy Emile himself was actually raised by a tutor, who served as Emile's constant guide after the earliest years of childhood. In our review of the stages, we will note key features of each stage and the typical recommendations given about how to treat the child so his development best matches nature's intended growth pattern.

---

*These additional writings include a portion of *The New Héloise*, parts of *The Confessions*, his *Memoir on the Education of the Prince of Wirtenberg's Infant Daughter*, and *Letters to the Abbé M. on the Education of a Boy* (Boyd, 1962).

Besides the growth stages, three aspects of Rousseau's theory are of particular interest today. These are the issues of *critical periods, discovery learning,* and *permissiveness.* The term *critical periods* identifies the belief that in child rearing, as in the blacksmith trade, one should strike while the iron is hot. Striking too soon or too late will ruin the product. Those who subscribe to a belief in critical periods say that before a child can profit from environmental influences—from instruction or experience—she must have attained a particular degree of internal maturation. That a child needs a certain amount of readiness or "growing up" before learning is not new. We waste our time if we try teaching a two-week-old infant to walk or a one-year-old child to read books. However, there is more to the critical-periods concept than this. There is also the question of when is the optimal time to provide experiences for each activity—walking, reading, analyzing concepts of algebra, engaging in sexual relations, and so forth. Furthermore, if you miss this optimum time, if you wait too long to begin the experiences, will the child fail to develop adequately? In other words, is there both a lower age limit and an upper age limit for the optimal—or even the possible—period in which environmental forces can interact with maturational preparation to produce development? These issues engage the active attention of researchers today, just as the matter of maturational readiness did Rousseau two centuries ago (Lerner, 1976, pp. 98–100).

Rousseau's concern, however, was not with the problem of parents' waiting too long before teaching children, and thus passing over the critical period for learning a particular skill. Rather, he was concerned about the parents' making the error of trying to teach too soon or of furnishing the wrong experiences and thus irreparably damaging the child for the future. Rousseau felt that each dimension of development (physical, mental, social, moral) flowered at a particular time, and he felt it important to protect the child's growth schedule to ensure that each dimension flowered in nature's intended way.

Linked to the matter of critical periods was Rousseau's belief in what is known today as *discovery learning.* In recent decades, educators have expressed strong convictions about the value of stimulating children to discover the operating principles of their physical and social worlds rather than memorizing principles given them by parents and teachers. These ideas of discovery or inquiry learning are not new but were advocated by Rousseau in *Emile* and illustrated by detailed examples of how to carry them out in practice.

Another current issue that has been partly credited to, or blamed on, Rousseau is that of *permissiveness* in child rearing. Rousseau's prime tenet was that children are born naturally good and will develop into models of wisdom and virtue if permitted to follow nature's way and not driven off the track by the meddling of a corrupt society. In modern times there have been various interpretations of Rousseau's permissiveness, and at least one of the more popular interpretations is clearly wrong. It is the interpretation that nature's proper course involves letting children do as they wish in all things, indulging them at every turn. But this is not what Rousseau intended. He believed that it is the mature adult's responsibility to analyze nature's way, as he himself did in *Emile,* and, on the basis of this analysis, manipulate the child's experiences so they suit the sequence of critical periods he pictured as comprising desirable development. Thus, within structured limits of opportunity that were devised by an adult, the child was permitted to grow the natural way. This was the Rousseauistic version of permissiveness.

With these matters of critical periods, discovery learning, and controlled permissiveness in mind, we are prepared to review Rousseau's scheme of developmental stages.

Infancy: Birth to Age 2   This was the critical period for establishing physical health and sharp senses. In Rousseau's opinion, newborn infants have vague feelings of pleasure and pain but no real *sentiments* (definite feelings about things), and during infancy they develop no ideas. They do, however, sense things in their environment and begin to store in memory the impressions of these sensations.

The goal of this stage was to produce a healthy young animal with keen senses of sight, hearing, touch, taste, and smell. Rousseau felt that nature intended the infant to be breast fed by its own mother and not turned over to a nurse, as was the practice in many upper-class European households of the day, so he stressed the virtues of mothers feeding their own offspring. Rousseau also believed that nature did not intend children to be fettered by heavy, tight clothing. With great conviction but little evidence, he contended that in countries where infants have the freedom of loose clothing, "the people are tall, robust, and well proportioned" (1773, vol. 1, p. 16). But where infants are confined in swaddling clothes, the nations "swarm with hunch-backed, crooked-legged, lame, rickety, and deformed persons of every kind" (1773, vol. 1, p. 16).

The purpose of these suggestions about food and clothing was not to indulge infants and maximize their comfort but rather to ensure that they were raised in nature's way. And often, as Rousseau interpreted it, this way was harsh indeed. For example, he suggested putting babies by gradual stages into extreme physical conditions so as to "harden their bodies to the intemperance of the seasons, climates, and elements; to hunger, thirst and fatigue" (1773, vol. 1, pp. 24–25).

The period of infancy ended when the baby was weaned, took her first steps, and mastered some rudimentary speech.

Young Childhood: Age 2 to Age 12   This was the critical period for developing physical strength and agility and for storing up sensations. Throughout this stage, the child—like the "noble savage" whom Rousseau admired from accounts he had read of "primitive peoples"—learns through direct experience related to daily needs and interests. He is also taught to make useful objects, such as toys and simple science mechanisms, with his hands.

Like his contemporaries, Rousseau assumed that the mind consists of faculties or functions that emerge at different times during childhood. He wrote that "of all our faculties, the senses are perfected the first; these therefore are the first we should cultivate; they are, nevertheless, the only ones that are usually forgotten or the most neglected" (1773, vol. 1, p. 217). In order to sharpen the senses and store up sensations, the child, he felt, was best reared in the countryside, in a pastoral setting undisturbed by the evil influences of city life and the child's own peers. Emile is not even around other children until he reaches the mid-teens.

The child's mentors during these years should place him in situations that exercise his body and senses. The method of instruction should be what Rousseau labeled *negative teaching.* Rather than teaching what is right (which is *positive teaching*), the wise tutor or parent protects the child from instruction in such improper things as rote or stock answers, clever repartee, religious doctrine. Negative teaching consists "neither in teaching virtue or truth; but in guarding the heart from vice. . . . Exercise the child's corporal organs, senses, and faculties as much as you please; but keep his intellectual ones inactive as long as possible" (1773, vol. 1, pp. 126–127).

With such treatment, the child would arrive at age 12 as a most honest youth—agile, keen of sight and hearing, animated, but socially naive.

Pubescence or Later Childhood: Age 12 to Age 15   This was the critical period for developing the first phases of reasoning. During these three years, the child no longer operates mainly on the sensations she collects, but begins to develop real ideas. Rousseau, like the Puritans, believed that sense impressions are carried to a processing center in the brain called the *common sense*. During pubescence this sense matures. It not only processes impressions from the external senses, but its impressions are "partly internal, being called *perceptions* or *ideas*. It is the number of these ideas that limits the extent of our knowledge; it is their perspicuity that determines the clearness of the understanding; and it is the art of comparing them with each other that is called human reason" (1773, vol. 1, pp. 275–276).

In his treatment of the source of ideas, Rousseau adopted a position on an old issue that continues to be of great importance to psychologists and philosophers today. It is the question of whether ideas are built up entirely of people's experiences or are partly determined by the nature of humans. The latter is asking, in other words, are there genetically determined ideas or, at least, genetically determined cognitive functions? Rousseau would say that indeed there are, and they begin to show themselves during pubescence.

The first stage of reasoning that Rousseau said manifests itself during pubescence is called *sensitive* or *puerile* reason. It consists only of forming "simple ideas from the concurrence of various sensations" (1773, vol. 1, p. 276). The child puts together sensations he receives at a given moment and draws some simple conclusions. These ideas are committed to memory. Later, in adolescence, the child advances to the age of *true* human reasoning, which consists of "forming complex ideas from the concurrence of many simple ideas" (1773, vol. 1, p. 276). (In Chapter 13 we will see that there are parallels between Rousseau's observations about reasoning and Piaget's.)

Pubescence was the period for stimulating the faculty of *curiosity*. Prior to this stage the child's motivation—his seeking behavior—was seated in a drive to achieve a sort of hedonistic happiness. This drive stimulated the child's seeking to exercise his body and senses. But during pubescence, the child started to display significant intellectual curiosity that became his "chief spring of action" (1773, vol. 1, p. 294). Rousseau's recommendations about how to take advantage of curiosity sound much like the suggestions about discovery learning or inquiry teaching today:

Direct the attention of your pupil to the phenomena of nature, and you will soon awaken his curiosity; but to keep that curiosity alive, you must be in no haste to satisfy it. Put questions to him adapted to his capacity, and leave him to resolve them. Let him take nothing on trust from his (tutor), but on his own comprehension and convictions; he should not learn, but invent the sciences. If ever you substitute authority in the place of argument, he will reason no longer; he will be ever afterwards bandied like a shuttle-cock between the opinions of others (1773, vol. 1, p. 296).

Rousseau would have tutors teach children to read and write, prior to pubescence, only those sorts of communications needed to fulfill the child's daily wants: "Children, when taught to read, learn that only; they never think; they gain no information; all their learning consists in words" (1773, vol. 1, p. 296). However, by the time of pubescence, he felt, children could comprehend ideas and not simply store up impressions. So they could begin reading about places and times distant from their own.

With such a regime, Emile arrived at the close of pubescence knowing only how to reason about the physical world he had been observing for more than a decade. "He knows not even the name of history, nor what is meant by metaphysics and morality. . . . He is ill qualified to generalize his ideas or form abstract nothings of things. . . . Emile is laborious, temperate, patient, resolute, and bold" (1773, vol. 1, p. 389).

Adolescence: Age 15 to Age 25   This was the critical period for becoming socialized and developing true morality. In Rousseau's scheme, the rise of powerful sexual passions in adolescence was accompanied by the flowering of the faculty of *imagination*, which stimulated social and moral (ethical) development and the formation of the *conscience*. At this time the faculty of the *will* also asserted itself in yearnings for greater independence.

Rousseau believed that youths become socialized and consciously moral when they are able to imagine themselves in the shoes of people who are suffering. So the task of parents and tutors was to introduce the adolescent to such suffering, but not through direct observation of human misery and vice since overexposure to suffering could cause the youth to become callous rather than humane.

I would show him mankind at a distance, in other times and other places; so that he might be a spectator of the scene without having it in his power to become an actor. This is the proper time to introduce history. . . . There he will behold mankind, not as their accomplice or accuser, but as their impartial judge (1773, vol. 2, 59–60).

The ethical feeling that developed during these years was not, however, solely a product of the adolescent's experiences. Part of it arose in his soul as "an innate principle of justice and goodness; by which . . . we approve or condemn the actions of ourselves and others; to this principle it is that I give the appellation *conscience*" (1773, vol. 2, p. 172). Though conscience, in Rousseau's view, was inborn, it could be dulled or heightened by social experiences.

Finally, we consider the most obvious developmental change of adolescence, the maturation of sexual functions, or as Rousseau called them, the *passions*. He believed that children, prior to adolescence, should be protected from situations that might stimulate sexual ideas. But once puberty arrived, the youth's questions should be answered truthfully, without fables or evasion. Later, during the closing years of adolescence, it was the tutor's or parent's responsibility to help the youth select a mate.

By the time the properly raised youth reached the mid-twenties, he commanded all the physical, intellectual, social, and moral virtues anyone could desire, and he was ready for marriage. At this time the development of the child was complete.

Two other aspects of Rousseau's theory warrant our attention: individual differences among children and differences between the sexes.

INDIVIDUAL DIFFERENCES

In his theorizing, Rousseau implied that nature's clock runs at the same pace for everyone. Each boy and girl reaches early childhood at age 2, enters pubescence at age 12, and adolescence at age 15. However, the condition of the child at each of these stages will be influenced by the sorts of experiences she has. Consequently, there will be marked differences among children in physical strength and agility, in acuity of their senses, in the contents of their memories, and in their moral and social traits.

However, it is not only the environment that accounts for variations among children of the same age. Rousseau proposed as well that children can be originally endowed with different capabilities. He suggested that tutors and parents give the young child many chances to investigate science, art, and music so that "by exciting his curiosity and training its tendency, we may be enabled to study his taste, inclinations and propensities" (1773, vol. 1, p. 367). Nevertheless, the most powerful cause of individual differences, he felt, was the quality of the growing child's environment.

SEX DIFFERENCES

Had Rousseau lived in the late twentieth century, he would have been a prime target of women's rights advocates, for he considered women intellectually inferior to men and properly subservient to them:

> Woman is framed particularly for the delight and pleasure of man. . . . His merit consists in his power; he pleases her only because he is possessed of strength. This is not the law of love, I grant you; but it is that of nature, antecedent to love itself (1773, vol. 3, p. 7).

The stages outlined for the growth of boys are the same for girls. In fact, "Till the age of puberty, there is little apparent difference between the sexes in children" (1773, vol. 3, p. 25). However, there needs to be a different emphasis in the upbringing of the two. For young boys, stress needs to be placed on gaining strength, but for girls the stress is on charm. After puberty, girls should not be expected to master the same intellectual material as boys. The young woman's concerns are not "abstract and speculative truths, principles and axioms of sciences. Their studies ought to be all practical; it is their business to apply the principles discovered by man. . . . Woman, honor thy chief; it is he that labors for thee, he that earns thy bread, he that nourishes thee; this is man!" (1773, vol. 3, pp. 71–72, 191).

SOURCES OF ROUSSEAU'S IDEAS

Now that we have inspected key features of Rousseau's theory, we can speculate briefly about the likely sources of his ideas. The main influences behind his theory seem to be four: memories of his own childhood, his experience tutoring boys of aristocratic families, his reading in philosophy and in books on "primitive peoples," and his casual observations of European peasant children.

In regard to his childhood, he wrote in his *Confessions:* "If ever child received a sound and reasonable education, it was I" (Boyd, 1963, p. 13). This education of which he boasted was a most erratic one. His mother had died shortly after his birth, so until later childhood he was raised mainly by his father, a sometime watchmaker and dancing teacher with romantic ideas he passed on to his son. Jean Jacques had learned to read by age 6, starting with romantic novels his mother had left him. At age 7 he began with philosophy and history. When the boy entered early adolescence, his father ran off from Geneva to escape punishment for breaking the law, and Jean Jacques was schooled by relatives. He then was apprenticed to an engraver, but soon quit the trade and moved from one job to another. Finally, he attached himself to upper-class families as a secretary or tutor. This childhood, unfettered by formal schooling or a strict home life, seems to have become his model for that of Emile.

In his writings on child development and education, Rousseau emphasized that parents should spend much time in supervising their children's development if a tutor could not be provided to do the job. But in his own life, Rousseau did not take fatherhood so seriously. He never married but lived many years with a young woman of servant status who bore him five children, all of whom Rousseau promptly sent off to foundling homes, despite the tears of their mother. Thus, at no time did Rousseau apply to his own offspring the advice he offered other parents. In describing the proper development of the girl Sophia in the novel *Emile*, Rousseau apparently drew at least some traits from the woman who bore his own children. She was devoted and loyal, but apparently a bit simpleminded. She seems to have satisfied Rousseau's needs without causing trouble over the other romantic attachments he established during their years together (Davidson, 1898).

A third influence on Rousseau's views was the books he read about the native peoples of the Americas, the South Seas, Africa, and Asia. The books were written either by adventurers who had visited these lands or by authors who imagined what such places might be like. While some writers deplored the state of the "primitive peoples," others praised the "noble savages" ' way of life. Rousseau admired certain traits of these fabled people so much that he sought to have Emile emulate their naivete and their close bond with nature.

The fourth main influence on Rousseau's theory was his observations of the European peasants' child-rearing practices in villages he frequented throughout his life. Although he did not approve of certain crudities of the common folk, he considered some of their practices laudable (such as breast-feeding infants) and incorporated them into his own recommendations on child rearing.

From such a background Rousseau fashioned his theory of child nature.

ROUSSEAU'S VIEW: AN ASSESSMENT

In appraising the strengths and weaknesses of Rousseau's theory of child development, we will use the same method used in assessing the Puritan viewpoint in Chapter 3. Rousseau's theory is first rated according to my estimates on each evaluation standard, then some explanation for the ratings is given. Again, you may wish to prepare your own rating sheet and appraise Rousseau's view of children according to your own criteria.

Rousseau's theory is rated highest on item 8 because he exerted such a strong influence on nineteenth- and twentieth-century educational practice. Four distinguished educational innovators who owed much to Rousseau's *Emile* were Heinrich Pestalozzi (1746–1827), Friedrich Froebel (1782–1862), Johann Friedrich Herbart (1776–1841), and Maria Montessori (1870–1952). Pestalozzi, a Swiss, refined basic Rousseauistic teaching methods and made them work in a practical manner in the classroom (Heafford, 1967). Froebel, a German, launched the kindergarten movement. He used Rousseau's predeterminist concepts as the foundation for learning activities for young children, and his influence is still apparent in kindergartens today, particularly in Europe (Froebel, 1889; Kilpatrick, 1916). Herbart, a German inter-

ROUSSEAU'S THEORY

How well do I think the theory meets the standards?

The Standards	Very Well	Moderately Well	Very Poorly
1. Reflects the real world of children		X	
2. Is clearly understandable	X		
3. Explains the past and predicts the future	Specifically X Accurately X		
4. Guides child rearing	Specifically X Accurately X		
5. Is internally consistent		X	
6. Is economical		X	
7. Is falsifiable	X		
8. Stimulates new discoveries	X		
9. Is self-satisfying		X	

ested in the education of older children, analyzed the ways ideas of the mind are built up, and then he translated his analysis into classroom teaching methods. Maria Montessori (Chapter 20), an Italian physician, based her system of teaching the mentally retarded partly on Rousseau's principles, then extended her scheme to include an instructional program for normal children as well.

Various writers on the history of education have credited Rousseau with being the father of other movements as well—of manual training, of modern pedagogy, and of the discovery method in science (Boyd, 1963, pp. 296–350; Davidson, 1898, pp.

211–244). In short, when Rousseau's work is judged by its effect on subsequent educators, he comes off with high marks.

As a guide to child rearing, Rousseau's theory gets two different marks, one for the number and specificity of his suggestions and the other for the likely accuracy of the suggestions. I gave a high rating for the fact that he offers many specific illustrations in *Emile* of ways his principles of child raising could be implemented. However, since I believe the content of some of his suggestions is highly questionable, I gave him only a moderate rating on accuracy of recommendations. In particular, I think he is wrong about how children are most effectively socialized, that is, how they develop skills of getting along with their peers. Rousseau isolated Emile from other children until the boy was an adolescent, then proposed that, as a teenager, he would immediately display all of the admirable skills in human relations that would make him recognized by his peers as their natural leader. It is unlikely, however, that any serious observer of developing children would accept such a proposition. Most early childhood education today is based on quite an opposite belief. An important role assigned to nursery schools and kindergartens is that of offering children guided opportunities for learning the skills of getting along with their peers. This proposition that children profit from social practice seems more convincing than Rousseau's belief in the value of isolation from peers in childhood as a means of socializing the child.

The two ratings on item 3 are given for similar reasons. Rousseau's predictions of a child's future as a result of different child-raising practices are relatively specific. Likewise, Rousseau could view a child's present behavior and appearance and offer confident estimates about the treatment the child received in the past. Thus, on specificity I rated his theory rather highly. But the accuracy of his explanations and predictions can be questioned in some instances. The most obvious is that of socialization. Another is his prediction about the effect of tight infant clothing on ultimate physical stature and fitness. With such reservations, I judged his accuracy to be moderate.

I rated Rousseau's description of his scheme (item 2), the theory's internal consistency (item 5), and the economy of its explanations (item 6) rather highly. Of these three, the economy rating (item 6) may be the most controversial. Rousseau does not propose an elaborate explanatory mechanism when a simpler one might suffice. His framework of development, for example, is not unduly complex: He explains the sequence of critical development periods simply as "nature's way," and he explains that distortions of development are the result of parents' misunderstanding the treatment each stage requires for natural development. On the other hand, if we wish to ask why the critical periods arise in such a sequence or why discovery learning is superior to indoctrination, then we find that Rousseau does not offer much of an answer. His scheme is too simple to answer such *why* questions. Thus, his theory is economical for answering questions about how certain child-raising practices are suited to each of his proposed growth stages, but not why the stages appear in such an order.

In regard to item 1, Rousseau's picture of childhood in *Emile* and other writings represents the real world of children only moderately well. I believe he was correct in reacting against the view that children are born naturally sinful, but I question his proposal that they are born naturally moral and will do right if left to their own inclinations. In his practical suggestions, he moderated this position somewhat by suggesting that the freedom allowed children not be boundless but have defined limits, and this moderated position appears to me to make sense. I agree with Rousseau's suggestion that it is desirable to give children many opportunities to exercise their bodies, to practice using their senses, and to draw conclusions from their observations of nature. But I question how realistic he is in concluding that exposing infants to inclement weather and pain promotes their optimum development by inuring them to hardships in the early months of life. Furthermore, present-day observations of girls' behavior and tests of their abilities cast serious doubts on Rousseau's contention that girls are inferior to boys intellectually. Rousseau's sketch of childhood, therefore, seems only partially realistic.

Item 7 focuses on the issue of whether the theory is falsifiable. Is it possible to perform experiments or observations that test the validity of Rousseau's scheme? To a considerable extent, I believe it is. If we were to conduct careful observations of children, following their development under different environmental conditions over a period of years, we could test Rousseau's contentions about (1) the effect of tight clothing, (2) the influence of interactions with peers throughout childhood on the ultimate social skills adolescents display, and (3) the effectiveness of negative teaching compared to direct instruction for achieving learning goals. Also, since modern day scientists have devised ways to investigate the concept of critical periods in development, the critical-period aspect of Rousseau's system can be tested as well

(Schneirla and Rosenblatt, 1963; Scott, 1963). Though Rousseau's basic tenet that children are born naturally moral is perhaps the most difficult of his ideas to test, it is conceivable that this belief is falsifiable as well. For example, comparisons could be made of young children's moral judgments both within a given culture and across cultures that hold different moral-value standards.

Finally, there is item 9, whether Rousseau's system overall is self-satisfying or not. To me his theory is at least moderately self-satisfying, particularly as seen in its cultural environment. Despite the aspects I have criticized as shortcomings, Rousseau did have some convincing insights not widely held in his day. These contributions include (1) his insistence that children are not simply undersized adults but are different in quality of mind and have different needs, (2) his emphasis on the importance of firsthand experience as the most basic foundation of learning in childhood, (3) his desire to allow children the freedom to exercise their bodies and explore their environment, (4) his suggestion that children profit from constructing useful objects with their hands, and (5) his technique of questioning and of arranging experiences that lead children to draw their own conclusions about what they observe.

For students of child development, some knowledge of Rousseau's ideas is useful since his work is an important source of the ideas currently found in several modern theories, particularly theories on teaching young children.

FOR FURTHER READING

Boyd, William. (1963) *The Educational Theory of Jean Jacques Rousseau.* New York: Russell & Russell. A description and critique of Rousseau's viewpoint.

Boyd, William (ed. and trans.). (1962) *The Minor Educational Writings of Jean Jacques Rousseau.* New York: Teachers College, Columbia University. A collection of segments on education other than from *Emile.*

Rousseau, Jean Jacques. *Emile; or, A Treatise of Education.* The novel is available in its original French version and in several English translations.

PART 3

THE PEOPLE'S VIEW OF A GROWING CHILD

A search for the underlying structure of commonsense ideas about development.

The cluster of ideas that most people hold about how children develop is usually called *common sense*. And according to such psychologists as Fritz Heider, this cluster is not just a disorganized conglomeration of opinions, but it has an identifiable underlying pattern that warrants its being labeled a theory of child development. One analysis of this pattern is offered in Chapter 5 as a commonsense model of development, or, as Heider called it, *naive psychology*.

Since the term *common sense* has different meanings for different people, it is important at the outset to clarify our definition of it.

In ancient Greece, Aristotle proposed that there were five external senses—sight, hearing, taste, smell, and touch—plus a common sense, located in the heart, that served as the coordinating center for the other five. Vestiges of this belief are still found in our language in such usages as, "She learned it by heart." But as we saw in Chapters 3 and 4, later philosophers relocated the common sense in the brain, where the Puritans and Rousseau, for example, thought it resided. In this chapter, however, common sense means something different.

For many people, common sense refers to convictions held by a person because the truth of the beliefs involved is self-evident. If you need no special training or special instruments to arrive at a conclusion about something you see or hear or smell, then you can say your conclusion is "just common sense." Anyone in his right mind would have come to the same conclusion. In Chapter 5, this sort of common sense, self-evident conclusions, is part of what we intend.

For the other part of our meaning we will equate common sense with the term *popular opinion*. To some people common sense means an idea that everybody, or nearly everybody, subscribes to, whether it is obvious or not. In our culture, for example, the fact that the earth is a sphere is common sense today, though that "fact" is not obvious to the eye. Nor was that "fact" common sense at the time of Columbus.

Thus, in Chapter 5 the phrase "a commonsense view of child development" identifies those beliefs shared by a large proportion of society—with many of the beliefs being self-evident conclusions.

Although at first this definition of commonsense theory may appear uncomplicated, we will see, when we analyze specific beliefs, that people do not all agree on what they believe about children's growth and development. Differences of opinion are especially apparent in large, complex modern societies in which scholars have both the time and desire to speculate and conduct research about the nature of humanity. These thinkers come up with ideas that sometimes conflict with the common sense of the populace. But as the novel ideas are communicated abroad, many people are convinced of their validity and become disciples of this new school of thought. Such splintering of common sense into different camps can be expected to occur more frequently in societies that are blessed, or burdened, not only with the leisure time for speculation but also with highly penetrating mass-communication devices—television, radio, newspapers, magazines, and books. Smaller, more isolated and cohesive societies will subscribe to a more commonly accepted set of convictions about children than will larger, more disparate ones. Therefore, as we consider one version of commonsense theory, there may be a problem of consensus.

Furthermore, the common sense outlined in this chapter applies chiefly to societies that have evolved from European roots. How closely this version represents common sense also in traditional African, Asian, American Indian, and Pacific Island cultures is not known.

Another aspect of naive psychology that deserves attention was described by Baldwin (1967, p. 38):

> It is important to realize . . . that naive psychology is not a stated theory but a body of beliefs about human behavior. Only the systematic description of naive psychology gives it the look of a theory.

Thus, we are interested, not just in the commonsense beliefs themselves, but in the systematic way they are analyzed. However, we may ask whether such everyday beliefs about children deserve a chapter in a book on formal theories. Are not naive assumptions too ordinary to warrant serious discussion? There are at least four reasons why they are not and why they do indeed deserve attention.

First, commonsense psychology is the sort that all of us use, either entirely or to a great degree, in dealing with children during the routine of daily living. A study of the structure and content of naive notions of development should help us analyze the strengths and weaknesses of such notions. As a result, we may be able to alter at least some of the least defensible aspects of our commonsense opinions and perhaps substitute more valid ones.

Second, the analysis of common sense can help us understand the nature of more formal theories of development, because those theories often include many commonsense assumptions. After we observe the way such psychologists as Heider analyze naive beliefs, we should be better prepared to recognize the naive-psychology aspects of other theories we study.

Third, formal theories, in a sense, are often the reactions of theorists against naive-psychology notions that they believe are in error. Thus, when we recognize the commonsense ideas theorists are reacting against, we are better equipped to understand the formal theories.

Fourth, an inspection of commonsense theory can help us gain some perspective about the historical roots of beliefs widely held in our society today. For example, when we learn about the old faculty-psychology concept of the human soul or personality we recognize that today's commonsense acceptance of beliefs in imagination, reasoning, and the will are held over from that supposedly discredited concept.

For these reasons, then, a chapter on naive psychology is of value in a modern-day book on theories of development.

CHAPTER 5

HEIDER AND COMMONSENSE THEORY

We could adopt any of several ways to construct a commonsense theory of development. We might conduct a poll, asking a sample of people to answer questions about children. We might collect folklore, proverbs, and traditional sorts of advice about child raising, and then search for the pattern of concepts that underlies them. We might observe adults as they interact with children or as they talk about children; then we could estimate what theory of child nature is implied in such action and talk. We might analyze laws relating to children, on the assumption that laws reflect a common set of beliefs for a society. Or we could use all of these approaches. However, due to space limitations, in this chapter we will use only two: an analysis of typical daily talk and an inspection of a few key laws that relate to children.

For the analysis of talk, we will use as a guide the work of Fritz Heider, a German who moved to the faculty of the University of Kansas, where he dedicated himself to tracing the framework of naive psychology, which undergirds the way most of us conduct our lives. The principles Heider derived have been described in his book, *The Psychology of Interpersonal Relations*. However, since his description focuses primarily on the adult, on the mature personality, and not on the child, it is necessary to extend Heider's treatment to show how commonsense psychology views a child's developmental changes from one age level to the next. In making this modest extension, we will depend not only on people's everyday language but also on civil and criminal laws commonly found in modern American communities.

It is important to realize that this chapter is designed only to suggest some of the main lines of naive theory and to illustrate the way a theorist such as Heider identifies such lines. The material included falls far short of describing the complexity of Heider's analysis.

THE CAUSES OF HUMAN ACTION

A key question that commonsense psychology seeks to answer is: Why do people act as they do? When this question is translated into child development terms it becomes: How and why does the pattern of a child's behavior change as he or she grows up?

In answer to the first question, Heider's analysis of daily language tells us that three factors determine whether or not a person carries out a given act. Two of these factors are inside the person: *personal power* (Can he do it?) and *effort* or motivation (Will he try to do it?). The third factor, which can be called *task difficulty*, is outside the person and is composed of all forces in the environment that influence the accomplishment of the act.

From this perspective of personal power, effort, and task difficulty, we can define the study of child development as: an investigation of the changes that occur in a child's power and efforts between the time of birth and the end of adolescence, that is, the changes as they relate to the different environments with which the child interacts over these years. We will analyze the three factors to illustrate how they can be used to explain human behavior at different age levels.

To suggest the flavor of the raw materials from which such a view of child psychology is constructed, I have prefaced the analysis with a fictitious conversation, a typical chat about children that might be overheard in many American neighborhoods. Phrases from this conversation will be used later to illustrate the assumptions or convictions about child behavior that underlie people's daily interaction according to commonsense theory.

TALK ABOUT CHILDREN—
GRIST FOR THE COMMONSENSE
PSYCHOLOGIST'S MILL

Mr. Young and Mrs. Campbell meet at the market.

> **Mr. Young:** What do you think of the kids' third-grade teacher? I think she's expecting too much of them. My son

Freddie says hardly anyone in the class can do the math. Have you seen the problems she gives?

Mrs. Campbell: Yes, Doris brings work home every day. But luckily she seems to get it done all right without my help.

Mr. Young: She must be pretty smart.

Mrs. Campbell: It's not just that. She works hard at it, too. I guess having to compete with her twelve-year-old brother has caused her to try hard. He's good in physical activities but kind of average in school work, so she seems to want to show that she's good with her brain. She tries to get her recognition that way.

Mr. Young: Oh, yes, your son. I saw in the paper that he's on the football team.

Mrs. Campbell: Well, he's crazy about sports. But getting on the team isn't much of a distinction. Nearly every boy who showed up was put in uniform.

Mr. Young: But isn't he some kind of a star?

Mrs. Campbell: Well, for the first couple of weeks he was the starting quarterback. He's quick and he throws the ball well. But then he had a streak of bad luck. First he hurt his ankle, and that put him out for over a week. And since then the coach hasn't given him a fair chance to show what he can do. The poor kid's spending every game on the bench.

Mr. Young: That's too bad. Say, I see you didn't bring your baby with you.

Mrs. Campbell: No, I left Doris with him at home.

Mr. Young: Really? Aren't you afraid to leave a nine-year-old in charge of such a small baby?

Mrs. Campbell: Oh, no. Doris is very good at it, and she likes it.

Mr. Young: Well, that's brave. I don't think I'd let my daughter Charlene try that, even at age 14. It's not that Charlene can't do it. It's just that she's always thinking of something else—mostly boys and loud music. Well, I'd better pay for my groceries and get going. I left Charlene out in the car. She's fiddling with all the gadgets, pretending she's driving. She just can't wait till she's 16 to get a driver's license.

With this conversation in mind, let us turn to the three main components of action. First we consider personal power, then effort or motivation, and finally environmental forces.

"CAN DO"—
THE FACTOR OF PERSONAL POWER

In daily conversation, the commonsense notion of personal power is reflected in the use of the terms *can* and *cannot* ("Hardly anyone in the class can do the math," "It's not that Charlene can't do it"). Personal power has several components. The most important of these is ability. Others that exert a minor influence on personal power are attitudes, social status, and such temporary personal conditions as fatigue.

During a typical day, a typical teenager uses many specific skills or abilities in performing tasks. However, in commonsense psychology, these abilities are not all discrete and unconnected. Instead, they seem to fall into two categories: physical and mental. And it is not uncommon for people to believe that a youth can have one level of ability in the physical realm and another in the mental. For example, it appears to surprise no one that a twelve-year-old boy might be a fine football player but not much of a scholar, or that his nine-year-old sister might be the opposite. But it seems less common for people to see that within either category a youth's subabilities may vary. In short, people seem to think that mental ability is all-encompassing, a unitary skill or aptitude that covers all intellectual task performance. So Mr. Young, on hearing of Doris's skill in mathematics, concludes that Doris must be smart in general. Mrs. Campbell, too, reflects this idea of an all-encompassing intelligence by saying that Doris is "good with her brain." This belief that abilities are divided into physical and mental realms that are each unitary rather than composed of discrete subskills has important implications for the way children are treated in school and at home. And though widely accepted, the belief is somewhat at odds with empirical evidence (Thomas and Thomas, 1965, pp. 4–10, 386–388, 425–428).

As people try to understand and predict their own and others' behavior, they are interested in knowing whether a person's ability is high, medium, or low. It is therefore useful for us to examine three kinds of information on which this judgment is based.

The first clue to ability level is the proportion of other people who can perform the task or tasks we have in mind. Specifically, if only a few people can perform the task, then any individual who does so is credited with having high ability. The main cause of success is thought to reside in the individual's personal power, and consequently she is accorded respect. But if nearly everyone can perform the task, then we conclude that it was easy, and those people who perform it successfully are not credited with much ability. In fact, the cause of success is not attributed to the person at all but to the environment. She succeeded because environmental factors were in her favor.

A second important factor in judging ability is a knowledge of the people who have already performed the task. This matter is far more significant for assessing ability in childhood and adolescence than in the adult years, because children's physical and mental skills increase noticeably with age, while adult skills are thought to be stable until the declining years. So in naive psychology we seek to learn the ages of the people with whom a given child is being compared. It is considered fairest to compare him with age peers—often age-mates of the same sex. However, it is frequently useful to compare him with older or younger children as well. A young child who performs as well as an average child several years older is credited with high ability and is labeled gifted, bright, or even genius. An older child who performs no better than an average child several years younger is said to be retarded, deficient, or handicapped.

A third sort of information that tells us about ability level is the amount of effort exerted to perform a task. The child who succeeds with ease is credited with greater ability than the one who has to struggle and strain to accomplish the same job.

As for whether or not people feel a person can perform a task at all, we noted earlier the tendency people often have to feel that a child who is apt at one physical (or mental) task will also be apt at other physical (or mental) activities. This belief in a high correlation among subabilities within a broad category enables people to predict whether a person can or cannot perform a task not actually tried before. Such was the case when Mr. Young stated that fourteen-year-old Charlene could care for a baby even though the girl had never done so. Mr. Young's opinion was apparently based on his knowledge that Charlene had succeeded in other physical and mental tasks as well as her age-mates who did care for babies. So Charlene could do the things necessary for child care. The girl's problem, in her father's eyes, lay not in a lack of ability ("It's not that Charlene can't do it") but in a lack of motivation ("She's always thinking of something else").

Although abilities are the most important constituents of personal power, several other elements affect power in lesser degrees. Three of these are attitudes, social status, and temporary personal conditions.

Attitudes, in the sense intended here, reflect the individual's estimate of how able he is to do tasks. If he feels generally incapable, he is said to be pessimistic, feel inferior, have a poor self-concept, lack confidence, have low self-esteem, or be shy. If he feels he can succeed, he is described as optimistic, confident, having a good self-concept, and displaying a positive approach. So a person's power is not only based on true ability, but is influenced by attitudes that determine how well ability and effort can be marshaled.

Social status affects personal power when it influences the attitude the individual has toward accomplishing a task. If he has the status of team leader, he can give directions to team members with the conviction that his directions will be followed. A girl who, along with her classmates, recognizes that she is from a lower social-class background may fare poorly at the class party because she lacks the confidence to try her social skills around others whose manners, dress, and speech differ from her own.

Temporary conditions, such as fatigue and illness, influence how a person performs on a given occasion, but these conditions do not decrease the true ability attributed to him.

To close this brief look at commonsense notions of personal power, we note three of the most significant assumptions underlying naive psychology's view of child development:

1. Abilities are considered rather permanent attributes of an individual. They do not change over the short term.

2. Abilities increase, sometimes regularly and sometimes in spurts, over the period of childhood and adolescence. To a great extent, the study of child development is the study of the manner in which abilities increase. A child described as a "problem learner" in school is usually one whose abilities are not increasing at the rate considered desirable.

3. Abilities are determined by both heredity ("His good memory is from his mother's side of the family") and environment ("It took a lot of practice for her to pronounce French properly"). However, the proportion that each of these two sources contributes to various abilities and the manner in which the two interact is not clear.

"TRY TO"—
THE FACTOR OF EFFORT

Not only must children have the personal power or ability to perform, they must also want to do it. So "can" and "try" are both necessary for action. Neither is sufficient alone. Doris was not only smart, she also worked hard.

The factor of trying, which psychologists usually call *motivation*, has two aspects: direction and amount. Direction refers to what the person is trying to do. It is often called her *intention*. Amount refers to how hard she tries and is called *exertion* or *intensity of effort*. Mr. Young's remarks about Charlene suggested that the girl would probably not look after a baby's needs seriously. On the other hand, it seems clear that Charlene intends to drive a car when she is permitted to do so, for she spends time in a car pretending to drive.

We noted earlier that in naive psychology abilities are expected to increase regularly with age. Effort is also expected to change in predictable ways as the child grows older. For one thing, the child's attention span, the time she dedicates to a given task, is expected to lengthen with age. As a youth matures, her interests are supposed to settle down and not jump from one thing to another all the time. Also, the child is expected to expend greater effort as she grows up, to give it her best and not be a quitter.

Compared to the other two factors of action, personal power and task difficulty, trying is considered to be more under the conscious control of the individual. Consequently, when she fails because of an apparent lack of trying, she is more liable to be blamed than if her failure were based on either a lack of ability or a task that was too difficult. Commonsense psychology thus holds the child personally responsible for laziness, for quitting a job before it is completed, or for daydreaming instead of working. In contrast, she usually is not blamed for being mentally retarded or physically handicapped.

The concept of motivation is crucial in daily social interaction as we try to understand and predict others' behavior. The matter of direction of motivation constantly arises in such queries as: "What's he up to?" "What does she want?" and "What's he after?" To a great extent, the way we react to others is based on the objectives we think they are trying to reach rather than simply on their overt actions at the moment. Commonsense psychology gives a larger role to this matter of predicting others' motives than do most other theories we will be considering.

TASK DIFFICULTY—
THE ROLE OF THE ENVIRONMENT

The last of the three factors that determine action is the environment. This factor can be labeled *task difficulty*. At any given moment, it consists only of those aspects of the environment that influence, either favorably or unfavorably, whether the child can accomplish a task she is attempting.

According to Heider, a person's efforts to understand the facts, principles, and laws by which the environment operates are motivated by his desire to "establish himself in a stable world in which the future can be anticipated and controlled" (Heider, 1958, p. 91). Thus, what we wish to learn about the environment are those stable, permanent conditions that influence task difficulty. However, predictions based on understanding such conditions sometimes turn out wrong because of unexpected influences. It is not always clear where the blame or credit for these influences should be placed, on the person or on the environment, but usually we do not attribute them to the person, particularly if we like the person. These surprising or unpredicted happenings are usually accounted for by chance, opportunity, luck, fate, or the breaks. Mrs. Campbell felt such temporary, unpredicted influences accounted for her son's losing his quarterback position: he had "a streak of bad luck" in the form of an injury and the coach's later overlooking him on the bench. The boy's loss of position has not lessened his ability in his mother's eyes. She feels he still can play well even though he no longer has the chance to show it in a game.

By following Heider's general line of reasoning about environmental influences, we can suggest two additional assumptions people make about development:

1. The difficulty of a task is judged by the number of children or youths of a given age level who can accomplish it and by the effort expended to carry out the task.

2. Environmental conditions are divided into two general categories: (a) those that are stable and operate in a predictable manner and (b) unexpected occurrences, which are usually called "opportunity," "chance," or "luck." In an effort to make life more predictable, people try to increase their command of conditions in category a and as a result to decrease the number of conditions in b.

Our analysis of task difficulty leads us to generate the following rule of thumb for child rearing: People who are in charge of children will best serve the children's welfare by adjusting the difficulty of tasks to the gradually increasing level of ability the children attain as they grow up.

IMPLICATIONS FOR THE
TREATMENT OF CHILDREN

From naive psychology's use of three factors to account for action, we can draw several implications about child rearing that appear to guide adults' treatment of children. For instance, if we want to help a child complete a task at which he is currently failing, we first need to estimate which of the three factors—ability, task difficulty, or effort—is causing his failure. Then we can try to remedy the faulty condition of the identified factor.

If we think the child is striving as well as he is able and that his ability cannot be improved very readily, then we logically attempt to reduce the difficulty of the task so he can succeed. To reduce the task's difficulty level, we can either do part of the task ourselves or break it down into smaller steps he can manage. However, in many cases we either cannot or do not wish to simplify the task. Then we may concentrate on improving the child's ability through training. In other cases we may conclude that the child's abilities are sufficient, but he either has not focused on the task (direction of motivation) or has not tried hard enough. So we try to convince the child that the task is something he really wants to do. We might try logic, cajoling, promises of rewards, or threats of punishment to motivate him to action (Heider, 1958, p. 123).

If this line of reasoning appears too obvious to be worth analyzing, it is not surprising. It's all common sense.

PRIVILEGE AND RESPONSIBILITY

Like other theories of development, the commonsense theory depicts child growth in terms of stages. The three most general stages are infancy, childhood, and adolescence. The borders between them are distinguished by relatively sudden physiological and psychological changes. An infant or baby crosses the border into childhood when she becomes "more of a real person" through learning to walk and talk around age 1½ or 2. The child crosses the border into adolescence or teenage status when the mature sexual functions ripen and such secondary sex characteristics as voice change, a spurt in height, body hair, and changes in skin texture show up around ages 12 to 15.

Paralleling these marks of physical maturation are a series of changes in privilege and responsibility that society regards as suitable for the growing child. Consequently, one way to analyze directions or stages of development from a commonsense perspective is to do so in terms of the sorts of privileges and responsibilities that are added at different age levels.

The phrase *growth in privileges* here means increased opportunities to engage in a wider variety of activities, particularly activities the child considers desirable. In other words, she can do more things that she would like to do. *Growth in responsibility* means that the child incurs the obligation to carry out, under her own initiative or supervision, additional tasks that society considers proper, constructive, and desirable. In naive psychology, responsibility is composed of what Heider has called *ought forces* (1958, pp. 218–243). These are attitudes regarding the duties people are to fulfill that are shared widely by a community. Such duties are necessary for providing the individual with a stable, predictable social environment in which to live, in the same way that "man can operate in the physical environment only when physical laws hold" (Heider, 1958, p. 229).

As suggested by the folk saying, "With each privilege you incur a responsibility," common sense conceives privilege and responsibility to be opposite ends of a balance scale. Throughout a child's development, his increasing abilities enable him to do more things by himself, so he gradually is permitted by his society to carry out a greater variety of actions and make more decisions on his own. But as privileges are gained by the child, society, primarily in the form of parents and teachers, adds oughts or duties. Much of the conflict between children and adults over the first two decades of life comes from (1) children wanting more privileges at an early age and (2) adults seeking to postpone the privileges or to impose responsibilities before the child wants them.

Since the most commonly agreed upon gauge of developmental level is chronological age, society uses age for defining when children's abilities (and sense of responsibility) are sufficient to permit them to try certain tasks or make certain decisions. Some of these age expectations are in the form of custom, such as the custom in certain Christian churches of having children gain church membership at around age 12. Other expectations are formalized as laws and regulations. By inspecting these laws, we can see what the common sense of the day considers to be proper steps or stages of development. For example, the stage of early childhood is typically distinguished from later childhood by school entrance laws. In the United States children are both permitted and obligated to attend school around age 5 or 6. Such formal laws reflect commonsense perceptions of steps in development; less formal regulations, such as the school's curriculum guidelines, delineate substages within the major steps. For instance, it is common in American schools to focus kindergarten activities on broadening the children's experience with their physical and social world and not on formally teaching them reading, writing, or arithmetic. But when children enter first grade at age 6 or so, they are expected to begin reading, writing, and formally analyzing quantitative concepts.

Criminal law reflects the commonsense belief that children before puberty are not yet reasonable or responsible beings, and even after they are not considered to be entirely reasonable. The California penal code states that children under age 14 are not capable of committing actual crimes unless there is "clear proof that at the time of committing the act charged against them, they knew its wrongfulness." So the excuse that "he didn't know what he was doing" is sufficient for not prosecuting a child as a "reasonable" adult would be prosecuted. Between ages 14 and 17, youths are still considered only partially responsible beings, so that when they commit unlawful acts they are labeled delinquents rather than criminals and are processed through special juvenile courts. Furthermore, many states prohibit the public press from publishing the names of youths under age 18 who are involved in crimes, under the belief that prior to 18 an adolescent is still not fully responsible and does not deserve public blame and shame.

The number of laws, both civil and criminal, that use age 18 as the cutting point for various privileges and responsibilities suggests that common sense today defines the period of childhood and adolescence as extending from birth through age 17, even though in American society many youths are still not economically independent of their parents by age 18. There is a general expectation, or hope, that all youths will graduate from high school, and this usually occurs around age 18. In recent years the legal voting age was lowered from 21 to 18. One result of this was to make the voting age more closely coincide with the age at which boys acquire the privilege or obligation to fight and die for their country (age 17—voluntary enlistment; age 18—registering for conscription).

In effect, laws and customs reflect common notions of steps in development, with each step representing a point at which abilities and children's acceptance of ought forces are sufficient for them to be accorded new privileges and responsibilities. However, reaching the designated age for taking a step is not a guarantee that a privilege or responsibility will actually be provided. Other measures of development are also used. Before a child is considered ready for first grade, for example, he is tested or observed to determine whether he has the abilities needed to succeed at typical first-grade tasks. And Mr. Young's daughter, Charlene, is not guaranteed a driver's license at age 16. The girl's driving skill and knowledge of traffic laws will also be tested, and she will be denied a license until she has proven her skill. On the other hand, privileges are sometimes given before the minimum age level is reached. An adolescent who is slightly underage but who can prove her driving skill and a compelling need to drive (such as to provide the family income) may be given a driver's license before age 16. In sum, age is the main criterion of developmental sufficiency in commonsense psychology, but other criteria are also used to accommodate individual differences in children's ability.

Thus, commonsense psychology proposes (1) generalizations that describe the average child and (2) minor amendments that describe children who deviate from the average. And these conclusions that form a society's naive view of development are found in the customs, regulations, and laws that apply to life in the home, in the school, and in the wider community.

NAIVE PSYCHOLOGY: AN ASSESSMENT

The appraisal of commonsense theory will be based on the nine evaluation standards used previously. My estimates of how well naive theory meets the standards are given as marks on the nine scales; then my explanations for the ratings are given. Again, because your value system or your weighing of the evidence may differ from mine, you may well arrive at a different pattern of ratings and may wish to prepare your own rating sheet.

The logic behind my ratings may be easiest to follow if we begin with item 5, the degree of internal consistency in the theory. There is necessarily considerable consistency among the assumptions on which people conduct their everyday treatment of chil-

NAIVE THEORY

How well do I think the theory meets the standards?

The Standards	Very Well	Moderately Well	Very Poorly
1. Reflects the real world of children	X		
2. Is clearly understandable		X	
3. Explains the past and predicts the future		X	
4. Guides child rearing	X		
5. Is internally consistent		X	
6. Is economical		X	
7. Is falsifiable		X	
8. Stimulates new discoveries	X		
9. Is self-satisfying		X	

dren. Otherwise child rearing would be far more chaotic than it is. However, as Heider has pointed out, one can also criticize naive theory and its sources of data for "the many contradictions that are to be found in this body of material, such as antithetical proverbs or contradictions in a person's interpretation of even simple events" (1958, p. 5). Which is the proper guide to child raising: "A little love and kindness goes a long way" or "Spare the rod and spoil the child"? How does a teacher reconcile the contradictions in her observation that "he really doesn't have the ability to do it, but he tries so hard that he is able to overachieve"? In judging item 5, then, the substantial consistencies in naive theory are bal-

anced against what seem to be a substantial number of contradictions, and the theory is rated in the upper portion of the
moderately well segment.

There are at least two ways of looking at item 2, regarding the
clarity of naive theory. First, naive psychology is not some scientist's creation. It is the set of assumptions upon which people
base their treatment of children. So a first way of viewing the issue
of clarity in item 2 is reflected in the question: Are the assumptions about children that comprise common sense clearly understood and agreed upon within a given society? I believe the
answer to this is that the contents of commonsense psychology are
only moderately clear. People in a society have different assumptions about what makes sense in terms of child development. Even
within a given person's set of assumptions there are contradictions, as illustrated in the discussion of internal consistency.
However, there is considerable clarity about many aspects of naive psychology. If there were not, we would have far more conflict
in our society than we do.

A second way to look at the clarity issue is illustrated by the
question: Have psychologists who analyze naive theory clearly
described all of its characteristics? Heider has made a good start
toward clarifying the structure of commonsense views, and such
writers as Baldwin (1967) have extended Heider's general system
to focus it more distinctly on childhood. However, the system is
still far from being completely clear, and numerous questions remain unanswered.

Therefore, from both points of view—from people's understanding and agreeing upon the nature of commonsense beliefs
and from psychologists' descriptions of the underlying structure—
I have estimated that naive theory is only moderately clear.

Now to item 1: Does naive theory accurately describe the real
world of childhood and adolescence? I believe that to a great extent
it does. As Heider has observed, "The ordinary person has a great
and profound understanding of himself and of other people
which, though unformulated or only vaguely conceived, enables
him to interact with others in more or less adaptive ways. . . .
Intuitive knowledge may be remarkably penetrating and can go
a long way toward the understanding of human behavior" (1958,
p. 2). However, there are, at the same time, some notably unrealistic aspects to commonsense views. One of the most obvious is
the tendency for people to attribute happenings in a child's development or behavior to a single cause. A careful analysis of events
illustrates that an event results from multiple causes, with some

causes exerting more influence than others. Past arguments about whether nature or nurture caused a particular development exemplify this commonsense tendency to attribute a happening to a single cause. Baldwin has written that "in many ways this feature of naive theory is its most insidious error and creeps most easily into attempts to develop a better, more scientific theory of human behavior" (1967, p. 75).

There are also numerous other aspects of naive theory that bring into question its accuracy in describing children. For example, studies in recent decades of intellectual abilities have furnished a mass of evidence that contradicts the commonsense notion that the level of ability in one subarea of mental life will be the same in all other subareas. As a consequence, psychologists have moved increasingly away from a single general intelligence test that yields one overall intelligence quotient and have moved instead toward the use of multiple-factor tests that yield separate scores for each of several types of mental skills (Guilford, 1967; Harris and Harris, 1971). Likewise, studies of children's reading readiness contradict the belief that the time when all children are ready to begin reading is when they enter first grade (Durkin, 1976).

Thus, balancing the strengths of naive theory against its weaknesses in terms of describing children realistically, I rated the theory in the upper portion of the moderately well segment.

Related to a realistic view of children are item 3 (explaining the past, predicting the future) and item 4 (guides child-rearing practices). Since naive theory is better prepared to explain past events than to predict future ones, it cannot achieve a top rating for its ability to guide child rearing. As Baldwin has pointed out, the theory's weakness in predicting the future behavior of children rests to a great extent on two of its prominent characteristics. First, it does not specify all of the conditions or causes that interact to bring about an event or an aspect of development. For this reason, if the cause it does identify is not the most powerful of those actually operating, then the prediction will be in error.

Second, naive theory assumes that the child has a free will. The issue of the free will is an old one in philosophy, one that has never been resolved satisfactorily. The concept of free will is usually discussed in connection with the contrasting or contrary concept of determinism, which has long been a basic tenet of the physical sciences or what is known as the *scientific method*. Determinism is a belief that everything that happens has been absolutely set or established by preceding conditions and could not have turned out any other way. In effect, if you know all the causal factors, you can make an exact, error-free prediction of what will happen. In contrast, the concept of free will holds that determinism may be true for strictly physical phenomena, such as thunderstorms and the growth of violets, but events that involve human decisions are influenced as well by the individual's freedom to make a choice. In effect, in human events a knowledge of preceding conditions or causal factors enables you to estimate likely outcomes, but you still must consider the individual's free will. The issue of determinism versus free will is a complex one. Here we will simply recognize that the idea of free will poses problems for naive theory when the theory is used as the basis for predicting future child behavior. No matter how much is known about causal conditions in a child's life, if the child has the freedom of choice, errorless predictions of future development or behavior are not possible. This fact limits the value of naive theory for child-rearing purposes. When you treat a child a given way, you never know for sure how he will interpret your actions and choose to respond.

Therefore, even though naive theory contains a lot of folk truths that, over the generations, have enabled people to guide children's development with some measure of success, it also has shortcomings that limit the accuracy of its predictions and child-guidance suggestions. Hence, naive theory is rated in the moderate range for items 3 and 4.

Item 6 was difficult to mark because in some ways naive theory is too economical. That is, it makes what appear to be simplistic assumptions about aspects of development that seem to require more complex explanations. You may recall from Chapter 1 that Morgan's canon states: A theory is better if it is economical in the sense that it is founded on as few unproven assumptions as possible and requires rather simple mechanisms to explain all the phenomena encompassed by the theory. Naive theory violates this standard by failing in some ways to provide the simple mechanisms and in other ways to explain all the phenomena. In failing to fulfill the attribute of simplicity, naive theory may be too complex—for example, it still accepts certain assumptions about the divisions of the mind held over from faculty psychology. In failing to fulfill the attribute of explaining all the phenomena, naive theory may be too simple or simplistic:

Let us consider this charge of oversimplification in more detail. Baldwin (1967, pp. 64–70) has illustrated this problem with examples focusing on matters of perception and intentional action. He points out that the assumption is made in naive psychology that everyone perceives things in the same way. In other words, the child's perceptual equipment is like a television camera, recording sight and sound the way "they really are." And everyone's camera records events in the same way. (This assumption underlies the practice in courts of having witnesses describe what they perceived so the judge and jury can determine what "really" happened.) But today a growing body of research suggests that perception is far more complex than naive theory would suppose. In effect, naive theory neglects the complexities of the phenomenon and proposes an overly simple picture of what apparently occurs.

Baldwin charges that in like manner, common sense fails to explain adequately the relationship between a person's intention and her actions. This objection leads us to the traditional philosophical issue of *teleology*. In a teleological explanation, the main cause of an event is found in the future rather than in the past or present. Instead of specifying the past and present conditions that have caused the young child to speak a few words, the teleological approach identifies some future purpose or outcome that has "caused" the speech behavior. For example, a child learns to speak because she now will be able to communicate her wants more adequately. Or, adolescents seek sexual mates out of a need to reproduce and thus preserve the human species for the future. Although this line of logic may at first appear reasonable, it is not in keeping with basic rules traditionally followed in the natural sciences. In the natural sciences, a cause does not appear in the future, that is, a cause does not appear before its effect. Thus, for people who want child development theory to adhere to the tenets of biological and physical sciences, then the teleological aspects of naive theory are an embarrassment, just as are the beliefs in a free will and single causal factors.

There are, of course, theorists who say that human behavior follows different laws (at least to some degree) from those governing nonhuman events. For these theorists, including the humanistic psychologists (Chapter 19), teleological causation and the free will are not objectionable features of commonsense psychology.

In terms of its economy of explanation, then, naive theory oversimplifies certain aspects of development, thus violating part of item 6, and I have rated it only moderately well.

As for item 7, concerning falsifiability, parts of the theory are testable or disconfirmable, and other parts are not. Although many research studies conducted over the past century on child development represent successful efforts to test the validity of commonsense views, some important aspects of the theory have not as yet appeared testable or falsifiable. These aspects have depended for their confirmation on personal opinion or faith. Two examples of such aspects are the concepts of free will and teleological causation. Balancing these positive and negative factors against each other, I rated item 7 in the moderately well range of the scale.

The highest rating has been given to item 8 in recognition of the great fertility of commonsense beliefs for stimulating new discoveries. In the last analysis, all new theories and new research have resulted from people's dissatisfaction with commonsense answers or from people's attempts to defend naive theory in the face of attacks on it. Furthermore, the sort of analysis of commonsense theory carried out by Heider and his disciples has itself led to a growing body of research called *attribution theory* (Kelley, 1973, pp. 107–128; Weiner, 1972; Weiner, 1974).

Finally, naive theory is, overall, moderately self-satisfying (item 9). Although much of my own treatment of children is based on commonsense notions, in many ways this common sense fails to answer my child development questions adequately and I am left discontented with naive theory. This discontent serves as a sufficient stimulus for learning what more formal theories, such as the ones in the following chapters, offer.

FOR FURTHER READING

Baldwin, Alfred L. (1967) *Theories of Child Development*. New York: Wiley. Baldwin reviews Heider's general theory to show the implications it holds for child development; he offers a detailed critique of naive theory and its relation to scientific method and other theories of development.

Heider, Fritz. (1958) *The Psychology of Interpersonal Relations*. New York: Wiley. Heider describes what he conceives to be a theoretical framework on which people's commonsense psychology is founded.

PART 4

DESCRIPTIONS OF
DEVELOPMENTAL MILESTONES

A search for typical steps of growth in many aspects of a child's life.

G. Stanley Hall, with the publication in 1891 of his study entitled "The Contents of Children's Minds on Entering School," is credited with starting a tradition that dominated child development investigation in America over the first half of the twentieth century. This is the tradition of measuring and observing groups of children, then summarizing the results in the form of averages for different age levels. Studies of this type have focused on a wide array of child characteristics, ranging from measurements of height and weight, through the testing of mental and physical skills, to observations of social relations, sleep habits, and outbursts of anger. The number of such published studies from around the world runs into many thousands. They have been called *normative, descriptive* investigations because they describe the normal, in the sense of average, status of children on specified characteristics at different age levels. The summarized results of these studies typically are labeled *descriptive norms* or *age norms*.

The theorist who best exemplifies the normative-descriptive school of child development is Arnold Gesell, a physician and child psychologist who studied under G. Stanley Hall at Clark University before setting up a clinic at Yale University to conduct descriptive research on children. Gesell's apparent intention was to chart with as great care and thoroughness as possible children's characteristics at each age level in a great many facets of their lives. A brief review of Gesell's work is given in Chapter 6.

A second approach to describing milestones on the road to maturity is illustrated in Chapter 7. The approach, known as *developmental-task theory*, grew up in the 1930s and 1940s in the United

States within the progressive education movement that dominated the educational thought of that era. Like Gesell, leaders of the developmental-task approach tried to identify the typical steps in development at different age periods in many aspects of growth —physical, intellectual, social, and emotional. But, unlike Gesell, developmental-task adherents did not systematically measure, test, and observe children who were chosen as typical representatives. Rather, the developmental-task theorists based their growth stages on data drawn from a great variety of sources: empirical studies like those from Gesell's clinic, anthropological and sociological investigations, observations by teachers of children in school, commonsense ideas about child raising, and others. Furthermore, whereas Gesell was most interested in describing what children are like at different age levels, the developmental-task theorists were more interested in speculating about what children are trying to accomplish during each successive age period. The term *developmental task* was created to reflect the theorists' conviction that growth should be viewed as the child's seeking to achieve new goals or perform new tasks at each new stage of development.

In sum, Gesell endeavored to describe what children are like. Advocates of the developmental-task approach not only wished to describe what children are like at each phase of growth, they also sought to infer from these descriptions the sorts of goals they felt children were pursuing or the needs they were seeking to fulfill by their behavior.

The tradition of normative-descriptive studies in which Gesell played such an important role continues very active today. Likewise, though the peak of developmental-task theorizing was reached in the 1940s, the movement continues to exert a significant influence on curriculum development in schools and on child development textbooks.

CHAPTER 6

GESELL'S GROWTH GRADIENTS

An early stage in the development of any natural science is that of describing phenomena and putting the descriptions into some sort of order. In the field of child development in America, such a task of describing and ordering was done over the first half of this century by Arnold Gesell and his colleagues at the Yale University School of Medicine.

Gesell was born in 1880 in Wisconsin, where he was schooled and eventually took a college degree in teaching before earning a Ph.D. in psychology at Clark University in Massachusetts in 1906. In 1911 Gesell was appointed to the Yale faculty as an assistant professor of education. At the same time he established the Clinic of Child Development, which he directed over the next thirty-seven years. While at Yale he earned a doctorate in medicine (1915), and his clinic was attached to the school of medicine. After Gesell's retirement, several of his co-workers set up a private institution near Yale in New Haven, naming it the Gesell Institute of Child Development. Gesell served as a consultant to the clinic from 1950 through 1958. He died in 1961, but the work of his clinic has continued since that time.

Throughout his professional years Gesell pursued the task of describing the observable changes in child growth and behavior from birth to adolescence. Although his principal concern was with development after birth, he also conducted studies on prenatal growth stages.* In our review of the theoretical themes that

---

* The following sample of titles of books he authored suggests the range of his interests: *The Normal Child and Primary Education* in 1912, *Guidance of Mental Growth in Infant and Child* in 1930, *An Atlas of Infant Behavior* in 1934, *The Embryology of Behavior* in 1945, *The Child from 5 to 10* in 1946, *Youth: The Years from 10 to 16* in 1956.

dominated Gesell's investigations, we will consider the following:
(1) the aspects of development on which Gesell focused, (2) the
primacy of genetic determinants, (3) cycles of behavior, and
(4) his manner of accounting for individual differences.

ASPECTS OF DEVELOPMENT

The work of Gesell and his colleagues consisted mainly of studying children brought to their clinic from families in New England
of varying socioeconomic status. The number of children studied
as representative of children in general was not specified in such
key volumes as Gesell and Frances Ilg's *Child Development* (1949),
nor were other characteristics of the group defined except in such
broad terms as: "The nursery school children have in general been
above an average level in intelligence. The parents of all these
children have assisted us with a high order of cooperation" (Gesell
and Ilg, 1949, pp. xx). The results reported in *Child Development*
were based not only on studies of the New England children but
also on data about "a special group of fourteen Swedish infants
. . . studied by Dr. Ilg in 1936–37 while she was in residence in
Stockholm" (Gesell and Ilg, 1949, p. xx).

To carry out their studies, Gesell and his staff created an array
of tests, measuring procedures, and techniques of observation
that would enable them to describe children's status precisely in a
wide range of growth areas. The research team gathered information about children in the clinic, and also interviewed parents to
learn about the children's behavior at home. These data enabled
the staff to describe the steps or *gradients of growth* for the typical
child at each age level. The array of developmental aspects for
which Gesell identified *maturity traits* and *gradients of growth* were
categorized into the following ten major areas, with several minor
divisions under each major category (Gesell and Ilg, 1949, p. 69):

1. Motor Characteristics
   a. Bodily activity
   b. Eyes and hands
2. Personal Hygiene
   a. Eating
   b. Sleeping

   c. Elimination
   d. Bathing and dressing
   e. Health and somatic complaints
   f. Tensional outlets

3. Emotional Expression
   a. Affective attitudes
   b. Crying and related behaviors
   c. Assertion and anger

4. Fears and Dreams

5. Self and Sex

6. Interpersonal Relations
   a. Mother-child
   b. Child-child
   c. Groupings in play

7. Play and Pastimes
   a. General interests
   b. Reading
   c. Music, radio, and cinema

8. School Life
   a. Adjustment to school
   b. Classroom demeanor
   c. Reading
   d. Writing
   e. Arithmetic

9. Ethical Sense
   a. Blaming and alibiing
   b. Response to direction, punishment, praise
   c. Responsiveness to reason
   d. Sense of good and bad
   e. Truth and property

10. Philosophic Outlook
   a. Time
   b. Space
   c. Language and thought
   d. War
   e. Death
   f. Deity

An inspection of this extensive list shows that Gesell adopted a multifaceted view of a child rather than concentrating on one or two aspects of growth. And the fact that the topics cover growth areas that are of daily concern to parents and teachers helps account for the popularity of his books in the mid-twentieth century. When a mother worried about whether a particular kind of behavior was typical or "normal" for her child, she could turn to one of Gesell's volumes for an answer. The writing style of the most widely read books was adjusted to the reading tastes of parents. The volumes were not composed of statistical tables, showing the frequency of certain behaviors or of the number of children above and below the average at a given level. Instead, Gesell and his staff digested the statistics and turned them into specific statements of what a child was like at a given age. For example, here are typical descriptions of an aspect of behavior—children's fears—for ages 5 and 6 from a volume by two of Gesell's closest co-workers, Frances L. Ilg and Louise Bates Ames.

> *5-year-olds:* Not a fearful age. More visual fears than others. Less fear of animals, bad people, bogeymen. Concrete, down-to-earth fears: bodily harm, falling, dogs. The dark. That mother will not return.
>
> *6-year-olds:* Very fearful. Especially auditory fears: doorbell, telephone, static, ugly voice tones, flushing of toilet, insect and bird noises. Fear of supernatural: ghosts, witches. Fear that someone is hiding under the bed. Fear of the elements: fire, water, thunder, lightning. Fear of sleeping alone in a room or of being only one on a floor of a house (1955, pp. 172–173).

Thus, the main body of books issued from the Gesell clinic was composed of such "typical traits and growth trends of each age . . . summarized in a 'Behavior Profile' " (Gesell and Ilg, 1949, p. 2). In addition, Gesell and his co-workers expressed three important convictions that warrant our attention: (1) that development is primarily a product of genetic factors, (2) that better and worse years alternate systematically in child growth, and (3) that there is a clear correlation between a child's body type and personality. These are the matters to which we now turn.

THE PRIMACY OF
GENETIC DETERMINANTS

In the heredity–environment controversy, Gesell is clearly a predeterminist. In his opinion, changes in children's structure and behavior are chiefly the result of their genetic endowment. The genes set the schedule by which the child's characteristics emerge over the first two decades of life, and the social and physical environments have little effect on these characteristics.

In light of this belief in the primacy of genetic determination, it is hardly surprising that Gesell and his staff saw as the most important mission in the field of child development that of cataloguing the physical and mental characteristics at each age level. This catalogue of average, normal characteristics could inform parents, teachers, and pediatricians of the traits they might expect to see unfold with each year of growth.

CYCLES OF BEHAVIOR

The Yale group also identified each year of development as either better or worse. They proposed that the better and worse phases appear in recurring cycles and are essentially the same for all children, or for nearly all. The term *better stage* was applied to any year in which the child appears to be in good adjustment or in good balance, both within himself and with the people in his world. The term *worse stage* was given to years during which the child is unhappy and confused within himself and at odds with his social and physical environments. Ilg and Ames termed these cycles "an alternation of stages of equilibrium and disequilibrium" (1955, p. 91).

As Table 6.1 shows, the first cycle of alternating better and worse ages begins at year 2 and ends at 5. The next cycle starts at 5 and lasts until age 10. Then a third cycle begins and continues through age 16.

Since the Gesell group envisioned the characteristics of the better and worse years to be determined by internal maturational factors, their advice to parents and teachers concerning what to do about the worse years was basically to be patient and wait until the inevitable bad times passed. Therapy, which Freudians might suggest, or retraining, which behaviorists would recommend, was not proposed. "We can try to smooth over the child's 'worse' stages. . . . But if we can accept . . . these extremes . . . as necessary parts of growth, and not blame them on somebody (teacher, other parent, neighbor, child himself), we will be looking at things realistically" (Ilg and Ames, 1955, p. 17).

Table 6.1   Alternation of Stages of Equilibrium and Disequilibrium

Stages of Child Behavior

First Cycle	Second Cycle	Third Cycle	General	Quality of
Age	Age	Age	Personality Trends	the Age
2	5	10	Smooth, consolidated	Better
2½	5½–6	11	Breaking up	Worse
3	6½	12	Rounded, balanced	Better
3½	7	13	Inwardized	Worse
4	8	14	Vigorous, expansive	Better
4½	9	15	Inwardized-outwardized, troubled, "neurotic"	Worse
5	10	16	Smooth, consolidated	Better

Table adapted from Ilg and Ames, 1955, p. 22.

INDIVIDUAL DIFFERENCES

When a system like Gesell's is described, with children at each age level depicted as so much alike in so many ways, the question of individual differences among age peers comes up. In acknowledging the existence of exceptions to their descriptions of typical characteristics, Gesell and his colleagues inserted in their writings such comments as:

> The prevalence of significant variations [is] recognized at every turn (Gesell and Ilg, 1949, pp. 1–2).

> Any description of age levels such as that which we have just given you is a gross oversimplification. When we describe characteristic behavior for any age, we do not mean that all children of that age will behave just that way all of the time (Ilg and Ames, 1955, pp. 22–23).

Seldom is more specific mention made in these writings, particularly in books written before 1950, of deviations from the typical traits. In one of the later volumes (1955), Ilg and Ames did give somewhat more recognition to individual differences by first describing typical traits, then describing two or three types of children that were deviations from or variations of these traits. In addition, the authors offered suggestions about what might be done to aid the deviant make a better adjustment. As an example, the following is part of the authors' discussion of eating behavior:

> Some children live to eat. They are the round, often plump children. They are rarely feeding problems. But there are others who rarely think of eating. They are the small, petite, or even scrawny children. Hunger may come often to them but it is usually sharp and short-lived. These children do better on small, frequent meals, even five or six a day. . . . They gain weight very slowly but are active and healthy, more healthy, often, than the larger robust children (Ilg and Ames, 1955, p. 91).

This passage illustrates three characteristics frequently found in publications emanating from the Gesell Institute. First, any differences among children at a given age are described in terms of two or three types of children, in this case the plump and the petite or scrawny, with the implication that all children fit into either the basic category for their age or into one of the deviant groups. Second, little or no attempt is made to suggest any environmental factors that might have contributed to a child's becoming one of these types, the implication being that children are naturally that way because of their genetic structure. Third, when advice is offered about what can be done for children whose type deviates from the average, the advice does not derive from principles inherent in Gesell's theory. Rather, the advice either qualifies as common sense or derives more logically from studies or theories of other workers in the field of child behavior.

In view of the dominant role the Gesell group has assigned to heredity in all aspects of development, it is easy to understand why they turned to William Sheldon's theory of *somatotypes* to account for personality differences among children. In Sheldon's opinion, there are three basic body types among people, or at least three tendencies. He labeled these the endomorph, the mesomorph, and the ectomorph (Sheldon, 1940 and 1942).

The person who is predominantly *endomorphic* tends to be fat, soft, and round. Sheldon proposed that this body build is accompanied by a personality type that displays a love of comfort and relaxation, of food, of the company of other people, and of affection.

The *mesomorph* has big bones and heavy muscles. This type

loves vigorous muscular activity and is assertive, wishing to dominate others in social situations.

The *ectomorph* is thin, fragile, poorly muscled. This personality is restrained, inhibited, oversensitive, and seeks concealment. He avoids social contact.

Though Sheldon agreed that few people are entirely one of these body types, he claimed that everyone tends toward one or the other. Ilg and Ames, subscribing to the Sheldon position, have stated that at each age level individual personality differences among children can be accounted for to a considerable degree by their body builds which, in turn, have been determined by their genes. The authors have allowed some room for the influence of the environment, however, by adding: "All of this does not mean that human behavior is *entirely* determined by hereditary factors. What it does mean is that the body structure provides the raw material out of which personality is formed" (Ilg and Ames, 1955, p. 55). Nevertheless, despite this passing notice of environmental factors, the dominant theme throughout all of the Gesell Institute work is that the prime factor in shaping development both for the average child and for types deviating from the average is the child's genetically set maturation schedule.

GESELL'S CONTRIBUTIONS: AN ASSESSMENT

In keeping with the system of assessment used in previous chapters, I first rate Gesell's work on nine scales based on the appraisal standards suggested in Chapter 1.

My ratings of Gesell's work may appear to form a strange pattern, since I have given his approach high marks on five of the nine criteria, yet have judged his theory overall as not very satisfying. To explain these conclusions, let us consider first the high ratings. With few exceptions, his beliefs are described (item 2) quite clearly. Also, with the exception of his position on the extent of and causes of individual differences among children in the same age cohort, his proposals are internally consistent (item 5).

His work is also falsifiable (item 7). His growth gradients and descriptions of behavior by age levels are the result of empirical findings, and their accuracy can be checked empirically. Likewise,

GESELL'S THEORY

How well do I think the theory meets the standards?

The Standards	Very Well	Moderately Well	Very Poorly
1. Reflects the real world of children		X	
2. Is clearly understandable	X		
3. Explains the past and predicts the future	Specifically X	Accurately X	
4. Guides child rearing	Specifically X	Accurately X	
5. Is internally consistent	X		
6. Is economical		Simplistic X	
7. Is falsifiable	X		
8. Stimulates new discoveries		X	
9. Is self-satisfying			X

the validity of the concept of better and worse years can readily be determined by a researcher who prepares careful definitions of *better* and *worse* behavior or adjustment and then observes children of different age levels to see how well the hypothesis about better and worse years holds up. In a similar manner, the proposed correlation between body build and personality characteristics is amenable to empirical testing.

Item 8 gets a rather high rating in recognition of the influence Gesell's work has exerted on other researchers in the field of development. During the years of his greatest productivity, he devised a variety of testing and observation procedures, particularly for use with very young children, that have been admired for their precision and ingenuity. His procedures have become part of commonly used scales for judging development over the first year or so of life. Not only are his research methods still used in normative studies, but much of what he learned about the early years of growth continues to be respected today. Burton L. White, a Harvard University authority on infancy, wrote in 1971, "In this country, the most widely utilized source of information on the behavior of the human infant is probably the work of Arnold Gesell" (White, 1971, p. 7).

The rating on item 6 for the degree of economy Gesell's system displays represents a compromise between (1) his extremely simple, and in that sense economical, explanation of the causes of development and (2) the oversimplicity of the explanation. Although Gesell did not devise an unduly elaborate array of untested assumptions on which to erect his explanation, he did ignore a mass of research evidence that suggested environmental influences were far more important than his system recognized. As Zigler has commented:

> It is difficult to refer to [Gesell's scheme] as a theory. It appears rather to be a grand view having but a single construct, maturation. . . . Within such a framework, no other choice exists than to make the norms discovered through empirical investigations into explanatory devices . . . [so that] explanation is thus reduced to a labeling process. . . . The vacuousness and conceptual inadequacy of such a procedure has frequently been noted (1965, pp. 359–360).

In effect, the system is not overly complex, so it appears economical. In reality, however, it is unconvincingly simplistic. So I have rated it rather low on item 6.

On item 1, concerning how well a theory reflects the real world of children, Gesell deserves credit as an empiricist for founding his beliefs on observations of actual children, not imagined ones. He did not speculate about what children might be like or should be like. However, his penchant for reducing his observations to convenient averages or statements concerning typical characteristics at each age level distorted the picture of the real world of children. At any age level, and on any dimension of development, there are marked variations among children. For example, studies of reading ability among American school children have shown that in grade 5 of elementary school (ages 10–11), the most apt pupils will read as well as the average tenth-grade student in high school, while the least adept will read no better than the average first grader in primary school (Thomas and Thomas, 1965, pp. 304–309). Most pupils will fall between these two extremes, with the greater number near the fifth-grade average. Gesell's reporting of only averages, or at best his noting of subtypes of children who deviate from the average, gives an unrealistic picture of the growth status of many children at every age level.

Besides the problems of Gesell's reporting only typical characteristics of children, there is also a question of how accurately his developmental norms represent children in general. The question concerns both the number and the cultural background of the children on whom he based the norms. The exact number of boys and girls studied in the clinic is not specified in Gesell's major publications, but the total at each age level apparently was no more than a few dozen. Furthermore, the children studied were from New England families interested enough in Gesell's research to bring their children to the clinic periodically for testing and observation. This method of sampling might well bias the results since there might be systematic differences between these families and those that did not participate in the clinic's studies. Indeed, Gesell pointed out that the preschool children in his group were above average in intelligence. Thus, there is reason to doubt that the typical behaviors recorded for this sample, even when supplemented by observations of fourteen Swedish infants, give a realistic picture of children from other geographic and cultural settings.

Of course, this question about the representativeness of the sample is really not a serious issue when viewed from Gesell's predeterminist perspective. Since he believed that development depends heavily on heredity rather than environment, he could reason that it is unnecessary to choose children from different cultural environments—environment has little influence. It is necessary only to observe enough children to convince yourself that you have included the few major genetic types that make up the population. Thus, Gesell was willing to generalize his observations to all children. But because I agree with those researchers who state that environment does exert an important influence on development, I have concluded that Gesell's sampling procedures were inadequate.

By balancing Gesell's admirable care in studying real children against his practice of describing only typical behaviors of a sample of New England children, I decided to rate his scheme only moderately realistic (item 1).

Both item 3 (explains past, predicts future) and item 4 (guides child rearing) are given two marks. The first mark in each case is for the degree of specificity of Gesell's system. In his system a child's past development is explained as the result of the natural unfolding of the preset genetic pattern. A child's future growth is described in terms of the typical characteristics of the age in which you are interested. Gesell's guides to child-rearing practices are equally definite. Basically you let nature take its course. If the child's current development seems unsatisfactory, it is because he is in one of the worse years, and patience on the part of adults is required until the stage passes. For such specificity Gesell's system rates high marks.

However, in terms of the accuracy of his explanations of the past, predictions for the future, and child-raising recommendations, he is rated further down the scales. I disagree with his practice of limiting his attention to "average" or "typical" behavior for an age group. Probably no child is average or typical in every way. Each child has a pattern of characteristics that makes up his individuality. Group averages are of limited use in explaining a child's past, predicting his future status, and suggesting what should be done to guide his development. The faith that researchers during the first half of the twentieth century placed in the value of normative group studies that yielded average scores (called *nomothetic* studies) has decreased in recent decades. More attention has been given recently to devising methods of investigating the growth of the individual child (called *idiographic* studies), particularly for purposes of prediction and child-rearing guidance.

Not only do I question Gesell's heavy dependence on typical behaviors, but I also question his crediting the environment with such a meager role in shaping development. In later chapters we will inspect the work of theorists who marshal evidence and a line of reasoning that suggest that environmental factors are extremely important in fashioning child growth, and much of this evidence I find convincing. (In particular see Lewin and Barker in Chapter 8, Vygotsky in Chapter 14, and the behaviorists in Part 9.) Gesell's neglect of children's physical and social surroundings reduces the accuracy of his explanations of the child's past, predictions of his future, and recommendations for guiding his upbringing. For these reasons I have marked items 3 and 4 in the low to moderate range for accuracy.

Finally, I judge Gesell's system overall to be in the low to moderate range in terms of being self-satisfying (item 9). I respect his practice of making careful firsthand investigations of children and his devising techniques for carrying out such study. However, these contributions do not sufficiently compensate for his overdependence on maturation and his overconcentration on "typical" behavior to warrant a higher rating.

FOR FURTHER READING

Gesell, Arnold and Frances L. Ilg. (1949) *Child Development: An Introduction to the Study of Human Growth.* New York: Harper. This volume contains the most complete, systematic summaries of typical developmental characteristics by age levels that have been drawn from the research of the Gesell group.

Ilg, Frances L. and Louise Bates Ames. (1955) *The Gesell Institute's Child Behavior.* New York: Dell. Two of Gesell's closest co-workers offer the results of the institute's studies in a popular form intended particularly for parents and teachers.

CHAPTER 7

HAVIGHURST'S
DEVELOPMENTAL TASKS

According to the developmental-task theory, the process of living, from birth to death, consists of an individual's working her way from one stage of development to the next by solving problems that are met at each stage. These problems, common to virtually everyone in a particular culture, are life's developmental tasks. If a person is successful in achieving each task, she is happy and receives the approval of her society. This success builds a good foundation for accomplishing later tasks. If the individual fails with a task, she feels unhappy, society does not approve, and she faces difficulty with later tasks (Havighurst, 1953, p. 2).

Examples of developmental tasks at the first stage of life, infancy, are learning to walk and learning to talk. Examples from middle childhood are learning the physical skills necessary for ordinary games and developing the fundamental skills of reading, writing, and calculating. Examples from later adolescence are achieving emotional independence from parents and preparing for an occupation.

The developmental-task theory is not the product of a single theorist. The basic idea underlying the scheme and the identification of important tasks began in the 1930s and evolved during the 1940s among groups of child psychologists and educators who played leading roles in the Progressive Education Association in the United States.* The theory was subsequently cast in its most

---

* Havighurst (1953, pp. 328–333) credits the following people with contributions to the developmental-task concept: Frankwood Williams, Lawrence K. Frank, Carolyn Zachry, Erik Erikson, Fritz Redl, Caroline Tryon, Jesse Lilienthal, Stephen M. Corey, Peter Blos, Daniel Prescott, Evelyn Duvall, and Reuben Hill.

systematic and extensive form by Robert J. Havighurst in his 1953 volume entitled *Human Development and Education* and by Carolyn Tryon and Jesse Lilienthal in two chapters of their 1950 work *Fostering Mental Health in Our Schools*. The picture of the theory sketched in the following pages is based mainly on these two sources.

Although the developmental-task model found its greatest popularity in the 1940s and 1950s in the field of education, it has continued to influence child psychologists and educators, and periodically has stimulated the publication of new books in Europe and America founded on the task concept.

The following brief overview of the theory treats three topics: (1) characteristics of tasks, (2) timing of tasks, and (3) evidence to support the theory.

CHARACTERISTICS OF THE TASKS

The term *developmental task* was apparently coined in the 1930s by people prominent in the Progressive Education Association. It was adopted and popularized by Havighurst in the 1940s and 1950s because, in discussions of adolescent development, he said he had "seen so much misunderstanding result from the use of the equivocal term 'needs' as a central concept" (1953, p. 330). He felt that the new term *developmental tasks* better described what young people were attempting to do as they grew up. According to Havighurst, the developmental tasks of life are pursuits that:

> constitute a healthy and satisfactory growth in our society. They are those things a person must learn if he is to be judged and to judge himself to be a reasonably happy and successful person. A developmental task is a task which arises at or about a certain period in the life of the individual, successful achievement of which leads to his happiness and to success with later tasks, while failure leads to unhappiness in the individual, disapproval by society, and difficulty with later tasks (1953, p. 2).

What are the tasks at different age levels? How many are there? Havighurst said that the number is somewhat arbitrary. It depends both on the way a person chooses to specify them and also on the particular society he is talking about. For instance, the task of learning independent locomotion can be seen either as a single complex task composed of subactivities (creeping, walking, trotting, running, hopping, jumping) or as six different small tasks.

Some tasks arise mainly from the biological nature of humans and thus will be found in all human societies. Their form is essentially the same in all cultures. Other tasks derive their characteristics from the unique cultural patterns of a given society; these either exist in different forms in different societies or else are found in some cultures but not in others. A task like learning to walk, which depends primarily on genetically determined growth factors, is essentially the same in all societies and arises at about the same time in a child's life. However, the task of selecting and preparing for an occupation is a complex one in highly industrialized societies that are characterized by much specialization and division of labor, while in nonindustrialized societies in which nearly everyone is a farmer or hunter or fisher, the task of choosing a vocation is perhaps simpler and is achieved at a younger age than in the industrialized society. Furthermore, the tasks of learning to read and write, which are so important in highly literate cultures, do not even exist in preliterate ones.

Consequently, lists of developmental tasks will not be the same for all cultures, and the items in the lists identifying a culture's tasks will be determined to some degree by the personal value systems of the people who prepare them. Havighurst admitted that the description of tasks he produced was "based on American democratic values seen from a middle-class point of view, with some attempt at pointing out the variations for lower-class and upper-class Americans" (1953, p. 26).

Havighurst felt that in applying the developmental-task approach to the education of the child, it is most useful to define between six and ten tasks at each stage of development. One such application is shown in Table 7.1, which was devised by Tryon and Lilienthal. The chart contains ten general categories or types of tasks. These categories are listed in the far-left column. To find the specific tasks in each category at each age level, look to the right of the category name.

For example, consider the first category, that of the child's achieving an appropriate dependence-independence pattern in growth. In the second column from the left, we find two specific tasks the infant faces in this category: (1) establishing one's self as a very dependent being and (2) beginning the establishment of self-awareness. For children at the stage of early adolescence (fifth

Table 7.1 The Tasks of Five Stages of Development in Ten Categories of Behavior

	Infancy (Birth to 1 or 2)	Early Childhood (2–3 to 5–6–7)	Late Childhood (5–6–7 to pubescence)	Early Adolescence (Pubescence to puberty)	Late Adolescence (Puberty to early maturity)
I Achieving appropriate dependence-independence pattern	1. Establishing one's self as a very dependent being 2. Beginning the establishment of self-awareness	1. Adjusting to less private attention; becoming independent physically (while remaining strongly dependent emotionally)	1. Freeing one's self from primary identification with adults	1. Establishing one's independence from adults in all areas of behavior	1. Establishing one's self as an independent individual in an adult manner
II Achieving an appropriate giving-receiving pattern of affection	1. Developing a feeling for affection	1. Developing the ability to give affection 2. Learning to share affection	1. Learning to give as much love as one receives; forming friendships with peers	1. Accepting one's self as a worth-while person, really worthy of love	1. Building a strong mutual affectional bond with a possible marriage partner

(continued)

Table 7.1 The Tasks of Five Stages of Development in Ten Categories of Behavior (continued)

	Infancy (Birth to 1 or 2)	Early Childhood (2–3 to 5–6–7)	Late Childhood (5–6–7 to pubescence)	Early Adolescence (Pubescence to puberty)	Late Adolescence (Puberty to early maturity)
III Relating to changing social groups*	1. Becoming aware of the alive as against the inanimate, and the familiar as against the unfamiliar 2. Developing rudimentary social interaction	1. Beginning to develop the ability to interact with age-mates 2. Adjusting in the family to expectations it has for the child as a member of the social unit	1. Clarifying the adult world as over against the child's world 2. Establishing peer groupness and learning to belong	1. Behaving according to a shifting peer code	1. Adopting an adult-patterned set of social values by learning a new peer code
IV Developing a conscience	1. Beginning to adjust to the expectations of others	1. Developing the ability to take directions and to be obedient in the presence of authority 2. Developing the ability to be obedient in the absence of	1. Learning more rules and developing true morality		1. Learning to verbalize contradictions in moral codes, as well as discrepancies between principle and practice, and resolving these

	problems in a responsible manner			
V Learning one's psycho-socio-biological sex role	authority where conscience substitutes for authority 1. Learning to identify with male adult and female adult roles	1. Beginning to identify with one's social contemporaries of the same sex	1. Strong identification with one's own sex mates 2. Learning one's role in heterosexual relationships	1. Exploring possibilities for a future mate and acquiring "desirability" 2. Choosing an occupation 3. Preparing to accept one's future role in manhood or womanhood as a responsible citizen of the larger community

*Tryon and Lilienthal, 1950, pp. 77–89. We have not dealt with the developmental tasks of relating to "secondary" social groups. As the child grows and develops, he must relate to groups other than the family and his peers—to school, community, nation, world. There are not yet sufficient data to enable us to delineate the specific developmental tasks in this area.

(continued)

Table 7.1 The Tasks of Five Stages of Development in Ten Categories of Behavior (continued)

	Infancy (Birth to 1 or 2)	Early Childhood (2–3 to 5–6–7)	Late Childhood (5–6–7 to pubescence)	Early Adolescence (Pubescence to puberty)	Late Adolescence (Puberty to early maturity)
VI Accepting and adjusting to a changing body	1. Adjusting to adult feeding demands 2. Adjusting to adult cleanliness demands 3. Adjusting to adult attitudes toward genital manipulation	1. Adjusting to expectations resulting from one's improving muscular abilities 2. Developing sex modesty		1. Reorganizing one's thoughts and feelings about one's self in the face of significant bodily changes and their concomitants 2. Accepting the reality of one's appearance	1. Learning appropriate outlets for sexual drives
VII Managing a changing body and learning new motor patterns	1. Developing physiological equilibrium 2. Developing eye-hand coordination 3. Establishing satisfactory rhythm of rest and activity	1. Developing large muscle control 2. Learning to coordinate large muscles and small muscles	1. Refining and elaborating skill in the use of small muscles	1. Controlling and using a "new" body	

VIII Learning to understand and control the physical world	1. Exploring the physical world	1. Meeting adult expectations for restrictive exploration and manipulation of an expanding environment	1. Learning more realistic ways of studying and controlling the physical world		
IX Developing an appropriate symbol system and conceptual abilities	1. Developing preverbal communication 2. Developing verbal communication 3. Rudimentary concept formation	1. Improving one's use of the symbol system 2. Enormous elaboration of the concept pattern	1. Learning to use language actually to exchange ideas or to influence one's hearers 2. Beginning understanding of real causal relations 3. Making finer conceptual distinctions and thinking reflectively	1. Using language to express and to clarify more complex concepts 2. Moving from the concrete to the abstract and applying general principles to the particular	1. Achieving the level of reasoning of which one is capable
X Relating one's self to the cosmos		1. Developing a genuine, though uncritical, notion about one's place in the cosmos	1. Developing a scientific approach		1. Formulating a workable belief and value system

column), we find one task described in this category, that of establishing one's independence from adults in all areas of behavior. In a similar manner we can find the specific tasks for each growth stage in any of the ten task categories.

Just as the number of tasks is somewhat arbitrary, so also are the stages through which an individual's development is traced. Tryon and Lilienthal identified five stages from birth to around age 20. Havighurst, however, divided the entire life span into six stages: (1) infancy and early childhood (birth through age 5), (2) middle childhood (ages 6 through 12), (3) adolescence (ages 13 through 17), (4) early adulthood (ages 18 through 30), (5) middle age (ages 31 through 54), and (6) later maturity (ages 55 and beyond).

No matter how the stages are defined in terms of age levels, tasks at each stage arise from three sources: (1) the biological structure and function of the individual, (2) the particular society or culture in which the individual lives, and (3) personal values and aspirations of the individual. Havighurst called these the biological, the cultural, and the psychological bases of development. Three examples of biologically based tasks are: (1) learning to control the elimination of one's bodily wastes, (2) learning to accept one's physical sex changes in adolescence, and (3) learning to behave appropriately toward the opposite sex. Three tasks originating mainly from the pressures of society are: (1) learning to read and write, (2) learning to respect other people's property, and (3) accepting the responsibility to do one's share of the work in group projects. Two tasks arising in later adolescence chiefly from the personal values and motives of the individual are: (1) selecting an occupation, and (2) establishing one's philosophical or religious convictions.

To guide people who wish to analyze the anatomy of each task for themselves, Havighurst recommended a series of questions that fall under five categories: task definition, biological basis, psychological basis, cultural basis, and educational implications. Specifically, he recommended that we try to answer these queries about a given task.

Nature of the task: How is it defined?

Biological basis: What can the biological sciences tell us about this task? How is a person's physical maturation related to achieving it? How do individual biological differences influence achievement of the task?

Psychological basis: What can psychology tell us about the task? How is the person's mental development related to it? How do the values and aspirations of the individual influence achievement of the task? How is the task related to individual mental and personality differences? How can success or failure in accomplishing the task influence personality?

Cultural basis: What can sociology and social anthropology tell us about the task? How does the task vary from one culture to another? How is the task defined in the upper, middle, and lower social classes?

Educational implications: What are the responsibilities of general education for helping children and youth accomplish this task? How well are these responsibilities now being met? How might the educational system do a better job of helping young people achieve the task? (Havighurst, 1953, p. 17)

To learn how Havighurst himself used these questions as guidelines for the complex job of delineating tasks, see his book *Human Development and Education* in which he offers detailed analyses of the key tasks he identified for six periods of the life span.

THE TIMING OF TASKS

For any theory involving stages of development, an important question to ask is: How crucial is it that a child pass through a stage at the time designated as normal or usual? In other words, are there critical stages? In his theory, Havighurst differentiated between two general categories of tasks: ones that arise only at a particular time and must be completed at that time and ones that are continuing tasks whose fulfillment the individual works on for many years. In the first category are such tasks as learning to walk and talk, learning how to eliminate bodily wastes in an acceptable manner, and selecting a vocation. In the second category are such long-term, recurrent tasks as learning to participate as a responsible citizen and learning a feminine or masculine role. These recurrent tasks, however, have substages that are to be completed at given times in the child's and adolescent's development.

According to Havighurst, it is critical that the child pursue and succeed with most, if not all, tasks at the time designated for them. To support this opinion, he cited studies of children "who were denied human companionship during their first few years of life and therefore did not learn to talk" (1953, p. 3). He suggested that such cases furnish at least some evidence that if the task of learning to talk is not accomplished during the second year of life, it may never be accomplished successfully. Hence, the second year of life is seen as the critical period for achieving initial speaking skill. Furthermore, failure with a task during its critical period causes difficulties in performing later tasks related to the one that was failed. Failure in learning to talk, for example, will prevent the child from learning to read and write and from understanding many concepts normal to children at later stages of growth.

The model for this concept of timing tasks was drawn by Havighurst from evidence about the biological development of humans, particularly development in the prenatal, embryonic stage. In the embryo, the organ that does not arise at its proper time not only damages its own chance of developing but "endangers the whole hierarchy of organs" (1953, p. 3). Havighurst then extended this generalization to all of the bio-socio-psychological tasks treated in his scheme. "If the task is not achieved at the proper time it will not be achieved well, and failure in this task will cause partial or complete failure in the achievement of other tasks yet to come" (Havighurst, 1953, p. 3).

EVIDENCE TO SUPPORT
THE TASK THEORY

Adherents of the developmental-task concept of child growth base most of their theorizing on normative studies and on their own casual observations of children and adolescents. Also, Havighurst acknowledged that the psychoanalytic ideas of Erik Erikson influenced the sorts of tasks he defined regarding the development of a self-concept in the early years of growth. And, as noted, Havighurst found it convenient to derive growth principles from biological studies, then to extend these principles to encompass social and psychological development as well. However, he regarded this extension more as a plausible hypothesis than a description of absolute truth.

In an effort to test the hypothesis that biological growth principles could be extended to other areas, he and his colleagues conducted a study of fifteen boys and fifteen girls in a small American town over a period of six years. The children were age 10 when the study began and age 16 when it was completed. To make the study broad in scope, the researchers used a variety of assessment techniques, including interviews with pupils and their parents, sociometric tests, projective tests (the Rorschach, Thematic-Apperception, and sentence-completion tests), observational reports by teachers and other adults, essays and checklists from the pupils, tests of aptitude and intelligence, ratings of personality, and measurements of physical growth.

The five developmental tasks on which the study focused were: (1) learning an appropriate sex role, (2) achieving emotional independence from parents and other adults, (3) developing a conscience and a set of values, (4) getting along with age-mates, and (5) developing intellectual skills.

At the end of the study, the researchers concluded that, in general, success with one task was correlated with success in others, though the amount of relationship varied with the types of tasks. For example, there was a high relationship between getting along with age-mates and developing a scale of values. However, the relationships were only moderately high for other tasks, such as learning an appropriate sex role (which correlated only $r = .61$ between ages 10 and 13). In most cases success with a task at one age would be followed by good performance on the task at later ages although the relationships were not so strict as to "rule out any possibility of improvement on the part of a poor performer as he grows older" (Havighurst, 1953, pp. 290, 325–326).

The research team also found some evidence to support the concept of compensation. A child might make up for poor performance on one task by good performance on another. However, such children seemed to be exceptions to the general rule, so that "the number of people who are using good achievement in one task to compensate for poor achievement in another must be quite small" (Havighurst, 1953, p. 322).

This investigation of developmental-task theory, conducted with a very small sample of children, is apparently the most intensive and best controlled study that was designed to test the theory. Thus, belief in the theory remains grounded mainly in normative studies—what the average child is like at different age levels—and in the logic or reasonableness of the scheme.

DEVELOPMENTAL-TASK THEORY: AN ASSESSMENT

In keeping with the mode of assessment used in previous chapters, the appraisal of developmental-task theory centers on the nine assessment standards described in Chapter 1.

I have rated developmental-task theory high on item 1 because Havighurst offers a realistic picture of the cultural group to which he restricted his particular list of tasks. That is, his list is intended to represent the developmental problems of mid-twentieth-century, middle-class, American children and youths. My observations of such children suggest that Havighurst's claim that these young people are seeking to accomplish his list of tasks is reasonable.

I have also rated the developmental-task system high for its clarity of explanation (item 2) and its internal consistency (item 5). Likewise, the theory appears to fulfill the criterion of economy (item 6), for it does not require a large number of untested assumptions as its foundation when a smaller number would suffice. While it is not unduly complex, neither is it overly simplified, as I feel Gesell's system is. Havighurst has gone to considerable length to analyze for each task the biological, social, and personal-psychological roots from which he proposes the tasks have grown.

On items 3 (explains past, predicts future) and 4 (guides child rearing) I have rated the theory in the moderately well range. It does, in a general way, predict the future for a child by describing tasks that seem common to all children in a given culture. Thus, it suggests on what areas of life children at different stages will be focusing attention. Likewise, if a child seems maladjusted at a particular stage, developmental-task theory suggests what tasks were possibly not achieved adequately in the past and are thus causing difficulties with present tasks. However, the theory is more a way of describing behavior, of telling what children are like in their interests and concerns at different age periods, than a way of explaining why a child is behaving in a particular manner at the present time. In short, the theory is more descriptive than explanatory, as is Gesell's system. If you ask how biological factors interact with environmental factors to yield a particular behavior, developmental-task theory does not provide a clear answer.

In terms of child rearing, the theory tells what sorts of problems children may be expected to face while growing up, but it does not offer much useful advice to parents and teachers about

DEVELOPMENTAL-TASK THEORY

How well do I think the theory meets the standards?

The Standards	Very Well	Moderately Well	Very Poorly
1. Reflects the real world of children	X		
2. Is clearly understandable	X		
3. Explains the past and predicts the future		X	
4. Guides child rearing		X	
5. Is internally consistent	X		
6. Is economical	X		
7. Is falsifiable		X	
8. Stimulates new discoveries			X
9. Is self-satisfying		X	

how to promote successful achievement of the tasks. The most useful implications for child rearing to be drawn from developmental-task theory seem to be that (1) we should recognize the nature of children's tasks at each age period and provide opportunities for them to practice solutions of the tasks, (2) we should be patient with children's attempts to solve the problems inherent in the tasks, and (3) we should furnish them information and training in skills that can promote accomplishment of the tasks.

As for item 7, the theory appears to be only moderately falsifiable. Some of its key hypotheses are testable, as was demonstrated in Havighurst's study of how satisfactory accomplishment of earlier tasks seems to influence the achievement of later ones. However, other aspects of the theory are not falsifiable. For example, how can we determine what the proper number of tasks and grouping of tasks should be for a given culture? Or, how do we identify with confidence which task or combination of tasks is being pursued in a specified segment of behavior, such as in a girl's agreeing to stay home and wash clothes for her mother rather than going to a movie with her friends? Identifying the tasks that are ostensibly motivating a particular series of actions or developmental changes involves a large measure of personal opinion. Testing the validity of personal interpretations made in matching tasks with behaviors would seem to be, in many cases at least, impossible. In this sense, then, developmental-task theory does not appear to be falsifiable, and the theory is rated moderately low on this scale.

In terms of item 8 (the fertility of the theory for stimulating new discoveries), the developmental-task approach has a mixed record. The theory has served as a guide to school systems in devising curricula that suit the needs of pupils at different stages of development. As curriculum planners have sought to improve the school's offerings in order to give students opportunities to learn what they need for succeeding with their current development problems, they have evaluated course work to see how well it matches the developmental tasks for the age level of the children under consideration. They have then made changes that strengthen those parts of the course of study that do not appear to contribute toward the achievement of important tasks (Tryon and Lilienthal, 1950). Furthermore, the developmental-task way of viewing growth continues to be presented in child development textbooks as a useful perspective from which to understand children's behavior (Bernard, 1970; Hurlock, 1968; Travers, 1977). So the theory has been fertile in the sense of providing a useful scheme for revising school curricula and for offering parents and teachers another way of looking at children's developmental needs. However, relatively little research has been stimulated by developmental-task concepts. When compared to Freud's psychoanalysis or Piaget's cognitive theory, the developmental-task approach ranks very poorly on this score, and it is here rated low for that reason.

Finally, how self-satisfying is the theory (item 9)? It is limited in terms of its capability to explain rather than just describe behavior. And it is not precise in identifying tasks and matching them to segments of behavior. Furthermore, it has not opened new vistas for investigation; or at least few researchers have seen it as a fertile source of new discoveries. Despite these limitations, though, the developmental-task perspective is useful for interpreting children's behavior. The idea that children are struggling to achieve the goals implied in the tasks makes sense to me. Balancing these shortcomings of the theory against its usefulness as a way of viewing children, I have rated it as moderately self-satisfying.

FOR FURTHER READING

Bernard, Harold W. (1970) *Human Development in Western Culture.* Boston: Allyn and Bacon. A child development book featuring developmental tasks at each stage of growth, infancy through adolescence.

Havighurst, Robert J. (1953) *Human Development and Education.* New York: Longmans, Green. The most complete analysis of the developmental-task approach available.

PART 5

MAJOR PATTERNS OF GROWTH

A search for general principles of development.

Kurt Lewin's topological psychology and Heinz Werner's orthogenetic model are considered together in Part 5 because the authors of these two theories have several things in common.

Both Lewin and Werner sought to identify general principles or patterns of development, principles that would be valid for all aspects of growth—cognitive, physical, emotional, and social. Neither of them proposed an overall system of growth stages, though both identified steps of development for certain specific phenomena that they investigated, such as stages of play behavior (Lewin) and language use (Werner). Both theorists conducted and stimulated innovative empirical research on children.

Furthermore, Lewin and Werner came from a European holistic or Gestalt background, which emphasizes the development of the child as a whole, integrated organism. This holistic view, typical of European theorists in many scientific disciplines, contrasts with the British associationism from which behaviorism partially derived. Associationism represents a tradition that conceives of development as proceeding by small, additive increments that gradually accumulate to form the personality or to form a child's repertoire of acts. But to the holistic or field theorist of European background, a new stimulus or experience does not simply add a new element to a child's store of actions or knowledge, leaving the previous elements undisturbed. Instead, each new experience alters the relationship of many or all the existing elements that have made up the personality to this point, so the patterning of the whole personality is influenced.

The holistic or field-theory concept of personality development is sometimes explained by the use of an example from astronomy. Assume that a new planet the size of Saturn is added to the solar system between Earth and Mars. This addition does not simply place a new speck of light in the sky of earthlings and martians, but its gravitational pull influences the paths of all planets in the solar system, having more effect on the closer planets than on the distant ones. So with the entire pattern of the solar system altered, the system itself becomes something new. In the realm of psychology, holistic or Gestalt (a German word meaning "configuration") theorists propose that a similar thing occurs in the development of a child's personality each time he encounters new experiences or each time an internal change is triggered by his genetic structure. In the following two chapters we will see that the field-theory concept is part of the systems proposed by Lewin and Werner.

Finally, Lewin and Werner are also alike in their having left Germany in mid-career, emigrating to the United States to escape the rising Nazi regime. Lewin (whose name is pronounced either in its original German as La-*veen* or in its Americanized version as *Lou*-in) came to the United States in 1932 and spent the next decade and a half as a university professor, mostly at the University of Iowa and the Massachusetts Institute of Technology. Werner (pronounced either *Ver*-ner or *Wer*-ner) came to America and established his child development research center at Clark University in Massachusetts.

Of the two theorists, Lewin has had the broader influence on the field of psychology. One example of this influence in the area of child behavior is the development of ecological psychology, a theoretical position described briefly in the latter portion of Chapter 8.

CHAPTER 8

LEWIN'S TOPOLOGICAL PSYCHOLOGY

Although Kurt Lewin (1890–1947) spent much of his professional life studying children, he was not strictly a child psychologist. He was more of a general theorist, and he applied his theories to the realms of social and industrial psychology as well as to child development. His focus on children was most evident during the 1920s in Germany and during the 1930s at the University of Iowa. Although his interest in social psychology was expressed in studies of children at Iowa, it became more pronounced when he moved to the Massachusetts Institute of Technology where he worked on group relations problems and industrial psychology in the later years of his career.

Baldwin (1967, p. 87) has written that it is more accurate to speak of the "Lewinian approach" than of the "Lewinian theory," because Lewin never did present a clearly structured description of his view of child development. He never wrote a book that pretended to give a complete picture of child behavior. Rather, in a number of speculative articles and research reports, he proposed theory in the form of interpretations of particular phenomena he was studying at the time, phenomena such as children's reactions to frustration in their play activities, the productivity of children's groups under different sorts of leadership, and psychological changes in a child's life as she moves into adolescence. In order to understand how Lewin conceived child growth, we must gather from his scattered writings the key elements of his viewpoint and piece together his interpretation of child behavior. Such a gleaning process has provided the material for this chapter.

Lewin made a number of notable innovations. Among them was his adaptation of topological concepts and diagrams to explain human behavior. *Topology* is a type of geometry that gives special attention to the relationships among spaces, especially to the distances between one space and another and to the barriers between the two. Lewin's psychological version of topology enabled him to draw maps of both: (1) a child's developmental condition at different points between birth and adulthood and thereby to illustrate principles of development and (2) the forces that cause a child to act the way she does at a given moment. These maps served Lewin as adjuncts to his verbal explanations of behavior.

In this chapter we will first inspect the sorts of growth principles Lewin conceived and then consider his ideas of growth stages. Still using his topological maps, we will next see how he diagramed the causes of a child's behavior in a decision-making situation. Finally, before considering an assessment of his theory, we will review the key concepts of a newer theoretical position devised by some of Lewin's colleagues and students, a position known as *ecological psychology*.

GENERAL PRINCIPLES
OF DEVELOPMENT

To understand Lewin's scheme, we must first learn what he meant by four of his favorite terms: life space, fact, region, and boundary.

A child's *life space* in Lewin's system consists of all the facts that influence the child's behavior at a given time. In this system a *fact* is not an objectively verifiable observation from the "real world." Instead, a fact is any element within the child's psychological environment that affects the child's behavior or thought; this includes both forces of which the child is unaware and elements the child accepts as real or true. If a second-grade girl believes her teacher dislikes her, while actually the teacher likes her well enough, then the child's impression that "I'm not liked" is still a fact within her life space. This misconception or illusion influences the child's behavior as much as if it were objectively true.

To illustrate the sorts of elements or facts that make up a child's life space, let us consider the second-grade girl during the arithmetic period just before noon on the last day of October. We can estimate many of the facts that are influencing her performance on this lesson, which concerns the metric system. One fact, of course, is the child's impression that the teacher dislikes her. Another is the child's physical condition—the girl ate only a doughnut for breakfast and is now hungry. Also, she missed school last week as the result of a cold, so she missed the week's lessons on weights and measures. However, over the past months she has done well in arithmetic and considers herself a good arithmetic student. Another fact is the child's knowledge that this afternoon the second-grade class will have a Halloween party and each child will wear a costume. Her own costume is in her locker waiting to be put on during lunch period. These, then, are some of the forces or facts in the girl's life space as she faces the lesson on measuring with meters and centimeters.

Based on this illustration, we can identify several important characteristics of the facts of life space. First, the facts can originate from various sources. The child's hunger, which disturbs her concentration on the arithmetic lesson, originates from a physiological condition. In contrast, her desire to have the teacher like her, along with her fear that the teacher actually does not, influences the girl to try to obey the teacher's instructions, but also causes her to hesitate to ask questions because this might suggest to the teacher that she does not entirely understand what the teacher wants the pupils to do. These feelings toward the teacher are not founded in physiological needs but in social needs—those of being liked and approved of.

Furthermore, some of the facts are from the past, some from the present, and some from the future. The girl's opinion of herself as good at arithmetic is based on her past successes with arithmetic assignments. The teacher's explanation of measuring with meters is in the present. And the child's plans for the upcoming Halloween party, which distract her from the measuring lesson, center on the future.

In speaking of the way past events affect present behavior, Lewin was careful to distinguish between his own approach and that of such historically focused theories as psychoanalysis. In the traditional Freudian model, the sources of a youth's or adult's psychological disorder lie in the past. To the psychoanalyst, therefore, the patient's dreams or free-flowing stream of memories is a means of digging into the patient's past to learn what incidents caused the present-day neurotic symptoms. A Lewinian, however, is not interested in such historical material. Although Lewinians agree that past experiences can influence the individual's present actions, they are concerned only with the vestiges of those experiences as they exist in the form of memory traces in the present-day life space. They are not concerned with the nature of the original incidents. Consequently, Lewinians seek to learn about present feelings, attitudes, and knowledge rather than past experiences that may have historical links with these present-day facts in the individual's life space.

Some people have mistakenly equated Lewin's concept of life space with the *phenomenal self* of humanistic psychology, which we will meet in Chapter 19. To humanistic psychologists, the phenomenal self is the "I" or "me" of which the person himself is aware. In contrast, life space consists not only of these conscious aspects, but also of all the forces of which the individual is unaware, forces which, nonetheless, influence the way he acts. In the case of the second grader, it is likely that traces of the illness she suffered last week remain within her system and will affect how well she completes her arithmetic assignment. A lingering infection, together with inadequate nourishment from today's doughnut breakfast, can reduce her ability to concentrate on the lesson. These physiological facts are significant influences that do not fall within the definition of the humanists' phenomenal self but are still part of the girl's life space.

The contents of life space differ also from the objectively observed environment of the behaviorist. As we will see in Part 9, the behaviorist is interested in those aspects of the "objective, observable or measurable environment" that serve as stimuli to the child. The Lewinian, on the other hand, is not so concerned with the objective "real world" as with the child's perceptions. In the Lewinian view, the child does not act on the basis of objective reality but on the basis of what he perceives is true, whether this perception is the same as "objective reality" or is an illusion or hallucination (Lewin, 1942, p. 217).

When the child's life space is thus constructed from a Lewinian viewpoint, we recognize that its contents are an amalgam of both nature and nurture. The second grader's success on the measurement lesson depends partly on her genetic endowment (the neurological structure of her sense organs and brain) and partly on her experiences with her environment (last year's arithmetic lessons as well as last week's absence from school). Lewin did not seek to make distinctions concerning which source con-tributes more to a child's life space, heredity or environment—he apparently saw both sources merging to produce its contents.

Two other terms needed to understand Lewin's concept of child development are region and boundary. A *region,* in the most frequent way Lewin used the word, is an element or a fact within the child's life space. Two aspects of regions are of particular im-portance. One is the *relationship* among two or more regions—they may be closely connected or distant. The other is the nature of the *boundaries* between regions. A boundary may be weak, permitting one region to influence the other quite easily, or it may be strong, serving as an effective barrier to the influence of adjacent regions.

With these definitions in mind, we can inspect Lewin's growth principles, that is, the principles governing the way the child develops into an adult. Lewin proposed that as the child develops, five sorts of changes occur in the life space. The grow-ing child becomes more *differentiated,* the boundaries between regions become more *rigid,* the space *expands,* regions increase in *complexity of organization,* and behavior becomes more *realistic* (Barker, Dembo, and Lewin, 1943, pp. 441–442). We will look at each of these principles and try to clarify their meanings.

DIFFERENTIATION

The first principle of development states that as a child grows older, his life space becomes more differentiated (Figure 8.1). This means that regions increase in number and in specificity of func-tion. Differentiation occurs as a result of the child's increased ex-periences in the world and his increased capacity to perceive differences between one situation and another. For example, as an infant, the child grasps a crayon in a single grip, his fingers tightly curled around it, and his only uses of the crayon are to wave it about and put the end into his mouth. But by age 6 he can hold the crayon in several different grips and can manipulate it in many ways, even coloring in such varied shapes as those of a dog, a star, and a triangle. Likewise, in the realm of language, the very young child uses the word *go* to include a wide variety of activities. The older child can differentiate these activities into an array of related concepts such as "let's go," "he went," "shall we go," "if we go," "they are still going," and many more.

RIGIDIFICATION

The second development principle states that as the child grows up, the boundaries between regions become stronger so that one region is increasingly less influenced by adjacent ones (Figure 8.1).

The phenomenon of rigidification was conceived by Lewin in terms of *tension* arising within a region that is in a state of need. Lewin used the physiological need for food as the model for what he believed happened in other regions of the life space. When hunger arises, tension builds up and motivates the individual to action. In the young child, the tension from the hunger region spreads easily to other regions, influencing other aspects of the life space. But in an older youth, the boundaries between one region and another are greater so that the hunger tension can be expected to exert less influence over other aspects of the life space. With the food analogy in mind, Lewin postulated that other sorts of needs or hungers arise in other regions—such as needs for the approval of other people or for novel and interesting experiences.

To test these ideas about the spread of tension over region boundaries, several of Lewin's disciples conducted a series of experiments that involved children drawing simple outline sketches of animals such as cats, turtles, and rabbits. Each animal was considered to represent a different subregion in the child's life space. The experimenters sought to determine how many copies a

Young child: few regions
with weak boundaries

Adult: many regions
with rigid boundaries

Figure 8.1   Life-Space Structure of the Young Child and the Adult (Adapted from Kounin, 1943, p. 181)

child would produce of a given animal before her need in that region was satiated and the tension generated by the need dissipated. They also attempted to judge how much of the tension developed in one region (cat drawings) would spread to another (turtle drawings) and influence the child's attention or interest in the second region.

In one such experiment, a colleague of Lewin's, Joseph Kounin, hypothesized that rigidity increased with chronological age, whereas differentiation increased with mental age (Figure 8.2). To test his hypothesis, Kounin tried the animal-drawing activities with a group of mentally normal children and also with a group of mentally retarded adults whose measured intellectual maturity was the same as the children's. The experiment confirmed the rigidity hypothesis. The feebleminded adults drew a new animal (turtle) for almost as long as they had the original one (cat). But the normal children, after drawing turtles until satiated, drew cats for a much shorter time. Kounin interpreted this to mean that the boundaries between regions in the adults were stronger or more rigid than those in the children. For the children, the satiation from drawing turtles passed more readily into the region of cats and reduced the children's interest in drawing cats (Kounin, 1943, pp. 194–196). Lewin used the term *co-satiation* to describe this process of the satisfaction (or boredom) of one region reducing the amount of activity needed to satiate the need of another region.

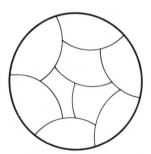

Ten-year-old of normal
intelligence: few regions
with weak boundaries

Retarded adult with mental
age of 10: few regions
with rigid boundaries

Figure 8.2   Life-Space Structure of the Normal Child and the Mentally Retarded Adult (Adapted from Kounin, 1943, p. 181)

EXPANSION

As a third principle of development, Lewin stated that the life space of the child enlarges in terms of both time and space as the years pass. Furthermore, the child gains access to increasing numbers of regions in her life space as she grows older.

Space expansion occurs for a number of reasons. Physically, the child grows larger, stronger, and more agile, able to coordinate individual movements into complex activities that permit her to move into more environments and accomplish more tasks. Intellectually she improves her knowledge of the environment and her problem-solving strategies so that she sees more ways to take advantage of more opportunities. Socially, she becomes more responsible, so that those in control of society permit her to engage in more activities under her own supervision. The older youth is allowed to drive a car, stay out late at night, and enter places of entertainment not open to children.

Time expansion occurs because the child has memories of the past and gains access to skills—such as reading and a growing concept of historical time—that extend her vision to include what happened decades and centuries ago. Likewise, the growing child achieves an increasing grasp of the future. She improves her ability to imagine, expect, hope for, and plan what may take place months and years ahead.

ORGANIZED INTERDEPENDENCE

According to this interdependence principle, regions of the life space, including segments of the child's behavior, become increasingly interlinked as the child grows older. On the surface this generalization appears to conflict with the principle of rigidification. If the boundaries between regions become stronger with age, does this not produce greater independence rather than interdependence of regions? Lewin sought to meet this objection by differentiating between *simple interdependence* and *organizational interdependence*. Simple interdependence is represented by weak boundaries between regions so that the tension or satiation of one region affects adjacent ones. Such simple interdependence decreases as the child grows up. In contrast, organizational interdependence consists of the arrangement of different regions into hierarchical systems or sequences of actions designed to accomplish a more distant or more complex goal. Whereas a one-year-old child has difficulty picking up a small ball and throwing it in a desired direction, a ten-year-old can scoop a baseball into a glove while on the run, can snatch the ball from the glove with the other hand, and can throw it accurately to another child a good distance away. In effect, the ten-year-old can coordinate a sequence of behaviors and regions in his life space to accomplish the goal of putting out a base runner. This is organizational interdependence. In the realm of nonphysical activity, such organization of life-space regions is exhibited in complex intellectual operations—in the child's acts of decoding puzzles, in his analyzing a diagram of how to build a model airplane, or in his creating a drama to be enacted by his classmates.

REALISM

Finally, normal growth is evidenced by an increase in realism. This is the development of distinctions between levels of reality, between (1) what might be or we wish to be or we imagine could be and (2) what things really are to us. As Baldwin has explained:

> Where realism is high, the boundaries between regions are relatively rigid; goals are not reached merely by wishing or imagining but only by behavior that conforms to some rules. It probably represents the child's acquiring the concept of an objective world external to himself (1967, p. 121).

In summary, then, Lewin saw development as movement toward greater differentiation of life space, toward more rigid boundaries between regions, toward expanded time and space, toward better organized interdependence of activities and regions, and toward greater realism.

STAGES OF DEVELOPMENT

Though Lewin considered the identification of growth principles more important than the description of growth stages, he did give attention to stages in two different ways. First, he acknowledged the popularly recognized growth periods, such as infancy, early childhood, and adolescence. Second, he identified phases through which children pass in several specific areas of their lives, such as the areas of play and of drawing activities. We can illustrate the way he applied topology to such matters by describing some examples of his work.

GENERAL GROWTH PERIODS

Lewin mentioned general growth periods in his essays and research reports and occasionally dedicated an essay to explaining how a given period could be analyzed by means of topological diagrams. He used two kinds of topological diagrams to illustrate his concepts of the difference between general stages of development. For instance, when he wrote about adolescence, he described it as a stage of instability, a time of locomotion from one stable period (late childhood) to another stable but as yet poorly comprehended stage (adulthood). Lewin believed that the adolescent's life space was forced into a labile, fluid state by the puzzling bodily changes brought on by puberty, by the youth's growing intellect, and by the new opportunities for social freedom offered by society. To compound his problems, the teenager in the modern Western world is not quite sure about how much freedom he really has or wants. In short, after late childhood, the terrain ahead is poorly mapped in the youth's mind. The "cognitively unstructured character" of his new situation causes the adolescent to act shy, sensitive, or aggressive. Emotional tensions arise from the conflict between the various attitudes, values, and styles of life of the period he is leaving (childhood) and the one he vaguely sees ahead (adulthood). He is apt to take extreme attitudes in politics or social behavior and to shift his position radically. He is like an emigrant to a new culture—the sociologist's *marginal man*—living with both old and new cultures but not completely accepted by either. Lewin illustrated this group belongingness aspect of adolescence by the sorts of diagrams shown in Figure 8.3.

While Figure 8.3 represents the relationships among groups in society, Figure 8.4 represents the shift within the life space of the individual as he passes from the clearly defined regions and boundaries of childhood through the shifting, vague regions of adolescence, and into the clearly delineated life space of mature adulthood.

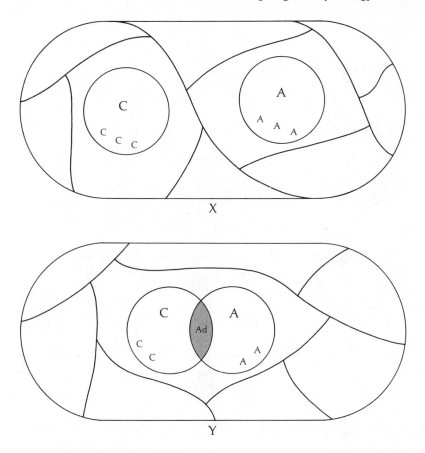

Figure 8.3   Society's Structure for Children, Adolescents, and Adults (After Lewin, 1939, p. 882)

As the upper (X) diagram in Figure 8.3 shows, the world of the child (c) is distinct from the world of the adult (A). Individual children (c, c, c) and adults (A, A, A) know their roles clearly. As the lower (Y) diagram shows, the adolescent (AD) is caught as the marginal man between the two worlds and thus does not clearly know his role or the "rules of the game."

In Figure 8.4a, the child's space of free movement is shown by white regions, which are clearly separated by rigid boundaries from the adult space (shaded). Regions 1–6 represent such activities as getting into the movies at half price and belonging to the Boy Scouts or Girl Scouts. For the adolescent (shown in Figure 8.4b), the space of free movement is not well defined in many instances. For some activities the expectations are clear. He can no

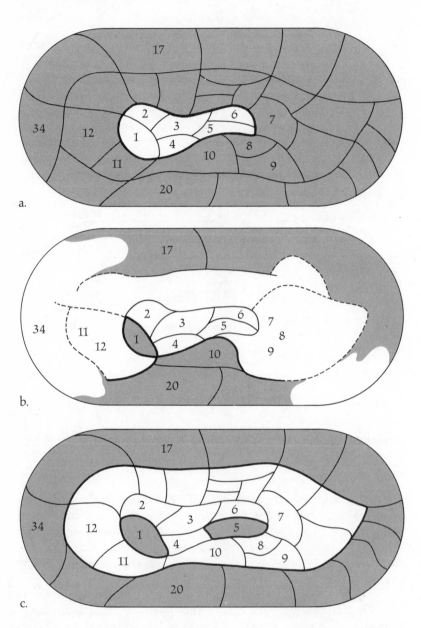

Figure 8.4   Space of Free Movement of the Child, Adolescent, and Adult (After Lewin, 1939, pp. 875, 877)

longer get into the movies at half price (region 1), nor can he yet vote or buy alcoholic beverages (10), but he does acquire new privileges (7–9, 11–12), such as a driver's license, a chance to stay out late at night, and freedom to smoke, although even these are not guaranteed. The adult space (Figure 8.4c) includes far more regions, regions that are clearly defined. However, some activities are prohibited, such as half-fare movies (1) and certain childish acts (5). Prohibited also are such activities as killing people he dislikes (20) and entering occupations for which he is unprepared (17, 34).

GROWTH STAGES IN A
SPECIFIC REALM OF LIFE

In an experiment entitled "Frustration and Regression," Lewin and his co-workers studied thirty children, ages 2 to 5 years, in free play with a variety of toys (Barker, Dembo, and Lewin, 1943). Each child was observed as she played alone with the toys in a room. Later, a transparent screen was lowered in the middle of the room, separating the child from the most attractive toys, while the experimenters observed her playing with the remaining, less appealing ones. This experimental arrangement enabled the researchers to note two things: (1) the level of constructiveness of play before and after the screen was lowered and (2) the extent to which the level of the child's play was influenced by separating her from the more appealing toys.

From the experiment, the research team concluded that play with toys like trucks, dolls, and a playhouse can be divided into at least eight levels of constructiveness, levels that are correlated with age. They also concluded that after the children experienced the frustration of the barrier being lowered, they regressed to a lower level of constructiveness during the subsequent play period (Barker, Dembo, and Lewin, 1943, pp. 452–456). The nature of these levels of constructiveness can be illustrated by the following three examples:

> Level 2: The toys are superficially examined. Example: The child sits on the floor and picks up the truck.

> Level 5: More complicated, elaborate manipulation. Example: Truck and trailer unloaded, detached, pulled in circles, reattached, detached, reattached, pulled in circles.

Level 7: Dramatic meaning given to play by composing a story involving a larger setting than the experimental room. Example: "Here's a car truck, and it's going out fishing, so we have to take the trailer off. First, we have to go to the gas station. Toot, toot." Gets gas, goes back for trailer and fishing pole, and attaches a motor boat to the truck and trailer. "Hummmm! There he goes" (Barker, Dembo, and Lewin, 1943, pp. 449–450).

In this way Lewin and his associates identified stages of development for specific realms of child behavior. However, the task of specifying such stages was not pursued for its own value but was incidental to the researchers' investigating theoretical issues of greater interest to them. For instance, in the play experiment the primary concern was the nature of children's reactions to frustration, and the play-constructiveness hierarchy was devised as a necessary instrument for measuring hypothesized regression following frustration.

THE ANALYSIS OF DECISIONS

Lewin used topology not only to illustrate growth principles and the nature of developmental stages, but also to explain why a child acts in a particular way at a given moment. To do this, he first assumed that children's behavior is goal-directed. A child acts in order to achieve a goal that will satisfy a need she feels. Achieving the goal, however, is not always easy, for the child may be caught between two incompatible needs seeking fulfillment at the same time. Or there may be physical, social, or psychological barriers to be overcome or bypassed before the goal is reached. Consequently, at any given moment, the child's life space consists of a variety of regions or elements, each exerting a particular amount of force in a given direction. The final decision about how to act is determined by which of these forces proves most powerful.

To illustrate the manner in which decision-making situations have been charted by Lewinians, we will examine the simple problem of a child's being faced with two desirable alternatives—a kindergarten girl is attracted by both the doll-play corner and the easel-painting corner of the classroom. As Figure 8.5 shows, the situation can be diagramed as three life-space regions. Region X is the doll-play corner, region Y the easel-painting corner, and re-

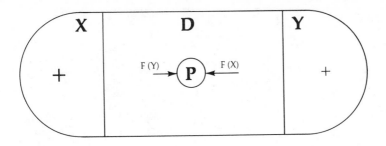

Figure 8.5   Choosing between Two Attractive Alternatives

gion *D* the decision-making condition in which the girl finds herself. She is symbolized by the circled *P* (for "person") in region *D*.
Lewin adopted the term *valence* from the physical sciences to represent the psychological power or strength of a region or fact in life
space. A positive valence attracts the child toward that region,
while a negative valence repels the child. The plus (+) signs in
regions *X* and *Y* represent their valence values. The heavier plus in
region *X* shows that doll-play has a stronger attraction for the girl,
so we can expect her to resolve the problem by going to the doll
corner. The arrows pointing at the child (*P*) suggest the comparative power of the forces toward *X* and *Y*. The force toward *X*—
shown as the long arrow *F(X)* —is stronger than the force toward *Y*
—the short arrow *F(Y)*.

Although the kindergarten example illustrates how decision
situations can be charted, it does not show how more complex
decisions are diagramed. A more complex step is shown in Figure
8.6, which introduces barriers (region B_A) into the life space. Figure 8.6 represents the problem of a boy, Harry, who is trying to
decide which of two girls to invite to the high school dance. He
likes both of them, so both are represented by positive valences
(regions *A* and *B*). But he finds Betty (region *B*) more attractive
than Ann (region *A*), partly because his friend Bart has dated Betty
and found her to be a lot of fun. Bart though is probably going to
ask Betty to the dance. Consequently, Harry faces the likelihood
that he will alienate his friend Bart if he tries to date the more
attractive Betty. This fear of alienation serves as a psychological
barrier (region B_A) to his asking Betty to the dance. The barrier,
therefore, is exerting a force on Harry opposite to that of the positive valence of Betty. This barrier force, which represents Bart's
interest in Betty, is symbolized by the $F(B_A)$ arrow and functions

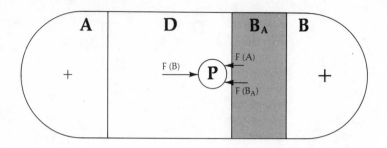

Figure 8.6　The Function of a Barrier in Decision Making

in two ways. It enhances Betty's attractiveness, making her a prize particularly worth winning, but at the same time it threatens the friendship with Bart. In the end, Harry resolves the problem by asking Ann to the dance, because the combined forces in Ann's direction, $F(A)$ and $F(B_A)$, overpower the single strong force, $F(B)$, in Betty's direction. Thus, Harry prefers Betty, partly because she is hard to get, but chooses Ann because the psychological price of getting Betty is too high.

Of course, most of life's decisions are not as simple as those pictured in our two examples. At any moment of decision there are multiple attractions and barriers exerting force on an individual. To diagram the life space under these conditions requires far more complex topological maps than those of Figures 8.5 and 8.6. Lewinians, in their theorizing, have produced many varieties of diagrams, each intended to elucidate a particular sort of decision or to propose new hypotheses.*

It is also important to recognize the connection between Lewin's view of decision making and his principles of development. As the child grows up and his life space changes, his decision-making mechanism is altered in ways described by these principles. For example, a seven-year-old boy and a seventeen-year-old boy who are ostensibly facing the same decision are actually facing quite different decisions because their life spaces are so different. Let us assume that in the case of each boy there is a girl at school who has invited him to visit her after school. She tells him the street on which she lives, a street more than a mile from his own home, but forgets to give him the house number. When the boy gets home after school, he must decide whether to visit the

* A sampling of Lewinian maps is found in Baldwin's third chapter (1967).

girl and, if he does, by what means of transportation. If we recall Lewin's main principles of development, we can estimate significant ways in which the seven-year-old's and the seventeen-year-old's life spaces will differ. Because the seventeen-year-old's life space is more *expansive* in space and time, he can be expected to see more realistic possibilities for modes of transportation to the girl's home than the seven-year-old, such as, he can walk, or drive the family car, or use his bicycle or his skateboard. He is also more likely to perceive possible ways of finding the girl's house number. Thus, his life-space regions of transportation possibilities and of finding his destination are more *differentiated* than those of the seven-year-old.

Let us also assume that when each boy was age 5, he became separated from his mother during a shopping trip, and for more than an hour had feared being abandoned. Now, as each boy faces this current decision, we may speculate that the seven-year-old is more likely to be influenced by this fear from the past than is the seventeen-year-old; the boundaries between subregions (the past and present incidents) are more *rigid* in the seventeen-year-old and he is more *realistic* in estimating consequences than is the younger boy. Finally, we might expect that the older boy would coordinate his activities in arriving at the decision and carrying it out more effectively than the younger one, because he has become more adept at *organizing* the complex of regions that compose his life space.

In short, the decision-making process is influenced by developmental differences that affect the structure of a child's space, as conceived in Lewinian theory.

Now that we have viewed some main features of Lewin's system, we will look briefly at an extension of the system that was devised by several of his co-workers after Lewin's group in Iowa dispersed to other institutions.

BARKER'S ECOLOGICAL PSYCHOLOGY

After Lewin's death in 1947, Roger W. Barker (1903—) and another Lewin enthusiast, H. F. Wright, made it their mission at the University of Kansas to investigate the role that a child's physical-social environment plays in her life space. In biology, the term *ecology* refers to the interrelationship between a plant or animal and its environment. Barker and Wright borrowed the term to describe their way of investigating how children's surroundings affect their behavior and development.

The most basic conviction behind ecological theory is that a child's behavior patterns and personality are, to a great extent, fashioned by the environments she inhabits. The task of an ecological theorist is to describe the anatomy and operating principles of such environments.

Barker has noted that traditional psychology shows ways in which people differ from each other, but fails to trace the great variations in thought, feeling, and action that an individual child experiences during a typical day. Furthermore, according to Barker, a large proportion of this variation within a single child's life can be accounted for by the environments or *behavior settings* through which the child commonly moves. In effect, ecological theorists contend that we can account for a great deal of a child's behavior if we know her current environment.

For example, we can predict that if a typical teenager is in church, she will not shout, but if she is at a basketball game, she will shout loud and long. We can predict that if she is in the middle of an ice-skating rink, she will not be sitting reading a book, but if she is home in bed at nine o'clock, she may very well be reading. If she is walking to the drug store, we can predict that she will not be walking in line, but if she is in the school band in the Fourth of July parade, she will be carefully keeping in line and in step with her companions.

To move ecological theory beyond these commonsense observations, Barker and his colleagues have identified and labeled a variety of components of behavior settings. Consequently, the nature of a child's significant surroundings can be analyzed more systematically. For example, ecological psychologists have proposed that a behavior setting (such as a history class or a dinner party) is composed of two main elements: (1) typical ways people act (called *standing patterns of behavior*) and (2) the *milieu*, which is made up of two components. The first component is *physical things*—desks and wall maps in history class, the dining table and silverware at the dinner party. The second is *time boundaries*—a forty-five-minute class period, a two-hour dinner party. The milieu is said to be circumjacent to—that is, it encompasses—the behavior of the people in the setting. These terms have been created by ecological theorists to help organize their observations of the environments in which children grow up.

Ecological psychology is not simply an intellectual pastime—it has proven to be a useful tool for answering practical questions. One of the most detailed applications of the approach has been the analysis of the way small and large high schools can differ in how they influence adolescents' development. During an investigation in several schools in the midwestern United States, Barker and his colleagues accurately predicted that students of smaller high schools engage in a wider variety of activities, assume more responsibility, hold more extracurricular positions of importance, and are more highly motivated to take active part in voluntary activities than students in larger schools. These discoveries led Barker and his co-workers to conclude that:

> The educational process . . . thrives on participation, enthusiasm, and responsibility. Our findings and our theory posit a negative relationship between school size and individual student participation. What seems to happen is that as schools get larger and (their behavior) settings more heavily populated, more of the students are less needed; they become superfluous, redundant. . . . A school should be small enough that students are not redundant (Barker et al., 1970, p. 42).

In this way, ecological theory has contributed to the literature on child psychology and furnished suggestions about how behavior settings might be arranged to promote children's more satisfactory development.

LEWIN'S TOPOLOGICAL THEORY: AN ASSESSMENT

Marks on the accompanying scales reflect my estimate of the ratings Lewinian theory deserves on the nine assessment standards previously described.

The interest of child psychologists in Lewinian theory reached a peak in the late 1930s and in the 1940s when the works of Lewin and his associates were first being published. Since then, the influence of topological child psychology has declined. Today it is represented by a few key concepts that have entered the general body of theory and by works of certain of Lewin's followers who have evolved their own variants of his approach.

The rather high mark on item 1 (reflects the real world of children) is based principally on my belief that one of Lewin's lasting contributions was his emphasis on the complexity of forces exerted on the individual child to determine his behavior at a given moment. The terms *life space* and *psychological field* have been accepted into the child psychologist's general vocabulary in recognition of this. The emphasis is in contrast to the simplistic notion that a single, isolated stimulus causes an individual's response. Furthermore, Lewinian theory has high potential for explaining individual differences among children the same age, since it proposes that the combination of facts comprising one child's life space differs from that of another. As further evidence of the real life foundations of Lewinian theory, we should note that he and his colleagues did not merely speculate about what children might be like, but they conducted an extensive series of experiments and observational studies of children's actual behavior.

However, there still remains some question about how truly the topological maps of life space are reflections of the real operation of children's development dynamics. This question about the validity of the theory has caused me to mark item 1 somewhat short of the highest rating. The issues that lie behind this question are discussed in the following paragraphs.

The high rating on item 8 (stimulates new discoveries) is based on Lewin's being credited with generating a large amount of innovative research on children. Lewin had a talent not only for developing his own research proposals but also for motivating students and colleagues to carry out novel studies. Reports of these investigations typically have included descriptions of the empirical results and interpretations of what the results mean from a topological-psychological viewpoint. However, there are psychologists who would question whether it was Lewin's theory or Lewin the man that deserves credit for such a high rating. For instance, Spence, as a leading behaviorist in the field of learning, has written that:

> Lewin employs very fragmentary parts or subsystems of topology. As for the formal system of dynamics, it remains thus far closeted . . . in Lewin's mind. Like so many of these field theorists, Lewin sets up a most attractive program for theory. Taken in conjunction with his interesting experiments the illusion is nicely created that there is some connection between them (1965, p. 168).

Spence's comment about the questionable relationship be-

LEWIN'S THEORY

How well do I think the theory meets the standards?

The Standards	Very Well	Moderately Well	Very Poorly
1. Reflects the real world of children	X		
2. Is clearly understandable		X	
3. Explains the past and predicts the future			X
4. Guides child rearing			X
5. Is internally consistent		X	
6. Is economical		X	
7. Is falsifiable			X
8. Stimulates new discoveries	X		
9. Is self-satisfying		X	

tween the theory and the experiments brings us to the matters of clarity of description (item 2) and internal consistency (item 5) of Lewin's system. I would agree with those psychologists who value Lewin's topological diagrams as a means of illustrating the dynamics of his conception of life space. The maps are helpful supplements to the verbal descriptions of concepts that most theorists use to explain their systems. Likewise, the empirical studies of children that Lewin used as the raw material for his theorizing function as real life bridges between his abstract ideas and his readers' own ways of looking at children. These, then, are factors in favor of marking Lewinian theory high on clarity.

However, at the same time, there is the kind of confusion criticized by Spence. Lewin has been criticized for not presenting his theory in a single book or essay, for not showing how all the parts fit together consistently. He drew ideas from various "hard science" disciplines, but did not define his concepts clearly enough or use them consistently (such as the concept of "region") so as to make them clearly understandable to a large number of his readers. Furthermore, the elements of life space are not sufficiently accessible to observation or measurement to permit scientists to determine their composition and power. Thus, Lewinians have frequently needed to turn to illustrative anecdotes, like the ones I created about the kindergarten girl and the high school dance, to convince their audience of the validity of their theory. To arrive at a rating on item 2, I matched the positive factors against the negative ones and decided the theory overall was only moderately clear.

This same evidence bears on the theory's internal consistency (item 5). As Baldwin has observed:

> Field theorists share a common approach to problems and much of the same terminology, but they have not exerted much effort to build a coherent total theory of a mechanism that governs human behavior. . . . Lewinian investigators often use some commonsense term as the starting point for research, without being too concerned about how the concepts will eventually fit others in the theory. They seem to have a faith that if individual problems are carefully investigated and analyzed, the working hypotheses will eventually fit together (1967, p. 142).

For these reasons, I have given Lewinian theory only a moderate score for its internal consistency.

Again for the same reasons—and particularly for inconsistences in the coordination among such concepts as regions and barriers—I have rated the theory only moderate in its economy of explanation (item 6).

On falsifiability (item 7) the theory deserves a low mark. If you wish to test the validity of a model of development, the terms it employs can be dealt with most readily if they have unequivocal definitions tied closely to observable events in the world. Furthermore, the connections hypothesized between terms or concepts need to be clear enough so that you are not likely to arrive at alternative or, in particular, at conflicting conclusions from your observations of child behavior. Lewinian concepts in many instances are not characterized by such clarity. It is true that Lewin's group have conducted controlled experiments and have carefully observed children in their natural habitats. These sources of data have been useful in estimating the validity of theoretical concepts.

However, Lewinian studies have also depended on phenomenological introspection by the subjects who participate in the experiments and by the researchers themselves. Such testimonial data furnish less secure bases for testing the theory's validity than does more objective, publicly observable child behavior, at least in the opinion of those who follow the research tradition of the physical sciences. It is not clear today how we can determine the accuracy or profitability of conceiving of life space as regions separated by barriers, with each region involving tensions or needs. How can we test this conception?

Lewin's system appears weak also in its ability to explain the past and predict the future (item 3) and guide child rearing (item 4). The very concept of life space as a highly complex field whose regions and forces shift each moment has contributed to the weakness of the theory in predicting and guiding a specific child's development. If we are to forecast how a child will act, we need to know what regions are currently active and how the forces among regions are patterned. If this idea of life space is an accurate representation of a child's psychological environment, then in the present imprecise state of psychological measurement, it is not possible to produce the data we need to make predictions. Our methods of assessing the types and powers of goals, needs, barriers, abilities, fears, fatigue, and the rest of the facts of life space are simply too primitive to furnish the information required for either predicting or guiding child development. In addition, our capacity to explain past behavior from a Lewinian viewpoint is nearly as inadequate. It is true that after Harry has asked Ann to the dance, we can safely conclude that the forces in her favor were greater than those in favor of Betty. But we still cannot specify all the regions of Harry's life space at the time he arrived at his decision, nor can we identify the amount and direction of force exerted by any given region. These problems of Lewinian theory with decision making have helped stimulate social psychologists over the past three decades to propose other ways of explaining the dynamics underlying decisions.

What, then, should be the overall rating for Lewin's system in terms of being self-satisfying (item 9)? On the credit side, Lewin opened new perspectives on development by adopting ideas from mathematics and physics. This adaptation helped stimulate a significant amount of novel empirical research with children. In

addition, Lewin's diagrams have helped people visualize his postulated psychological forces and, consequently, understand his
proposals more easily. Furthermore, the general growth principles he proposed—differentiation, rigidification, expansion, organized interdependence, and realism—have furnished developmentalists with ways to view the trends in change from infancy to
adulthood.

On the debit side, the key concepts of the theory are a mixture
of commonsense ideas and more precisely defined theoretical constructs. The theory is somewhat segmented, with gaps and inconsistencies among the parts, and the elements of life space are not
sufficiently accessible to appraisal to permit researchers to determine their composition or power. In sum, the Lewinian theory is
only moderately self-satisfying.

We might note that an appraisal of Lewin's theory like this
would not likely distress him very much, for he did not consider
his scheme a finished product. He saw theorizing as a continuing
process or strategy for guiding investigation, not as a completed
structure depicting the true anatomy of development. When
viewed from this perspective, Lewin's theorizing apparently did
fulfill his expectations.

FOR FURTHER READING

Baldwin, Alfred L. (1967) *Theories of Child Development*. New York:
    Wiley. Pp. 85–166. Chapters 3 and 4 present a detailed de-
    scription and critique of Lewin's position.

Hall, Calvin S. and Gardner Lindzey. (1970) *Theories of Personality*.
    2d ed. New York: Wiley. Pp. 209–255. Chapter 6 describes and
    appraises Lewinian theory.

Lewin, Kurt. (1936) *Principles of Topological Psychology*. New York:
    McGraw-Hill. An early statement of Lewin's general
    viewpoint.

CHAPTER 9

WERNER'S ORTHOGENETIC THEORY

For many of the theories we consider in this book, the developmental aspect of personality is not the main interest. Rather, any principles or stages that theorists identify are incidental to some more important purpose they have in mind. Such is true of Puritan philosophers, Freud, behaviorists, and others. But it is not true of Heinz Werner (1890–1964). Werner's self-imposed mission was to discover principles and processes that account for why children develop from their infant condition to adulthood. In effect, he spent his professional life seeking out the principles of correct (*ortho*) development (*genetic*).

In pursuing his mission, Werner carried out an extensive series of experiments, many of them focusing on children's perception and language use. From these experiments he was able not only to derive support for the general growth principles he sought, but also, incidentally, to identify specific phenomena of perception and language use that have since been added to the body of knowledge in these particular subfields of psychology. Another incidental product of his research was the creation of new or revised experimental techniques for use by psychologists.

In this chapter we will consider Werner's orthogenetic principles, his ideas on stages of development, and then his research methodology and some of his specific findings in the areas of perception and language.

PRINCIPLES OF DEVELOPMENT

Poets and theorists alike adopt observations from one aspect of life to explain phenomena in another aspect. The poet Tupper did this when he wrote that the friendship of a child is a "jewel worth a world of pains." Heinz Werner did it when he proposed that the growth of the child's intellect followed the same pattern as (1) the biological evolution of organisms and (2) the development of a society from a primitive state to an advanced condition.

The general features of Werner's plan were not new. They dated back to the recapitulation theory of zoologists of the nineteenth century. This theory, known to biology students as *ontogeny recapitulates phylogeny*, suggests that the evolutionary stages through which species develop (phylogeny) are paralleled by stages in the development of the individual animal or human (ontogeny). This notion had been proposed occasionally by natural scientists and philosophers in earlier centuries, but it acquired its greatest appeal after Darwin traced the steps through which the human species apparently evolved from simpler forms of life over eons of time. Zoologists also observed that the foetal development of more advanced animals and of humans progressed from a single fertilized cell (which might represent a single-celled, simple organism) through many stages that simulated the mature states of increasingly complex organisms or animals. In Sidgwick's words, "the developmental history of the individual appears to be a short and simplified repetition, or in a certain sense a recapitulation, of the course of development of the species" (1959, p. 268).

The British philosopher Herbert Spencer (1820–1903) was not content to have the recapitulation theory apply only to biological development. He extended it as well to both psychological and sociological phenomena. In Spencer's opinion, the child developed intellectually from a primitive to an advanced condition. Likewise, primitive societies, he said, represented early stages of the social evolution that eventually produced advanced societies.

In America in the 1890s and early 1900s the chief protagonist of the recapitulation theory in child development was G. Stanley Hall, president and professor of psychology at Clark University (Hall, 1904). During the early decades of the twentieth century the recapitulation theory fell into disrepute as the result of criticisms by biologists, psychologists, and sociologists. By the 1930s and 1940s developmentalists generally no longer accepted the discredited view that the growing child lives through the same developmental stages as the species but at a highly accelerated pace.

When Heinz Werner arrived at Clark University from Germany a half century after Hall had begun his work there, Werner's own views of development looked curiously like a modern version of the recapitulation theory. But Werner pointed out that the similarities were superficial and that he was not espousing Spencer's and Hall's position (Werner, 1961, pp. 24–25). In order to make clear the distinctions he had to offer, let us first consider some of the similarities between Spencer's and Werner's views, then inspect in greater detail the nature of Werner's scheme.

Spencer had defined three basic principles of evolution that he felt applied to all things in the world—to materials organic and inorganic, to psychological growth, and to societies. He proposed that as something develops, it becomes increasingly differentiated in parts and functions, better integrated in the way the parts work together, and more segregated. By segregation, he meant that each part attained more individualized qualities that distinguished it from other parts as time passed (Royce, 1959, p. 392). (Spencer's three principles are not unlike Lewin's principles of differentiation, organized interdependence, and rigidification.)

Just as Spencer sought to identify general principles of evolution, so Werner, with a strong background in both biology and anthropology, set for himself the task of identifying the principles that proper development (orthogenesis) follows in the realms of biological and intellectual growth, with special emphasis on the area of human perception. Werner's studies led him to this general conclusion:

> We assume that organisms are naturally directed toward a series of transformations—reflecting a tendency to move from a state of relative globality and undifferentiatedness towards states of increasing differentiation and hierarchic integration. It is this tendency, formulated as "the orthogenetic principle" which serves for us to characterize development as distinct from other types of change over time (Werner and Kaplan, 1963, p. 7).

Does Werner's subscribing to such a view mean that he believed in the recapitulation theory? Werner said that it does not:

> There exist certain similarities between developmental series. These similarities, for instance between the child's mentality and that of

primitive man, cannot be reduced to conform with any law of re-capitulation. It is the very fact of development itself, in so far as it implies a change from generalized to more specialized forms, which gives the false impression of a recapitulation and occasions certain parallel phenomena in two related genetic series. For all practical purposes one may speak of a principle of parallelism: development in mental life follows certain general and formal rules whether it con-cerns the individual or the species. Such a principle implies that, apart from general and formal similarities, there do not exist material differences in the comparable phenomena (1961, pp. 24–25).

As implied in Werner's terms *naturally directed* and *tendency*, he believed that it is the nature of the species to grow in the direction of "some preordained end." Werner and his colleague Bernard Kaplan called this belief the *directiveness assumption* and explained that they did not intend directiveness to mean "con-scious effort toward an end, so-called 'subjective teleology.' Direc-tiveness in the sense of 'objective teleology' is an observable characteristic of organismic behavior irrespective of any con-sciousness of ends on the part of the organism" (Werner and Kap-lan, 1963, pp. 5–6).

In the concept of directiveness Werner expressed his vision of the human being being activated by a drive to survive and to master his fate. People, compared to other living things, are par-ticularly advanced in their skill of adapting to various environ-ments, a skill that depends to a great extent on the use of symbols that represent objects and ideas—symbols that can be manip-ulated into new configurations, recorded for later use, and sent from one place to another. Werner and Kaplan wrote:

> Man, destined to conquer the world through knowing, starts out with confusion, disorientation, and chaos, which he struggles to overcome. . . . Man lives constantly in a world of becoming rather than in a world of being. Now it is our contention that in order to build a truly human universe, that is, a world that is known rather than merely reacted to, man requires a new tool, the symbol (Werner and Kaplan, 1963, p.5).

So it was that Werner pictured development as movement toward greater differentiation, improved integration of the differentiated parts, and ever clearer understanding of the world, an under-standing that depended to a large extent on the use of symbols.

In addition to sketching these general outlines of develop-ment, Werner embellished the orthogenetic principle with subterms and subaspects. For instance, he used the phrase *syncretic to discrete* in speaking of the child's progressing from an undifferentiated to a differentiated being. *Syncresis* refers to global actions or concepts, in which terms a child acts or perceives things early in life. As he grows up, these general actions or ideas separate out into more discrete, identifiably different constituent parts. For example, a one-year-old infant's attempts to pick up a pencil are marked by a single gross movement of arm and body and hand, but a ten-year-old's attempts show far more differentiation of parts. The body does not move at all, only the arm and hand move. The wrist bends, and the thumb and forefinger easily grasp the pencil in a pincer movement that does not require the rest of the fingers. In addition, the ten-year-old's grasp can be altered to accommodate different objects, such as a tennis ball, a pebble, a worm, a hammer, and a wet orange seed. Differentiation of parts of the arm and hand makes such accommodation possible.

Syncresis that develops into greater discreteness is seen in intellectual growth as well. The young child displays *holophrasis* in her speech. That is, she uses one word to represent an entire situation or series of actions that an older youth would describe in a variety of words that more completely delineate the elements of the situation. For example, the two-year-old may say "Go car" to encompass the request that the adolescent might express in these terms: "If Dad's driving to town this morning, I'd like to go along."

Although Werner believed that development proceeds from the syncretic to the discrete, he did not propose that the adult loses the ability to perceive in a syncretic manner. For example, an adult can grasp the general impression of a room she enters, or can take in the general panorama of a mountain landscape in addition to analyzing it discretely, part by part. Furthermore, as Baldwin has explained:

> Syncresis is primitive, in the sense that it is characteristic of children and primitive man and of perception under conditions of impoverished input, but it is not, per se, maladaptive, disordered, or incompatible with the more discrete varieties of perception that characterize everyday adult life (1967, p. 502).

Not only does development move toward discreteness, but the parts become increasingly articulated. This factor of *articulation* is like Lewin's organized interdependence. As the child grows older, the increasingly differentiated aspects of physical and mental life arrange themselves into hierarchies and interlinked sequences that permit complex thoughts and actions. The young child who wishes to ride in the car with his or her father cannot smoothly string together a series of interdependent thoughts that take into consideration past and future conditions, as can the teenager when he says:

> If Dad's driving to town this morning, I'd like to go along and take my skis to be fixed. And since Caroline got to take Linda last time, I think it's my turn to take friends—like Frank and Ted, or at least Frank, if he doesn't have to work today.

As another orthogenetic subprinciple, Werner proposed that development moves from a state of rigidity toward greater flexibility. On first consideration, this principle appears in conflict with Lewin's concept of rigidification. Does Werner say children become less rigid and Lewin claim they become more rigid as they grow older? Closer inspection of their definitions shows that the answer is no. They really are not in conflict, for the two theorists used *rigid* in quite different ways. Whereas Lewin coined *rigidification* to identify an increasing discreteness of life-space regions (stronger barriers between regions), Werner used *rigid* to indicate the young child's inability to adapt present concepts or skills to suit new environmental demands. To Werner, the older child is more flexible, more sensitive to subtle changes in surroundings, and better prepared to select from his repertoire of behaviors those that can adequately handle these changes. The older child not only draws from a broader repertoire of ideas and actions, but is better prepared to alter existing ideas and skills to meet new demands. For instance, when a young child plays the game of checkers, she typically conceives of a very limited number of ways to move her discs, and she cannot predict very well what influence a present move may have on subsequent moves. In contrast, the older, more experienced child plays a more flexible game. She can readily conceive of several possible present moves and can more accurately foresee the likely consequences for future moves. She is also assisted by her greater ability to imagine her opponent's responses to her moves.

Another direction of orthogenetic growth in Werner's model is from instability toward stability. This characteristic is readily illustrated in the area of children's interests and attention. The young child's interests and concentration are labile, shifting easily from one thing to another. But by the time he reaches adolescence, he is able to concentrate longer on one thing, he can conceive of long-term goals to pursue, and his interests become increasingly stable.

Finally, Werner believed that the passing years allow the child to differentiate more clearly between self and the world. The infant at first fails to distinguish self from non-self. And when he begins to do so, he perhaps feels that satisfying things are self and nonsatisfying ones are non-self. So the oppositeness or separateness of self and the world "is relatively lacking in early childhood and increases with age. . . . The fundamental nature of the 'self:world' polarity is particularly evident under those circumstances where it breaks down, for example, in pathology," with *pathology* referring to such states of confused identity as schizophrenia (Wapner and Werner, 1965, p. 10).

Thus, as the foregoing examples illustrate, Werner believed that it is the nature of humans to develop physically and psychologically toward increased (1) differentiation of parts and their functions, (2) integration of individual parts to form complex behaviors and intricate thought patterns, (3) flexibility in adapting actions and thoughts to changing environmental conditions, (4) stability of interest and intention, and (5) distinctions between self and the world.

STAGES OF DEVELOPMENT

Like Lewin, Werner's main concern was with identifying growth principles or directions rather than spelling out the nature of growth stages. However, he did not entirely neglect the matter of stages. To understand his position, we can cast the opposite sides of the continuity–discontinuity argument as a pair of questions: Do new forms of development emerge gradually and continuously out of old forms, so that there are no discernible steps or stages? Or do novel forms spring up to replace the old, producing discontinuous steps or levels? In Werner's opinion, both of these processes occur. The general movement of development is continuous and unbroken, but periodically, along this growth incline, steps are seen. "On the one side, the orthogenetic principle in *overall terms* . . . necessarily implies continuity. On the other hand, concrete forms and operations, novel functions and structures 'emerge,' and in this respect changes are discontinuous" (Werner and Kaplan, 1963, pp. 7–8).

However, in Werner's system, when a new form of behavior or thought replaces an earlier one, the earlier form is not lost. It is simply subordinated to the newer form. In a sense, it is put on a back shelf to be retrieved if needed. Under ordinary circumstances the growing child uses the newer, more advanced behavior pattern. However, under special internal or external circumstances the old, discarded patterns may come to the fore again. Samples of such internal circumstances are dream states, pathological conditions, or intoxication by certain drugs. Unusual external conditions most often take the form of difficult or novel tasks. In facing a novel task, the child frequently returns to a more primitive mode of functioning before progressing toward "full-fledged higher operations; we may refer to this tendency as a manifestation of the *genetic principle of spirality*" (Werner and Kaplan, 1963, p. 8).

In a number of subrealms of development, Werner identified growth stages. However, unlike Gesell, he did not attach specific age designations to the stages. We can illustrate the way he treated such growth steps by citing those he proposed for two sorts of communication—gesture and speech. As indicated in Table 9.1, when a child gives a close representation (by gesture) of the shape or use or (by speech) of the sound of an object he sees, a low level of communication is involved. As he matures, his reference to the object becomes less and less a direct representation. The symbols he eventually uses will typically have no apparent similarity to the objects they represent at all. This developmental trend was labeled *distancing* by Werner (Werner and Kaplan, 1963, pp. 82–83).

In summary, Werner identified stages in various realms of behavior. However, he did not formulate these into a single system, as did Piaget, nor did he specify ages when the typical child would be in each stage.

WERNER'S RESEARCH PROGRAM

Werner spent much of his professional life conducting experiments or aiding his co-workers with experiments in development, particularly development in perception. This research served his theory in two ways. It enabled him to test or illustrate hypotheses

Table 9.1 Stages of Development of Communication Skills

General Stage	Motor-Gestural Communication	Vocal-Articulatory Communication
Stage III	Gestures are less reflective of object's shape.	Words have no apparent similarity in sound to the objects they represent (examples: *banking, pleasant, obvious*).
Stage II	Gestures closely reflect shape or use of object.	Words reflect some characteristic of the object, such as a long word means a big object and a high-pitched word a tall object. These are *physiognomic depictions.*
Stage I	Gestures referring to objects begin in infancy with such acts as reaching-to-touch or turning-to-look.	Words echo or imitate the sound the object makes or would seem to make (examples: *clunk, buzz, murmur*). These are echoic or *onomatopoetic expressions.*

Werner and Kaplan, 1963, pp. 82–83.

derived from his orthogenetic principles. And on the basis of the tests, he was able to refine his principles and identify the conditions that affected their operation. The research also provided ideas for new subprinciples that should be incorporated into his overall scheme if it was to explain development adequately. In order to demonstrate this interaction between experiments and theory, we will look at two typical studies in perception that he and his co-workers at Clark University included in their extensive research program. The first concerns a person's perception of his body position in relation to the world outside his body. The second focuses on perceptions of meaning in sentences.

Perceiving Body Position The experimental conditions were these. In a darkened room, a person was placed in a special chair that could be tilted to either the left or right by 30 degrees. In front of the person was a luminous rod which he observed. During the first phase of the experiment the individual was tilted 30 degrees to the left, and then was to instruct the researcher how far the luminous rod should be tilted to the right or left in order to make the rod exactly vertical. The same task was then performed with the individual tilted 30 degrees to the right. In the second phase of the experiment the individual was once again tilted, but in this instance he was to direct the tilt of the rod so that it was at the same angle as his own body.

The purpose of this experiment was to determine (1) how people perceive the position of things in the environment (an ostensibly vertical rod), (2) how they perceive the position of their own body, and (3) what discrepancy may exist between these two perceptions. Werner tried the tasks with children and youths between ages 6 and 18 to see if there were developmental trends in such perceptions of body and outside space. He discovered that the discrepancy between judgments of the luminous rod at the perceived vertical and judgments of it at the perceived body angle differed significantly with age. Children from age 6 to almost 12 on the average perceived the difference between the vertical and their body position as being around 34 to 36 degrees (while the true difference was 30 degrees). But by ages 15 to 18 the judgments jumped up markedly to between 44 and 46 degrees. In other words, in middle and later adolescence, the difference between perceived body angle and the outside space (represented by the supposed vertical) was markedly overestimated. Werner interpreted this finding as support for his orthogenetic subprinciple that *differentiation between self and non-self (self and world) increases with age.* Adolescents exaggerated the difference between their body position and "vertical" in the outside world far more than did children who had not reached puberty (Wapner and Werner, 1965, pp. 12–16).

Perceiving Meaning in Sentence Contexts   A markedly different sort of experiment is illustrated by Werner's scheme of inserting a nonsense word into each of a series of sentences. The child's task is to analyze the sentences to determine which familiar English word might properly substitute for the nonsense word. Here is one such series (Baldwin, 1967, p. 511):

1. You can't fill anything with a *contavish*.
2. The more you take out of a *contavish*, the larger it gets.
3. Before the house is finished, the walls must have *contavishes*.
4. You can't feel or touch a *contavish*.

5. A bottle has only one *contavish.*

6. John fell in a *contavish* in the road.

The experimenters asked children of different age levels to insert a single word that would fit reasonably into each sentence in the series; they also asked the children to explain how and why they arrived at the answers they gave. By analyzing children's responses, Werner and his staff were able to identify sorts of thinking that appeared to follow orthogenetic principles.

For example, some children thought of a word that would make sense in the first sentence—such as *smile* or *space.* However, they considered this a final solution, applicable to all the rest of the sentences, rather than as a tentative or trial word that had to be tested in all six sentences before it could be accepted as the proper solution. When they came to subsequent sentences, these children either blindly inserted their first word or engaged in specious logic to force the fit, such as, "People are happy that the walls are all up, so they smile at their new house." This is the argument they used to defend the use of *smile* in sentence 3. Werner found that younger children more often stayed with their first guess, while older children more often considered their first try as a tentative estimate that might need adjusting or eliminating as later sentences were faced. The researchers interpreted this trend as support for the orthogenetic direction of growth from the rigid to the flexible.

Other patterns of answers that children offered seemed, in Werner's opinion, to illustrate the principle of greater differentiation as the child got older. For example, some children could not conceive that the key word for which they were searching could assume different meanings in different sentences. Furthermore, some of the younger elementary school children in the experiment felt that the word they were hunting for had the meaning of the entire sentence. This is the phenomenon of holophrasis mentioned earlier. For these children *contavishes* meant "having something in the walls when the house is finished." Or a *contavish* was "a bottle with something in it." The older children were far more capable of differentiating the word's meaning according to its context and also of seeing the word as a unit by itself—as part of the sentence and not as the conveyor of the entire meaning of the sentence.

In these ways and in a variety of others, Werner used the results of such experiments to support and illustrate orthogenetic theory. In addition, his experiments provided data for use by other psychologists and suggested new phenomena for Werner and his colleagues to investigate and to integrate into orthogenetic psychology.

ORTHOGENETIC THEORY:
AN ASSESSMENT

My assessment of Werner's theory in terms of the nine appraisal standards introduced in Chapter 1 is reflected by the marks on the accompanying set of rating scales.

I concluded that Werner's theory is clear (item 2) and internally consistent (item 5), and I gave these the highest marks. The theory is also economical (item 6), in the sense that it does not propose a complicated set of concepts when a simpler set will do. Werner's general growth principles are few in number, and he applies them in a reasonable manner to explain the results of his experiments.

Furthermore, Werner's theory appears to closely reflect the real world of children, a result of his carrying on a continuing series of empirical studies of children's language and perceptual behavior (item 1). Thus, I rated him highly on this scale.

I believe Werner also deserves a rather high rating on item 8 (stimulates new discoveries). In books written by developmentalists, his name appears often, attesting to other authors' recognition of his contributions. Furthermore, he developed such research tools as the series of sentences containing a nonsense word and techniques for testing perception, all of which have added to the experimenters' arsenal of investigative methods. Also, students of Werner like Seymour Wapner and Jonas Langer have contributed significantly to the field of development using orthogenetic theory.

However, items 3 (explains past, predicts future) and 4 (guides child rearing) are a different matter. Only in a most general sense do Werner's contributions enable us to predict a child's future development or explain her past growth. And they offer little or no advice about how to raise a child. This is not surprising, for Werner's goal was to discover general developmental principles, not techniques for guiding the treatment of individual children. Thus, I have rated the theory low on these items.

WERNER'S THEORY

How well do I think the theory meets the standards?

The Standards	Very Well	Moderately Well	Very Poorly
1. Reflects the real world of children	X		
2. Is clearly understandable	X		
3. Explains the past and predicts the future			X
4. Guides child rearing			X
5. Is internally consistent	X		
6. Is economical	X		
7. Is falsifiable		X	
8. Stimulates new discoveries		X	
9. Is self-satisfying		X	

In terms of falsifiability (item 7), orthogenetic theory seems to me to rank low in the moderately well range. Whenever a theory is composed of general principles of development whose application depends to a considerable degree upon personal interpretation, then it is difficult to conceive of tests that would show unequivocally whether the theory is true or false. Such is the case with orthogenetic theory. It is not difficult for advocates of the theory to cite instances of behavior that can serve as evidence that the principles are true. But at the same time, people who are critical of the theory can take the same instances and, by interpreting them differently, claim that the principles are false or in need of some revision.

For example, a mother brings her five-year-old daughter to kindergarten on the first day of school. As they enter the room, the daughter dashes immediately to a rocking horse, while the mother pauses to gaze about the entire room. A critic of orthogenetic theory might cite this incident as evidence that Werner's syncretic-to-discrete principle does not explain such behavior. If behavior progresses from the syncretic to the discrete (from the undifferentiated or global to the differentiated or specific), then why did the girl focus immediately on the rocking horse and her mother look generally around the room? A supporter of Werner's theory, however, might suggest that this is the wrong interpretation of the incident. In the first place, the supporter might say that moving from the undifferentiated to the discrete in visual perception is a momentary developmental trend—the person first sees the whole, then the parts that comprise it, all in a moment or two. So just seeing the mother's and daughter's gross actions does not tell us that they failed to perceive in a syncretic-to-discrete manner, nor does it tell us that the daughter's move in perception from syncretic to discrete occurred as rapidly as her mother's. Furthermore, a defender of orthogenetic theory might say that the incident in the kindergarten could be instead an example of the rigidity-to-flexibility principle. The child's running to the rocking horse might suggest less flexibility of behavior than the mother's looking around the room to observe many possibilities for interesting activities.

Regardless of whether an advocate would argue the case in this way, the point is that general principles that allow considerable leeway for personal interpretation make it difficult to test a theory in order to determine its validity. Of course, Werner and his followers did derive hypotheses from the theory and conduct studies to test these hypotheses, thereby helping estimate the validity of the theory's general principles. And these studies were a step in the right direction. However, I believe that the theory's form is as yet in a state that makes it weak in terms of falsifiability.

Finally, there is the question of how self-satisfying (item 9) Werner's theory is overall. For me, his identification of general growth principles and his convincing examples and experimental demonstrations of them are valuable. The principles help me comprehend general lines of development. Furthermore, his studies of language and perception, along with the research techniques devised to conduct these studies, are positive contributions. However, when I seek aid in understanding the past and predicting the future of individual children in order to be better prepared to guide their development, I find little or no help from Werner. Providing such information was not his mission. So overall, I find the results of orthogenetic theory just moderately self-satisfying.

FOR FURTHER READING

Baldwin, Alfred L. (1967) *Theories of Child Development*. New York: Wiley. Pp. 495–533. Chapter 17 offers a description and critique of orthogenetic theory.

Lerner, Richard M. (1976) *Concepts and Theories of Human Development*. Reading, Mass.: Addison-Wesley. Pp. 113–122. Werner's position on the issue of the continuity or discontinuity of development is presented.

Werner, Heinz. (1948) *Comparative Psychology of Mental Development*. Rev. ed. Chicago: Follett. An early statement of orthogenetic theory.

Werner, Heinz. (1957) "The Concept of Development from a Comparative and Organismic Point of View" in Dale Harris, *The Concept of Development: An Issue in the Study of Human Behavior*. Minneapolis: University of Minnesota.

PART 6

BIOLOGICAL SOURCES
OF DEVELOPMENT

A search for principles that describe
how genetic determinants of behavior
evolve.

An underlying theme of this book is that one reason theories differ from each other is that theorists do not all use the same questions to guide their search. It is true that all investigators appear to share in common the two broadest questions: (1) In *what ways* do living things, such as children, develop and (2) *Why?* In this respect, all theorists are trying to describe and explain development. But if we move from this general level of query to those more precise questions that actually define what will be studied and how, we find significant differences between one theorist and another.

This matter of the way theorists' questions guide their inquiries is particularly striking in the case of theories that can properly be assigned to Part 6. Theories in other parts of this book use guide questions focusing primarily on *ontogeny*, meaning the course of development during the child's lifetime. The authors of such theories ask: How does the child change from the time of conception until maturity, and why do such changes come about? In contrast, the key questions directing theorists belonging in Part 6 go beyond ontogenetic queries to search out more basic phylogenetic answers, with *phylogeny* meaning the evolutionary development of any species of plant or animal, in this case, the human species. Phylogenetic issues are defined by such questions as: In the evolution of the human species from one-celled organisms over hundreds of millions of years, what types of changes have occurred (meaning description) and why have they come about (meaning explanation)? In what way is human development similar to and different from the development of other living things, and what are the reasons for these likenesses and differences?

The people who have been proposing theories to answer such phylogenetic questions in recent decades come primarily from the disciplines of biology and psychology. The biologists labor in the subrealms of comparative zoology, developmental biology, and population biology. The psychologists have been chiefly from the subrealm of comparative psychology. In each of these disciplines, the term *comparative* indicates that the investigator is concerned with comparing the characteristics of one species with those of others. So the studies they conduct involve such varied subjects as worms, starfish, army ants, honey bees, white rats, goldfinches, ringtailed monkeys, chimpanzees, and many more. Often a theorist takes the final step and compares these living things to the last species in the evolutionary hierarchy, human beings. Comparative zoologists and psychologists who include this final step are the ones belonging in Part 6.

Theorists who have pursued issues of phylogenetic development in recent decades have been located in various parts of the world. Familiar names from Europe have been Lorenz (1965), Eibl-Eibesfeldt (1975), and Hinde (1974). Those from America include Lashley (1960), Hebb (1949), Schneirla (1972), and Wilson (1975). To illustrate the line of reasoning developed by the strongly committed evolutionists among these scholars, I have chosen for Chapter 10 the sociobiology of Edward O. Wilson.

It is impossible to understand the evolutionists' position unless we first recognize assumptions they hold in common. So in the following discussion we will review in an elementary fashion a number of the assumptions, asking your forebearance if the review is unduly reminiscent of a class in high school biology.

At the outset it is important to establish the definitions of two terms: species and population. A *species* is a collection of individual organisms capable of interbreeding under natural conditions. The phrase "natural conditions" is an essential part of this definition, for it requires that we establish separate species categories for two organisms that can be induced to mate under experimental conditions but that do not interbreed in a natural setting. Hence, lions and tigers form two separate species, even though they can be successfully interbred in captivity (Wilson, 1975, pp. 8–9).

A *population* is a set of organisms of the same species occupying a clearly delimited geographical area at the same time. Thus, a single hill of ants is not an entire population—a population in this case is all the colonies of ants of the same species in that particular area. Or a population can comprise all the indigenous people living in a cluster of interlinked islands of the South Seas.

With these definitions of species and population in mind, we turn to the five propositions to which our theorists appear to subscribe as underlying assumptions.

1. Species Reproduction   For humans, as well as for all other species that require two parents as the source of reproduction, a new member of the species is conceived when a sperm cell from the male combines with an ovum from the female. This combination produces a new cell that immediately divides. The resulting pair of cells also divide, and this process of dividing to produce increasing numbers of cells continues over and over. Each step in the sequence creates cells of slightly different properties, cells capable of specialized functions, until finally they represent a fully constructed new member of the species, including such variegated, coordinated parts as heart and spleen, throat and lungs, skin and hair, eyes and brain.

2. The Genetic Plan   The architectural design for this new fish or fowl or human is provided by thousands of genes carried by chromosomes contained in the sperm cell of the father and in the ovum of the mother. In humans the chromosomes total 46, with 23 contributed by the mother and 23 by the father.

The genes inherited from one's parents determine both (1) the border limits within which development normally can occur and (2) potentialities for variation within these limits. By *border limits* I mean the identifying features of the species, the common elements that all normal individuals in the species share. As a simple example, humans normally are born with two eyes in front of the head, one on each side of the upper bridge of the nose. In contrast, rabbits and frogs are normally born with eyes farther to the side of the head. By *potentialities for variation* I mean that within these limits particular gene combinations determine some variation of the general characteristic. So eye color and acuity of sight can vary from one normal child to another, depending on the specific mix of genes received from the father and mother.

The connection between a gene and a given characteristic, such as skin color, intelligence, or competitiveness, is not a simple one. A chromosome does not merely contain a skin color gene or competitiveness gene that by itself determines the hue of the person's skin or his degree of competitiveness. Rather, the inherited foundation of such characteristics is determined by a number of genes located at various places among the chromosomes. Within the same family, one child will inherit a different mix of genes than her siblings, except in the case of identical (monozygotic) twins. Hence, it is obviously not only the variations in the environment that cause differences among children in the same family, but variations also in the combination of genes received by each child.

3. The Network of Species   The theorists belonging in Part 6 subscribe to Darwin's proposition that none of the species, human or otherwise, is a separate creation, unrelated to the others. Rather, all species are links in a network of living things. The network extends from the simplest one-celled organisms—or from even more primitive stages of matter—to the most mature, advanced species, that of the human being.

4. The Natural Purpose   If there is a natural purpose to life, a goal toward which all living things are driven by their nature, then that is survival. In its most basic sense, this is not the survival of the individual organism, since all individuals die. Nor is it even the survival of the species, for species are eliminated or altered with the passing of time. Rather, the basic aim seems to be the survival of the genes, which are the carriers of life itself (Wilson, 1975, pp. 3–4).

5. Natural Selection   Living things obviously do not develop in a vacuum. They develop in environments that can vary in temperature, humidity, oxygen content, food supply, type of predator, and the like. Only those species survive and thrive that are well suited to changes that occur in their environments. Those poorly suited to environmental changes die off. This is the process of natural selection, the survival of the fittest. Such a point of view, refined since Darwin published his theory of evolution in 1859, is the new Darwinism that undergirds much of the work conducted today on the biological origins of human behavior, and thus is the foundation for the origins of child development.

The work of Wilson that we will consider in Chapter 10, like that of other investigators in this realm, draws most heavily on studies of life forms below humans on the evolutionary ladder. And the question is often asked: Why use studies of animals to elucidate the development of humans? A typical answer is that taken from the preface of Hinde's *Biological Bases of Human Social Behaviour:*

> Understanding human behaviour involves problems infinitely more difficult than landing a man on the moon or unravelling the structure

of complex molecules. . . . If we are to tackle them, we must use every source of evidence available to us. Studies of animals are one such source. Sometimes such studies are useful to the extent that animals resemble man, and sometimes they help just because animals are different and permit the study of issues in a simplified, isolated, or exaggerated form. They may assist us in understanding the behaviour of man not only through factual comparison between animal and man, but also by helping us to refine the categories and concepts used in the description and explanation of behaviour and social structure. But the use of animals involves dangers: it is so easy to make rash generalizations, to slip from firm fact to flight of fancy, to select examples to fit preconceptions. Studies of animals must therefore be used circumspectly, and the limitations of their usefulness specified (1974, p. xiii).

With Hinde's caution in mind, we now move on to Wilson's version of sociobiological theory.

CHAPTER 10

WILSON'S SOCIOBIOLOGY

Edward O. Wilson (1929—), a Harvard University biologist, has defined *sociobiology* as the "systematic study of the biological basis of all social behavior" (1975, p.4). In his book, *Sociobiology: The New Synthesis* (published in 1975), Wilson focused attention on animal societies as well as on early man "and the adaptive features of organization in the more primitive contemporary human societies" (p. 4). He did not take on the task of explaining the complexities of modern "advanced" societies, but he expressed the hope that scientists soon might be able to reformulate the foundations of the social sciences (particularly sociology) and the humanities, so these disciplines could be drawn into the "modern synthesis" of neo-Darwinian evolutionary theory. By *modern synthesis* he means that each phenomenon, such as each social act, is analyzed to show how the action helps the organism adapt to its environment. Then this analysis of adaptation is used for drawing inferences about the genetic composition of the population being discussed. In other words, sociobiologists seek to answer the questions: What is the genetic nature of the organism, such as the child, that enables it to make an observed social adaptation to its environment, and how has this particular genetic nature been brought about?

It is not my purpose in this brief chapter to describe Wilson's theory in its considerable detail. Rather, the purpose is only to identify the main theme of his argument and to illustrate several of the forces that Wilson proposes are chief determinants of social behavior. Near the end of the chapter, we will hazard some speculations about the implications a theory such as Wilson's can have for explaining the development of children in modern societies.

LEVELS OF CAUSE

Some theorists, such as Gesell (Chapter 6) and Koppitz (Chapter 20), are very concerned with how people behave but are little interested in the causes of behavior. Others, however, make causes their main concern. Wilson is very much this second kind. He searches for why people and other organisms act as they do. Although Wilson's theory describes the social acts of many species, none of his description is offered for its own sake. Instead, it serves to illustrate from real life observations the principles he believes explain social behavior.

Besides proposing causes, Wilson differentiates between two levels of cause, the apparent ones and the basic determinants underlying them. As indicated in Table 10.1, he begins with types of observed social acts. Then he suggests first-level factors that he believes cause organisms to adopt such acts in their efforts to survive as a genetic strain. Finally he proposes two, more fundamental second-level variables that he thinks underlie these factors. We will analyze his model by first considering observed social behaviors, then describing second-level causes, and finally discussing the first-level variables.

OBSERVED SOCIAL BEHAVIOR

The term *social behavior* refers to the degree and kind of interaction among organisms, interaction both within species and between them. Thus, social behavior includes relationships between boy and dog as well as between boy and mother. It includes interactions between prey and predator as well as among cooperating members of a colony.

In his scheme, Wilson distinguishes between more advanced and more primitive social behavior. The more complex the social interaction, the more advanced it is considered to be. The simpler the interaction, the more primitive or lower it ranks on his behavior scale. By applying this criterion, we would rate starfish quite low, ants much higher, and humans at the top.

The sorts of social behavior that sociobiologists commonly study can be categorized in various ways. One common category is that of competition and cooperation. Under this heading are such concepts as social roles, division of labor, tribalism, and dominance and submission. Another popular category is commu-

Table 10.1   Causes of Social Behavior

Types of Social Behavior	First-Level Causes That Determine Social Behavior	Basic or Second-Level Causes That Determine First-Level Causes	
		Phylogenetic Inertia (interacts with)	Ecological Pressure
Cooperating or competing, acting selfishly or altruistically, caring for offspring, dominating or submitting, dividing the labor and performing a role, defending a territory, engaging in sexual behavior, living communally, bartering, communicating, and others	Major determinants include: 1. Demographic variables: birth rates, death rates, equilibrium population size 2. Rates of gene flow into and out of the population 3. Coefficients of relationship (fraction of genes in two individuals that are identical by descent)	Aspects of a behavioral category that determine the degree of inertia include: 1. Genetic variability 2. Antisocial factors 3. Complexity of social behavior 4. Effect of evolution on other traits 5. Others	Aspects of the environment that urge changes on the species' genetic structure include: 1. Changing food supplies 2. Predators 3. Changing temperature and humidity 4. Intrusions by other populations 5. Others

nication. Others are the socialization of the next generation, altruism, barter, sexual relations, and territoriality (the use and protection of a given region). Typical questions asked about these phenomena are: Under what conditions do individuals and groups cooperate rather than compete? Why do members of some species live alone or in small family groups while members of other species live in densely populated colonies? How do different roles and divisions of labor arise in a society? Why do species engage in altruistic behavior?

To answer such questions Wilson has proposed two layers of determinants, which we will call first- and second-level causes. The nature of these levels can be explained most readily by starting with the second, more basic one.

SECOND-LEVEL CAUSES:
INERTIA VERSUS PRESSURE

According to Wilson, the two fundamental factors that interact to cause the development of all behavior, social and otherwise, are nature and nurture.

The nature portion of the formula is called *phylogenetic inertia*. It is the tendency for the genetic composition of a population of organisms to continue unchanged generation after generation. Or, said another way, inertia is the resistance of a species to alter its heredity pattern from one generation to the next.

The nurture side of this interaction is labeled *ecological pressure*. It consists of all those aspects of the environment, both animate and inanimate, that push a species, over successive generations, toward altering its genetic structure in order to better survive. These aspects are the forces that constantly or periodically threaten the organism's existence. They include dwindling food supplies, extremes of temperature and humidity, poisons, competition for sexual partners or rest sites, and many more.

From the sociobiologist's viewpoint, all social behavior, like every other form of biological response:

> . . . is a set of devices for tracking changes in the environment. No organism is perfectly adapted. Nearly all the relevant parameters of its environment shift constantly. Some of the changes are periodic and predictable, such as the light-dark cycles and the seasons. But most are episodic and capricious, including fluctuations in food items, nest sites, and predators, random alterations of temperature

and rainfall within seasons, and others. The organism must track
these parts of its environment with some precision, yet it can never
hope to respond correctly to every one of the multifactorial twists and
turns—only to come close enough to survive for a little while and to
reproduce as well as most (Wilson, 1975, p. 144).

So it is in this struggle to track and adapt to environmental
pressures that species evolve their social characteristics. In his
effort to identify and illustrate the principles that govern such
evolution, Wilson has drawn upon examples of the behavior of
many species, and in doing so has required hundreds of pages to
make his case. However, for the sake of economy of explanation
we will look at one fictitious population whose fate is traced over
eighty generations. The mythical species is a type of primate, not
unlike the chimpanzee or gibbon though somewhat smaller. By
means of this fictional creature we can save space but still remain
true to sociobiological theory by taking our items of social behavior from similar behaviors observed in several real species.

This primate is called a *lamina*. We will view it at two times
during its evolution. On the first occasion, the population of laminas consists of 4000 members living on the slopes of a cluster of
volcanic mountains (Figure 10.1). Soon an extensive series of volcanic eruptions pours lava flows down the slopes, destroying half
the lamina population and much of their traditional territory. The
surviving members are split by a broad lava field into two groups
of nearly equal size. One group is gradually driven up the mountain slope by subsequent flows; the other group is driven down
into a jungle region. Thus the two groups are prevented from any
future interaction (Figure 10.2). The second time we view the laminas is eighty generations later, when they have evolved into two
subspecies. On this second occasion we note similarities in their
development over the generations, particularly in regard to four
interlinked social characteristics: cooperation, altruism, territoriality, and parental care.

Table 10.2 summarizes the "facts" about the original and later
forms of laminas and their environments. These data are the phenomena we will try to explain by concepts from Wilson's theory.
However, before turning to the explanation, let us review some
key aspects of the three lamina societies charted in the table. In
this review and throughout the subsequent analysis, we will embellish, as needed, on the characteristics listed in the table.

The Original Laminas   The original laminas enjoyed moderate
temperatures during most of the year and enough rainfall to en-

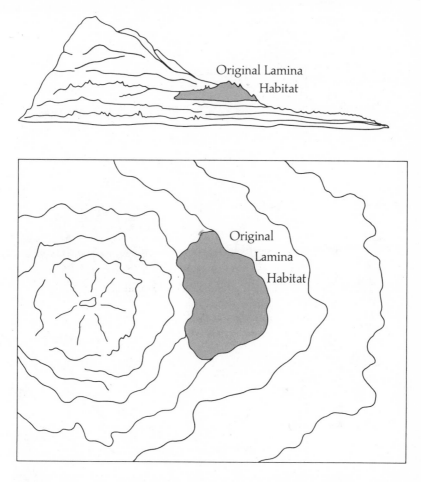

Figure 10.1 Two Views (Elevation and Aerial) of Original Lamina Habitat

sure a fairly adequate supply of berries and nuts. In terms of social organization, they fed and rested in the forest groves in groups of one or two dozen related adults and young. When traveling across the plains to another grove, they stayed in a close-ordered troop so the larger adults could shield the young from marauding hawks. The very young clung to their mothers' backs when traveling or when the troop climbed to the lower branches of trees to sleep at night. The laminas' cooperative behavior (working together toward a common goal) included (1) traveling in groups to locate suitable feeding and resting sites and (2) screaming to warn the others when a wolf appeared. Altruistic behavior (sacrificing one's

Figure 10.2   Lamina Populations after Eighty Generations

own welfare for the sake of someone else's) included (1) adults sheltering the young from diving hawks and (2) mothers softening hard nuts and berries for the young by chewing before they themselves ate. In regard to territoriality (using and protecting a given area), one or two dozen family-related laminas cooperatively used adjacent groves within a four-mile area. Parental care consisted of mothers feeding, carrying, and grooming the young. Any adult felt free to discipline the young. A male adult would occasionally play with his offspring.

Now: Eighty Generations Later   The Type-One population continues isolated on the rocky, cold upper slopes of the mountains,

Table 10.2 Social Evolution of a Fictitious Primate

Aspects of the Species and Their Environments	The Original Laminas	Eighty Generations Later	
		Type-One Subspecies	Type-Two Subspecies
Topography	Lower mountain slopes with mixed woods and grassy plains	Upper boulder-strewn mountain sides broken by crags and rocky canyons. Plant growth includes stunted evergreen trees, bushes, and coarse grass.	Tropical rain forest on the flat lands below the mountain slopes
Temperature and humidity	Moderate temperature and regularly spaced rain. Cooler in winter, but snow rarely falls.	Generally chilly, except when bright sun strikes the rather barren rocky hillsides. Frost and frequent snow in winter.	Hot and humid, with rain almost daily
Predators	Great hawks attack smaller, young laminas that cross the plain from one woods to another.	Great hawks attack smaller laminas seen on the open mountainside. Night-roaming wolves all year hunt smaller animals, including laminas.	At dusk and throughout the night jungle cats the size of leopards hunt mostly on the ground but will climb trees if hungry enough.
Lamina food	Red berries from bushes in woods and peanut-like legumes dug from the ground	Mostly soft bark of roots from young bushes, and black-berries when available briefly in summer	On the jungle floor, tender shoots of new plant growth. In high tree branches, buds and tender shoots.

(continued)

Table 10.2 Social Evolution of a Fictitious Primate (continued)

Aspects of the Species and Their Environments	The Original Laminas	Eighty Generations Later	
		Type-One Subspecies	Type-Two Subspecies
Resting and nesting sites	Sleep in crouches of trees where lower branches extend from trunk 3 or 4 meters above the ground	Sleep in caves or in niches between rocks	Sleep 9 to 12 meters above the ground in tall trees. Each lamina finds as high as possible a resting crouch that provides both comfortable support and an umbrella of leaves to deflect the rain.
Protection from predators	Avoid hawks by staying in groves. Cross the plains in groups, with adults guarding the young. Avoid wolves by sleeping in trees.	Mothers travel with young to ward off hawks. Adults, particularly males, sleep at the cave entrance to fight off intruding wolves.	A group of thirty or forty sleep in the same cluster of trees, as high as possible to avoid cats. When a lamina detects a cat, the lamina screeches, wakening the rest who screech in chorus and discourage the predator.
Rate of gene flow into population from outside	Low to moderate rate from occasional interbreeding with primates entering lamina territory from jungle below the mountain slopes	Zero rate of gene flow because lava fields isolate population from other primates. Population is entirely inbred.	Moderate rate of flow from some interbreeding with another population of similar laminas in lower jungle area

driven there by periodic lava flows. Originally numbering 1000, the population has been currently reduced to less than 300. In terms of cooperative behavior, they feed, sleep, and travel mostly in family groups of four or five. But when food is scarce, the females with their young drive off the males during feeding hours and dig for roots on their own. Altruism has increased since the time of the original laminas. Adults still protect the young from hawks and mothers feed their offspring before they themselves eat, but now both male and female adults sleep at the opening of their caves or rock crevices to fight off wolves that might appear. No longer do Type-One laminas scream at the sight of a wolf. Instead, they remain deadly still unless the wolf is obviously about to attack. As for territory, Type-Ones range across more than five times the area their ancestors did, for food is difficult to find on the high mountain slopes. Parental care is much the same as before, though fathers are more attentive guards of the young and will play with them more often.

While the Type-One subspecies is on the high mountain slopes, declining in population, the Type-Twos are down in the tropical rain forest, eating tree buds and shoots of new plant growth on the jungle floor. Compared to the Type-Ones, they are numerous (over 12,000) and also live in larger groupings, fifty or sixty of them in a colony. A colony is centered on a grove of "sleeping trees" whose great height offers nighttime protection from jungle cats and whose broad top leaves ward off rain. The Type-Twos gather at the grove at dusk to find sleeping spots, then at dawn they disperse in groups of four or six to areas where shorter trees offer more tender buds and shoots. Though mothers care for their young much as they did eighty generations ago, altruism in the population is less than among the Type-Ones. For example, while Type-One adult males guard the cave entrance against marauders, Type-Two males scramble in competition for the highest, safest tree perches, with larger laminas ousting smaller ones from choice spots. They do not roost at night on the lower branches so as to take the brunt of possible attack from a climbing cat. However, they do cooperate in screeching together at any predator one of them senses in the area. Since food is plentiful, a community can usually subsist in a territory of a square mile. Though Type-Two maternal care much resembles that of Type-One and their ancient ancestors, Type-Two fathers are less attentive to the young than Type-One fathers.

These, then, are the Type-One and Type-Two subspecies that hypothetically could have evolved from a common ancestral population. Wilson's theory explains how such social development could come about. We already noted Wilson's proposal that all social behavior results from the interaction of phylogenetic inertia and ecological pressure. Let us now consider the nature of such inertia.

Wilson states that inertia can range from high to low. High inertia means strong resistance to evolutionary change, and low inertia means a ready tendency to such change. He says that the amount of inertia varies greatly from one type of social behavior to another. Complex learning and parental care display high inertia while territoriality and nest-building patterns display low. In the lamina example, high inertia was suggested in the similarities of the subspecies in parental care, and low inertia was shown in their marked differences in territoriality; that is, the Type-Ones roamed abroad in small groups while the Type-Twos kept to a limited area in a large colony.

The question now is: What aspects of behavior determine its degree of inertia? Wilson has proposed that there are at least four aspects: (1) genetic variability, (2) antisocial factors, (3) the complexity of the social behavior, and (4) the effect of the evolution on other traits.

1. Genetic Variability   To understand how variability occurs and what its consequences can be, we need to review some elements of genetic theory. As a new organism, such as a lamina, is conceived, the thousands of genes of which it is composed from the mother's and father's germ cells establish the range of possibilities for its subsequent development. This genetic constitution is called the organism's *genotype*. Then, as the organism grows up in its particular environment, it displays, in its structure and behavior, certain of its genotypical potentialities. This environmentally and genetically determined appearance—what it looks like and how it acts—is its *phenotype*. The two terms can also be applied to a population of organisms. Within the population there is a pool of genes that consists of all the different varieties of genes possessed by the members of that population. For a given phenotypical trait, such as hair type or ability to engage in complex learning, the genes that contribute to the development of that trait occur in particular proportions. For example, within the original lamina population's gene pool there may have been genes with the potential to cause coarse body hair and others with the potential to cause fine body hair. The genes causing coarse hair may have been twice the number in the population's gene pool of those causing fine hair. Another population of laminas might have the same two sorts of genes but in the opposite proportions. Thus, the two populations are alike in the type but not in the incidence of hair texture genes in the population pool. And, other things being equal, we can expect to see more coarse hair in the first than in the second population.

But other things are not equal. Some genes are dominant, others neutral, and still others recessive. The ways such genes can interact at the genotypic level to cause a particular phenotype can become quite complex, particularly in traits or behaviors that are caused by not one or two but a combination of a number of genes located at different points on chromosomes. But, in general, if a dominant gene from one parent and a recessive one from the other exist in the genotype of the organism as potential determinants of a given trait, such as hair texture in laminas, the dominant gene will determine the phenotype, and the recessive gene's potential will go unrealized in that particular lamina. But the lamina can pass the recessive gene along to the next generation in its germ plasm, and it may combine with a similar recessive gene in a subsequent offspring, allowing the "hidden" recessive trait to show up phenotypically in that offspring.

Of course, in real life, the genes contributing to physical traits, like those contributing to social behavior categories, are very complex. And the complexity is considerably increased by the phenomenon of *mutation*. So far we have been assuming that genes are passed from one generation to another unchanged. We have also been assuming that the differences in the phenotypes from parents to children are simply a result of the particular mix of genes the children inherited from their parents or of changing environmental pressures as well. But sometimes, for reasons not completely understood, genes themselves change. These altered genes—these *mutants*—are different determinants in the children than were the original, unaltered genes in the parents.

As Wilson points out, most mutants are undesirable ones. They do not enhance the fitness in the species. And often they are dominated by more constructive genes already in the population's gene pool. Thus, most mutants tend to drop out of a population, for people who carry them tend not to survive or to thrive sufficiently as reproducers of the species to pass the mutants on to future generations. Other mutants, however, enhance the fitness of the species to adapt to ecological pressures. And when these are viable in terms of heredity—that is, they do not die out in the first generation but pass on in their mutated form to subsequent generations—they make a long-term contribution to the survival of the genetic strain.

Now, what does all this have to do with the genetic variability of a population and with phylogenetic inertia? Consider the problem faced by a population when a change in the environment, such as a lava flow among laminas, exerts sufficient ecological pressure to threaten the population's existence. The old behaviors are no longer good enough. New ones must be generated. For example, the Type-One laminas, forced by lava flows out of their forest groves, found that their habit of sleeping in trees in groups of a dozen or more to avoid wolves no longer worked. If they slept in the few stunted evergreens on the mountain slopes of their new habitat, wolves could leap up and snatch them. Now imagine that when they had lived in the forest, a few of the larger males and females not tending the young displayed the rudiments of the behavior of sleeping in a protected place on the ground. Sometimes they would not climb into trees at night but would push into a bushy thicket and nest there. If a wolf appeared, the lamina was protected in the rear by the thicket and was large enough and sufficiently pugnacious to fight off a frontal attack. Imagine further that this deviant sleeping tendency had a genetic basis. That is, a particular combination of genes in these few laminas' genotypical makeup is what determined their ground sleeping and pugnacious inclinations. The majority of the population did not have this particular mix that fostered sleeping in thickets and fighting wolves. In short, there was variability within the population in the genetic combinations supporting nesting and fighting behavior.

When the Type-Ones were forced to the rocky slopes, this small proportion of rudimentary ground sleeping genotypes promoted the evolution of the entire Type-One population to the pattern of sleeping in small family groups in caves or crevices with the larger adults guarding the cave entrance from intruders. The chief process that brought about this evolutionary transformation was natural selection. In the Type-Ones' new environment, the members who adapt to sleeping on the ground with their flanks protected by natural barriers will survive best. Thus, their gene combinations will pass on to subsequent generations, which will produce the desired phenotypical fitness. In effect, the genetic evolution of social behavior has been made possible by the genotypical variability in the original population. If there had been no variability in nesting and protection techniques with a genetic basis in the population, the species would not have evolved in the small family, adult male protected, cave sleeping direction. If the Type-Ones could not have assembled from within the population's existing gene pool the genetic base for other appropriate nesting and protection behaviors, the species would have been wiped out.

Thus, the amount of genetic variability related to a category of social behavior within a population influences phylogenetic inertia. Little or no variability means high inertia. The sort of behavior that is not well suited to ecological pressures is not going to evolve into a more suitable form. But if there is considerable variability related to a behavior category, inertia is lower, and the species has a better chance of putting together gene combinations that promote evolution to more fitting forms of behavior. In regard to how rapidly the transition to the more fitting forms will take place, Wilson has written that:

> . . . the population will proceed to the new mode at a rate that is a function of the product of the degree of superiority of the new mode, referred to as the intensity of selection, and the amount of phenotypic variability that has a genetic basis (1975, p.33).

Greater genetic variability, and hence greater chance of evolving new adaptive behaviors, can also be produced by mutations (if the mutants are hardy and inheritable) and by gene flow. *Gene flow* is the introduction of new genes into the population by interbreeding with members of other populations. Thus, a species does not have to depend entirely on the existing gene pool for the variability needed to create a gene mixture that supports new social patterns. Since the mountain dwelling Type-One laminas were isolated from other primates, they could not depend on gene flow as a source of more fitting genetic material. The jungle dwelling Type-Twos, however, could profit by the immigration of genes from a different lamina population that bred into the Type-Twos from the periphery of their territory.

2. Antisocial Factors   Any condition that presses a population toward reduced sociality and hence toward greater phylogenetic inertia is considered to be an antisocial factor. As an example, scarcity of food in the Type-One laminas' barren mountain habitat pressed them to reduce the number of individuals comprising a foraging group. A small group could more readily roam a wide territory in search of roots and berries than a large troop. As a further antisocial act, female Type-Ones, at times of food shortage, would drive males away from feeding sites so the females and their young might find enough roots and berries to survive.

Antisocial behavior can also arise from the differences in size and in mating activities between males and females in societies featuring polygamy; the largest, most aggressive males fight to dominate the harems. Such males usually are less integrated into the society of the females and young than are males in primarily monogamous populations (Wilson, 1975, p. 36).

3. Complexity of the Social Behavior   According to this principle of inertia, the more elaborate the elements that comprise a behavior, the more resistant the behavior is to change. As an example we might assume that the behavior pattern of mother care among the original laminas would, other things being equal, display higher inertia than the laminas' feeding habits, since mother care involved a more complicated array of components than did feeding behavior.

4. Effect of the Evolution on Other Traits   Wilson has further proposed that resistance to evolution of a given social behavior will increase in the degree that the behavior interferes with other valued characteristics in the population. For instance, if the Type-Ones' tendency to forage ever farther afield will expose the laminas to greater danger of attack by hawks and wolves, then the tendency will slow or stop. In like manner, if the trend among Type-Twos to form ever larger colonies starts to cause food shortages in familiar and convenient eating sites, then the trend will diminish or cease. Such is the inertial effect of any social evolution that impairs other aspects of the species's life.

To summarize, Wilson has stated that some environmental conditions affect social evolution a great deal, while others affect it not at all. Highly potent influences are such things as changes in food supplies, in types and amounts of predators, in available resting sites, and in climate. Furthermore, the form and complexity of a society is decided chiefly by "only one or a few of the principal adaptations of the species" (Wilson, 1975, p. 37). For instance, we can account for essentially all of the social differences between Type-One and Type-Two laminas on the basis of the differences in only four characteristics of their environment—available food, the traits of their most dangerous predators, available resting sites, and atmospheric temperature. Many other differences in the two populations' environments, for example, the sorts of flying insects, the types of grasses, the mineral contents of the water, the variety of flowers, and more, exert little or no influence on their social development.

FIRST-LEVEL CAUSES:
THE IMMEDIATE DETERMINANTS

According to Wilson, underlying, second-level causes—phylogenetic inertia and ecological pressure—determine a higher level of variables that are the immediate determinants of social development. In effect, the basic causes are linked to social behavior by means of this first-level set of conditions that he labels *demographic variables, rates of gene flow,* and *coefficients of relationship.* To explain how these conditions function, we will first discuss their nature and see how the more basic level of determinants produces them; then we will examine how these first-level conditions influence the form and function of a species's social characteristics.

Demographic Variables   These variables include birth rates, death rates, and equilibrium population size. Both birth and death rates are clearly a function of the genetic composition of a population interacting with such environmental forces as food supplies, types of predators, and climactic conditions. A population size at which a species can achieve stability within its particular habitat is a function of these same underlying forces. In our case of the fictitious laminas, Type-Ones had a population of 300 members and Type-Twos had 12,000. They had ostensibly reached a size that was in balance with the current conditions of their environments. Scarce food, more successful predators, and cold winters brought death earlier in the Type-Ones' mountain habitat than did conditions in the Type-Twos' jungle home. In effect, the Type-Ones, with their particular genetic composition, could not sustain a population of greater size in the rigorous mountain setting.

Rate of Gene Flow   The most potent force behind evolution is selection, which means that certain genes become increasingly frequent in the population because the organisms carrying them possess the favored ability to pass the genes along to the next generation. This ability can be the result of any number of factors: greater skill in besting competitors for food or sex partners, superior methods of avoiding predators and disease, greater re-productive competence, and others (Wilson, 1975, p. 67). As certain genes increase and others decrease, the population's potential for evolving new forms of social organization increases as well.

Next to selection, the fastest way that gene frequencies can be changed is through gene flow—"the immigration of groups of genetically different individuals into the population" (Wilson, 1975, p. 64). The lamina case illustrates two different rates of gene flow occasioned by two markedly different environments. The Type-Ones, isolated from other primates by lava fields, had a zero rate of gene importation. The Type-Twos, with a population of sexually compatible laminas on the periphery of their jungle habitat, experienced a moderate rate of interbreeding, resulting in new genes that added variability to the original pool.

Coefficients of Relationship   As indicated in Table 10.1, these coefficients show the fraction of genes in two individuals that are identical by descent. In other words, the coefficients tell the extent to which members of the population are genetically alike. A small, heavily inbred population, like that of the Type-One laminas, would have higher coefficients of relationship than would a larger population that maintains greater genetic variability by means of gene flow and an environment that does not so readily eliminate the less hardy members. So we would expect the coefficients of relationship among the Type-Two laminas in their tropical rain forest habitat to be somewhat lower than those among the Type-Ones in their chilly mountain setting.

The great importance in sociobiological theory of the degree of similarity among members of a population (as reflected in relationship coefficients) is seen in Wilson's belief that:

> most kinds of social behavior, including perhaps all of the most complex forms, are based one way or another on kinship. As a rule, the closer the genetic relationship of the members of a group, the more stable and intricate the social bonds of its members (1975, p. 73).

In effect, then, inbreeding encourages social evolution. Our case of the laminas illustrated this by suggesting a greater degree of altruism among the inbred Type-Ones than among the Type-Twos, especially in the greater self-sacrifice displayed by the cave dwelling Type-One males as they guarded the females and young at night.

But the results of inbreeding are not all happy ones for the species. While inbreeding promotes sociality, it tends at the same time to disseminate through the population traits that impair the fitness of individuals, that diminish genetic adaptability, and that reduce the group's chances of survival. On the basis of this principle we could speculate that the small size of the Type-One laminas' mountainside population is at least partly a result of a diminished hardiness and adaptability of the stock as a consequence of inbreeding.

Wilson presumes that, to some extent, the direction of social evolution is the interplay of these positive and negative features of inbreeding or high coefficients of relationship (Wilson, 1975, p. 80). When these features are combined with particular birth rates and death rates in the population, and with migration tendencies that influence gene flow, we have a complex of factors determining the particular sorts of social behavior displayed by the population under study. According to Wilson (1975, p. 5), the principal goal of the emerging discipline of sociobiology should be the ability to predict characteristics of social organization from a knowledge of the first-level causal factors we have discussed— demographic variables, gene flow, and coefficients of relationship.

Now that we have traced some key features of Wilson's model, we can estimate its implications for understanding child development.

IMPLICATIONS FOR CHILD DEVELOPMENT

Wilson has not directly described what consequences his theory might have for explaining how children develop in present-day societies, but it is possible to draw a number of inferences from his model. In the following discussion, we will see one way this can be done. As background for such speculation, we will look at three interlinked notions that Wilson has proposed about social organization and the human condition.

First, Wilson proposes that the goal of life, and hence the goal of child development, is to increase the chances that the genetic line will survive.

Second, he proposes that this goal is pursued on different levels of social organization. By *levels* he means that a person functions as a member of different social groupings that vary in size and generality. The first level is the individual himself, operating alone and in competition with other individuals. A second level is the family, a third, the colony or tribe, a fourth, the population, and a fifth, the species. Wilson (1975, p. 4) has pointed out that an action or habit a person exhibits may contribute to the fitness or welfare of one of these levels but at the same time detract from the fitness of another. An action, for example, that may be good for the individual's survival may be destructive to the family, a behavior that promotes the family's fitness may weaken the tribe, and what may help the tribe may harm the broader population. So at a time of food shortages, if a child steals the food rations of other members of the family, he enhances his own chance of survival but damages the family's fitness as a social unit. But if, altruistically, he shares his food allotment with younger members who have little or none, he enhances family fitness at his own expense. From this viewpoint, social interaction can be interpreted as a negotiating of compromises in the welfare of one level for the welfare of another. And from the vantage point of sociobiology, this negotiating represents the attempt of members of the species to find the combination of selfishness and altruism or cooperation that promises the survival of the genetic line within an environment of continually shifting pressures.

The third notion he proposes is that the variety of conflicting emotions and behaviors that plague or enliven daily human existence is the result of the way people have been programmed by evolution to pursue genetic survival under complicated, puzzling environmental circumstances. Wilson has depicted the human condition by first giving a biological label—hypothalamic-limbic complex—to what the layman might call "mind" or the "thinking mechanism." Then he explains:

> The hypothalamic-limbic complex of a highly social species, such as man, "knows," or more precisely has been programmed to perform as if it knows, that its underlying genes will be proliferated maximally only if it orchestrates behavioral responses that bring into play an efficient mixture of personal survival, reproduction, and altruism. Consequently, the centers of the complex tax the conscious mind with ambivalences whenever the organisms encounter stressful situations. Love joins hate; aggression (joins) fear; expansiveness (joins) withdrawal; and so on; in blends designed not to promote the

happiness and survival of the individual, but to favor the maximum transmission of the controlling genes (1975, p. 4).

With this picture of the purpose of human behavior in mind, what implications can we draw from sociobiology about child development? Among the variety of implications we might suggest, three in particular illustrate directions that seem useful. These involve the explanation of (1) group differences among children in their social behavior, (2) individual differences in social behavior, and (3) the basis of altruism among children. Each of these topics is first given as a general proposition or hypothesis that seems to derive logically from Wilson's model; then it is discussed as an issue in child development theory and research.

Proposition 1: Group Differences in Social Behavior. Children from one population (such as a particular racial or ethnic line) may be genetically more inclined to exhibit a given social behavior than children from another population.

If we should substitute in this hypothesis the words *physical features* for *social behavior*, there would be no question that the proposition is true. People generally agree that such differences among children as skin color, hair type and distribution, and certain facial features are the result of genetic differences in the children's population lines or ancestries. Furthermore, it is generally agreed that the genetic determinants of these characteristics do not allow the usual environmental forces to alter the characteristics. (Plastic surgery and skin or hair transplanting would be considered "unusual" environmental forces.)

But when we turn from such readily observed physical traits, and from such special population-linked diseases as sickle-cell anemia and certain forms of skin cancer, the truth of this first proposition is not at all clear. In the realms of psychological and social characteristics, the great debate continues as to whether observed differences between groups of people are more the result of genetic than of environmental factors. And particularly in the political-social climate of today's world, questions of this type are debated with great emotion. No ethnic or social class or religious subgroup wishes to have uncomplimentary traits that are found among its members attributed to a genetic base shared by everyone in the subgroup. They would much prefer that undesirable characteristics be blamed on environmental forces, on unfavorable or disadvantageous circumstances that can be improved, thus transforming the undesirable into the desirable. So questions raised within sociobiological theory are not simply theoretical scientific curiosities; they are among the most incendiary of the political-social issues faced in the world today.

In the area of psychological characteristics, the most recent, prominent illustration of the nature-nurture question arose in the late 1960s when Arthur R. Jensen, a University of California psychologist, made an extensive survey of intelligence test results for children and youths of different ethnic lines. He concluded that white children on the average score as much as 15 I.Q. points higher than black children. This finding came as no surprise to people in academic and political circles in America. Indeed, it was widely known that children of certain ethnic and social-class groups generally fared poorly in school and in competition for the more desirable occupations. Leaders in government and in philanthropic organizations generally attributed this deficit in school and occupational progress to disadvantageous social conditions—unsuitable environment, inadequate experience with those activities and objects that prepare middle- and upper-class white children to do well in school and in finding and holding jobs. Consequently, the government and philanthropic groups in the 1960s furnished large sums of money for special educational activities. At the preschool level, Head-Start programs were developed to prepare minority children for entering the primary grades with a background of experience that would enable them to read, write, and compute as well as their majority age-mates. Upward-Bound programs were designed to do the same for teenage youths who wished to enter college.

So Jensen's discovery of intelligence test score differences between the average black and average white student did not greatly surprise or distress either the general populace or the scientific and political communities. Rather, what disturbed political liberals among educators, scientists, and social activists was Jensen's citing genetic endowment as the chief cause for the differences. Translated into sociobiological terms, his contention was that the gene pool from which modern blacks have drawn their inheritance does not equip them as well for developing symbolic reasoning skills (as measured on the typical intelligence test) as does the pool from which white children have drawn their inheritance. And when many Head-Start programs reported disappointing results from their attempts to upgrade the school performance of minority-group children, Jensen suggested that the children's genetic endowment rather than an inadequate background of experience was mainly to blame. His computations led him to propose that 80 percent of the difference in I.Q. scores among members of certain groups is attributable to genetic rather than environmental influences (Jensen, 1969, 1973; Scarr-Salapatek, 1971a, 1971b).

After Jensen reported his conclusions, social activists and scientists arrayed themselves on both sides of the controversy, and others positioned themselves in the middle. Many who entered the fray were armed chiefly with emotional rhetoric and name calling. But others have deserved more serious consideration, for they founded their arguments on data and thoughtful lines of reasoning. While some scientists, including some geneticists, have supported Jensen's proposal, a larger number who have expressed themselves in print have either (1) directly opposed him, contending that he is wrong and that differences in average test scores between groups are the result of environmental factors and the shortcomings of the intelligence tests used in the studies or (2) taken a middle position, claiming that faults in Jensen's methodology or line of logic cast such serious doubts on his conclusions that the issue must be considered still unsettled (Hebb, 1970; Hirsch, 1970; Layzer, 1974; Lerner, 1976). (At present, my social conscience inclinations dispose me to hope that Jensen is wrong; but after reading the arguments on both sides, I find that for me the issue remains unresolved. The sort of data needed to give unequivocal answers to the questions still do not seem to be available.)

The purpose in mentioning here this nature–nurture controversy over the sources of intellectual skill is not to analyze the arguments of both sides in detail, but rather, the purpose is twofold. First, it is to point out that from the viewpoint of Wilson's sociobiological theory, what Jensen has proposed is not at all impossible. In sociobiology, the idea that different populations carry different gene pools that result in different characteristics for the two populations is not limited to such physical features as skin color or proneness to certain diseases. Populations can differ as well in the pools of genes that contribute to differences in both psychological (such as intelligence or emotional reactions) and social (competitiveness, cooperativeness, gregariousness, and so on) characteristics. So theoretically, human populations, like subhuman populations, *can* display social differences that have a genetic base. Whether they actually *do* exhibit such genetically based social differences is a question to be settled, not by armchair argument, but by empirical investigation.

The second purpose in mentioning the intelligence score debate is to suggest that the task of investigating proposition 1—that differences in certain social behaviors among groups may have a genetic base—can be expected to be as complex and engender at least as much public controversy as the intelligence score issue. Many social activists, including some members of the scientific community, are not likely to endorse the study of the proposition if the results might fail to support their political-social proclivities. However, in the long run, avoiding the investigation of such questions will do nothing to solve the social problems to which the questions are related. Instead, people will continue to base their beliefs about the causes of social behavior differences on the sources of belief they have always used—the opinions of their elders, their own experiences with people of different social groups, and the voices or writings of people they regard as authorities. Constructive social action might better be founded on more secure empirical evidence than is generally available today.

To summarize these implications about the first proposition, we can conclude that:

1. From the viewpoint of sociobiological theory, it is possible that differences in social behavior among children whose inheritance derives from different populations may be caused, at least partly, by differences in the gene pools of those populations.

2. The question of which, if any, of the social behavior differences among groups of children do have a genetic base needs to be settled by empirical investigation. Such investigation can be expected to encounter major difficulties, not only because of the technical problems involved but also because of the opposition of political activists.

3. Constructive social action, designed to help achieve the ideals of nations and their citizens, would appear to be more efficient if based on more valid data about proposition 1 than is currently at hand.

Proposition 2: Individual Differences in Social Behavior. Some children within a given population may be genetically more inclined to exhibit a given social behavior than other children in that same population.

As indicated in our earlier discussion of Wilson's theory, no two members of a population (except monozygotic or identical twins) inherit exactly the same mixture of genes. Each child in a population (except identical twins) develops according to her own unique genetic map. Likewise, each child's environment (including each monozygotic twin's) is different from every other child's, at least in its details. Thus, no two children are alike. But when we try to account for why a given child differs from another, we come back to the nature–nurture question. To what extent has a given difference resulted from genetic as compared to environmental influences? In other words, has the genetic endowment that underlies a particular trait or behavior provided narrow boundaries or wide boundaries within which environment can exert influence?

In proposition 1 we were asking such questions about group differences in social behavior. Is one population group genetically more prone than another to exhibit a particular social characteristic, such as altruism, competitiveness, pugnacity, peaceful means of settling disputes, communal living, nomadic living, and many others? Under proposition 2 we are asking the same questions about individuals within the same population. And the implications to be drawn about the issue are basically the same. According to sociobiological theory, individual differences among children in social behavior can be seated, at least partly, in differences in the gene combinations the children have inherited. The technical difficulties in sorting out heredity and environmental forces through empirical investigations of children are great, and political-social opposition to such research can be expected to arise as it has in the past. But people who are responsible for guiding children's growth—parents, teachers, pediatricians, social workers, and the like—are likely to make better judgments toward promoting each child's social development if they have more valid information than is now generally available about the genetic bases of various social behaviors.

The significance of this last point about the usefulness of better information can perhaps be illustrated by a sample of the questions a typical parent or teacher or club leader faces when working with children.

To what extent are a child's submissive or dominant or cooperative or introversive actions a result of a genetic or "natural" tendency to behave in such a manner? How much room is there for environmental forces to alter the course of such traits or tendencies?

To what extent does an inner genetic time clock, such as the one that appears to determine the advent of puberty, determine the time at which children can be expected to acquire particular social behaviors? In other words, is there a time when the child becomes ready, as a result of genetic timing, to profit most from experiences designed to promote particular social traits or skills, such as altruism, verbal communication, abiding by group rules, and sharing the labor in group endeavors?

Is there any truth at all in beliefs of the past that antisocial acts of children and youths are based, at least partly, on "a bad blood line" or "bad seed"? Or, in more modern terminology, are there actually such phenomena as "psychopathic personalities," meaning people whose underlying genetic endowment so predisposes them to antisocial acts that efforts to teach them prosocial behavior are destined to fail?

These are the types of questions additional evidence about human sociobiology and child development might answer and thereby help us manage our social institutions and child-raising practices to better achieve our social ideals.

Proposition 3: Expectations for Altruism. The greater the genetic similarity between two individuals, such as two children, the greater the degree of altruism they will display toward each other.

Whereas our first two propositions illustrated implications drawn from the general structure of neo-Darwinism, this third proposition illustrates an hypothesis of a more specific variety. It is an extension to humans of a kinship theory that zoologists have recently built from studies of altruistic (self-sacrificing) behavior among insects—ants, bees, wasps, and termites—that differ in the extent of their sociality (Hamilton, 1964; Wilson, 1975; Trivers and Hare, 1976; Alexander and Sherman, 1977).

In this kinship theory, an act is called "altruistic" if it benefits another organism while harming the organism performing the act. And to make *benefit* and *harm* easy to measure objectively, benefit and harm are assessed in terms of the reproductive success of an organism, that is, the organism's success in producing its own offspring. An act is altruistic if it harms the individual's chances of producing its own offspring while aiding another organism in producing and maintaining its own. At this point the line of reasoning will not make sense unless we recall that within sociobiology the goal of nature is not the survival of the individual but the survival of the genetic line. And in some cases in which organisms are struggling against difficult environmental circumstances, a self-sacrificing act will better ensure that the organism's genetic line, as carried by a close relative of the individual, will prosper than if each individual behaved entirely selfishly without regard for the welfare of others. When the males of the tribe array themselves in the front line of defense against dangerous predators, each of them is reducing his chances of personal survival and reproductive success more than if he tried to escape on his own, leaving the females and young at the mercy of the predators. But this cooperative, altruistic act helps maximize the chance that the large proportion of his genes, which are also carried by the close relatives he is defending, will survive through future generations.

This general line of logic suggests why natural selection over the centuries encourages the development of altruistic behavior by promoting the survival and reproduction of individuals that carry genes particularly conducive to such acts. However, in such a general form, the logic does not help us specify the conditions under which an altruistic act rather than a selfish act can be expected. And it is here that zoologists' recent work on kinship theory may offer some help. Scientists have now devised formulas for estimating under what conditions natural selection will favor genes conducive to altruistic acts. The formulas include two main factors: (1) the degree of genetic relatedness of the two organisms concerned (that is, the proportion of genes common to the two individuals) and (2) the comparative cost and benefit to the organism carrying out the act and to the recipient of the act. As Trivers and Hare have put it:

> For natural selection to favor an altruistic act directed at a relative, the benefit of the act times the altruist's r (degree of relatedness) to the relative must be greater than the cost of the act (1976, p. 249).

In other words, the theory proposes that, through the evolutionary process, genes have been selected that encourage an organism to engage in more self-sacrificing behavior for the benefit of close relatives than for distant relatives. But in all instances, altruism has limits. The individual will bear a higher personal cost for the sake of closely related individuals, but when the cost becomes so high that it exceeds the product of (a) benefit to the relative times (b) the degree of relatedness, then the actor can be expected to behave selfishly rather than altruistically.

Such, then, is the general direction of reasoning and the beginnings of specifying conditions in kinship theory as based on and tested in altruistic-versus-selfish behavior among social insects. But what might this all have to do with child development? It provides some hypotheses about the bases and conditions of altruism in humans. It suggests some lines of inquiry for investigating such hypotheses as proposition 3, the hypothesis that natural selection for the human species has operated in such a way as to genetically predispose children to display more altruism toward others who are closely related to them than toward people more distantly related. The proposition implies such questions as the following:

1. To what extent do children exhibit self-sacrificing behavior toward members of their family because the children have been taught to do so, and to what extent is such behavior a result of genetic predisposition?

2. A common ideal of social democracy is to have children treat other people on the basis of each person's individual behavior rather than a person's membership in some subgroup of society (a family, tribal, religious, ethnic, or socioeconomic subgroup). Does this mean that in order to achieve the ideal, those people in charge of child rearing must counteract a natural (genetically based) propensity of children to behave more altruistically toward people who are closely related to them than toward people with whom they have fewer genes in common?

Thus, studies of animal behavior provide suggestions about issues to investigate in the field of child development and about some of the possible answers or solutions to those issues. But this shift from hypotheses or principles regarding the social behavior of ants and bees to those regarding children is accomplished only in the face of some large and potentially dangerous *ifs*. If this kinship theory is really valid for social insects, and *if* its general principles apply to humans, and *if* there are not too many other conditions involved that affect altruism among humans, then kinship theory may contribute to an understanding of child development. In any case, the theory points the direction for interesting investigations of children's social behavior. Though the idea that people may "naturally" act more favorably toward those who are in their own close "blood line" is not at all new, ways of explaining and specifying such relationships, and of testing the validity of the idea, are being produced today by zoologists in more promising forms than have been available in the past.

To close this discussion of the implications of sociobiology for child development theory, we will again note the words of Hinde from the opening pages of Part 6:

> Sometimes such studies [of social behavior in animals] are useful to the extent that animals resemble man, and sometimes they help just because animals are different and permit the study of issues in a simplified, isolated, or exaggerated form. . . . But the use of animals involves dangers: it is so easy to make rash generalizations, to slip from firm fact to flight of fancy, to select examples to fit preconceptions. Studies of animals must therefore be used circumspectly, and the limitations of their usefulness specified (1974, p. xiii).

We turn now to an assessment of Wilson's sociobiological theory from the viewpoint of the standards described in Chapter 1.

WILSON'S SOCIOBIOLOGY: AN ASSESSMENT

In explaining my reasons for the ratings on the accompanying chart, I begin in general with items awarded high marks, and then consider the ones with lower ratings.

Item 1, concerning how closely the theory reflects the real world, is divided into two subscales, the first focusing on Wilson's chief interest and the second focusing on the main subject of this book. I rated Wilson's model high on item 1a because in his very large volume he has profusely illustrated each concept in the theory with examples from field studies of a broad variety of species. However, many sociologists and social psychologists would probably rate Wilson lower on this dimension because they would charge him with crediting a population's genetic composition with too great a role in determining the social patterns in the population. In other words, they would accuse him of being too much an hereditarian and of ignoring the role of experience or learning. Although it is not true that Wilson ignores the place of learning in social organization, he does see genetic structure as setting narrower boundary lines within which learning can take place than many social scientists would likely accept. In Wilson's opinion, what evolves is a set of genetically based capacities to

WILSON'S THEORY _____

How well do I think the theory meets the standards?

The Standards	Very Well	Moderately Well	Very Poorly
1. Reflects the real world of: **1a.** Subhuman species and more "primitive" humans	X		
1b. Children			X
2. Is clearly understandable	X		
3. Explains the past and predicts the future		X	
4. Guides child rearing			X
5. Is internally consistent	X		
6. Is economical	X		
7. Is falsifiable		X	
8. Stimulates new discoveries	Potential X		Actual X
9. Is self-satisfying		X	

learn certain things rather than others and with a certain degree of ease:

> Pavlov was simply wrong when he postulated that "any natural phenomenon chosen at will may be converted into conditioned stimuli." Only small parts of the brain resemble a tabula rasa; this is true even for human beings. The remainder is more like an exposed negative waiting to be dipped into developer fluid (1975, p. 156).

Thus, while Wilson might be criticized for taking a position toward the hereditarian camp in nature–nurture controversies, when more data have been compiled, it may turn out that he is correct, or nearly so. In any event, I have given him the benefit of such doubts in marking item 1a on the basis of the wide range of field studies with which he has buttressed his description of sociobiological theory.

In judging the model's clarity (item 2), internal consistency (item 5), and economy of explanation (item 6), I have agreed with a book reviewer who, in *Contemporary Psychology*, called Wilson's volume "a lucid, superbly crafted zoological text" (Cairns, 1977, p. 1). As for the theory's clarity, even the more complicated parts of Wilson's explanation should be easily understood by anyone with a moderate level of knowledge in genetics, mathematics, and probability theory. In regard to economy, his model does not seem encumbered with more concepts than the minimum needed to explain the phenomena he discusses.

The ratings on items 1b and 4 (children's real world and guidance for child rearing) are low, since Wilson did not deal directly with any issues of child life. But if the theory were to be assessed for its potential to generate ideas about children's social behavior and child-raising practices, I would rate it higher. Wilson's model holds numerous implications for child development issues, but it requires the efforts of child psychologists to identify these implications and devise ways to investigate them. To illustrate, here are three questions that logically derive from sociobiological theory:

> To what extent does the development of cooperation and competition depend on children's social training in contrast to their genetic similarity?

> From one generation to the next, do certain kinds of social behavior develop increasingly early in children's lives? And if so, to what degree is such precocity the result of changes in the genetic composition of the population?

> How much are children from a given population (such as an inbred tribal or ethnic group) genetically predisposed to display one pattern of social behavior (such as a tendency to settle disputes by reasoning) than another (a tendency to settle disputes by physical violence)?

Items 3 and 7 (explains past and predicts future; is falsifiable) can conveniently be considered together, for they share a weakness in common. The weakness is that sociobiological theory, at its present stage of development, is composed of a set of broad concepts and principles intended to explain the evolution of all social behavior in all species; but as yet the theory is not sufficiently detailed and precise to produce an unequivocal description of any population's past social development or future social evolution. It is still at the stage of a natural history, with theorists observing social behavior in one or two species, proposing concepts that could explain such behavior, then extending the application of these concepts by "logical reasoning" to other species without rigorously testing the validity of this extension. As Wilson has pointed out:

> The greatest snare in sociobiological reasoning is the ease with which it is conducted. Whereas the physical sciences deal with precise results that are usually difficult to explain, sociobiology has imprecise results that can be too easily explained by many different schemes (1975, p. 28).

The cure for this shortcoming, Wilson says, lies in adopting methods of "strong inference." This means deriving alternative hypotheses from the theory, creating crucial experiments or field observations that will reveal which of the competing hypotheses is the most tenable, and then accepting or revising the theory's concepts in light of these test results (Wilson, 1975, p. 28). Until sociobiological models reach this stage of postulational-deductive methodology, they will continue to be nonfalsifiable and will furnish inconclusive explanations of the past and future.

On item 8, I have marked Wilson's theory for both its actual and its potential value in stimulating new discoveries. His book *Sociobiology* (1975) is too recent a publication to have had a chance to motivate much new research, thus my low rating for its actual impact. But if the early lively response in both scientific and popular periodicals is a good indicator of the theory's ultimate impact, then *Sociobiology*'s potential for stimulating new discoveries deserves a high rating (Cairns, 1977, p. 1).

For the final assessment standard—how self-satisfying the theory is—I have marked Wilson's sociobiology in the moderate range to reflect a counterbalancing between (1) the strengths of the theorist's line of reasoning about species in general and (2) the weaknesses that surface when he applies this reasoning to explain complex human behavior. In particular, I would like the kind of detailed extension of the theory that would account for why children's social behavior develops as it does during the first two decades of life. Or, stated another way, I would hope the future development of sociobiology might bridge the gap that currently exists between theories of (1) how social organization evolves among different species and (2) how the social behavior of individual members of a species develops during their lifetime.

FOR FURTHER READING

Wilson, Edward O. (1975) *Sociobiology: The New Synthesis*. Cambridge, Mass.: Belknap Press of Harvard University Press, 1975. This is the volume on which the present chapter is based.

For a sample of the way other contemporary zoologists explain the biological sources of social development, consult the following two books, the first from Germany and the second from Britain:

Eibl-Eibesfeldt, Irenaus. (1975) *Ethology: The Biology of Behavior*. 2d ed. New York: Holt, Rinehart, and Winston.

Hinde, Robert A. (1974) *Biological Bases of Human Social Behavior*. New York: McGraw-Hill.

PART 7

THE PSYCHOANALYTIC TRADITION

A search for developmental causes and cures of neuroses.

From the viewpoint of the general public, the most unsettling theory of child development proposed over the past century has been Sigmund Freud's psychoanalysis. In the late 1800s and throughout the 1900s many people have been shocked by Freud's contention that sexual motives—with sex interpreted in a broad sense—underlie much if not all human behavior. More shocking still has been the notion of infantile sexuality. To the lay public and medical profession of the late 1800s and early 1900s, the idea that little children have sensuous thoughts that are important determinants of their personal-social adjustment was clearly a distortion of the truth at the hands of a dirty-minded neurotic (S. Freud, 1917, pp. 323–325; S. Freud, 1938, p. 9; Hartmann, 1959, p. 11).

Not as morally shocking but no less disturbing personally was Freud's suggestion that much of the time we do not consciously know why we act the way we do. Instead of behaving as rational beings, we are driven and manipulated by primitive urges and by traumas from our past that reside in what Freud called our *unconscious mind*. In the sixteenth century, Copernicus had already insulted mankind by suggesting that the earth was not the center of the universe. Darwin had carried the insult further by proposing that man was a descendent of lower forms of life and therefore not the divine, unique being that man had led himself to believe. Now Freud pushed insult another step by contending that man's conscious mind was neither master of his fate nor captain of his soul; instead, man was a victim of his own unconscious drives.

However, over the years since Freud first put forth his theory, he has gained a substantial following of believers. His work, and the revisions of it by later generations, now represents a major branch of psychology. Indeed, many of his key ideas have nearly achieved the status of common sense. For these reasons, the psychoanalytic tradition deserves a prominent place in a survey of theories of child development.

Chapter 11 presents central concepts of the theory as Freud himself devised them. At the end of the chapter is a brief description of contributions subsequently made by Freud's daughter Anna specifically concerning the childhood portion of the overall theory.

Chapter 12 illustrates a major extension of psychoanalysis by a disciple of Freud, Erik Erikson. Of the various revised versions of psychoanalysis fashioned during the twentieth century, Erikson's has been the most significant for the field of child development, particularly for the years of adolescence.

CHAPTER 11

SIGMUND FREUD'S PSYCHOANALYSIS

Often we best understand how a theorist arrived at his model of development if we recognize the sequence of experiences that were instrumental in guiding the direction of his theorizing. Since this seems particularly true in the case of psychoanalysis, we will begin the account of Freud's model by looking briefly at the medical puzzles that stimulated him to speculate about the nature of children and the forces that determine their development.

Sigmund Freud (1856–1939) was an Austrian neurologist who, early in his career of private medical practice in Vienna, encountered some very perplexing cases. Patients came to him with a variety of ailments, such as paralysis of the hand or aches or blurred vision, that could not be explained by traditional physiological knowledge. Although the patients' symptoms suggested the nerve tissue had been damaged, examination showed the nervous system to be intact.

How could people suffer such ailments without any organic impairment of the nervous system? While Freud was pondering this problem, he learned about the work that Jean Charcot was conducting on hypnotism in Paris. Charcot had shown that under hypnotic spell people could be told that they would have one or another bodily symptom after they awakened from the hypnotic state, but they would not remember the cause of this symptom. They would not recall that they had received a suggestion under hypnosis. And, indeed, after coming out of hypnosis, they did exhibit the suggested symptoms, such as paralysis of a leg, numbness of the skin, or deafness. Charcot, in addition, was able to use hypnosis to relieve people of certain symptoms. Under hypnosis, patients were told that they no longer suffered the ailment that

225

had brought them to the clinic. Upon awakening, at least some of these patients had lost the symptom of which they had complained (S. Freud, 1910, p. 21).

Freud's interest in Charcot's experiments was so great that he spent the year 1885–1886 in Paris studying the methods and effects of hypnosis. At the same time, he asked the more basic questions that might explain these curious phenomena: What relation might there be between the strange cases Freud faced in his medical practice and the cases Charcot exhibited in his clinic? How must human personality be structured and how must mind be related to body in order to cause such things to occur (S. Freud, 1910, pp. 16–22)?

In answer to these queries, Freud, over the next several decades, developed his psychoanalytic theory of personality. Included in the theory is a conception of child development that has exerted significant influence over a number of areas of child psychology today—child psychiatry, counseling children and adolescents, nursery school teaching methods, and research in child development. Certain concepts from Freudian theory have now been generally accepted by psychologists, educators, and social workers, even those who reject most of psychoanalytic theory. In effect, Freud's views have had a decided influence on people concerned with raising children.

Psychoanalytic theory in its entirety is quite complex. Not only does it have many ramifications, but adherents of psychoanalysis often disagree with each other on important issues. Freud himself altered the theory in major ways on several occasions. For these reasons, the following discussion presents only a simplified sketch of the theory's main elements.

The early part of the chapter is divided into descriptions of: (1) levels of consciousness, (2) the apparatus of mental life, (3) psychosexual stages of child development, and (4) the development of consciousness and ego strength. After these, there is a brief review of some contributions to psychoanalytic theory and practice by Anna Freud.

LEVELS OF CONSCIOUSNESS

Early in the process of formulating his theory, Freud proposed that each person has an unconscious aspect of mind in addition to the conscious aspect of which the individual is aware. By *unconscious* Freud meant a sort of mental receptacle for ideas, a receptacle from which the individual cannot recall ideas at will. These ideas, of which we are unaware, influence our actions just as much as if they were conscious. In effect, much of what we do arises from unconscious motivation (S. Freud, 1923, p. 4).

The concept of an unconscious state of mind was not entirely new in the field of philosophy. An occasional theorist over the centuries had postulated such an aspect. However, it was Freud who elaborated the concept and assigned it a central role in behavior.

By proposing the unconscious, Freud was able to account for otherwise unexplainable disorders suffered by his patients. He hypothesized that a person who faces a distressing, unsolved problem in her daily life will find the problem psychologically painful. So the individual's personality, to escape this pain of unresolved conflicts, automatically resolves the problem by pushing the distressing thoughts out of consciousness. The patient actively "forgets" the matter. But Freud believed that such forgotten material does not leave the mind. Instead, it is only relegated to an unconscious condition—in other words, it is "repressed"—to keep the sufferer unaware of its existence and, consequently, enable her to feel more at peace. But the problem, now unconscious, continues to agitate, and it expresses itself in devious ways. One mode of expression can be a bodily ailment, such as a headache or paralysis of some part of the body. So it was that Freud concluded that the strange symptoms displayed by his patients were caused by unresolved mental conflicts that seethed insistently in their unconscious minds. Not only were these bodily disorders, which he called *conversion hysteria symptoms*, the consequence of repressed mental conflicts, but so, Freud believed, was the entire array of neurotic symptoms, an array including phobias, obsessions, compulsions, and anxieties.

To alleviate such symptoms—in effect, to cure the neuroses—Freud proposed that the repressed conflict, which had originated in a problem of development earlier in the patient's life, had to be brought into consciousness. The patient had to recognize the origin of her difficulties and verbally relive the original conflict situation, but now working out the conflict in a constructive, emotionally satisfying manner and thus being cured of the neuroses.

In order to make his therapeutic scheme work, Freud had to devise a process for uncovering the unconscious conflicts and presenting them so that patients would accept the conflicts as true and deserving of serious attention. Early in his career Freud tried different means for uncovering unconscious conflicts. He began with hypnosis but, as he later reported, "I soon came to dislike hypnosis, for it was a temperamental and . . . mystical ally" (S. Freud, 1910, p. 22). Hence he gave it up in favor of free association and dream interpretation.

The process of *free association* consists of encouraging the patient to relax, usually on a couch, and to describe his free-flowing thoughts without editing them. The analyst listens to hours of such narration in order to locate underlying themes of conflict that are hints or symbols of hidden problems. By using the process of relaxed, free association, the therapist is assuming that "the repressed wishful impulse . . . is on the look-out for an opportunity of being activated, and when that happens it succeeds in sending into consciousness a disguised and unrecognizable substitute for what had been repressed" (S. Freud, 1910, p. 27). It is the analyst's task to unmask the significant elements of the patient's narration and reveal them for what they really are in the individual's past development.

In a like manner, Freud used *dream interpretation* as a window, albeit murky and distorted, for viewing the contents of the unconscious. He believed that during sleep, a censor force, which seeks to prevent unconscious conflicts from entering consciousness, is not as alert as during waking life. So dreams, in Freud's scheme, are products of the person's trying to satisfy wishes and solve problems during sleep. The dream serves as an audiovisual symbol of unconscious urges pressing for expression into consciousness. The clever analyst is a person skilled in interpreting dreams in a way that reveals the nature and source of the patient's unconscious conflicts (S. Freud, 1900).

The significance of Freud's reliance on free association and dream interpretation is twofold. First, both techniques were tools crucial to the conduct of his system of therapy. Second, and more important for our present purposes, they served almost exclusively as the sources of data about childhood on which he erected his model of development. Rather than spending his time directly observing children in the process of their development, Freud spent endless hours listening to adult neurotics produce memories of childhood. On these memories, extracted from free associations and dreams, he built his picture of sexual growth.

In addition to introducing a view of the mind as consisting of both conscious and unconscious aspects, Freud also distinguished two levels of unconsciousness. One level, he said, contains those ideas that are not in consciousness at the moment but that are latent. We can recall them, "bring them to mind," if we choose even though it may take a bit of effort. This first level Freud labeled the *preconscious*. The second level contains the truly repressed ideas, those held down purposely by the personality's resistance forces, because allowing them to enter consciousness would be too painful for the conscious personality to face. This second level, deeper and less accessible than the preconscious, is the *true* or prototype unconscious in the Freudian scheme. In a sense, then, the preconscious is a shadow zone between the open, bright conscious and the closed, dark unconscious (S. Freud, 1923, pp. 4–5). A person has thoughts or ideas at each of these levels.

THE PSYCHICAL APPARATUS

The levels of consciousness serve as a sort of three-tiered arena in which a person's psychic life takes place. Within the psychical arena, the three main functionaries that compete and cooperate to produce this performance were conceived by Freud to be the *id*, the *ego*, and the *superego*. In the course of a child's development, these three do not appear simultaneously. The id comes first—it is already present at birth. The ego develops out of the growing infant's efforts to satisfy his needs through transactions with the environment. Some years later the superego develops as an internal representative of the rules and values of the environment.

The way the development of the id, ego, and superego becomes intertwined with stages of the child's psychosexual growth is rather complex. In order to make this development easier to grasp, we will divide the explanation into two parts. The first, which comprises this section on psychical apparatus, treats the nature and functions of the id, ego, and superego. The second, in the next section, describes their relation to the psychosexual growth stages that Freud proposed.

As a preface to these matters, we need to recognize that all behavior, physical and psychological, needs energy to activate it. In psychoanalytic theory the sources of all energy are the instincts, with *instinct* defined as an inborn factor that gives force and direction to psychological activities. For at least three decades Freud experimented with various conceptions of instincts. Then in 1920 he settled on a basic pair of motivating forces, the *life* and *death* instincts, which he thought vied for expression and supremacy in directing psychic behavior throughout a person's life span. The influence of the life instinct is reflected in constructive acts, in acts of love and altruism. The influence of the death instinct is displayed in destructive acts, in hate and in aggression. Freud applied the word *libido* to the psychic energy deriving from the life instinct, but he coined no parallel term for the energy emitting from the death instinct (S. Freud, 1920).

From the viewpoint of the instincts, the process of living consists of a continual competition between the opposing life and death forces—love against hate, life preservation against self-destruction. Often a mode of behaving represents a fusion of the two, as when aggression against a threatening enemy (motivated by the death instinct) preserves one's life and promotes one's welfare (which is the objective of the life instinct). Although throughout childhood and well into adult life the evidences of the life instinct appear to be the more prominent, the ultimate victory obviously goes to the opposing force, when, at life's close, the organism loses all animation and returns to the passive inorganic state that is the ultimate aim of the death instinct.

Now that we have the pair of basic instinctual energy sources in mind, we turn to the psychical apparatus through which the forces are invested or expended. In psychoanalytic theory, the personality of the newborn consists of a single operating component called the *id*. It is at the unconscious level and "contains everything that is inherited, that is present at birth, that is laid down in the constitution—above all, therefore, the instincts" (S. Freud, 1938, p. 2). It is within this id that libido builds up as a sort of pressure, searching for expression. Seen another way, libidinal energy arising from the id assumes the form of *needs* that demand fulfillment. The expenditure or release of libido is experienced by the infant as pleasure. The blocking of libidinal release is experienced as pain. So the id operates on the *pleasure principle*, which says: "Get as much pleasure as possible as soon as possible without regard for anyone else or anything else in the world." In its converse form the principle becomes: Avoid as much pain as possible.

Hence, psychoanalysis pictures the newborn baby as all id, seeking only to satisfy its needs for food, for drink, for warmth, for elimination of body wastes, for freedom from skin irritants, and for affection, affection in the sense of being cuddled by its mother or mother substitute. The newborn's awareness of its condition and of the world is ostensibly very fuzzy. Freudians suppose that a baby does not distinguish among objects in its environment, nor does it recognize a difference between itself and other people or things. The newborn is aware only of discomfort or pain which signals unfulfilled needs that require attention. The only observable methods the infant has for reacting to these pain or tension signals are crying, mouthing, and randomly moving its arms and legs.

But as time passes and the infant's experience with the world increases, more precise awareness of the environment begins to develop. The earliest level of awareness results in the *primary process,* which is the baby's act of creating in its memory an image of an object that will fulfill a need. For example, when the newborn feels hunger pangs, he automatically cries until someone feeds him. The food reduces the tension of hunger, and the baby experiences pleasure. As days pass, this cycle of hunger, feeding, and tension reduction is played over and over, so that gradually the taste, smell, feel, and sight of the food and of the feeder (usually the mother) are stored as images in the baby's memory. As a result, the infant, by means of the primary process, can now imagine those things that will bring a particular variety of satisfaction or a particular mode of expending libidinal energy.

It is important to recognize that the primary process is a rather chaotic, irrational mode of thought that does not distinguish between reasonable and unreasonable need-fulfilling images. The concern of the id and its primary process thinking is to gain satisfaction, regardless of whether or not the method of satisfaction is practical or will be tolerated by the environment. What the personality next requires, then, is a component that recognizes the nature of the environment, as well as the demands of the id, and can, therefore, provide realistic methods of investing energy. This second component of the psychical apparatus is called the *ego.* Freud postulated that the ego arises from, or separates out of, the id and is fueled by libidinal energy from the id. In effect, the id's primary process develops images of things that fulfill needs, but the image is only an initial, incomplete step toward satisfaction. Another agent, the ego, is required to bring the dream into reality. Freud explained that "the ego is that part of the id which has been modified by the direct influence of the external world through the medium" of conscious perception (S. Freud, 1923, p. 15). Furthermore, he proposed:

> It is to this ego that consciousness is attached; the ego controls the
> . . . discharge of excitations into the external world; it is the mental

agency which supervises all its own constituent processes, and which goes to sleep at night, though even then it exercises the censorship on dreams (1923, p. 7).

Hence, the ego serves as a decision maker that tries to negotiate a satisfactory solution to the conflicting demands that come on the one side from the id (which says "I want") and on the other side from the environment or "real world" (which says "You'll get it with a minimum of cost or pain only under these conditions"). Whereas the id works on the pleasure principle, the ego operates on the *reality principle,* which can be stated as: Recognize the conditions and demands of the real world, then seek methods of fulfilling the id's needs that are acceptable in such a world.

To play its role of negotiator, the ego is constantly assessing the kinds and strengths of needs arising from the id and at the same time is assessing the conditions of the environment. From this assessment, the ego attempts to devise behaviors that represent the best compromise between the id and the outside world. Or, as is sometimes the case, the ego must negotiate a compromise among several demands coming simultaneously from the id, such as the demands of hunger and fatigue arising at the same moment.

We noted that the id, by means of the primary process, associates certain objects with need fulfillment. These associations are stored as memory images. It is now up to the ego to turn the images into reality. This problem-solving act is called the *secondary process.* The individual's skills of perceiving, remembering, analyzing, and taking action develop from this constant interaction among (1) the id's needs, (2) the maturing bodily organs, such as eyes and ears, and (3) the ego's increasing awareness of the complexities of the world.

Our next concern is with the third component of the psychical apparatus, the *superego.* Early in a child's life the rules of the world —the rules of *do* and *don't*—are enforced by the environment. The infant, in Freud's system, has no inborn inner voice telling her what is right and what is wrong. In effect, the child is born neither moral nor immoral, but is *amoral.* She has no knowledge of good or bad. Her morality is simply that of getting pleasure (as demanded by the id) in a manner that will avoid punishment or pain (a manner arranged by the ego). The very young child, therefore, does not automatically feel bad or guilty or ashamed when she transgresses one of society's expectations. She feels bad only when the consequences of her behavior are either the withholding of rewards or the application of punishment. It is usually the child's parents who produce her good and bad feelings by manipulating the system of rewards and punishments she will experience.

Although children are not born with knowledge of what is good and what is evil, they are born with a capacity for two things: (1) to develop internal values and (2) to feel good (pleased and proud) when they abide by these values and to feel bad (sad, ashamed, and guilty) when transgressing them. Over the years of childhood and adolescence this capacity acquires contents in the form of moral values the child adopts from her environment. It is this third component of the growing personality that Freud labeled *superego*. How and why the superego appears and grows are matters intimately involved in the psychosexual stages of development and will be discussed in connection with them. For the present we will restrict our attention to the role the superego plays in the mental life of the older child and adolescent.

Just as Freud pictured the ego as developing out of the id, so he saw the superego arising from the ego (S. Freud, 1923, pp. 18–29). He explained:

> This new psychical agency continues to carry on the functions which have hitherto been performed by the people in the external world: It observes the ego, gives it orders, judges it and threatens it with punishments, exactly like the parents whose place it has taken (1938, p. 62).

Freud conceived of the superego as having two aspects, the *conscience* and the *ego ideal*. The conscience represents the "should-nots" of the child's world, the things for which he has been punished. The ego ideal represents the "shoulds," the positive moral values the child has been taught. Whereas the very young child must be punished for transgressions and rewarded for good behavior by his parents, the maturing child gradually does not need outside sanctions. His superego plays the punishing and rewarding roles for him. For disobeying the values he has now accepted as his own, the child's conscience punishes him with guilt, shame, and fear. For abiding by his moral values, his ego ideal rewards him with feelings of self-righteousness, self-praise, and pride.

With the addition of the superego to the id and ego, the apparatus of the mind is complete. The behavior of older children and adolescents is thus a result of the way the ego has negotiated a settlement among three conflicting sources of demands: (1) the id, which insists on immediate fulfillment of wishes, (2) the environment, which sets conditions under which wishes can be satisfied without punishment, and (3) the superego, which presses the youth to live up to a set of moral values he has incorporated from his parents and from other significant people in his world.

As the ego develops over the years, it evolves techniques or habits for accommodating the conflicting demands made on it. A strong, mature ego uses direct means to accomplish this. It frankly admits the nature of instinctual demands, environmental forces, and the superego's commands. Then it proposes forthright, reasoned ways to effect a solution that satisfies each source of demand to an acceptable degree. But an ego that is weak, still childish and immature, slips into using more devious techniques of adjustment, techniques that Freud called *defense mechanisms.* The ego, in effect, seeks to fool itself and others concerning the state of affairs it faces, for it feels inadequate to solve the conflict among the demands that confront it.

The most significant defense technique, *repression,* has already been described. It is the automatic, nonconscious process of pushing distressing matters out of the consciousness and into the unconscious. Though repression clears the conscious mind of worries, the repressed material continues to foment distress in the unconscious and produce the sorts of neurotic symptoms that Freud met in his medical practice.

A second mechanism is *sublimation,* the substitution of a culturally higher, socially more acceptable mode of expressing sexual or aggressive energy. Such altruistic acts as caring for children or aiding the sick, or such artistic endeavors as writing poetry or performing a ballet, are viewed by Freudians as substitutes for direct sexual behavior.

A third defense technique is *regression,* which consists of returning to an earlier, more primitive mode of adjusting to problems. A person turns to this device when facing a new or distressing situation in which her more advanced techniques are not readily applied. As a simple example, a twelve-year-old girl feels frustrated when her mother criticizes her in public, so the girl begins sucking her thumb or the corner of her handkerchief as she did when she sought solace as an infant.

A mechanism that has been readily adopted into common-sense understanding is that of *projection.* When a child senses within his own personality a motive of which he is ashamed or which he fears, he may not admit its existence consciously to himself, but instead he may constantly see this motive in other people. He attributes to others those unacceptable acts and feelings that his own id urges him to express. Thus, the child who harbors hate in his own unconscious will accuse others of hating him, claiming at the same time that he himself bears no malice. Likewise, a person who is repressing strong sexual desires of which he is ashamed will assume that others are trying to seduce or assault him sexually.

The device called *reaction formation* has been particularly useful to psychoanalysts, for it enables them to explain behavior that would otherwise appear to refute typical predictions that derive from the theory. Reaction formation consists of a child's adopting behavior that is just the opposite of his instinctual urge. For instance, a child may act compulsively clean, avoiding dirt and frequently washing his hands and changing his clothes. The direct interpretation of such behavior is that the child desires to be clean —cleanliness is his basic need. But Freudians would suspect something different. Since in their theory the basic drives involve such sensuous pleasure as sexual stimulation and bowel and urinary functions, they would propose that the child is not motivated by a basic cleanliness need. Instead, he really wants to become soiled, to mess around in dirt and feces, but he has been punished by his parents for expressing such desires so now he feels his basic urges are wicked. To control them, he represses the original desires and in his conscious life adopts the opposite sort of behavior as a desperate means of mastering the urges of which he is ashamed. In short, his behavior represents a reaction against his instinctual drives.

Three more defense mechanisms can be briefly described. *Compensation* is a device by which the child seeks to overcome a personal or environmental barrier by substituting success in some other realm of life than the one in which she suffers the weakness. *Rationalization* consists of giving a socially acceptable reason for a behavior that actually was motivated by a less honorable reason. *Escape* is leaving the scene of a distressing experience. The escape can be either physical, such as a girl's running away from home, or psychological, such as a youth's retreating into daydreams in school when the lesson is confusing.

These defense mechanisms, which are only some of those identified by Freud and his followers, illustrate the kinds of strategies the ego employs to satisfy, as well as possible, the conflicting demands made on it.

Now that we have identified the main components of the psyche and their functions, we can look at the psychosexual growth stages involved in the development of these components.

PSYCHOSEXUAL STAGES OF DEVELOPMENT

To account for the sorts of dreams and memories of childhood that his patients described, Freud produced a model of child development that featured a series of growth stages. The current neuroses of his patients, he thought, were the result of inadequate solutions to the problems the individual had faced as a child at one or more of these stages. He labeled these growth steps *psychosexual phases* because he believed the development of the personality—the psyche—was crucially influenced by the manner in which the child learned to expend sex energy (*libido*) from one period of life to the next. In other words, Freud proposed that the most significant emotional experiences during childhood and adolescence are those associated with expending libido in relation to a series of particularly sensitive zones of the body on which children's attention focuses at different points of development. These *erogenous zones*, in chronological sequence, are the mouth, the anus, and the genital organs. At the time a particular zone is the chief focus for the release of libido, the child not only derives sensuous (sexual, in a broad meaning of the term) pleasure from use of the zone, but his relationships with other people are heavily influenced by the way they respond to his attention to the zone. In essence, Freud proposed that the personal-social relationships the child develops—his feelings about himself and others, and his ways of treating himself and others—are founded in the experiences the child has at each psychosexual stage. Personality problems that arise as the child seeks to work his way through a stage may go unresolved, be repressed by the frantic ego, and continue to agitate within the unconscious so as to cause neuroses for years afterwards.

Although the number of developmental periods identified between birth and adulthood may vary slightly from one psychoanalytic theorist to another, all of them cite at least five major stages: oral (ages 0–1), anal (ages 2–3), infantile-genital (ages 3–4 or so), latency (ages 4 or 5 to puberty), mature-genital (from mid-teens to adulthood). We will examine these stages and the substages involved in several of them.

BIRTH:
THE TRAUMATIC BEGINNING

Birth is not a stage of growth, but it is a highly significant event in psychoanalytic theory because it is regarded as the first great shock of the child's life. In the Freudian view, the newborn is overwhelmed with stimulation from the environment into which he or she emerges from the womb. The reaction is intense fear, for the undeveloped ego has no means to cope adequately with such a flood of stimuli. The birth trauma, then, is the prototype of all subsequent fear-producing situations the child will meet as she grows to old age. When later in life she is confronted by extreme stimuli, either extreme instinctual demands or extreme pressures from the environment, and her existing ego techniques are ineffective for mastering the stimuli, the original fear occasioned by the birth trauma is reactivated, and she reverts to infantile behavior. Consequently, according to Freudian theory, an easier birth, involving less shock upon entering the world, can be expected to build less fear into the unconscious of the growing child, and she may be able to face frustrating experiences later in life with greater emotional control.

STAGE 1: THE ORAL PERIOD
(AGES 0–1)

The psychoanalytic model of the child pictures the newborn not as a passive slab of damp clay on which environmental experiences will engrave a personality structure, but as a dynamic energy system pressing to expend its energy. Or more precisely, the id of the neonate is seeking to invest libidinal energy in images of objects that will satisfy the instinctual needs and bring the pleasure of release. This act of investment (the primary process of the id) is called *cathexis*. When the id channels energy into an image of an object, it is said to *cathecting* that object.

Following birth, the natural initial object for cathexis is the mother's breast or a suitable substitute, because it is through his mouth that the newborn must now obtain his life-sustaining nourishment. So also must he use his mouth and nose for breathing. The nerve endings in the lips and mouth are particularly sensitive and offer the infant special pleasure. Freud wrote:

> The baby's obstinate persistence in sucking gives evidence at an early stage of a need for satisfaction which, though it originates from and is instigated by the taking of nourishment, nevertheless strives to obtain pleasure independently of nourishment and for that reason may and should be termed *sexual* (1938, p. 11).

The adequacy with which the child satisfies the need for food, drink, and breath gives him his first impressions of the world and of his relation to it. Not only is his personality influenced by how soon and how completely the pent-up libidinal energy is released, but the atmosphere associated with how these needs for release are either met or neglected affects him also. If his mother holds him affectionately and soothingly during the feeding process, the child will pass through the oral period in a happier, more confident state than if he is never cuddled and if there are distressing sounds and sights bombarding him while feeding.

In addition to taking in food and drink, the oral zone is used by the infant to investigate the parts of the world he can reach. He examines most objects by putting them to his lips or into his mouth. Freud suggested that the basic reason the child mouths objects is that he wishes to *incorporate* them and thus to control and master them.

The infant's personality, being mostly pleasure-seeking id, begins to distinguish *me* from *not-me* (evidence of a growing ego) by regarding pleasure-giving objects as *self* and non-pleasure-giving objects as *non-self*.

Some psychoanalysts divide the oral period into two sub-stages, the early or *receptive stage* and the late or *biting stage.*

The receptive stage covers the first few months of life when erotic pleasure is derived from sucking, swallowing, and mouthing. At this time the infant is rather passive and plays an extremely dependent role. If his feeding and other dependency needs are not adequately met or if great conflict is associated with them, a residue of unfulfillment and conflict is repressed into the unconscious to reveal itself in subsequent years, often as neurotic overdependency or a compulsive habit of trying to "take in" other people and objects. In essence, Freudian theory sees the experience the child has with satisfying instinctual drives at a particular psychosexual stage as forming a model for attitudes or relationships he may carry over to later times in his life.

The biting stage occurs during the latter portion of infancy when teeth erupting and gums are harder. The dominant zone of gratification is still the mouth, but at this point the act of touching things with the lips or of swallowing is not as satisfying as biting or chewing. As the infant's perceptual skills mature, he begins to recognize the features of outside objects more clearly. He now recognizes that one object, such as mother, can have both pleasure-giving and pain-giving functions. Mother gratifies hunger when the baby cries. But mother also has to carry out other activities in her life, so she cannot satisfy baby's demands immediately all the time, and baby finds this postponement painful.

As a result, the infant develops his first *ambivalent* feelings. He both loves and hates the same object. Freudian theory proposes that the child's early ambivalent feelings and sadistic tendencies are expressed in biting—biting his mother's breast, people's fingers, toys, and the like. If progress through this stage is incomplete, so that the infant experiences insufficient satisfaction of biting needs and has inadequate opportunities to express ambivalence without unduly painful repercussions, then a residue of conflict remains in the unconscious to disturb the individual in later life. If the child's progress through the latter oral stage is arrested —that is, if he becomes *fixated* at this point in psychosexual growth—then he may evidence such fixation as an adult through a pattern of "biting" criticism of others or by frequently "chewing out" people around him.

This phenomenon of fixation can occur at any of the psychosexual stages. Freudians hold that fixation, carrying into later life those modes of libidinal gratification suited to an earlier stage, can be the result of either too little or too much satisfaction at the stage in question. If the child's attempts at libidinal investment in an erogenous zone are frustrated, so there remains pent-up energy and inadequate satisfaction, then fixation may occur in the form of a constant seeking to gain the satisfaction in symbolic ways in subsequent years. In contrast, if so much satisfaction with a given erogenous zone is experienced so that the child does not wish to abandon this pleasure by moving ahead to mature forms of libidinal expression, then fixation may again be the result. At each psychosexual stage, the child progresses most satisfactorily if he gains enough pleasure to move ahead without dragging along a residue of unfulfilled needs, yet does not gain so much satisfaction that he is unwilling to advance.

STAGE 2: THE ANAL PERIOD (AGES 2–3)

During the second and third years of life, much of the attention of the child and his parents typically focuses on establishing proper control of the bowels. This time of life is usually called the "anal period" because the prime concern is with expelling and retaining feces. However, it is sometimes referred to as the *anal-urethral period* because the control of urinary functions is also involved. Thus the dominant zones of gratification or libido investment become the anal cavity, the sphincter muscles of the lower bowel, and the muscles of the urinary system.

The shift of the child's attention to the anal area does not mean that the expression of instinctual energy via the oral zone has stopped. It means, rather, that anal activities usually become of major concern for both child and parent. In response to questions about the sequence of the oral, anal, and genital stages, Freud wrote:

> It would be a mistake to suppose that these three phases succeed one another in a clear-cut fashion. One may appear in addition to another; they may overlap one another, may be present along side of one another (1938, p. 12).

In the anal period, much of the child's important contact with adults and much of the emotion adults express toward him are related to toilet training. Like the oral stage, the anal period can be divided into two subperiods, the first concerned with pleasure in expelling feces and urine and the second with retaining these materials.

During the *expulsion stage* the child meets his first serious experience with an external barrier (parents' coercion to have the child control the bowels) to an instinctual cathexis (wishing to defecate). If the child is to accomplish bowel and bladder control, the ego must apply resistance to the child's urge to eliminate at the moment he feels the need. Thus, the ego must borrow libido from the id to energize the resistance. Such a use of libidinal force by the ego—or at a later stage, by the superego—is called *countercathexis* or *anticathexis*. In short, the cathexis or energy investment of the id in the pleasurable release of defecation must be countered by an opposing cathexis of the ego if the child is to meet the parents' demands for cleanliness and thus retain their love.

This is a crucial time for the child to learn to earn love, praise, and approval. If the period is not handled properly by parents—if they harshly impose cleanliness standards before the child is physiologically prepared to control the bowels and bladder, for example—then the child's personality will retain vestiges of fear, guilt, and defiance. The repressed conflict may produce an adult who is compulsively regular and clean or, in contrast, one who is bitter and, in a symbolic sense, voids and urinates on others in his social interaction. The frequent use of the words *crap, shit,* and *bullshit* among adults is said to reflect a measure of fixation at the anal stage.

In the second half of the anal period, the child has learned to *retain* feces and urine at will. He now gains sensuous satisfaction by holding in, that is, by keeping the product he values. Freudians suggest that the child's idea of things having value comes from this period, and inadequate passage through the stage may show up later in life in acts of hoarding and collecting things.

STAGE 3: THE INFANTILE-GENITAL PERIOD (AGES 3–4 OR SO)

The boy's penis and the girl's clitoris and vulva become the key objects of erotic pleasure during the third major psychosexual period. It, too, can be divided into two phases.

During the first phase, called the *phallic stage*, the child discovers that fondling the genitals, titillation, and masturbation (but without orgasm) give erotic pleasure. The child next associates the use of the genitals with a love object with whom he or she would wish to have some sort of sexual relations. For the boy, Freud says:

> The object that has been found turns out to be almost identical with the first object of the oral pleasure-instinct, which was reached by attachment (to the nutritional instinct). Though it is not actually the mother's breast, at least it is the mother. We call the mother the first *love*-object (1917, p. 329).

While the boy is viewing his mother as the desired object, he is at the same time recognizing that he cannot have her all to himself, for his father is the successful competitor for her affections. The resulting psychological conflict—wanting to possess mother but prevented from doing so by the powerful father—has been labeled the *Oedipus complex* or *Oedipus conflict*. The girl is in the opposite situation, wanting father as her love partner but being defeated in this contest by mother. The resulting conflict for the girl has been called the *Electra complex,* but both the boy's and girl's problems are usually subsumed under the Oedipus label.

During this period the child experiences strong ambivalent feelings, seeking the parent of the opposite sex as a lover, but at the same time both fearing and loving the parent of the same sex. An adequate resolution of the Oedipus situation occurs when the child rejects the sexual feelings toward the taboo object, the opposite-sex parent, and, at the same time, identifies with the parent of the same sex. By identifying with the same-sex parent, the child both assuages feelings of fear of reprisal and incorporates the traits of the same-sex parent, the traits that made that parent win the love of the other. In effect, the boy identifies with his father and seeks to adopt his father's characteristics. The girl does the same with her mother. This is the way Freudian theory accounts for the development of masculine and feminine characteristics that fit the mode of the society into which the child is raised.

It is during this process of solving the Oedipus conflict by repressing sexual desires and adopting parental characteristics that the superego evolves. To control what he now considers his dangerous sexual urges, the child incorporates parental values into his personality. These values, in the form of a superego that separates out of the ego, enable the child to reward and punish himself and thus control his own behavior in the absence of outside authority figures.

If the Oedipus conflict is not adequately resolved through repression of sexual impulses and identification with the like-sex parent, remnants of the conflict remain in the unconscious to distort the personality of the adolescent and adult. For instance, homosexuality sometimes has been explained as the child's identifying with the other-sex parent and thus modeling his or her subsequent living habits and sexual tastes after the opposite-sex parent rather than the same-sex one.

The resolution of the Oedipus complex leads into the second portion of the infantile-genital stage, called the *latency period*. Since this time of latent eroticism is so different in its manifestations from the early infantile-genital stage, we will treat it as a major period by itself.

STAGE 4: THE LATENCY PERIOD (AGES 4 OR 5 TO PUBERTY AT AGES 11–13)

During this period, the dominant zone of gratification is still the genital area, but this is usually not displayed in the child's behavior, for both the boy and girl are repressing expressions of sex in order to solve the Oedipus conflict. The child has cathected or adopted both the gratifying and punishing parts of the parents and thus considers talk and displays of sex to be "nasty." The boy stops masturbating because he is afraid of being punished by having his penis cut off, and the girl stops because she is afraid of losing parental love. According to Freud (1938, p. 10), the child falls "victim to *infantile amnesia*" and "forgets" (by use of repression) the sex urges and activities of the first five years of life.

Throughout the years of latency the child's interests in working and playing primarily with children of his or her own sex is a manifestation of efforts to control sexual thoughts. This period has sometimes been called the *gang age* because children seldom voluntarily form groups that include the opposite sex. Because of this same-sex tendency in social relationships, the period is also referred to as the *homosexual phase,* though the homosexual relationships often do not involve any overt sexual acts. Indeed, the rejection of "sex" which the child so strongly evidences at this time in order to control Oedipal tendencies can preclude the child's allowing himself or herself any thoughts of physical displays that might be construed as sexual, whether the object of these displays is a same-sex or opposite-sex peer. In effect, the superego serves as a strong, moralistic internal representative of parental, and thus societal, rules. Playing by the rules both in games and in other daily activities becomes a matter of great importance to children in this phase of growth.

Solving the Oedipus conflict and working through the latency phase successfully is a difficult, stressful task, and often children fail to complete it successfully. Some become fixated at this stage, so that in adult life they never feel comfortable around the opposite sex, and they may avoid sexual relations with the opposite sex or else perform sexual activities in an emotionally detached or aggressive manner.

STAGE 5: THE MATURE-GENITAL PERIOD (FROM AGES 14–16 TO 18 OR 21)

The maturing of the sex functions at the time of puberty and beyond is signaled in girls by menstruation and such secondary bodily changes as the rounding of the breasts and the growth of underarm and pubic hair. The parallel maturation in boys is shown by growth of the genital organs, the appearance of sperm cells, nocturnal emissions of semen (often accompanied by erotic dreams), lowering of the voice pitch, and the growth of underarm, facial, and pubic hair.

The primary zone of erotic pleasure or libidinal cathexis is still the penis in the boy and the vaginal area in the girl, but now the gratification involves sexual orgasm. Whereas during the latent period the child was interested primarily in peers of the same sex, now the attention turns to the opposite sex. In mature sexuality the dominant erotic activity becomes copulation with a partner of the opposite sex. To make the transition from the rejection of sex at the latency phase to the wholehearted pursuit of heterosexual activity is typically a psychologically demanding challenge, particularly in societies that have erected moral barriers against intercourse between unmarried people, especially between adolescents. And such was the case in the late nineteenth-century Viennese society from which Freud drew so many of his patients on whose psychoanalytic histories he erected his theory.

The process of working through the problems of this transition successfully not only enables the youth to gratify his sexual instincts in a mature fashion, but also gives him a less egocentric, more objective perspective of the world in general. The superego has been well formed, with its appropriate conscience and ego ideal. The ego operates on the reality principle, having developed direct modes of solving life's problems and not depending unduly on defense mechanisms.

However, it is during this final stage of psychosexual development that society's rules about the conditions under which sexual intercourse is permissible often press youths to adopt sublimation as a defense mechanism. That is, the adolescent abstains from copulation and substitutes instead artistic or philanthropic activities to express sexual drives indirectly. The substitute may be writing poetry, reading literature, singing or playing a musical instrument, caring for children, aiding the handicapped, or the like. (The question of whether such sublimation actually does satisfy sexual urges is an unsettled issue, still debated among psychoanalysts and among psychiatrists of other persuasions.)

THE STAGES AND THERAPY

Freud's concept of stages is the key to the practice of psychoanalysis as a method of aiding both children and adults who suffer neuroses. The task of the therapist is to use free association and dream interpretation to search back through the patient's psychosexual history to locate the stage at which unresolved conflicts were repressed. Through analysis the therapist hopes to reveal to the patient the original causes of her repressed problem and, by consciously reviewing the original conflicts, to recognize them for what they are and to integrate this new understanding into the personality. In short, the conflict is dug up and relived both intellectually and emotionally. When this process is complete, the neurotic symptoms that brought the patient to the psychoanalyst are expected to disappear. Thus psychoanalysts do not attempt to change neurotic symptoms directly, which they believe is folly, but rather, to find the repressed conflict that is causing the symptom. They believe that when the conflict is resolved and psychologically integrated, the symptoms will evaporate. Treating a symptom directly, they say, does not solve the problem but at best only causes the patient to substitute a different symptom for the one that has been treated. The underlying cause, they insist, must be found and relived realistically. (As we will see in Part 9, behaviorists believe quite the opposite.)

TWO FACETS OF DEVELOPMENT

Now that the main features of Freud's model have been described, we will consider two aspects of it in more detail. The discussion will illustrate something of the complexity of Freud's speculation about development and also show how these aspects—the development of consciousness and of ego strength—fit into the overall framework.

DEVELOPMENT OF CONSCIOUSNESS

In Freud's system, the conscious aspect of mental life does not burst forth in its mature, ultimate state at the time of birth or during infancy. Instead, both consciousness and the preconscious develop over the years as personality is influenced by increasing internal maturation and by ever-widening experiences with the world. This development is perhaps best explained in terms of the relationship that evolves between the levels of awareness (conscious, preconscious, unconscious) and the apparatus of mental life (id, ego, superego).

One of the major challenges Freud faced over the last two or three decades of his life was that of describing clearly the way levels of consciousness interacted with the id, ego, and superego as the child grew up. As he admitted, his attempts at solving this riddle met with only partial success because of the difficulty of penetrating such tangled and clouded territories as the preconscious and unconscious. "And the profound obscurity of the background of our ignorance is scarcely illuminated by a few glimmers of insight" (Freud, 1940, p. 20). Nevertheless, he did depict something of what he saw with the aid of such glimmers, and Figure 11.1 attempts to diagram this.

The diagrams, based on Freud's opinions about the course of personality development in the Western industrialized society he knew best, sketch the anatomy of the mind at three age levels—one month, three years, and twelve years.

Shortly after birth the mind of the newborn in Freud's system is nearly all unconscious, with the unconscious dominated by the instinctual urges arising from the core of the id. Indeed, throughout life the commanding functionary in the unconscious is the id, operating on the pleasure principle without regard for the rules of the outside world. At this beginning stage of life the ego, as arbitrator between instinctual demands and the realities of the outside world, is as yet very small and weak. Only a tiny part of the ego can properly be called conscious, for the young infant has but an embryonic, vague awareness of its existence.

When we identify the ego as the operative of the personality that takes action in the real world to expend instinctual energy from the id, then it is reasonable to assume that the predominant portion of the ego shortly after birth must be preconscious and/or unconscious. This assumption is based on the observation that most—or perhaps all—behavior of the newborn is performed without conscious intent. The neonate does not have to decide to make the heart beat, the lungs breathe, the lips suck, the eyelids close under strong light, or the arms and legs wiggle. These are all done automatically. But as time passes, the internal maturation of the neural system and sensations from the outside world press the infant to become increasingly aware of what possible actions may fulfill needs arising from the unconscious sources. The child also becomes more skilled in choosing from among these possibilities acts that are likely to bring the greatest satisfaction at the least expense in terms of pain. In short, the reality principle on which the ego operates is beginning to guide more of the infant's behavior.

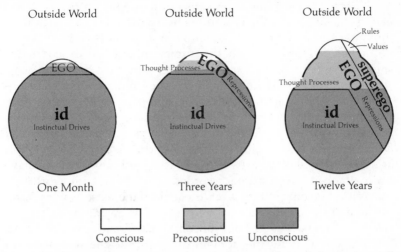

Outside World   Outside World   Outside World

One Month   Three Years   Twelve Years

Conscious   Preconscious   Unconscious

Although Freud did not apparently cast developmental trends in the form of a sequence of diagrams, he did on several occasions diagram his conception of the anatomy of the adult mind. Each of his diagrams differed somewhat from the others, reflecting some recent innovation in his beliefs about the relationships within the mental apparatus. (See Freud, 1900, 1923.)

Figure 11.1   Developmental Trends in the Structure of the Mind

By age 3 the child's transactions with the world have improved the clarity of consciousness and greatly expanded the area of the preconscious. At this point we can identify more precisely the characteristics of the conscious and the preconscious and describe their interactions.

The conscious—sometimes called the *system perceptual conscious*—is what the individual is attending to at the moment. It is what we are presently aware of seeing, hearing, feeling, or thinking about. The conscious is the outermost surface of the mental apparatus, the part in immediate contact with the outside world. The conscious is the nucleus of the ego (Freud, 1923, pp. 9, 18).

The images or ideas on which our attention is focused at the moment are limited in number and scope. We cannot keep many things in consciousness at one time. Rather, the images are like a sequence of individual pictures; each appears momentarily, then shifts in form or passes by to make way for the next. This notion of the kaleidoscopic nature of the conscious is reflected in the phrase *stream of consciousness*. However, once the images pass, they are not gone forever. Either we can purposely bring them to mind again by recalling them to the stage of consciousness, or else they may intrude from without (as sense impressions on the eyes and ears from sources in the environment) or extrude from within (as thoughts and feelings that rise into our awareness from we know not where). However, whether from an outside or an inside source, these things that catch our attention must have one characteristic: They must be *perceptible*. They must assume a recognizable form as an image or a verbal symbol or word construction. In other words, amorphous, raw sensations from one's unconscious cannot be perceived until they are cast either as *mental images* (pictorial or auditory forms as in dreams) or as *verbal symbols* or *word presentations* (words, phrases, and sentences that have been attached to sensations recorded from the outside world).

With this logic in mind, let us consider the reasons why Freud postulated the existence of a *preconscious* as an intermediary between the conscious and the unconscious. Freud envisioned the unconscious (chiefly the domain of the id) as the receptacle for instinctual energy, for ill-defined needs and urges. But he also needed a receptacle for material that was not in the mind at the moment but that could be recalled at will. So, as the storage area for memory traces of conscious perceptions from the past, for material not at the moment "conscious" but yet available to be retrieved if desired, he created the preconscious. Whereas the unconscious was pictured mainly as the operating arena for the id, the preconscious was described as basically under control of the ego.

In addition to being the storage area for retrievable memory traces, the preconscious was pictured as the processing chamber in which the ego receives amorphous urges from the id and recasts them into the image or verbal form required for their perception by the conscious ego. Recall that before the conscious ego can find ways to satisfy inner needs through trafficking in the real world, the needs must be put into perceptible shape. Freud proposed that this act of translating was performed by preconscious molding procedures that "we may—roughly and inexactly—sum up under the name of thought-processes" (Freud, 1923, pp. 9–10). It seems likely that what he meant by *thought-processes* was those mental acts known as analyzing, synthesizing, denoting, identifying, evaluating, and such.

In speaking of things arising from the unconscious and seeking expression, Freud distinguished between the route taken by ideas and the route taken by feelings. While ideas need to be processed by the preconscious, clothed by it in the recognizable raiment of familiar images or word presentations before they can appear in consciousness, feelings do not. Rather, they emit directly into consciousness from the unconscious (Freud, 1923, pp. 12–13).

Having identified conscious and preconscious roles performed by the ego, we can now understand more clearly the differences between the mental maps for the one-month-old and three-year-old in Figure 11.1. The neonate's preconscious barely, if at all, exists, and the conscious is very limited in scope and clarity. But by age 3 the conscious is more extensive and acute, and the preconscious is far larger, in the sense of containing rapidly increasing numbers of memory traces drawn from experiences in the world. Furthermore, the preconscious has acquired certain of its contents—particularly its thought processes—from the unconscious. As the hypothetical twelve-year-old mind also illustrates, this trend of the preconscious becoming more complex over the years continues throughout the period of child and adolescent development. Greater internal maturation of the neural system interacts with more and more experiences in the outside world to produce more memory traces and more sophisticated thought processes.

A comparison of the diagrams of the one-month-old and three-year-old minds also shows that the ego has now added something of its own to the unconscious. This something consists of psychologically painful thoughts that have been repressed into an unconscious condition by an apparently frantic ego, because it found them too unbearable to maintain in consciousness or preconsciousness but did not know how to eliminate or solve them in a satisfactory conscious manner. We assume that these repressed materials at age 3 are seated in anxieties that arose during the oral and anal stages (from birth through about ages 2–3) from conflict the child experienced with her parents. For example, in Freud's view parents' unreasonable and often harsh demands for bowel and bladder control when the child is not yet ready for such control can cause the child to feel inadequate and to fear the loss of parental love. Since the child's weak ego cannot solve the conflict on the conscious level, the ego frantically relegates the painful events to the unconscious. And, as the diagram of the twelve-year-old mind suggests, we can assume that the amount of repressed material will increase by that age due to the psychic conflicts experienced during the Oedipal period around ages 3 to 5 and thereafter.

In summary, then, throughout the early years of life, the child's conscious grows in clarity, and the ego builds up a supply center of recallable memories from past perceptions, memories deposited in an expanding preconscious. At the same time, particularly painful problems that the immature ego is ill prepared to master are pushed out of consciousness to be actively held in the unconscious by means of energy borrowed from the id. The supply of psychic energy available for conducting conscious and preconscious affairs is thus depleted by this diverting of energy for purposes of repression. Furthermore, as noted earlier, such repressed problems are really postponed rather than solved, for they continue to seethe and to express themselves out of the unconscious in deviant ways, such as in the form of neuroses.

The third diagram, the hypothetical twelve-year-old mind, also shows the new functionary, the superego, which has grown out of the ego during the Oedipal period of middle childhood. Freud proposed that the superego starts developing around age 3, or perhaps slightly earlier, in which case a sliver of its influence could have been included in the diagram of the three-year-old mind. The superego at the conscious and preconscious levels appears as the set of conscious values or rules of living that guide the older child's behavior even when parents, teachers, and police are not present. But the existence in the adolescent's psyche of free-floating anxiety and of vague feelings of guilt and shame that are not attached to any particular event suggests that the superego has an unconscious aspect as well. In effect, the older child or adolescent can "feel bad" without knowing why. This means, in Freud's scheme, that the youth has incorporated into her personality certain parental expectations that she does not consciously recognize. Apparently these expectations or standards are ones associated with traumatic early experiences that have since been repressed.

Thus, as the child grows up the relationships between levels of consciousness and the psychic operatives (id, ego, and superego) shift so that the child gains increasing control over her fate. At the same time, she is victimized by repressions that sap her psychic energy, divert her attention from reasonable conscious action, and cause distressing, illogical thoughts and behavior.

DEVELOPING EGO STRENGTH

Closely tied to the processes we have just discussed is the matter of developing a strong ego. Although Freud did not describe ego strength in exactly the terms used here, it seems reasonable to assume, from all he wrote about the ego, that the following definition faithfully reflects his opinion: A strong ego is one that has at its command sufficient adjustment techniques to: (1) fulfill the id's instinctual needs without neglecting or unduly postponing any need and, at the same time, (2) satisfy the expectations imposed on the individual by both (a) the physical and social environments and (b) the individual's superego.

A weak ego, in contrast, is one that lacks sufficient conscious methods of expending instinctual energy that are acceptable to the environment and superego. A weak ego, faced by conflicting demands that it cannot consciously satisfy, reverts to its emergency technique of repression. Consequently, the weaker a person's ego, the more repressions we can expect to accumulate in the unconscious to plague him—unless, of course, some outside agent, such as a parent or other caretaker, intervenes to reduce the number of demands pressed upon the ego from the environment. It is in this matter of intervention that Freud's concept of ego strength bears important implications for child-raising practices.

The newborn's ego is very weak. It has only a few, simplistic methods for arbitrating the conflict between id demands and environmental requirements. The child will require far greater neural maturation and experience with the world to develop the broad array of sophisticated adjustment methods that mark the strong ego. If the neonate is to survive and is to avoid storing up a dangerous cargo of repressions to bear through life, then he requires a lot of outside help from parents and others. Although there is nothing these outside agents can do to control the instinctual drives arising from the id, they can do something about the environment. Their aid in reducing the weak ego's burden of decisions can take two general forms. First, parents can provide the infant with certain things that he cannot obtain by himself, such as food and warmth. They can also furnish, in gradual steps, opportunities for the child to exercise his body and his perceptual system so that he learns to comprehend and act on his world in increasingly effective ways. Second, parents can protect the infant from intense stimuli that could overwhelm his perceptual capacities, stimuli that frighten him because he cannot understand or control them. Examples of such stimuli are loud noises, flashes of light, loss of support so the child suddenly drops, angry arguments and fights, and the like. But perhaps even more important is the parental role of protecting the young child from societal expectations that are beyond the child's capacity to fulfill. It was in relation to this role that Freud particularly criticized European child-rearing practices of his day. He felt that since nothing could be done to lessen the instinctual-drive demands on the weak ego, it was necessary for society to permit these drives freer direct expression in the early years of life instead of strictly censoring such expression.

> From a biological standpoint the ego comes to grief over the task of mastering the excitations of the early sexual period, at a time when its immaturity makes it incompetent to do so. It is in this lagging of ego development behind libidinal development that we see the essential precondition of neurosis; and we cannot escape the conclusion that neuroses could be avoided if the childish ego were spared this task— if, that is to say, the child's sexual life were allowed free play, as happens among many primitive peoples (Freud, 1938, p. 57).

While Freud proposed that fewer repressions and subsequent neuroses would develop if sexual urges (including sucking and biting in the oral stage and bowel and urinary activities in the anal stage) were allowed "free play," he proposed as well that civilization as we know it would not have developed under such free-expression conditions. He believed that the early "damming up" of the sexual instinct forced the growing child and subsequently the adult to redirect at least a portion of this energy into other channels through the adjustment technique of sublimation. This redirecting or sublimating process, he felt, caused many of the developments of our culture, since diverted libido was put to the task of fueling inventions, art works, literary creations, social service, and the like (Freud, 1938, p. 58). So in this sense, the variegated culture that we enjoy has been paid for, at least partially, by repressions by a weak ego early in life.

What, then, does all this mean for parents and other caretakers who wish to guide child growth in ways that promote the development of a strong ego and keep at a minimum repressions that will cause distressing neurotic symptoms? The answer, from a psychoanalytic viewpoint, consists of five principles. Both actual parents and surrogate parents should:

1. Recognize the nature of instinctual urges and accept the desirability of permitting expression of the urges.
2. Recognize the normal psychosexual stages of development and the sorts of conflicts the child faces at each stage.
3. Provide at each developmental stage enough opportunities for the child to satisfy instinctual drives within an atmos-

phere of understanding, but not furnish so much satisfaction that the child becomes fixated at that point and is unwilling to move ahead to the next stage.

4. Furnish plenty of service and protection to the infant in the early years so that the child's weak ego is not overwhelmed by the physical environment and societal standards.

5. As time passes, provide increasing amounts of guidance (teaching) in problem solving so that the ego develops an ever-expanding repertoire of conscious adjustment techniques to fill all kinds of instinctual demands under all sorts of environmental conditions.

In summary, the theory Freud devised to explain the origins of adult neuroses yielded, as a by-product, a number of general principles for guiding the normal personality development of children at all stages of the growth process, including the development of a strong ego.

Now that we have considered key elements of Freud's model of child development, we will look briefly at the sorts of contributions his daughter Anna made to his work.

ANNA FREUD'S CHILDHOOD PSYCHOANALYSIS

Sigmund Freud's model of child development was not constructed from direct observations of children. It was fashioned from the free associations and dreams of the neurotic adults he treated. However, Freud's daughter Anna (born 1895) spent a major part of her adult life as a psychoanalyst working directly with children. She was a rather strict adherent of her father's theory, but she found it desirable to clarify and embellish certain aspects of it on the basis of her experience treating childhood neuroses. Her additions to Freudian theory were not published as a single, comprehensive treatise, but appeared instead as occasional articles and speeches over a period of forty years, from the 1920s to the mid-1960s. These scattered works have now been brought together in five volumes as *The Writings of Anna Freud* (1974).

The kinds of contributions she made can be illustrated with three examples; these concern: (1) the psychoanalytic treatment of the child while his superego is still being formed, (2) the value of direct observations of children, and (3) implications of psycho-analysis for raising the normal child.

STATUS OF THE SUPEREGO

Like her father, Anna Freud explained that many adult neuroses result from an overly punitive superego. It is the task of the psychoanalyst to help the patient reorganize the contents of the superego so they fit reality more adequately and do not pose un-reasonable standards to which the individual is forced to aspire. In the adult neurotic, this rebuilding task is long and painful, for the superego has, since the time of early adolescence, become a powerful component of the personality, highly resistant to alter-ations. But in the older child or early adolescent, the superego is yet in the process of formation. The child is still in a state of transition between (1) receiving orders or values from his actual parents and (2) receiving orders from the evolving superego, which has not yet separated from either the ego or its external sources (parents, peers, teachers).

Adult psychoanalysis need involve only the patient and the analyst. However, in Anna Freud's opinion, childhood neuroses are best treated by the analyst working both with the child and with such important agents of his environment as parents and teachers. By changing parents' expectations for, and treatment of, the child, the analyst hopes to influence the contents of the as-yet-dependent superego and cure the neurosis with greater speed than would be possible in an adult, whose overly demanding superego has already solidified. Thus the analyst who works with children manipulates the environment in addition to re-forming the relationships within the child's personality among the id, ego, and superego (A. Freud, 1974, vol. I, pp. 57–58).

DIRECT OBSERVATIONS OF CHILDREN

In adult psychoanalysis, the source of the therapist's information is almost exclusively the patient's talk about himself. However, children are not as adept at explaining, upon command, their past history, worries, and fantasies. Thus, Anna Freud recommended that in child analysis dream interpretation should be supplemented with information provided by the child's family and by the therapist's observations of the child's actions. By noting patterns of feeding, sleep, illness, play, and the like, the analyst can select items of behavior which, according to psychoanalytic theory, grew out of the earlier oral, anal, and infantile-genital periods. Therefore, in child analysis certain types of observations can serve as substitutes for the free-association data on which the analysis of adults' psychological problems is usually founded (A. Freud, 1974, vol. V, pp. 95–101).

PSYCHOANALYSIS AND CHILD-REARING PRACTICES

In 1956 Anna Freud said, "While we are unable to alter the innate givens of a human being, we may be in the position to relieve some of the external pressures which interact with them" (1974, vol. V, pp. 265–266). She believed that psychoanalytic theory could make a major contribution toward the relief of such external pressures by helping parents gain "insight into the potential harm done to young children during the critical years of their development by the manner in which their needs, drives, wishes, and emotional dependencies are met" (1974, vol. V, p. 266). She then explained that the types of help psychoanalysis had already provided included: (1) the sexual enlightenment of children, (2) recognition of the role of conflict, conscience, and anxiety in the development of the child—a recognition that resulted in parents' limiting their authority over the child, (3) freedom for the child to express aggression, (4) recognition of the importance of the mother–infant relationship, and (5) an understanding of the mother's role as an auxiliary ego for the growing child.

In summary, Anna Freud extended psychoanalytic theory by adding to it a variety of conclusions she extracted from her direct observations of, and therapy sessions with, children at several stages of their development.

FREUDIAN THEORY: AN ASSESSMENT

My assessment of psychoanalytic theory in terms of the nine appraisal standards is given on the accompanying rating scales. My

FREUDIAN THEORY _____

How well do I think the theory meets the standards?

The Standards	Very Well	Moderately Well	Very Poorly
1. Reflects the real world of children		?	
2. Is clearly understandable	X		
3. Explains the past and predicts the future	Specificity X	Accuracy ?	
4. Guides child rearing	X		
5. Is internally consistent		X	
6. Is economical		X	
7. Is falsifiable			X
8. Stimulates new discoveries	X		
9. Is self-satisfying		X	

explanation for these ratings begins with the item I rated the highest and then moves to those I rated lower.

There can be little doubt that Freudian theory deserves high marks for its success in stimulating new discoveries (item 8). It has been the basis for hundreds of articles reporting clinical studies of children's development, usually in the form of analyses of deviant types of development. It has also motivated investigators to launch new journals dedicated entirely to psychoanalytic topics and to write scores of books that offer extensions, embellishments, or revisions of the theory. Furthermore, the Freudian model has furnished ideas that have become the focus of investigations by experimental psychologists, including such prominent behaviorists as Dollard and Miller (1950) and Sears (1965).*

The second highest rating, on item 4, is my estimate of the substantial influence psychoanalytic suggestions have exerted on the child-rearing views of ostensibly "concerned and well-read" adults in Europe and America during recent decades. These suggestions have focused on children's emotional needs, principally those in the areas of sex and aggression. For instance, from the Freudian conception of the oral stage comes the recommendation that infants be given plenty of opportunities to be cuddled and to satisfy their sucking needs, especially at feeding time. From beliefs about the anal phase of development comes the recommendation that toilet training should not be attempted too early, nor should it be enforced in a punitive fashion. Furthermore, toilet training should not be accompanied by distressing emotional outbursts from parents or even by half-disguised expressions of disgust, which the child interprets as threats of the withdrawal of parents' love if the child does not perform how, when, and where the parents desire. There are also suggestions offered about how parents and teachers can best react to sexual curiosity and expression throughout the years of childhood and adolescence. In effect, specific beliefs about child raising that are derived from Freudian theory appear as topics in both professional and popular publications and in the mass media.

However, although psychoanalytic theory offers guidance for handling children's emotional growth, it offers little or no help for directing children's academic (cognitive) development or physical growth, except in cases of physical ailments suspected of having a psychological origin. The rating on item 4, therefore, is a balance between Freudian suggestions about emotional development and a lack of suggestions about cognitive and physical growth.

As for the theory's clarity (item 2), I estimate that it deserves a mark slightly above the middle of the scale. Freudians explain the system's main components rather clearly, I feel, at least in general. And Freud's practice of illustrating these components with examples from cases of people undergoing psychoanalysis helps communicate what he intends. But when we move beyond the basic outline of the theory's structure, many puzzles appear, calling for greater clarification. As one illustration of confusion, Nagel has complained that the Freudian:

---

* For summaries of experimental studies, see Frenkel-Brunswik (1954), Hilgard (1952), Kris (1947), and Sears (1943).

Sometimes describes the main theoretical components of the mental apparatus as "units of functions," and suggests that unconscious drives are like dispositions. But he also declares that these components possess energies and conflict with one another—though without explaining in what sense functions can be charged with energies or dispositions can be engaged in conflicts (1959, p. 46).

In short, when we inspect the psychoanalytic model of child development in detail, we find it can profit from a good deal of additional clarification.

The issue of clarity is also related to item 1 (reflects real world of children), which I have rated slightly below the center. I believe that in Freud's favor are his (1) bringing to public view the importance and commonality of sexual interests in childhood and adolescence, (2) identifying defense mechanisms children develop, (3) describing children's ambivalent feelings—hate combined with love—toward parents and others close to them, and similar proposals. Observations of children's behavior would appear to substantiate these findings as phenomena in real children's lives (Hilgard, 1952).

But balanced against such items, which are confirmable by direct observation or assessment, is a large portion of Freudian theory that has not been substantiated in such an open or public manner. Some critics have been particularly blunt in their charges that psychoanalysts have failed to conduct the investigations that will convincingly test the theory's proposals. Scriven has written that:

> As a set of hypotheses it was a great achievement 50 years ago; as no more than a set of hypotheses it is a great disgrace today. . . . It is in fact the most sophisticated form of metaphysics ever to enjoy support as a scientific theory (1959, pp. 226–227).

Part of the difficulty with Freud's model as an accurate reflector of real children's development lies in the source of data on which he founded his theory. He did not directly observe, test, or measure children during their years of growth, as did many other theorists. Actually, there were at least four somewhat "slippery" steps between his data and the growing child. That is, his process of collecting data during therapy sessions with neurotic adults involved: (step 1) the analyst's *interpreting* from his viewpoint or through his "lens" (step 2) ostensibly *symbolic* material derived from (step 3) reported *dreams* and *memories* of neurotics about (step 4) *ostensible experiences* from their childhood one or more decades earlier. In view of this mode of gathering information, the theory's data base might be a distortion of typical children's actions, thoughts, and emotions during each phase of growing up. I am skeptical about how well it represents real children's development, and I share the opinion of those critics who ask that the Freudian model be supported more adequately with publicly verifiable evidence.

Probably the main reason psychoanalytic theory has been difficult either to verify or to refute is not that its adherents are stubbornly defensive or are inept researchers (though in some instances this may be the case), but that many of its key elements, including the unconscious, repression, reaction formation, and symbolism, seem to render it nonfalsifiable. These elements have caused critics to harbor "the suspicion that Freudian theory can always be so manipulated that it escapes refutation no matter what the well-established facts may be" (Nagel, 1959, p. 44). Since I share this suspicion, I have rated psychoanalysis at the bottom on item 7 (falsifiability).

Imagine that we wish to check the validity of the concept of the Oedipus conflict, and will do so by interviewing adolescents about the sexual ideas they had during their earlier childhood years. If the adolescents' answers corroborate the notion that the father–daughter, mother–son "family romance" is widely spread, we might consider these answers as evidence supporting the Oedipus-complex concept. But let us say that we get just the opposite results from our interviews. The adolescents, seeking to be as truthful as possible, rarely have any memories of Oedipal strivings. Can we then interpret this as evidence against the notion of a universal Oedipus conflict? Freudians would say no. They would contend, instead, that the negative responses show that the earlier sexual urges have been repressed into the unconscious, so the adolescents' denial of such thoughts is proof of both the Oedipus complex and of the defense mechanism of repression. Under these conditions, there is no way to test the validity of the Oedipus concept through the retrospective interview that Freudians use as the source of evidence about how children develop.

The concept of reaction formation poses the same problem for assessing the theory. Reaction formation is the defense mechanism that occurs when a person is driven by an urge or wish (id) that conflicts with his moral values (superego), and to solve the conflict he (ego) represses the urge and behaves as if his motives were just the opposite. A child's overt sex play is seen as direct evidence of the proposed libidinal energy. But the opposite behavior—puritanical avoidance of sex—is interpreted as an expression of exactly the same libidinal or sexual energy but expressed through the mechanism of *reaction formation*. Likewise, both the child who habitually fights (displaying direct aggression) and the one who is the habitual pacifist (showing reaction formation) are seen as driven by the same aggressive urge (death instinct). Once more, an appraiser of the theory is at a loss in deciding how to handle a model that derives identical conclusions from diametrically opposed data.

The role of symbols in Freud's scheme presents other puzzles. Freud proposed that a person's ego, in cooperation with the superego, censors repressed material that seeks to arise from the unconscious into consciousness. But he also said that repressed wishes can sneak past the censor in disguise, that is, in symbolic form. For instance, we noted in Chapter 1 that Freud considered any elongated, projectile-shaped object that appeared in a dream to be a symbol of the male penis. An open, container-like object symbolized the female vagina (Freud, 1900). So Freudians, with this notion of symbolism in their analytic armory, can interpret all sorts of thoughts that people express as support for their theory.

So, Freud's model of child development and personality structure may be correct, but the game of verification is unmanageable if it must be played with the elastic ground rules permitted by the inclusion of such concepts as the above. The fairly low mark given for item 5 (internal consistency) is also primarily a result of these considerations.

On item 6, is the theory economical, I have marked Freud's theory near the middle. While some aspects of his model appear to be direct, economical ways to explain the phenomena on which he focuses, others appear to me unduly complex. There should be simpler ways to account for the phenomena in question. For instance, there should be less confusing and simpler ways to account for fixations than to claim that they are caused by both over- and undersatisfaction of needs at a given psychosexual stage. Furthermore, there should be simpler ways to account for the prepuberal child's personal-social behavior than the Oedipus complex that Freud proposed. This is not to say Freud is wrong, but the same phenomena can be attributed to simpler sets of factors.

The difficulty experienced in giving a reasonable rating on item 3 (explains the past and predicts the future) is reflected by the two marks on the line. The mark for specificity is at the high end of the scale, principally because Freudian explanations of what psychosexual events occurred earlier in an individual's life, and why they occurred, are quite specific. Psychoanalysis emphasizes the past history of development as uncovered through free association and dream interpretation. But psychoanalytic predictions of the future are usually sketched in a more general way, often in terms of possible deviant development that might occur if the child's needs during upcoming psychosexual stages are not dealt with wisely by the adults who most affect her life. In consideration of the theory's very specific explanations of the past and more general predictions of the future, I have marked it relatively high for *specificity*.

However, *accuracy* of explanation and prediction is quite a different matter. For the sorts of reasons given in the discussion of falsifiability I am skeptical about the validity of explanations founded on the theory. On the basis of this skepticism, I have used a question mark as a rating in the lower ranges of item 3. The theory wants better validation.

Finally we come to the self-satisfying quality of Freud's model (item 9). In the case of psychoanalytic theory, this ninth standard is of particular importance because Freud's proposals have depended so heavily on personal affirmation for their acceptance. By *personal affirmation* I mean the "feeling" that psychoanalytic theory does indeed describe the way one's personality evolves and functions. Or as Hook has noted (1959, p. 213), some Freudians' response to criticism has been that "psychoanalysis may be unscientific, but it is true." And to some degree I must admit to sharing such a feeling. Despite the shortcomings of Freudian theory when judged against common scientific criteria like the foregoing standards, much of the theory makes a kind of existential sense to me. I believe in the unconscious, in repression, in our use of defense mechanisms, and in many other concepts the theory includes. But I remain skeptical about still other aspects of the model. For these reasons, I have rated it in the middle of the scale for item 9.

FOR FURTHER READING

The first two books are paperbacks offering concise, simplified, and accurate accounts of psychoanalytic theory.

Hall, Calvin S. (1954) *A Primer of Freudian Psychology*. New York: World. This is a systematic description of psychoanalysis as a theory of personality development. Hall has based his account on material drawn from a variety of Freud's writings.

Stafford-Clark, David. (1967) *What Freud Really Said*. London: Penguin. A description of the evolution of Freud's ideas, including summaries of several of his most significant publications.

The next two items are translations of Freud's own writings. The first of these is a seventy-five-page summary of psychoanalytic theory written near the close of his career. The second is a thirty-volume edition of his complete works, useful for its detail and for the picture it offers of Freud's revisions over a period of nearly five decades.

Freud, Sigmund. (1938) *An Outline of Psychoanalysis*. London: Hogarth, 1973.

Freud, Sigmund. (1964) *The Standard Edition of the Complete Psychological Works of Sigmund Freud*. James Strachey, translator and editor. London: Hogarth Press. In 30 volumes.

The most complete source of Anna Freud's works is the following five-volume collection:

Freud, Anna. (1974) *The Writings of Anna Freud*. New York: International Universities Press.

CHAPTER 12

ERIKSON'S VARIATION ON FREUD'S THEME

Erik Homburger Erikson (born 1902) is a German-born psychoanalyst whose self-imposed mission has been to extend and refine Freud's notions of personality development, with particular attention to child development.

Three of the most significant features of Erikson's refinement have been his proposals regarding:

1. The development of the *healthy personality*, in contrast to Freud's emphasis on the growth and cure of neurotic behavior.

2. The process of socializing the child into a particular culture by passage through a series of innately determined *psychosocial stages* which parallel Freud's psychosexual stages.

3. The individual's task of achieving *ego identity* by means of solving specified identity crises at each psychosocial stage of growth.

Erikson's professional career began in Vienna, where he graduated from the Vienna Psychoanalytic Institute before coming to the United States in 1933. He entered clinical practice in the United States, became a citizen in 1939, and over a period of four decades made significant contributions to the literature on psychoanalysis, personality theory, educational practice, and social anthropology.

Much of Freud's theory—the existence and nature of the unconscious, the tripartite composition of the mind (id, ego, superego), psychosexual stages, and more—was accepted by Erikson as valid. Since he accepted these concepts, Erikson wrote relatively little about them. Instead, he focused his work on those facets of psychoanalytic theory he believed required extension and, to some degree, revision. In discussing Erikson's contributions, we will center our attention only on the key additions he proposed, not on his entire system of beliefs. These additions are: (1) the nature of a healthy personality and of ego identity, (2) the epigenetic principle, and (3) stages of psychosocial growth and the identity crises. Finally, we add an assessment of Erikson's ideas from the viewpoint of someone who works with children and is interested in theory construction.

EGO IDENTITY AND
THE HEALTHY PERSONALITY

Erikson agreed with those critics of Freud who claimed that Freud had focused only on neurotic personalities and, in consequence, had neglected to define the nature of healthy personalities or to trace their pattern of development. Erikson sought to right this imbalance of psychoanalytic theory, and he began by identifying the characteristics of the healthy personality. These characteristics would be the goals and signs of desirable human development.

One statement of such characteristics that Erikson found suitable was that of Marie Jahoda, who believed that a healthy personality *actively masters* his environment, shows a certain *unity of personality*, and is able to *perceive* the world and himself *correctly* (Erikson, 1968, p. 92). The newborn child displays none of these characteristics. The healthiest adult personality displays them all. Thus, in Erikson's view, "childhood is defined by [the characteristics'] initial absence and by their gradual development in complex steps of increasing differentiation" (1968, p. 92).

Phrased in a different way, "growing up" is a process of achieving *ego identity*. In Erikson's system, ego identity has two aspects. The first or inner-focused aspect is the person's recognition of his own unified "selfsameness and continuity in time" (Erikson, 1959, p. 23). It is knowing and accepting oneself. The second or outer-focused aspect is the individual's recognition of and identification with the ideals and essential pattern of his culture; it includes sharing "some kind of essential character with others" (Erikson, 1968, p. 104). The person who has attained ego identity has a clear picture and an acceptance of both his inner essence and the group culture in which he lives.

Since, in Erikson's view, human development consists of moving from non-ego identity to ego identity, his picture of the developmental process features a description of "conflicts, inner and outer, which the vital personality weathers, re-emerging from each crisis with an increased sense of inner unity, with an increase of good judgment, and an increase in the capacity 'to do well' according to his own standards and to the standards of those who are significant to him" (Erikson, 1968, p. 92).

THE EPIGENETIC PRINCIPLE

Studies of the development of the human organism while it is still in the mother's womb have suggested that it develops from a single fertilized cell and follows the same general stages as all human organisms, until, after about nine months, a highly complex, multicellular baby with many differentiated but coordinated parts is born. The entire pattern of development, it is believed, is governed by a genetic structure common to all humans. In other words, the genes establish a construction plan and timetable for the development of each part.

Studies of physical development after birth suggest that the genetic plan does not stop with birth. Rather, the sequence of development of such skills as crawling and walking and such characteristics as adolescent breast growth in girls and facial hair in boys has been established by the genetic plan. These characteristics arise at a particular time in life according to a pre-established time schedule that is little affected by environmental influences.

The term *epigenetic principle* has been given to this belief that everything that grows is governed by a preset construction plan: "Out of this ground plan the parts arise, each part having its time of special ascendency, until all parts have arisen to form a functioning whole" (Erikson, 1968, p. 92).

Many people have accepted the principle as a guide to understanding physical growth. But Erikson extended the principle to social-psychological growth as well, proposing that personality appears to develop also according to steps "predetermined in the human organism's readiness to be driven toward, to be aware of, and to interact with a widening radius of significant individuals and institutions" (1968, p. 93). He recognized that this interaction would be somewhat different from one culture to another since the different cultures in which children grow up can vary in many significant ways. However, he held that personality growth follows a sequence of "inner laws" that set the potentialities for the kinds of significant interaction the child will achieve with the people and institutions she does meet in her particular culture.

In short, Erikson proposed that it is the nature of the human species to pass through an identifiable series of psychosocial stages as the individual grows up, stages determined genetically, regardless of the culture in which the growth occurs. The social environment, however, does have a significant effect on the nature of the crises arising at each stage and on the success with which the child and adolescent will master the stage.

THE GRID OF PSYCHOSOCIAL STAGES

Erikson accepted Freud's set of psychosexual stages as a basically valid description of the key concerns of personality development from infancy to adulthood. However, Erikson felt that the Freudian formulation was incomplete in at least four respects.

First, he thought Freud gave too little recognition to the socialization of the child, particularly to the various patterns of behavior that different cultures consider desirable—patterns the child needs to adopt or adapt if she is to be given the approval of the group within which she grows up.

Second, Erikson believed there are stages of development after adolescence which Freud failed to recognize. Thus, Erikson defined more clearly four additional levels from puberty and beyond.

Third, Erikson believed the interaction of the individual with her social environment produces a series of eight major *psychosocial crises* the individual must work through in order to achieve eventual ego identity and psychological health. Since Freud had not defined crises in a clear fashion, Erikson did so.

Finally, Erikson believed that the concepts of development could be better understood if they were cast in the form of a grid or matrix; such a grid had not been employed by Freud. Erikson produced a number of such grids to clarify the interaction and correlation among various aspects of development. One of these "worksheets," as he called them, is produced in an adapted form as Table 12.1.

Among Erikson's most significant additions to child development theory is his proposal that an individual undergoes eight psychosocial crises during development. These are listed in column A of Table 12.1. Each crisis or stage is phrased as a struggle between two opposite or conflicting personality characteristics. The trait of *trust* vies for dominance over *mistrust* in the infant's personality. At the next stage, the trait of *autonomy* struggles for ascendancy over *shame* and *doubt*. Six subsequent crises mark the next six stages of psychosocial growth to full ego identity or psychological maturity in the adult.

Although these conflicting traits or tendencies are cast in the form of absolutes, such as "absolute trust" versus "absolute mistrust," in reality they form graduated scales in the personality. Complete trust appears at one end of the scale line and complete mistrust at the other. Between these extremes are gradations that the individual may attain. In reality, no one reaches either extreme. Each personality represents some mixture of self-trust and mistrust, as well as some combination of trusting and mistrusting other people and the world in general. Consequently, one way of describing the configuration of a given child's or adolescent's personality within Erikson's system would be to identify where, along each of these scale lines, the individual stands at any particular time.

Before we consider each of the stages in more detail, we will examine the other columns in Table 12.1 so the relationship between this material and the psychosocial crises is clear.

Column B of Table 12.1 lists the expanding circle of significant people with whom the growing child interacts. The particular crisis the child or adolescent faces at a given stage is worked out through interaction with the people or the social setting identified in column B as appropriate to the crisis.

Column C suggests those acts on which the growing child's attention concentrates at each crisis stage, and column D indicates which psychosexual step correlates with each act. Thus, during Freud's oral stage of earliest infancy, the baby concentrates on the acts (psychosocial modalities) of getting and giving in return. At the psychosexual stage of puberty, stage V, the young person concentrates on the acts of being oneself and sharing being oneself.

Keeping this worksheet in mind, let us now consider in more detail the nature of Erikson's eight successive psychosocial crises or phases (Erikson, 1959, pp. 65–98).

Table 12.1 A Psychosocial Development "Worksheet"

Stage Number	Column A — Psychosocial Crisis	Column B — Radius of Significant Relations	Column C — Psychosocial Modalities	Column D — Freud's Psychosexual Stages	Column E — Approximate Ages in Years
I	Trust versus Mistrust	Maternal person	To get To give in return	Oral-Respiratory, Sensory-Kinesthetic (Incorporative Modes)	0–1
II	Autonomy versus Shame, Doubt	Parental persons	To hold on To let go	Anal-Urethral, Muscular (Retentive-Eliminative)	2–3
III	Initiative versus Guilt	Basic family	To make (going after) To "make like" (playing)	Infantile-Genital, Locomotor (Intrusive, Inclusive)	3–6
IV	Industry versus Inferiority	"Neighborhood" and school	To make things (completing) To make things together	Latency	7–12 or so

(continued)

Stage Number	Column A Psychosocial Crisis	Column B Radius of Significant Relations	Column C Psychosocial Modalities	Column D Freud's Psycho-sexual Stages	Column E Approximate Ages in Years
V	Identity and Repudiation versus Identity Diffusion	Peer groups and outgroups; models of leadership	To be oneself (or not to be) To share being oneself	Puberty and Adolescence	12–18 or so
VI	Intimacy and Solidarity versus Isolation	Partners in friendship, sex, competition, cooperation	To lose and find oneself in another	Mature Genitality	The 20s
VII	Generativity versus Self-Absorption	Divided labor and shared household	To make be To take care of		Late 20s to 50s
VIII	Integrity versus Despair	"Mankind" "My kind"	To be, through having been To face not being		50s and beyond

Adapted from Erikson, 1959, p. 166.

BASIC TRUST VERSUS BASIC MISTRUST

Erikson proposed that a sense of trust—being able to predict and depend upon one's own behavior and the behavior of others—is derived primarily from the experiences of the first year of life. In other words, a child's fundamental attitude about the dependability of the world is built chiefly on the relationship the infant establishes during the oral stage or incorporative stage when feeding and mouthing objects is of prime importance. The most important person in the infant's life at this juncture is the mother or a mother substitute. The particular point on the trust-mistrust scale that the child ultimately reaches will depend to a great extent on the quality of his relationship to the maternal figure during this first year out of the womb. If the child's need for food, for exercising the lips and gums and the sucking mechanism, is frequently frustrated, the infant will begin life more toward the mistrust end of the scale. If the quality of affectional relationships at this time is poor, with the mother emotionally rejecting the baby while tending to its physical needs, the sense of trust is damaged. This sets a poor foundation for the trust-mistrust ratio on which the child is to build the rest of his life.

As to how permanent the damage done at this early stage will be, Erikson said that the manner in which this first crisis, like the succeeding ones, is settled at the crisis period is not necessarily unalterable for the rest of the person's life. Damage to the sense of trust that occurs by an unsatisfactory infant–mother relationship during the first year of life can be repaired somewhat in later years by the child's enjoying a particularly trustworthy social environment. However, the damage is not completely undone by later positive experiences. In like manner, an infant who establishes a secure attitude of trust during the first year may have this attitude shaken in later years by experience with undependable people who are significant to him. But he will still retain a measure of self-trust and feel a trust of others founded on his success in passing through the trust-mistrust crisis of infancy. These same principles of permanence of influences during a crisis period are valid as well for the other crises faced at subsequent stages of growth.

AUTONOMY VERSUS SHAME AND DOUBT

In parallel with Freud's psychosexual anal stage during the second year of life, Erikson proposed a second psychosocial crisis. This second stage is influenced by the child's maturing muscle system, with his increased ability to expel or retain things, particularly bodily wastes. Evacuating the bowels and bladder not only causes him to feel good but gives him a growing sense of power through control over the evacuation system.

In Erikson's opinion, the child's new sense of power is the basis for his developing a sense of autonomy, of being able to do things for himself. At the same time he runs the risk of trying too much too soon and thereby attracting the censure of those around him. Thus, during this period he requires a delicate balance between (1) parental firmness that lets the child know he has a trustworthy world that will prevent him from overstepping the bounds and (2) parental flexibility and patience that allows him gradually to gain bowel and bladder control at a pace commensurate with his understanding and the conscious control of his sphincter muscles. If outer control is too rigid or too early, demanding he control bowel and bladder before he is able, the child will be faced with "a double rebellion and a double defeat" (Erikson, 1959, p. 68). He is powerless to manage his bowels and powerless to control his parents' actions. So he either seeks satisfaction by regressing to oral activities—sucking his thumb, whining, and demanding attention—or he fakes progression by becoming hostile and willful. He may pretend that he has achieved control by rejecting others' aid, even though he really lacks the ability to be so independent.

Erikson proposed that parents who impose strict bowel training on the two-year-old may influence the child to become an overcompulsive adult who is stingy and meticulous with his love, energy, time, and money. This overcompulsive behavior is accompanied by a lasting sense of doubt and shame. In contrast, firm but gradual and kindly bowel training can aid the child in developing a sense of *self-control without loss of self-esteem* and produce an adult with a strong but socially acceptable sense of autonomy (Erikson, 1959, p. 68).

INITIATIVE VERSUS GUILT

During the fourth and fifth years of life, the child gains more skill in using language, in moving about, and in handling things. As a result, his imagination expands to encompass "so many things that he cannot avoid frightening himself with what he himself has dreamed and thought up. Nevertheless, out of all this he must emerge with a sense of *unbroken initiative* as a basis for a high and yet realistic sense of ambition and independence" (Erikson, 1959, p. 75).

This is the time of the Oedipus conflict, when the conscience develops and serves as a control on initiative. Fear of sexual impulses toward the opposite-sex parent causes feelings of guilt. In order to navigate through this period successfully, the child needs the guidance of parents and teachers who understand the trials the child is facing. Through such understanding, the important adults in the child's life can alleviate the hatred and guilt the child may feel. This permits the "peaceful cultivation of initiative, a truly free sense of enterprise" (Erikson, 1959, p. 82). The child's mental and physical skills, unfettered by overbearing guilt, permit him to go after life in a self-confident way.

INDUSTRY VERSUS INFERIORITY

Throughout the Freudian latency period, in the years before puberty, the child wants to get busy with activities worth his attention and to pursue these activities with his peers. In Erikson's opinion, children during the elementary school years need and enjoy hours of make-believe games and play, but they become dissatisfied with too much of this and want to do something worthwhile. They want to earn recognition by producing something, to gain the satisfaction of completing work by perseverance.

If adults pose tasks for the child that he can accomplish and that he recognizes as interesting and worthy, and if the adults furnish him the guidance needed for completing the tasks, then he has a better chance to come through the latency period with a sound sense of industry. However, if the child has not solved the Oedipal conflict or if family life has not prepared him well for school life, the period can produce just the opposite—a sense of inadequacy and inferiority. Feelings of inferiority may also occur if the things the child has already learned to do well are considered insignificant by the teacher and classmates. Furthermore, in Erikson's opinion, the child may have potential abilities which, if not evoked and nurtured during latency, may "develop late or never" (1959, p. 87).

conclusion

IDENTITY VERSUS IDENTITY DIFFUSION

Of all the growth stages, the one on which Erikson focused the greatest attention in his writings is the period of adolescence, particularly the onset of adolescence. During the early teens, with the arrival of puberty, the body grows rapidly and changes in curious ways. These changes are disturbing to the girl and boy. Their social roles take on new form, and the views they held of themselves in childhood no longer fit their new appearance and their new feelings for the opposite sex. In addition, adults and peers adopt new expectations for them as they move from childhood into youth. The confusion this creates for the incipient adolescent has been labeled the *identity crisis* by Erikson.

During this period the results of earlier years' experiences should lead to a successful integration of the individual's basic drives with his physical and intellectual endowment and with his opportunities in life. In effect, the child's development over the first dozen or so years should now synthesize to give him a sense of *ego identity* or self-definition.

> The sense of ego identity, then, is the accrued confidence that one's ability to maintain inner sameness and continuity is matched by the sameness and continuity of one's meaning for others. Thus, self-esteem . . . grows to be a conviction that one is learning effective steps toward a tangible future, that one is developing a defined personality within a social reality which one understands (Erikson, 1959, p. 89).

Furthermore, the young adolescent should gain an increasing strength of purpose and understanding of reality as he recognizes that his own way of dealing with life—his way of mastering reality —is a proper variant of the ways in which other people successfully deal with their lives.

The great danger of this period has been termed either *role confusion* or *identity diffusion* by Erikson (1963, p. 261; 1959, p. 92). The youth does not know who he is to himself or to others. As a defense against a sense of identity diffusion, adolescents may overidentify with heroes or cliques and with crowds and causes; they can temporarily lose their own individuality. They help one another during these years of confusion and of unclear occupational direction by clustering together, by stereotyping themselves in their clothes and speech, in their ideals, and in their idols and enemies. They are frequently intolerant of others outside their clique. In search of self, they often come into conflict with parents, siblings, and others close to them while refighting "many of the battles of earlier years, even though to do so they must artificially appoint perfectly well-meaning people to play the roles of adversaries" (Erikson, 1963, p. 261).

Youths who solve the problems of the adolescent years come through with a strong sense of their own individuality and a recognition that they are acceptable to their society. Those who fail to work their way through the identity crisis continue to display in later life such marks of immaturity as intolerance, clannishness, cruel treatment of people who are "different," blind identification or loyalty to heroes and idols, and the like.

THREE ADULT STAGES

With his description of the adolescent identity crisis, Erikson carried the narrative of psychosocial development through the second decade of life. However, unlike Freud, he did not stop at this point in describing personality growth. Rather, he added three more stages, depicting key conflicts faced by adults in their early, middle, and later years. Since our chief concern in this book is with growth through the teenage years, we will not dwell on the three adult stages, but will simply mention the nature of the crises faced at those levels.

The transition from adolescence to adulthood is accompanied by the crisis of *intimacy and distantiation versus self-absorption*. Or, phrased another way, it is a crisis of intimacy and solidarity versus isolation. In Erikson's view, the youth who emerges from adolescence with a reasonable sense of his own identity is then prepared to establish a nonexploitative intimacy, sexually and intellectually, with a companion of the opposite sex. The youth whose identity is secure is also prepared to defend his or her rights and individuality against attackers. This ability to defend oneself is termed *distantiation* by Erikson. In his words, distantiation is the readiness to "repudiate, to isolate, and if necessary to destroy those forces and people whose essence seems dangerous to one's own" (1959, p. 95). Youths who fail at this stage are unable to establish intimate relations with a companion, so they retreat into self-absorption.

During the second adult stage, the psychosocial conflict involves *generativity versus stagnation* (or generativity versus self-absorption). The sexual mates who find true genitality (capacity for orgasmic potency with a love partner of the opposite sex) wish to combine their personalities in producing and caring for off-spring, a condition that Erikson labeled *generativity*. Such mates are not simply absorbed in their own welfare.

In later years of adulthood the crisis involves *integrity versus despair and disgust*. The older person who achieves integrity is one who accepts his own life cycle and "is ready to defend the dignity of his own life style against all physical and economic threats" (Erikson, 1959, p. 98).

These, then, are the eight stages of development as conceived by Erikson in his theory of psychosocial periods. Since he intro-duced this scheme in 1959, he has periodically embellished it with additional propositions. For instance, in *Insight and Responsibility* (Erikson, 1964) he expanded his picture of positive ego develop-ment by describing a series of human *virtues*, which he identified as "qualities of strength."

> I . . . speak of Hope, Will, Purpose, and Competence as the ru-diments of virtue developed in childhood; of Fidelity as the ado-lescent virtue; and of Love, Care, and Wisdom as the central virtues of adulthood (Erikson, 1964, pp. 113, 115).

These virtues, he said, are an expression of the integration of the psychosexual and psychosocial growth schedules we have just reviewed. Each virtue has its particular time of arousal and em-phasis in the hierarchy of epigenetic growth stages. For example, Erikson has postulated that the virtue of *hope* arises during early infancy, that of *will* around ages 2 and 3, and that of *purpose* in the preschool years of age 3 to 6. Furthermore, each virtue builds upon those that have developed before it. "Will cannot be trained until hope is secure, nor can love become reciprocal until fidelity has proven reliable" (Erikson, 1964, p. 115). The meanings assigned to these virtues by Erikson and their relationship to the psychosexual and psychosocial stages are displayed in Table 12.2.

When a theorist suggests that such traits as hope, fidelity, and wisdom trace their essential development to specified age periods that are universal for all children, two questions arise about the theorist's beliefs concerning the roles or heredity and environment. First, does the theorist.mean that all children inherit a time-schedule mechanism that preordains the sequence in which character traits evolve and the time when each trait be-comes of primary developmental import? Second, does he or she

Table 12.2 Stages in the Development of Virtues

Stage Number	Column A Freud's Psychosexual Stages	Column B Erikson's Psychosocial Crises	Column C Erikson's Virtues or Qualities of Strength	Column D Approximate Ages in Years
I	Oral-Respiratory	Trust versus Mistrust	*Hope:* The enduring belief that fervent wishes can be fulfilled despite "the dark urges and rages which mark the beginning of existence"	0–1
II	Anal-Urethral	Autonomy versus Shame, Doubt	*Will:* The constant determination to exercise both free choice and self-restraint, despite the shame and doubt experienced during infancy	2–3
III	Infantile-Genital	Initiative versus Guilt	*Purpose:* The "courage to envisage and pursue valued goals uninhibited by the defeat of infantile fantasies, by guilt and by the foiling fear of punishment"	3–6
IV	Latency	Industry versus Inferiority	*Competence:* The free use of skill and intelligence in completing tasks, "unimpaired by infantile inferiority"	7–12 or so

(continued)

Stage Number	Column A Freud's Psychosexual Stages	Column B Erikson's Psychosocial Crises	Column C Erikson's Virtues or Qualities of Strength	Column D Approximate Ages in Years
V	Puberty and Adolescence	Identity and Repudiation versus Identity Diffusion	*Fidelity:* Sustaining freely pledged loyalties despite contradictions in value systems	12–18 or so
VI	Mature Genitality	Intimacy and Solidarity versus Isolation	*Love:* "Mutuality of devotion forever subduing the antagonisms inherent in divided function"	The 20s
VII		Generativity versus Self-Absorption	*Care:* Concern for obligations "generated by love, necessity, or accident"	Late 20s to 50s
VIII		Integrity versus Despair	*Wisdom:* "Detached concern with life itself, in the face of death itself"	50s and beyond

Adapted from Erikson, 1964, pp. 115–134.

mean that the actual form each trait assumes is inherited, and that, consequently, the child's social environment has little or no effect on the nature of the hope, fidelity, and wisdom that she will display in her personality?

In response to these queries, Erikson would say yes to the first and no to the second. Yes, he does mean that the epigenetic principle establishes the sequence and the general time when particular psychosexual and psychosocial concerns appear in center stage, demanding primary attention. But no, the form that a given trait assumes is not determined by the child's genetic nature. Instead, the way a psychosocial concern is resolved and the way the personality characteristics that the child or youth comes to display are formed depend on the way she interacts with the social institutions of her particular culture. So while Erikson postulates that the crucial time for the development of hope arises during infancy for all of mankind, he says that the degree of hope or optimism the child achieves is determined by the way the child is treated during the first year of life. And such treatment varies greatly from one society to another and from one family to another. In effect, Erikson accords a very prominent role to the culture as an influence on the form that psychosocial traits assume as the child grows up.

The importance of social institutions in the sculpturing of the child's personality has also been emphasized in another, more recent extension of Erikson's theory, an extension described in *Toys and Reasons* (Erikson, 1977). The general subject of Erikson's attention in this book is human play, with the term *play* used in a very broad sense. According to Erikson the child is engaging in play when she uses her imagination to devise mental models of her place in her expanding world. These models are visions designed by the child to make sense out of her feelings and skills in relation to the array of puzzling stimuli that impinge on her from without. At each stage of development such play or the creation of such visions functions as a tool to help the individual solve the psychosocial conflict on which she is focusing at that stage.

Three aspects of Erikson's conception of play are of particular note. First, play in this sense is not an activity limited to the period of childhood, but rather is pursued throughout the entire life span. Nor are these imaginative, playful acts simply pastimes —something nonserious to do when we are not engaged in the work of life. Instead, such acts, during either working time or leisure time, are marks of the lifelong "human propensity to create model situations in which aspects of the past are re-lived, the present re-presented and renewed, and the future anticipated"

(Erikson, 1977, p. 44). Therefore, the child is playing when she builds a structure of blocks or dramatizes with dolls an encounter in the life of a family, but the physicist is also playing when she fashions a model of the universe, and the army general is playing when devising a battle strategy and conducting war according to the "rules of the game."

Second, though the psychological purpose of play is to enable the individual to organize and master her own existence, play cannot fulfill this purpose if conducted only in a solitary setting. There is an essential social quality to much if not all play. In Erikson's view, the individual's imaginative models or mental pictures of herself in her world need to be shared with and affirmed by others. The growing child does not achieve identity or self-concept in isolation but through the interplay of her imaginative creations with those of significant people in her environment. For the preschooler, this interplay can be the child's producing a visual construction with toys and blocks in the presence of an understanding observer. In spontaneous dramatic play with peers, the child has her model situation affirmed and clarified by other children participating in the drama in a way that makes sense to them all—they have produced a shared vision of their world. The games of school-age children are also microcosms —miniature, imagined worlds with defined roles, goals, boundaries of time and space, and rules that define the right way to do things. So also are the games of adults, whether in the form of sporting events and parlor pastimes or in the form of maneuvers in national politics and war (Erikson, 1977, pp. 53–64).

Third, within any society, as time passes, the dominant shared visions or world views assume rather permanent form. Each individual or each generation does not create entirely new ones. The dominant models become traditional and ritualized, and people who share these ways of viewing themselves within their world become convinced that theirs are the right ways or best ways. To perpetuate such models, the institutions of the society—the family, church, school, social club, mass communication media, judiciary, business organizations, and government—teach the viewpoints and rituals to the young. In this way one group of people perpetuates a different culture or pattern of rituals and world views than another.

Whereas the biologically inherited genes differentiate the human species from such other species as chimpanzees and hummingbirds, it is the set of socializing institutions within a given culture that causes differences between the people in that society and the people in another society. These resulting groups of people, each marked by the attitudinal and ritual signs of its own culture, are what Erikson has called *pseudo-species*.

> By pseudo-speciation, then, we mean a sense of irreversible difference between one's own and other "kinds," which can attach itself to evolved major differences among human populations or, indeed, to smaller and smaller differences which have come to loom large. In the form of man's "in"-group loyalties, such a specific sense of being elect—as a tribe or nation, creed, class, or ideology—can contribute to the highest achievements in citizenship, courage, and workmanship and can, in fact, weld together in new loyalties (*civis Romanus*, Christian love) previously inimical entities. In the form of new "out"-group enmities, on the other hand, it can express itself most variably—in mortal hatred as well as in phobic avoidance, or in sheer clannishness (Erikson, 1977, pp. 76–77).

Of the various aspects of play, as Erikson has used the term, the one facet on which he centers particular attention in *Toys and Reasons* is that of ritualization. He has fitted various forms of ritualization into his stages of the life cycle, tracing each form from its beginnings in childhood and adolescence to its form in the adult world. Erikson's chart of the ontogeny of ritualization is shown in Figure 12.1. As the chart suggests, the evolution of ritualization according to the epigenetic schedule proceeds as follows.

The earliest beginning of ritual in infancy has been labeled *mutuality of recognition* by Erikson, for the first social interaction in the infant's life involves his needs being cared for by parents, particularly by the mother. By means of the child-care ritual—the mother's touch, her smile, the name she gives the child—a mutual mode of recognizing each other and of affirming their identities and relationship develops. This initial ritual serves as the foundation for subsequent rituals of mutual recognition and bond that will mark later stages of life: the relationship between teacher and pupil, club or gang leader and group member, chieftain and warrior, statesman and citizen, God and the true believer. Erikson proposes that people are born with the need for such "regular and mutual affirmation and certification" and that its absence can radically harm an infant (Erikson, 1977, p. 88). He has called this aspect of ritualization the *numinous*, for it represents reassurance for the individual through familiarity and mutuality in relation to an object or personage of devotion. Among the institutions of adult society, that of organized religion is most obviously responsible for the numinous:

Infancy Age 0-1	Early Childhood Age 2-3	Play Age Age 3-6	School Age Age 6-12	Adolescence Age 12-18	Elements in Adult Rituals	Principal Societal Institutions in Adult Life*
Mutuality of recognition				⬆	Numinous	Church, family
	Discrimination of good and bad			⬆	Judicious	Court of law
		Dramatic elaboration		⬆	Dramatic	Stage, movies, television, literature
			Rules of performance	⬆	Formal	School, craft training agency, licensing agency for vocations
				Solidarity of conviction	Ideological	Political group, church, military
					Generational sanction	Marriage, guardianship, professional training and licensing agencies (for teachers, physicians, clergy, etc.)

*The institutions in adult life are partly quoted directly from Erikson and partly the present author's extrapolations from the general tenor of Erikson's analyses.

Figure 12.1   Stages in the Development of Ritualization (Adapted from Erikson, 1977, pp. 85–114)

> The believer, by appropriate gestures, confesses his dependence and his childlike faith and seeks, by appropriate offerings, to secure the privilege of being lifted up to the very bosom of the divine which, indeed, may be seen to graciously respond, with the faint smile of an inclined face (Erikson, 1977, pp. 89–90).

This first aspect of ritualization, the numinous, thus develops throughout life, and combines with subsequently developed rituals to form the complex that makes up the cultural patterns the child's personality acquires.

The second aspect, arising at age 2 or 3 in relation to the toilet-training stage, is that of discriminating good from bad. From these early years the rituals involved with making judgments develop until they reach their most formal version in the procedures of judicial courts. Hence, Erikson has applied the word *judicious* to this second sequence of imaginative models of a culture.

The third sort of ritualization is seated in the dramatic play of the preschool years, ages 3 through 6, when the child's new sense of guilt at the time of the Oedipus conflict motivates him to seek a resolution of his conflict through imagined dramas. For example, in his clinical experience with children, Erikson has observed them use toys as elements in creating a narrative with a plot that includes conflicts that are finally resolved. These are the elements —plot, conflict, resolution—that make up the sophisticated adult versions of ritualization performed on the stage, in motion pictures, and on radio and television. The effective drama is a vision of reality condensed in space and time and experienced by the audience as "unbearably personal and yet miraculously shared" (Erikson, 1977, p. 102).

A fourth element of ritualization, emphasized during the elementary school years (ages 6–12), is that of *methodological performance*. During this stage the child is assigned a series of tasks that prepare him to master the skills and work habits that will enable him to participate in the economic and technological life of the society, be it agricultural, industrial, commercial, or literary. This stage is the beginning of the child's learning to gain satisfaction through competently performing the formal tasks of the society. This "work role which we begin to envisage for ourselves at the end of childhood is, under favorable conditions, the most reassuring role of all, just because it confirms us in skills and permits us to recognize ourselves in visible works" (Erikson, 1977, p. 106).

A fifth element that enters at the time of adolescence is the adoption by the growing youth of a set of convictions that tie together in a coherent manner (1) the psychosocial identity he has achieved up to this point and (2) the structure and expectations of the adult culture. Erikson has identified two varieties of ritual prominent during these years. First are the *spontaneous "rites"* by which adolescents ritualize relations with their peers and mark their subculture as distinct from childhood and adulthood. Second are the *formal rites,* such as school graduation and joining the church, that represent the passage into, and adoption of, adult status and values. The solidifying of convictions during adolescence leads to the development of the mature ideologies of adult life.

The final stage in the evolution of ritualization is *generational sanction,* because as the youth achieves adult status he is officially authorized through such rituals as marriage and guardianship to take on the teaching, productive, and curative roles for a new generation of children. Whereas the child and adolescent are the objects of rituals supervised by adults, the new adult now becomes the ritualizer for the young. The evolution of ritualization for the growing years is now complete.

With this brief review of the place of ritualization in Erikson's epigenetic schedule of development, we close our inspection of his *vision of reality*—his *playful model*—and turn to an assessment of the overall theory.

ERIKSON'S VERSION OF PSYCHOANALYSIS: AN ASSESSMENT

Since Erikson's theory is an extension of the psychoanalytic model and is in essential agreement with it, the evaluation of Freudian theory at the end of Chapter 11 is also applicable to Erikson's theory in most respects. Therefore, rather than repeat the assessment from Chapter 11, I will confine my appraisal in the following paragraphs to ways in which Erikson's views and contributions differ from Freud's.

Not only has Erikson been acclaimed for his detailed definitions of psychosocial stages and the proposed identity crisis of adolescence, but he has been credited as well with significant contributions to psychoanalytic research methodology. Among the complaints that critics have lodged against Freud is the charge that he was anthropologically naive. By this they mean that he based his theory on a very narrow range of personalities, assuming that the themes of neurotic behavior and thought he found in his patients were an accurate reflection of the modes found in the rest of mankind. In effect, critics have questioned how accurately the patients met in a late-nineteenth-century Viennese psychiatric practice, that drew heavily from women of upper-middle-class Jewish society, represent people in general. Erikson, in contrast, drew the cases on which he based his speculations from a far wider geographical sampling than Freud. Erikson was a psychoanalyst in Europe, but he also participated in intensive studies of cases at the Harvard Psychological Clinic, of infants suffering neuroses at the Yale University Department of Psychiatry, of normal adolescents in Northern California, of Sioux and Yurok Indians, and of numerous other Americans. Furthermore, he focused more attention on normal development than did Freud, particularly the normal development of the healthy self or ego in personal-social relations.

Erikson also furthered the development of *psychohistory*, which is the analysis of the psychological development of individuals by use of what they have written and said and of reports of their actions. Perhaps the most notable of his analyses of world figures have been those of Martin Luther (1958) and Gandhi (1969). His purpose in these endeavors was to identify significant relationships between the life histories of great leaders and "the historical moment of their emergence" (Erikson, 1975, p. 10). In particular, he concentrated on "the powers of recovery inherent in the young ego" (Erikson, 1958, p. 8).

This same concern for the influence of the broad social setting on personality development caused Erikson to seek ways for elucidating and verifying impressions derived by means of the psychoanalytic interview. He saw sociological and anthropological research techniques as serving to help clinicians recognize the importance of the social environment in which their data are obtained.

> Clinical evidence, finally, will be decisively clarified, but not changed in nature, by a sharpened awareness (such as now emanates from sociological studies) of the psychotherapist's as well as the patient's position in society and history (Erikson, 1964, p. 80).

All of the foregoing points I would put on the credit side of the assessment ledger. On the debit side I find the same basic problems of scientific validation described in the assessment of Freud's theory. For example, not everyone has found the evidence cited in support of Erikson's proposed psychosocial crises to be convincing. Some of the difficulties with the evidence are reflected in the following questions: Is not the major evidence in favor of Erikson's scheme mainly in the form of his interpretation of selected, illustrative clinical cases—cases of individuals in therapy, of such figures as Luther and Hitler, and of such groups as Sioux Indians? And could not another theorist find as convincing a variety of illustrations as these to suggest that psychosocial crises come in quite a different order than that suggested by Erikson? For example, why is the crisis of autonomy versus shame necessarily set in the second year of life? Could we not easily find behaviors at other ages that might be reasonably interpreted as symptoms of an autonomy crisis, behavior such as the striving for independence that appears to mark the years of adolescence? And do all children necessarily go through the same series of crises? If a large number were studied, is it not likely we would find marked differences in the sorts of crises they encounter as a result of their unique social environment?

These are the kinds of questions that have not yet been answered adequately by the investigative methods Erikson used. Like Freud's system, and for somewhat the same reasons, Erikson's model has been difficult to translate into a form that permits experimentation or controlled observations that produce convincing evidence about the validity of the theory's components and principles.

In conclusion, Erikson's writings about development have generated much discussion in psychological circles and have attracted the admiration of many readers who have found his insights true in their own experience. But many of his proposals, like Freud's, must be accepted on faith, faith in the theorist's interpretive skills and in his authority rather than on experimental and observational evidence that would more clearly compel readers to arrive at the same conclusions. Of course, this charge can be made against many other theories of development as well.

FOR FURTHER READING

The two books by Erikson that most directly describe his overall theory of development are:

(1963) *Childhood and Society.* 2d ed. New York: Norton.
(1968) *Identity: Youth and Crisis.* New York: Norton.

A recent volume illustrating the manner in which Erikson embellishes his basic theory with further proposals is:

(1977) *Toys and Reasons.* New York: Norton.

For a biographical study of the theorist, see:

Coles, Robert. (1970) *Erik H. Erikson: The Growth of His Work.* New York: Little, Brown.

PART 8

THE GROWTH OF THOUGHT AND LANGUAGE

A search for patterns of development in children's cognitive and verbal skills, and for the mechanisms that bring these patterns about.

The title "The Growth of Thought and Language" is not meant to suggest that other theorists have neglected these matters. Indeed, what children say and think has an important role in all the theories. Rather, the title here points up the fact that the major emphasis of the work of the four theorists included in this section has been the growth of children's cognitive and verbal abilities.

The first of the four, Jean Piaget, is a Swiss who has often been acclaimed the most influential researcher in the field of child development in the twentieth century. He gained this position of distinction for proposing a novel model of children's mental development, a model founded on a great quantity of ingenious research on children from the time of birth to adolescence. Beginning in 1921, and continuing for well over fifty years, he published hundreds of journal articles and books on all sorts of questions related to the development of children's thought processes: how dreams and play evolve, how symbols develop, ways moral judgments grow, how perceptions change, how intelligence improves, ways numbers are conceived, what causes physical events, and many more. In recent years, interest in Piaget's theory has reached a high level all over the world. A search of the most widely used books and journals on child development over the past two decades has shown that Piaget is by far the most frequently cited author in the field (Wadsworth, 1971, p. 2).

Although Piaget wrote on a variety of topics, a basic theme or model of intellectual growth connects all of his work. The view of Piaget offered in Chapter 13 focuses on the most fundamental elements of his basic model.

The second theorist is a Russian, Lev Semenovich Vygotsky, a brilliant young scholar who pursued an active career from 1915, prior to the Communist Revolution, until his death in 1934 at age 38. Although he conducted his studies more than four decades ago, his work did not become widely known in English-speaking nations until recently, when English translations were published: *Thought and Language* in 1962 and *Psychology and Art* in 1971 (the form of art is that of literature). A description of Vygotsky's model of the development of children's thought and speech is given in Chapter 14, directly following Piaget's theory in order to point up contrasts between the two models.

Chapter 15 reviews the work of Roger Brown, an American social psychologist who has concentrated his attention on how children's speech develops and, consequently, on how children's thought processes develop as reflected in what they say. It would be inaccurate to call this chapter "Brown's Theory," for he does not propose a single integrated model of growth in speech. Rather, the chapter describes theory in the making, illustrating the mode of research pursued by one of the leaders in the field of psycholinguistics as applied to the speech of young children.

Chapter 16 reviews a theory of the development of children's moral values as formulated by an American psychologist, Lawrence Kohlberg. He has built on groundwork laid by Piaget and others to show how children's ways of defending value judgments change systematically over time.

CHAPTER 13

PIAGET'S GENETIC EPISTEMOLOGY

Jean Piaget (born 1896) was a precocious boy who, in his teens, had already developed an intense interest in biology, particularly in the biological bases of knowledge. By age 21 he had earned a doctorate at the university in his hometown of Neuchatel, Switzerland, and had published more than two dozen professional papers on biological studies, most of them concerning mollusks. This early specialization in biology has had a lasting influence on his conceptions of the development of the mind.

Upon finishing his doctorate, he shifted his attention to psychology, which he studied in Swiss psychological clinics and at the Sorbonne in Paris. While in Paris (1919–1921) Piaget worked on standardizing tests of children's abilities in the laboratory school of the French expert on intelligence measurement, Alfred Binet. During this time Piaget was not as interested in whether children got the test items correct as he was in the thinking processes that led children to produce the answers they gave, especially the incorrect answers. This interest set the focus for his research during the rest of his career.

Although Piaget is commonly referred to as a child psychologist, he has characterized himself instead as a *genetic epistemologist*. This means that the central question guiding his investigations is not "What are children like?" but "How does knowledge develop in humans?" Or more precisely, "How does the relationship between the *knower* and the *known* change with the passing of time?" So the term *genetic* (meaning the genesis or the mode of development) and *epistemology* (the theory of knowledge) does indeed describe the field of his endeavors. Children of different age levels just happen to be the instruments by which his investigations in this field might properly be carried out.

In the following review of Piaget's work, we will consider: (1) his methods of research, (2) his conception of knowledge, (3) his conception of the process by which children's knowledge grows, (4) stages of intellectual growth, and (5) educational applications of the theory.

PIAGET'S CLINICAL METHOD

While working at Binet's test-construction laboratory, Piaget devised the basic technique of studying children that would become the mainstay of his methodology over the next fifty years. His approach, known as a *clinical method*, involves a researcher posing problems for children and then observing how the children go about finding a solution. For children who have not yet reached puberty, the problems usually involve objects the child can see and manipulate, such as two lumps of clay that can be formed into different shapes or two glasses of water of different sizes. By the time the child can use language at age 3 or 4, the experimenter asks the child questions about solutions to the problems being posed. During the adolescent years, children are more often given verbal problems and questioned about how they arrived at their solution.

Unlike some other experimenters, Piaget has not limited himself to asking each child a preconceived set of questions. Rather, after beginning an interview with a standard question or two, he has felt free to create, on the spot, additional questions for the child designed to probe the thought processes that produced the initial answer. Piaget has defended this deviation from a single, standard set of questions by explaining that all children do not interpret a given question in the same way. Thus, the experimenter probes the child's understanding and may then cast the problem in a different form to help ensure that the problem situation is the same for each child, though not necessarily identical in wording each time (Phillips, 1975, pp. 4–5).

A typical interview is illustrated in the following passage in which eight-year-old Per is being questioned about some flowers —primulas and other varieties—that the woman interviewer has placed before the child. The interviewer's purpose is to discover how Per classifies objects into a general set (flowers) and into subsets within the general set (primulas, violets, tulips). At the point we enter the discussion, Per has already devised three levels of classes: yellow primulas, primulas, and flowers (adapted from Inhelder and Piaget, 1964, p. 107).

> **Interviewer:** Can one put a primula in the box of flowers (without changing the label)?
> **Per:** Yes, a primula is also a flower.
> **Interviewer:** Can I put one of these flowers (a tulip) in the box of primulas?
> **Per:** Yes, it's a flower like the primula.

When the experimenter does so, she changes her mind and puts it back with the other flowers.

> **Interviewer:** Can one make a bigger bunch with all the flowers or with all the primulas?
> **Per:** It's the same thing, primulas are flowers, aren't they?
> **Interviewer:** Suppose I pick all the primulas, will there be any flowers left?
> **Per:** Oh, yes, there will still be violets, tulips, and other flowers.
> **Interviewer:** Well, suppose I pick all the flowers, will there be any primulas left?
> **Per:** No, primulas are flowers, you're picking them too.
> **Interviewer:** Are there more flowers or more primulas?
> **Per:** The same number, primulas are flowers.
> **Interviewer:** Count the primulas.
> **Per:** Four.
> **Interviewer:** And the flowers?
> **Per:** Seven.
> **Interviewer:** Are they the same number?
> **Per** (astonished): The flowers are more.

In effect, then, Piaget's research methodology consists of his first observing children's reactions to their surroundings. Then, on the basis of these observations, he composes hypotheses about the sorts of biological and mental structures that underlie their reactions. Finally, he casts the hypotheses in the form of problems or questions that he poses to children in order to reveal their thinking processes and thus test the hypotheses. Over the years he has produced large numbers of problem situations that subsequently have been used by researchers in many parts of the world to investigate matters that Piaget studied, as well as other aspects of development.

PIAGET'S CONCEPTION OF KNOWLEDGE

A useful step toward understanding Piaget's theory is to learn how he defined knowledge, because his conception differs from most popular beliefs. We can perhaps best see this difference by beginning with a review of four commonsense ideas about knowledge and how it is acquired.

First, common sense holds that knowledge is a body of information or beliefs a person has acquired, either through instruction or through direct experience with the world. This idea of a collection of information is reflected in such everyday phrases as "She's a storehouse of knowledge" and "I wish I had all his knowledge."

Second, it is also a commonsense conviction that a person's knowledge is a fairly faithful representation of what she has been taught or what she has witnessed. It is assumed that if two people, both with good eyesight, observe an event from the same vantage point, their knowledge of the event will be essentially identical. The great dependence on witnesses in court cases is founded on this conviction.

Third, common sense indicates that our storehouse of knowledge is increased if we add to it from our daily experiences item upon item. We take in bits of information and pile them onto the proper heap in the storehouse, with each heap related to a different aspect of life.

Fourth, common sense tells us that whenever we need to recall an item of knowledge from the storehouse of memory, the item can be recovered in essentially the same condition as it was when first acquired. Of course, some details of the item may now be a bit vague, but if we can recall the item at all, it will be basically in its original form.

How do Piaget's views differ from such commonsense notions? To begin, he does not agree that knowledge is a body of acquired information or a state of possessing such information. Instead, he conceives of knowledge as a process. To *know* something means to *act* on that thing, with the action being either physical or mental or both. The two-year-old child's knowledge of a ball consists of his picking it up, pressing it with his fingers, tossing it, and observing it bounce away. As children grow up, they gain more experience with such direct, physical knowing, and they mature internally so that they are increasingly freed from having to carry out direct physical behavior in order to know something. They become able to produce mental images and symbols (words, mathematical figures) that represent objects and relationships. Hence, the older child's knowledge increasingly becomes mental activity. He "thinks about" things by carrying out *interiorized actions* on symbolic objects (Piaget, Apostel, and Mandelbrot, 1957, pp. 44–45). So to Piaget, knowledge is a process or repertoire of actions rather than an inventory of stored information.

Piaget also disagrees with the commonsense idea of perception, that is, with the way objects or events are recorded in the child's mind. In Piaget's opinion, the child does not take in a picture of objective reality. Instead, as the child perceives or takes in the world, the picture he obtains is biased by the condition of his perceptual mechanism. If we adopt the analogy of viewing the world through glass, then in the Piagetian model the child does not record events through a clear window. Rather, he views events through a colored lens that is given its present focus and tint by both (1) the child's past experiences and (2) his current stage of internal maturation. The way that two children know (act on) the same object will not be identical, for the lens of one will have a somewhat different focus and tint than the other's.

But if knowledge is a process of acting on percepts rather than a collection of information, then what is memory and how does it operate? Piaget agrees that the results of a person's past actions can be stored as memories to be retrieved when needed. He also agrees that the quantity of memories increases with maturation and experience. But he does not believe that the act of remembering is simply a matter of summoning images of past events from memory and placing them in the showcase of consciousness so that, like museum pieces, they can be viewed in their passive, original condition. Rather, retrieving stored vestiges of the past, which he has labeled *active memory*, is "interiorized recitation" or "a reconstitution of the past" (Piaget, 1946, pp. 5, 261). Remembering is a reenacting of the original process of knowing. However, it cannot simply be a repetition of the original knowing, because the child's mind has subsequently been altered by additional experiences and further internal maturation. So the interiorized recitation or rehearsal of the stored event is, as it were, now performed on a somewhat altered mental stage according to revised stage directions.

To summarize, in Piaget's system, knowledge is a process of acting—physically and/or mentally—on objects, images, and symbols that the child's perceptual lens has cast into patterns that are somewhat familiar to him. The objects are found in the world of direct experience, while the images and symbols can be derived not only from the "real world" but from memory as well.

One way to conceive mental growth or the development of intelligence is to picture it as a constant effort on the part of the child to expand and refine his knowledge, his repertoire of mental actions. Or, in different terms, "All knowledge is continually in a course of development and of passing from a state of lesser knowledge to one which is more complete and effective" (Piaget, 1972, p. 5).

This idea that a child's knowledge improves with age is hardly a noteworthy discovery. Everyone knows that already. But what everyone does not know is the specific ways knowledge changes, at what times it changes, and for what likely reasons. These are the things Piaget has provided. In our review of his stages of development, we will consider such matters in some detail, but as an indication of the aspects of knowledge on which he focused attention, Table 13.1 has illustrations of five categories of behavior he treated. In the description, we are using the verbals *recognizing* and *constructing* as synonyms, believing that the more passive *recognizing* is the familiar way people refer to such mental behavior but that *constructing* more accurately reflects Piaget's conception of knowledge as a process of active production on the part of the child.

These, then, are some of the directions of intellectual development that Piaget's theory is designed to depict and explain (Piaget and Inhelder, 1969). Our next task is to identify the mechanisms which, in Piaget's opinion, bring about these kinds of development.

THE MECHANISMS OF DEVELOPMENT

The purpose of all behavior or all thought, according to Piaget's system, is to enable the organism—the child—to adapt to her environment in ever more satisfactory ways. The techniques of

adaptation have been called by Piaget *schemes* or, in older translations of his writings from the original French, *schemas* or *sche-
mata*. A scheme or technique of adjustment can be biological or
mental or both. In Piaget's words:

> A scheme is the structure or organization of actions as they are trans-
> ferred or generalized by repetition in similar or analogous circum-
> stances (Piaget and Inhelder, 1969, p. 4).

The *grasping* movement of the infant's hand is such a scheme,
a physical organization of actions that he can generalize to grasp
a bottle, a rattle, or the edge of his crib. On the intellectual level,
an adolescent girl's concept of *a series* is also a scheme, a mental organization of actions. She can apply it in constructing a series
of numbers, arranging a series of sweaters according to shades
of color, or arranging a series of young men by height or
attractiveness.

A scheme can be very simple, such as the action pattern involved in the child's putting his thumb into his mouth. Or it can
be complex, comprising physical and mental subschemes, as in
the chain of acts required for starting a car and driving it down the
street or in the mental chain needed for solving quadratic
equations.

Schemes always include accompanying feeling tones. When
Piaget speaks of *affective schemes*, he does not mean schemes distinct from mental structures, but "simply the affective aspect of
schemes which are otherwise also intellectual" (Piaget, 1962, p.
207).

The newborn's schemes are very limited in number, consisting of reflex action patterns—sucking, crying out, sneezing,
flexing the limbs, and the like. But as the days pass, other sensorimotor actions build out of these beginnings. Then, still within
the first year of life, identifiable intellectual schemes evolve and
over the following years multiply enormously. Thus, when you
conceptualize child development in terms of schemes, you picture
it as the child's acquiring ever greater quantities of schemes that
become interlinked in ever more sophisticated patterns.

How does this process of evolving schemes come about? To
understand the process, we need to learn the meanings Piaget
assigned to the words *assimilation* and *accommodation*. To help
explain these matters, we will liken schemes to musical themes or
tunes, for tunes are organizations of sounds just as schemes are
organizations of sensorimotor and mental actions.

At every point in her life, the child's adaptation to her envi-

Table 13.1   Growth in Sample Aspects of Knowledge:
Infancy to Adolescence

From Infancy	Through Early and Middle Childhood	To Adolescence
Egocentrism versus Objectivity		
Not distinguishing between self and the environment	Partially distinguishing between self and the environment	Clearly differentiating self from objects of the environment
Object Permanence (Conservation)		
Not recognizing (not constructing) the permanence of objects whose location is changed	Recognizing (constructing) object permanence when location is changed, but failing to recognize (to construct) which characteristics of objects go unchanged (or are conserved) when objects are transformed	Recognizing (constructing) which aspects of objects go unchanged (are conserved) when the objects are transformed
Symbolic Functioning		
Not recognizing (not constructing) that one thing can represent something else	Recognizing (constructing) symbolization through such acts of imitation as gesture, play, drawing, and oral echoing	Recognizing (constructing) complex written and spoken symbols and signs

From Infancy	Through Early and Middle Childhood	To Adolescence
Internalization of Action		
Adapting to the environment solely by physical acts	Beginning to act internally on objects (manipulate them mentally) while observing them	Accomplishing faster, more complete adaptation by internally (mentally) manipulating objects of the environment, their classifications, and their relationships
Classes and Relationships		
Not recognizing (not constructing) classifications of objects or relationships among objects	Recognizing (constructing) classes and relationships among objects that are directly touched, seen, or heard	Not only recognizing (constructing) classifications of and relationships among objects directly perceived but also (1) of imagined objects and events and (2) of classification and relationship systems themselves

ronment in order to satisfy her needs is accomplished by means of her schemes. Her repertoire of schemes at any given time is like a collection of melodies she already knows. When she faces a problem of satisfying needs, she inspects the environment to perceive how its apparent structure seems to fit schemes currently in her armory. It's as if she listens to the sounds coming from her surroundings to determine if they match, or nearly match, a tune she knows. When she finds what she considers a good match, she has achieved her adaptation. When the infant in the crib drops her doll onto the floor, she inspects the scene to decide if the conditions of her problem match any scheme or strategy in her repertoire of solutions. A twelve-year-old boy assigned to draw a map of the route from home to school must likewise search his available action structures to find ones appropriate to the task. A high school girl listening to her English teacher lecture about the plot structure in Hamlet must incorporate the ideas from the lecture into suitable schemes already in her mind if she is to comprehend, or mentally construct, the meanings intended by the teacher.

This process of matching environmental stimuli to existing mental patterns is not simply a matter of ingesting objective reality from the world. Rather, the child reshapes the events of the world somewhat to fit the pattern of her existing schemes. It's like the child hearing several tones, then deciding they sound enough like a familiar melody to indeed be that melody. So she comprehends or takes in these sounds as her familiar tune or scheme.

Piaget applied the label *assimilation* to this process of taking in or understanding events of the world by matching the perceived features of those events to one's existing schemes. As Piaget put it: "To assimilate an object to a schema means conferring to that object one or several meanings" (Piaget, Jonckheere, and Mandelbrot, 1958, p. 59).

However, often the perceived structure of events does not readily fit the child's available schemes, even with some perceptual bending or shaping of that structure. When this occurs, one of two consequences can be expected. The first is that the event is not assimilated at all. It is ignored or passed by, like a person's rejecting several sounds as meaningless noise instead of recognizing them as a familiar tune. The encounter with the environment simply does not register on the child. Such is the case when a father tries to teach his young daughter to draw with proper visual perspective but finally concludes, "She can't do it at all. She just doesn't catch on."

The second possible consequence of a poor match between the perceived environment and available schemes is not outright rejection but dissatisfaction and continued efforts to achieve a match.

> New objects which present themselves to consciousness do not have their own qualities which can be isolated . . . they are vague, nebulous, because unassimilable, and thus they create a discomfort from which there emerges sooner or later a new differentiation of the schemas of assimilation (Piaget, 1963, p. 141).

So it is that schemes, under pressures from perceived realities of the environment, are altered in form or multiplied to accommodate for the lack of an adequate match. In effect, a tune from the child's existing store of melodies is revised to become a variation of the original theme, a variation that better fits the sounds of the world. Piaget used the term *accommodation* to identify this process of altering existing schemes to permit the assimilation of events that otherwise would be incomprehensible.

Since no new event is perfectly identical with those past events that were used in the formation of schemes, there is always some degree of mismatch of schemes with new events. But this is cared for by the balancing counterplay between assimilation and accommodation, which are two of the basic innate acts Piaget called *functional invariants*. Assimilation reshapes the environmental input to fit existing schemes, whereas accommodation revises or adds to the schemes to readjust for environmental features that cannot conveniently be ignored or distorted.

Just as adaptation to the world is achieved by the functions of assimilation and accommodation, so within the child's biological-mental self a process of *organization* operates to ensure that all schemes are properly interrelated, properly adjusted to each other to form an integrated person.

> It is sufficiently well known that every intellectual operation is always related to all the others and that its own elements are controlled by the same law. Every schema is thus coordinated with all the other schemata and itself constitutes a totality with differentiated parts. Every act of intelligence presupposes a system of mutual implications and interconnected meanings (Piaget, 1963, p. 7).

Therefore, a child's development according to Piagetian theory seems somewhat like a progressively complex symphony. Its multiple melodies are the schemes formed from the balanced counterpoint of assimilation against accommodation. And the interweaving of themes produces a coordinated whole.

All these matters can be summarized in three quotations from Piaget:

> The filtering or modification of the input is called *assimilation;* the modification of internal schemas to fit reality is called *accommodation* (Piaget and Inhelder, 1969, p. 6).

> Adaptation is an equilibrium between assimilation and accommodation (Piaget, 1963, p. 6).

> The "accord of thought with things" (adaptation) and the "accord of thought with itself" (organization) express this dual functional invariant of adaptation and organization. These two aspects of thought are indissociable: It is by adapting to things that thought organizes itself and it is by organizing itself that it structures things (Piaget, 1963, p. 8).

We next face the question of what factors or forces determine how this adaptation-organization system will operate in a given child's development. What causes a child to acquire his particular schemes and at what times in his growing up? How does environment as compared to heredity influence the kinds and rate of scheme formation?

In responding to such questions, Piaget has proposed four underlying causal factors: (1) heredity (internal maturation), (2) physical experience with the world of objects, (3) social transmission (education), and (4) equilibrium.

1. Heredity   In the continuing debate among developmentalists over the roles of nature and nurture, Piaget has been classified by most writers as an interactionist, and certainly he considers himself so. He does not accord either heredity or environment greater power in determining development. Instead, he sees each playing a distinct part that is necessary to complement the part of the other.

What role does Piaget see nature playing? He says that not only does heredity provide the newborn with the initial equipment to cope with problems he will meet in the world, but heredity also establishes a time schedule for new development possibilities to open up at periodic points throughout the child's growing years. This is the internal-maturation factor in heredity. It functions rather like a legislative body, which from time to time passes a new act of *enabling* legislation. Each such act, or maturational change, creates possibilities for new schemes to be created that could not have been generated earlier, but this action neither requires nor guarantees that the potential schemes will materialize. The extent to which the potentialities are actually realized is determined by the sorts of experiences the child has with his environment. So internal maturation is a necessary but not sufficient condition for development to proceed.

Much of the practical use of Piaget's findings for educators and parents lies in his identification of approximate age levels at which the maturation needed for developing particular schemes or intellectual operations occurs. If suitable maturation has not yet taken place, it is futile to try to teach the child the particular skill you have in mind. The probable reason the father failed to teach his young daughter proper visual perspective was that the maturation necessary for developing the required schemes had not yet occurred.

Piaget (1973, p. 27) has viewed as folly the efforts of some psychologists to dissociate the effect of heredity from that of the heredity–environment amalgam in seeking to decide which of the two is more important for development: "If a maturation effect intervenes everywhere, it remains dissociable from the effects of the exercise of learning or of experience."

2. Physical Experience   It is essential to recognize that Piaget, unlike most theorists, has separated the child's trafficking with the environment into two varieties: (a) direct and generally unguided experience with objects in the world—called physical experience—and (b) the guided transmission of knowledge, that is, education in a broad sense—called social transmission. We will discuss direct experience first, for it is the type on which he has focused the greater part of his attention.

In this case, the child directly manipulates, observes, listens to, and smells objects to see what occurs when they are acted upon. From such investigation he generates a logic or knowledge of the properties of things and how they work. Piaget stresses that it is not the observation of the passive objects themselves that develops the child's logic or intelligence, but the set of conclusions he draws from those actions that bring about events and influence objects. So it is not simply seeing a feather or brick or lump of clay. But it is the experience derived when physically or mentally participating in such events as the following:

> A chicken feather and a metal bolt are simultaneously dropped from the same height.
>
> A brick is put into a bucket full of water, and a pine block the size of the brick is put into a second bucket of water.

Three lumps of clay are rolled into shapes: the first into a ball, the second into a sausage, the third into a long snake.

The child tries to cut a board—first with scissors, next with a knife, and then with a saw.

These sorts of experiences contribute to the aspect of intellectual development that Piaget (1973, p. 2) has called *spontaneous* or *psychological:* "the development of the intelligence itself —what the child learns by himself, what none can teach him and he must discover alone."

Though such physical experience with the action of objects is essential to mental growth, by itself it is, like maturation, insufficient to bring about development.

3. Social Transmission   This is the educative factor in the broad sense, the transmission of knowledge to the child from without. Like the first two factors, this one is important but is insufficient by itself to effect mental growth, for it depends upon both maturation and direct experience to prepare the schemes that permit assimilation of what parents, the school, and the general social milieu seek to teach the child. This factor contributes what Piaget calls the *psychosocial* aspect of cognitive development (1973, p. 2).

4. Equilibrium   This last factor is the one that maintains a balance among the other three, fitting the maturational, direct experience, and social transmission influences together harmoniously. Piaget (1973, p. 29) felt the need for such a factor because "a whole play of regulation and of compensation is required to result in a coherence."

In summary, then, the sorts of knowledge the child acquires in terms of mental schemes, and the time at which they are acquired, depend upon the factors of maturation, physical experience, social transmission, and equilibrium. These factors regulate the stages of cognitive growth through which, in Piaget's system, all children normally develop. It is to this series of levels or stages that we now turn.

LEVELS AND STAGES OF DEVELOPMENT

As noted in Chapter 2, one of the traditional issues in the field of child development is whether growth proceeds continuously—by imperceptibly small increments—or advances by stages. And if a theorist proposes that it does indeed move by stages, then what criteria does he apply in identifying a stage?

Piaget, like apparently all developmentalists, recognizes that from day to day, growth is continuous, with no major leaps ahead from one day to the next, leaps that are followed by extended plateaus of dormancy in growth. At the same time, when he viewed the entire span of the growth years, Piaget was able to distinguish breaks in the process. These breaks suggested to him that the child has at each such point completed one phase of development and is now engaged in a further one.

To say that Piaget proposed *a* series of developmental stages would be oversimplifying his work. Actually, he identified a number of different series, each related to a different aspect of personality or mental life. For example, one series concerns steps in understanding physical causality (1930), another the steps in imitation and play (1951), still another in the conception of moral principles and justice (1948), and others in understanding number (1952), space (1956), and movement (1969). But underlying these and other specific series of stages is a basic set that provides the framework for overall sensorimotor-intellectual development. It is this underlying set that we will review.

There is some measure of confusion in the writings of Piaget and of his interpreters about how many major stages, and their constituent substages, best reflect the growth process. Some authors picture three major levels, others four, and some even five. In the following discussion I have cast the scheme into one of its most familiar forms, with four major levels or periods, each divided into subperiods designated as stages. In this fourfold division, the levels are called: (1) the sensorimotor period, (2) the preoperational thought period, (3) the concrete operations period, and (4) the formal operations period. As we trace the child's progress through the stages, we will see her grow from being (a) an entirely self-centered infant with no realistic knowledge of her environment to become (b) an adolescent who employs logic and language with facility to intellectually manipulate the environment and thus comprehend, ever more realistically, how the world functions.

Although age designations are attached to each of the four periods in the following discussion, they should be regarded as only approximations, as rough averages, for as Piaget has pointed out:

> They are not stages which can be given a constant chronological date. On the contrary, the ages can vary from one society to an-

other. . . . But there is a constant order of succession . . . that is, in order to reach a certain stage, previous steps must be taken. The prestructures . . . which make for further advance must be constructed.

Thus we reach a hierarchy of (mental) structures which are built in a certain order of integration and . . . appear at senescence to disintegrate in the reverse order (1973, pp. 10–11).

LEVEL 1:
THE SENSORIMOTOR PERIOD
(BIRTH TO AGE 2)

During the first two years, the infant is unable to verbalize very well any thoughts he may have, so it is necessary to estimate his intellectual growth by the manner in which he senses (sees, hears, feels, tastes, smells) his environment and by the manner in which he subsequently acts upon it (motoric behavior). Piaget's observations of children in this age period enabled him to distinguish six stages through which they develop (Piaget and Inhelder, 1969, pp. 4–12).

The first stage (0–1 month) features the baby's adapting to his environment by means of his inherited, ready-to-operate, unlearned *reflexes*. It is by reflex activity that he sucks, cries, breathes, coughs, urinates, defecates, and makes gross bodily movements.

The second stage (1–4 months) is marked by the infant's gradually acquiring adaptive actions as the result of experience. During the first stage there was no distinction between the functions of assimilation and accommodation. But during the second, assimilation and accommodation begin to dissociate themselves as the infant starts to alter his sensorimotor action patterns (his schemes) on the basis of the response of his environment. He accommodates or alters schemes somewhat on the basis of the reactions of his environment to his acting upon it. "For instance, when the child systematically sucks his thumb, no longer due to chance contacts but through coordination between hand and mouth, this may be called acquired accommodation" (Piaget, 1963, p. 48).

During this second stage the child engages in a great deal of repetitive activity, such as grasping and letting go of something over and over again. These actions, labeled *primary circular reactions*, have been interpreted by Piaget as evidence that learning new associations or acquiring knowledge is not accomplished by the environment's imposing them on the child's mind. Rather, as noted in our earlier discussion of Piaget's concept of knowledge, intellectual development even during the sensorimotor period involves understandings "discovered and even created in the course of the child's own searchings" (Piaget, 1963, p. 55). So the repetitious activity of the infant is purposive, designed either to preserve or rediscover an act or skill. In other words, it functions as practice.

The third stage (4–8 months) marks the beginning of the infant's distinguishing between self and outside objects. It also marks the start of intentional acts, of consciously acting to attain a goal. The intention, however, is of a transitional type. The child does not foresee a goal, then attempt an act designed to achieve the goal. That sort of "true" intention comes at the fourth stage. But during the third stage the child will repeat an act that he happens to have performed with satisfaction. The primary circular reactions of the second stage were movements not designed to produce a particular result in the environment, but were simply self-centered acts evidencing no apparent awareness of an environment. However, at this third stage, the repetitive behavior that occurs—the *secondary circular reactions*—suggests a beginning awareness of the environment, for the acts seem directed toward reproducing a result which, by chance, has just been effected. For example, when the infant happens to hit a rattle hanging within reach in his crib, he may enjoy the sound. Then by gradually moving his hands and occasionally hitting the rattle, he begins to distinguish between his hand, the rattle, and other objects, so he comes purposely to grasp or hit the rattle directly and not by chance.

The fourth stage (8–12 months) signifies the emergence of clear acts of intelligence. The infant anticipates people and objects. He searches for objects that are out of sight, thus showing that objects have now attained a quality of permanence for him. Prior to this time, if a toy was moved from one location to another, he apparently felt that it had dissolved into the nothingness around him and that a new toy had appeared from the nothingness at the second location, even though the toy had been shifted from the first spot to the second within the baby's presence. Along with this initial step in recognizing qualities of permanence of objects, the infant also begins to comprehend cause and effect, that certain acts will bring about predicted results. Consequently, he can conceive of an end result ahead of time, then fashion an act to bring the result about. His behavior now can be called truly intentional and thus qualifies as the beginning of *practical intelligence,* which consists of envisioning goals or desired ends, then employing existing schemes as means for achieving the ends (Piaget and Inhelder, 1969, pp. 10–11).

The fifth stage (12–18 months) involves the child in *tertiary circular reactions.* We recall that primary circular reactions (1–4 months) were events repeated over and over simply to preserve them, a kind of practice. Secondary circular reactions (4–8 months) were the purposive repetition of acts the infant found satisfying the first time, and so chose to repeat again and again, even in new settings—a kind of application of known means to new situations. In contrast, tertiary reactions are not exact repetitions of the original act. Rather, they consist of reproducing the original event in modified form—a kind of variation on the original theme. The one-year-old, according to Piaget (1963, p. 266), tries, "through a sort of experimentation, to find out in which respect the object or the event is new. In other words, he will not only submit to but even provoke new results instead of being satisfied merely to reproduce them once they have been revealed fortuitously."

Prior to the fifth period, acts of intelligence involved only an application of existing schemes to new situations, that is, assimilating new events into already acquired schemes by attending only to the features of the object or event that were similar to existing schemes. But now, in the fifth period, the child pays greater heed to the ways the new object or event differs from his present mental constructs, and he employs the process of accommodation to differentiate existing schemes and construct more suitable new ones. So tertiary circular reactions involve "reproductory assimilation with differentiated and intentional accommodation" (Piaget, 1950, p. 104).

The sort of "discovery of new means through active experimentation" (Piaget, 1963, p. 267) that marks this fifth stage has been illustrated by Piaget with the case of a child who, sitting on the floor, seeks a toy that is out of reach. During his grasping, he pulls the edge of the small rug on which the toy lies, an act that is either an accident or a substitute for getting the toy. When he notices how his tug on the rug made the toy move toward him, he then intentionally pulls the rug as the instrument for obtaining the object (Piaget and Inhelder, 1969, p. 11).

Up to this point in our discussion of mental growth stages, we have implied but not addressed directly one of the most important dimensions of development in Piaget's system. It is that of *object relations,* meaning the way the child conceives of himself in relation to the objects of the world as well as the way he sees the objects' relationships to each other. In the beginning, the infant's universe is centered entirely on his own body and actions. There are no objects but only a world of what Piaget has called "unsubstantial tableaux" that vaguely appear and then dissolve, never to reappear, or else they come back in some altered form (Piaget and Inhelder, 1969, p. 14). Nor is there a single space and time within which sensations of sight, sound, touch, temperature, taste, and smell are coordinated. Being lifted into mother's arms and fed is, in Piaget's estimation, sensed by the baby as separate impressions of postural change, pressures on various parts of the body, the touch of the lips to the nipple, voice sounds, shifting light patterns, and the ingesting of milk—none of which has any connection with the others. When the infant's mental organization of the universe is so unstructured, he does not—indeed could not —conceive of cause and effect relationships among objects. Even during the advance of infancy, as he begins to differentiate objects from himself and invest them with some permanence in time and space, his conception of cause remains egocentric: Nothing happens in the world except as a result of his own wishes and actions. But by gradual steps over the coming years he recognizes more accurately objective causality in the world.

In summary, an important perspective from which to view child development is that of object relations. Among researchers, Piaget has been particularly noted for his contributions in tracing developmental changes in children's conceptions of the permanence of objects, their position in space and time, and causal relations among them. In our continuing discussion of mental stages, this should become readily apparent.

At the sixth and final stage (18–24 months) of the sensorimotor period, the child no longer has to experiment with objects themselves to solve problems, but can represent them mentally and can cognitively combine and manipulate them. In effect, he is now mentally inventive. For example, a child at this stage sees a toy outside his playpen out of reach. He also sees a stick within arm's reach. He decides that he can use the stick as a tool for pulling the toy to the playpen, and he then uses the stick for this purpose. Prior to the sixth stage he might have gotten the toy if the stick had already been in his hand and he had groped for some time and happened to touch the toy. But he would not have preplanned the act by mentally combining the stick and the toy's distance before picking the stick up. Attainment of this new inventiveness makes intelligence now "capable of entering the framework of language to be transformed, with the aid of the social group, into reflective intelligence" (Piaget, 1963, p. 356).

LEVEL 2:
THE PREOPERATIONAL THOUGHT PERIOD
(ABOUT AGE 2 to AGE 7)

In our review of this level of preoperational thought, we need to understand what Piaget meant by *operations*. Such understanding will make clear what sorts of "operational thought" this level 2 thinking precedes, that is, what sort it prepares the child to perform at a later level of growth.

Operations, in Piaget's system, are ways of manipulating objects in relation to each other, such as arranging them in a series according to size or putting them in classes according to color. If the objects are actually before you, like actual colored blocks or ponies, the manipulations you perform on them, either by physically moving them or by observing how you might move them, are called *concrete operations*. We will meet these operations when we come to the third major period of development, which follows the preoperational level. However, when concrete operations are transposed into verbal propositions about the relationships that exist or might exist among objects, and these propositions are mentally manipulated, the intellectual actions that are performed are called *formal operations* (Piaget, 1969, p. 206). These we will meet at the fourth level of intellectual growth.

An operation, however, is not just any manipulation of objects. Indeed, as the term *preoperational thought* indicates, the mental activities of most children under age 7 do not yet qualify as operational. To be classified as operations, actions must be internalizable, reversible, and coordinated into systems that have laws that apply to the entire system and not just to the single operation itself. As Piaget has explained, operations:

> are actions, since they are carried out on objects before being performed on symbols. They are internalizable, since they can also be carried out in thought without losing their original character of actions. They are reversible as against simple actions which are irreversible. . . . Finally, since operations do not exist in isolation they are connected in the form of structured wholes (1972, p. 8).

The characteristics of operations should become clear when we review the third and fourth periods of intellectual growth, for then we will discuss in some detail illustrations of children displaying operational thinking. For the present we will review the preoperational thought period knowing that it leads to children's performing concrete and formal operations.

This preoperational period can be divided into two stages. The first extends from age 2 to about 4 and is characterized by egocentric use of language and a heavy dependence on perception in problem solving. The second lasts from about age 5 to around 7 and is marked by more social or communicative speech and greater dependence on intuitive thinking rather than just on perception.

Before inspecting these two stages in detail, we should recognize the great importance Piaget attributed to language in the development of intelligence during this period. Language, he said, performs three roles: (1) It enables the child to communicate with other people, thus opening the opportunity for socialization of action; (2) it enables the child to internalize words in the form of thoughts and a system of signs; and most important, (3) it internalizes action so the child does not have to depend on manipulating things physically to solve problems. Instead, she can represent them by mental images with which she conducts experiments. She becomes less bound by time and space. She can increasingly imagine things that are out of sight, far distant, and in the past. She can experiment with these things in different mental combinations far quicker than she could manipulate them physically.

Over the years 2–4, the child learns an increasing variety of words. She begins to talk a lot, and the talk is two varieties. Some of her talk is *social communication*—asking parents to reach a toy she cannot get, telling her sister she wants the doll back, or telling mother she wants to go to the toilet.

But a far larger proportion of the child's talking and listening is *egocentric*, a running oral commentary that accompanies what she is doing at the moment, and is not intended to communicate anything to anyone else. Since this kind of talk often appears in social situations, such as in a group of children at play, it can at first glance be mistaken for social communication. However, on closer inspection it becomes apparent that everyone is talking to herself or himself without listening to the others. For this reason, Piaget has labeled such speech *collective monologues*. An important causal factor behind this discourse, in Piaget's opinion, is the child's lingering self-centeredness. The child still views life from her own perspective and has difficulty seeing things from the perspectives of others. Hence, she does not try to comprehend what others say and then to respond from the viewpoint they express.

To check this hypothesis, Piaget observed preoperational children in situations requiring them to explain something to another child, and then noted, from the other child's behavior, how well the explanation or directions had been understood. The observations revealed a systematic egocentricity in the sense that the child giving directions had great difficulty adopting the other's viewpoint, casting the explanation in a form readily comprehended from the second child's perspective (Piaget and Inhelder, 1969, pp. 120–122).

While the child's growing language skills aid her mental development, they do not free her reasoning abilities from the influence of immediate perception. Children of age 2 through 4 or 5 base their problem solving heavily on what they see or hear directly rather than on what they recall about objects and events. What they perceive about an object is what dominates their conclusions, not what they conceive about the object based on the memory of the permanent characteristics of that object. Children at this age suffer from the limitations of what Piaget called *centration*. Presented with a visual stimulus, a child centers on one aspect and believes that this aspect completely characterizes the stimulus. He cannot consider two dimensions, such as height and width, at the same time. For instance, if there is the same amount of water in two glasses of identical size and shape, the four-year-old will agree that both contain the same amount of water. But if the child sees the water from one glass poured into a taller and thinner glass, he will center on the height dimension only and conclude that the taller glass contains more water. It may be apparent that centration is not the only factor involved in the child's error of judgment. Other characteristics of immature logic also contribute to the error. For example, the preoperational child fails as well to comprehend the principle of *compensation*, that is, that the dimensions of an object can operate in coordination so that one dimension compensates for another. The greater width of the original glass compensates for its lack of height.

By the time the child reaches age 5 or 6 or so, he enters a stage Piaget labeled that of *intuitive thought*. It is a transition period between depending solely on perception and depending on truly logical thinking. An experiment with beads illustrates the characteristics of such transitional thinking. Six red beads are lined up on a table, and the child is told to put as many blue beads on the table as there are red ones. At age 4 or 5 the typical child makes a row of blue beads about the same length as the red row, without bothering to make sure there are six blue ones. But a child a year or two older lines up six blue beads opposite the red ones, thus displaying progress toward recognizing equivalent quantities. But there are still shortcomings in his logic, for if the experimenter then spreads out the red beads to form a longer line, the six-year-old thinks the number of red and blue beads is no longer equivalent (Figure 13.1). He is still unduly influenced by perception of line length rather than the logic of quantity. In the terminology used by Piaget, the child has not recognized that the number of beads has been *conserved* or is *invariant* even though the length of the two lines has been altered (Piaget, 1950, p. 132).

Another Piagetian experiment also illustrates the transitional —between dependence on perception (on how things look) and on logic (on what principles govern their operation)—nature of the child's thinking during this stage of intuitive understanding. Three beads—one red, one blue, one yellow—are on a string that passes through a cardboard tube (Figure 13.2). A child is asked to observe the order of the beads before they are slipped into the cardboard tube where they cannot be seen. Then the child is asked to predict the order in which the beads will emerge from the other end of the tube. All children can predict correctly. But if asked to tell in what order they will emerge if poured back out through the same end they entered, the child under age 4 or 5 will be confused. She fails to see that they will emerge in the opposite sequence if

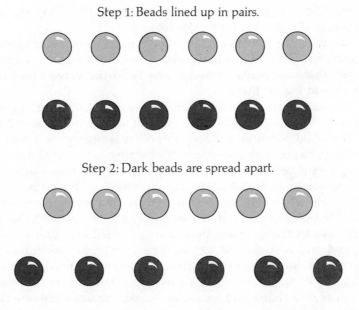

Step 1: Beads lined up in pairs.

Step 2: Dark beads are spread apart.

Figure 13.1   A Piagetian Experiment in Conservation

Figure 13.2   Piaget's Beads and Tube Task

they are backed out of the tube. Further, while the beads are in the tube, if the apparatus is turned 180 degrees and the child is asked the order in which the beads will emerge, the child from about age 4 to about age 7 will fail to see that half a turn will change the order of emergence from red-blue-yellow to yellow-blue-red. She then is given a chance to try it and see what happens. Intuitively she comes to recognize what the half turn will do. By experimenting further, she finally admits that if given two half turns, the order of emergence will be the same as it was originally. She intuitively gets the idea, yet still does not understand the principle that an even number of half turns keeps the emergence as it was origi-nally, but an odd number reverses the order of emergence. This is shown by the fact that even after the experiments, the child is no better able to predict the effect of three half turns than she was originally (Piaget, 1950, pp. 135–136).

In short, the intuitive stage marks a movement toward greater *decentration*. The child is better able to see more than one factor at a time that influences an event. She is on the verge of a major advance in logical thought.

To summarize, the child makes several important growth gains during the preoperational thought level between ages 2 and 7. The child acquires facility in spoken language as a tool for communicating with others and for helping himself think aloud. By age 7 his communicative language greatly increases as collec-tive monologues decrease. He also gains skill in solving problems intuitively when the objects involved in the problems are before him. He becomes less self-centered in that he recognizes that ob-jects have an existence and permanence of their own that does not depend on his wishes or actions. Specifically, he recognizes the permanence of an object's substance when its location or shape is changed. Water poured from a bowl into a tall glass is still water. A ball of clay rolled into a sausage shape remains the same clay. But the preoperational child is still in the process of transition toward decentering, for he does not yet recognize that volume, weight, and mass are also conserved in the acts of pouring and rolling. Even though he has made great advances by age 7 in comprehending how the universe of things operates, he is still strongly dependent on perception (how events seem to the eye) rather than on logic (what principles govern events).

LEVEL 3:
THE CONCRETE OPERATIONS PERIOD
(ABOUT AGE 7 TO AGE 11)

At the concrete operations stage, the child becomes capable of performing operations that are directly related to objects. In the formal operations period, which comes later, he will learn to perform operations on verbally stated hypotheses and propositions that are not limited to particular objects (Piaget and Inhelder, 1969, p. 100). The term *concrete* does not mean the child must see or touch the actual objects as he works through a problem. Rather, "concrete" means that the problems involve identifiable objects that are either directly perceived or imagined. In the later formal operations period the child is able to move ahead to deal with problems that do not concern particular objects. To illustrate this difference, we can consider the following two items, the first suitable for the concrete operations child, the second for the more advanced formal operations child or adolescent:

> **Concrete:** If Alice has two apples and Caroline gives her three
> more, how many apples will Alice have altogether?
> **Formal:** Imagine that there are two quantities which together
> make up a whole. If we increase the first quantity but the
> whole remains the same, what has happened to the second quantity?

It may be apparent that even though the child does not need to see the objects in order to carry out the operations, in the early transitional phase toward learning and mastering such operations, he will be aided by viewing the actual objects or pictures of them.

In our earlier brief introduction to the term *operations*, we defined it but did not illustrate its several characteristics. We will do so now. Piaget said that for an action of the child to qualify as an operation, it had to be internalizable, reversible, and coordinated into overall systems. Furthermore, operations are not unique to an individual child but are common to all people of the same intelligence level. Finally, an operation assists the child not only in his private reasoning but also in his "cognitive exchanges" which bring together information and combine it in various ways (Piaget, 1953, p. 8; Piaget and Inhelder, 1969, pp. 96–97).

By *internalizable* Piaget means the actions can be carried out in thought "without losing their original character of actions" (1953, p. 8).

By *reversible* he means they can be readily inverted into their opposite. For example, two groups of apples that have been combined (added together) to form a whole group can as easily be reduced (subtracted from the whole) to their original status. Hence, adding is an operation. In contrast, Piaget says, writing from left to right is only a simple action and not an operation, for it cannot be inverted into writing from right to left without the child's having to develop an entirely new set of actions (1953, p. 8).

Reversible transformations may be of two varieties: *inversions*, where $+A$ is reversed by $-A$ (addition reversed by subtraction, multiplication reversed by division) and *reciprocity*, where $A < B$ is reciprocated by $B > A$ (the width of the bowl of water compensates for its lack of height, and the height of the glass of water compensates for its lack of width). When an object is moved or transformed in some way, in a transformation that qualifies as operatory, not everything about the system changes. Some features remain constant. As we have seen, Piaget gave the label *conservation* to this feature of constancy or invariance of objects. So we can say that a child's scheme or idea of a permanent object consists of that combination of features of the object that do not change when the object is moved or acted on. How adequately the child's scheme matches that of adult logic or "reality" can be judged if you assess which aspects of objects the child believes have been conserved during the transformation. Many of the problem situations Piaget contrived for children to solve in his clinical method of investigation are designed to test children's notions of conservation. And his investigations have shown that the particular aspects a child sees as being conserved depend on the child's age, or more accurately, on the child's developmental level.

For example, when two lumps of clay the same size and shape are shown to the child, then one lump is rolled into a sausage form, the child of age 7 or 8 discovers that the substance has been conserved. But not until age 9 or 10 does he discover that the weight has been conserved as well. And not until age 11 or 12 does he discover the conservation of volume which occurs when an object is immersed in water and the displacement measured (Piaget and Inhelder, 1969, p. 99).

Thus it is during the concrete operations period, from age 7 to around 11 or so, that children gradually discover more of the properties of objects and transformations and thus master mental operations that can be applied to their concrete world.

The concrete operations child not only gains greater command of the notions of conservation and reversibility, but also becomes capable of decentering his attention, of recognizing the way two or more dimensions of an event interact to produce a given result. He no longer centers his attention solely on the height of the water glass or only on its width, but considers both dimensions simultaneously and recognizes their interaction. When presented with twelve wooden beads (nine red, three white), the child no longer will say there are more red beads than wooden beads when asked to compare red ones with wooden ones. At the concrete operations level he now recognizes that color and construction material are two different classifications, and he is not stuck by centering on only color or material. He also can now order things in a series according to a stated criterion, such as size or number.

Whereas the preoperational child focused on the static beginning state and final state of an object in a transformation, the concrete operations child can comprehend the transformation as a process. For example, typical preoperational children at age 3 or 4 think there is more clay in five small balls than in the original large ball from which the five were made. Even when the transformation, and its reverse of recombining the five into one, is performed before their eyes, three- and four-year-olds still say that the five contain more clay than the one. But by age 6 or 8, children agree that the quantity remains the same in the change from one to five balls and back again.

The egocentrism that caused the younger child to see things only from his own viewpoint changes as the older child achieves the aspects of cognitive growth mentioned above and as his increased facility with language leads to greater socialization. The child in the concrete operations period now has a more objective view of the universe and better understands how others see things.

Children's concepts of causation also mature during this period. For instance, a comparison of a child age 6 years, 8 months and a child 10 years, 3 months can illustrate the development of the concept of displacement of volume. The experiment involves dropping a small stone into a container of water (Piaget, 1930, pp. 169–172).

When the experimenter asks the six-year-old what will happen if the stone is dropped into the water, the child says the water will rise *"because it is heavy in the water."* The experimenter says, "You see the pebble hanging on this thread: if I put it in the water as far as this (half-way), will it make the water rise?" *"No, because it is not heavy enough."*

In contrast, the ten-year-old says the water will rise *"because the pebble takes up space."* The experimenter asks, "If I put this wood in, what will happen?" *"It will lie on the water."* "And what will the water do?" *"It will rise because the wood also takes up space."* "Which is the heavier, this pebble (small) or this wood (large)?" *"The pebble."* "Which will make the water rise the most?" *"The pebble takes up less space, it will make the water rise less."*

So the child arrives at the early teen years with increased skill in accounting for the cause of physical events, and is ready to solve not only problems that involve objects, but also problems concerning hypotheses and propositions about relationships.

LEVEL 4:
THE FORMAL OPERATIONS PERIOD
(ABOUT AGE 11 TO AGE 15)

In adolescence the typical child no longer is limited by what she directly sees or hears, nor is she restricted to the problem at hand. She can now imagine the conditions of a problem—past, present, or future—and develop hypotheses about what might logically occur under different combinations of factors. For example, if we begin a problem with "Imagine that water in the river ran up hill . . . ," the child younger than 12 will claim that the subsequent problem cannot be solved because water does not run up hill. But by the close of the formal operations period the teenager can accept the hypothetical condition of upward flow and can apply it in solving the problem that is posed.

Another of Piaget's favorite examples further illustrates the difference between the concrete operations child and the one who has attained formal operations ability. This is a problem involving *transitivity*, meaning that a relationship between two elements or objects is carried over to other elements logically related to the first two. For example, the child has solved the problem of transitivity if she recognizes that when $A = B$ and $B = C$, then $A = C$. Or if $A < B$ and $B < C$, then $A < C$. So the question posed to the child is this: "Edith is fairer than Susan; Edith is darker than Lily; who is the darkest of the three?" Piaget (1950, p. 149) found that before age 12 children rarely could solve this. Instead, they engaged in such reasoning as: "Edith and Susan are fair, Edith and Lily are dark, therefore Lily is darkest, Susan is the fairest, and Edith in between." However, the adolescent in her midteens can solve the problem accurately, for she comprehends the transitivity it involves.

Prior to early and middle adolescence, therefore, children are still bound by their perceptions. But during the formal operations period they are able to engage in *"pure* thought which is independent of action" that they see or carry out themselves (Piaget, 1950, 149). Adolescents can hypothesize and draw deductions from the hypotheses. They can understand general theories and can combine them to solve assumed problems. In effect, by age 15, the framework of the average youth's thinking has evolved into its mature state. The types of thought of which the adult is capable are now all within the youth's repertoire of mental functions.

Does this mean, then, that there is no intellectual growth beyond mid-adolescence in Piaget's model of the mind? No, it does not. It means that the framework of thought is complete, but the framework is not all filled in. Further experience over the years of youth and adulthood fill in the outline with additional, more complex schemes or greater knowledge, so the adult *does* know more than the adolescent. However, the adolescent is capable of all the forms of logic that the adult commands.

According to Piaget, the most obvious distinction between adolescent and adult thought is the greater lingering egocentrism displayed by adolescents. The teenage youth, with her newly acquired skills of logical thought, is an idealist who expects the world to be logical. She fails to recognize or accept the reality that people do not operate solely on the basis of logic, and she becomes a reformer and critic of the older generation, foreseeing a glorious future in which she and her peers will right today's wrongs. In Piaget's opinion, this egocentrism and idealism is rendered more realistic and social by the youth's entering the occupational world or by her taking on serious professional training.

> The adolescent becomes an adult when he undertakes a real job. It is then that he is transformed from an idealistic reformer into an

achiever. In other words, the job leads thinking away from the dangers of formalism back into reality (Inhelder and Piaget, 1958, p. 346).

This move from adolescence into adulthood, then, completes the sequence of stages through which the intellect develops over the first two decades of life.

EDUCATIONAL APPLICATIONS OF THE THEORY

Over the past two decades Piaget's writings have exerted a growing influence on the conduct of education in many parts of the world. Piaget himself has on numerous occasions suggested educational implications of his model. However, by far the greater part of this application of Piagetian thought to child rearing and schooling has been performed by others. To illustrate something of the educational implications drawn from the theory by Piaget and a variety of educators, we will inspect the Piagetian model's application to questions of: (1) the choice of learning objectives, (2) curriculum sequencing, (3) grade placement of topics, (4) the assessment of children's intellectual functioning, and (5) teaching methodology.

THE CHOICE OF LEARNING OBJECTIVES

As educators have selected learning goals for pupils to pursue, they usually have based their choices on tradition or on analyses of what children need to learn in order to succeed in the culture in which they are growing up.

The word *tradition* in this context refers to the curriculum of the past. Members of the adult generation recall what they were taught in school and assume that this same pattern of facts, concepts, skills, and values will be equally proper for the coming generation of children. This might be called a conservative approach to selecting objectives, since it emphasizes the conservation or retention of traditional goals.

The phrase *analyses of what children need to learn in order to succeed* identifies the practice of educators who inspect present-day society and predict changes that will likely occur in that society over the coming decades. On the basis of such analyses, they estimate the knowledge, skills, and values that will best equip the growing child or youth to become a happy, constructive member of that society. This could be called a *personal-social adjustment* approach to establishing objectives, for it emphasizes the achievement of objectives that enable the individual to fulfill his own needs within a culture that is continually evolving. A curriculum produced by such a process of analysis can be expected to retain some of the goals of the past, but it also will offer new objectives that result from changes in the society.

In contrast to these first two approaches, there is a third tack, which derives from Piagetian theory and might be called a *cognitive development* approach. To understand the educator's main focus when he uses this approach, we need to consider once again (1) the distinction Piaget made between *spontaneous* or *psychological* development and *psychosocial* development and (2) his ideas about the interaction of nature and nurture.

As explained earlier, several factors determine when a child will develop through the levels of sensorimotor reactions, of concrete operations, and of formal operations. The first factor is internal maturation of the neural system. The time at which the maturational steps needed for a given level of cognitive functioning occur is established by nature, by the child's genetic time schedule. But the developmental potential that this maturation provides cannot be realized unless the child obtains suitable direct experiences in life, experiences that bring the potential to fruition. As we have noted, Piaget called such unguided experience (the second factor) *psychological* or *spontaneous* development. A third factor is that of more formal instruction, the sort that goes on in school. It needs to be preceded by the first two, maturation and psychological development, if it is to be successful. This third factor is the one Piaget called *psychosocial* development.

This Piagetian view of intellectual growth is the foundation for a cognitive development approach to selecting instructional goals. From such a perspective, the central goal of the school is not to teach particular facts and concepts, nor is it to teach solutions to personal-social adjustment problems. Instead, the purpose of schooling is to promote optimal development of thinking skills appropriate to each level of growth. As a result of such schooling, by the time the child reaches adolescence he can efficiently apply formal operational thinking in understanding life and in solving whatever problems he faces. In such a curriculum the child does indeed learn facts and concepts. However, those he learns are not selected for any inherent value they might have but rather for their worth in fostering the development of the particular level of cognitive growth that he currently is working toward.

CURRICULUM SEQUENCING

Piagetian theory not only furnishes a vantage point from which to select objectives, but it suggests as well the sequence in which these objectives and their associated learning tasks should appear in the curriculum. For example, in reasoning about scientific and mathematical phenomena, children at the preoperational level can consider only one dimension at a time, such as only the height or only the width of an object. At the concrete operations level they can comprehend the interaction of two dimensions, such as height and width, simultaneously. Not until they reach the formal operations level can they consider the interaction of more than two variables. A similar sequence has been identified in the realm of moral or ethical judgments.

> At the egocentric stage in the logic of feeling, the self becomes the single dimension around which feelings and social interaction revolve. The second, sociocentric stage corresponds to concrete operations, in interacting with peer-group norms as the other dimension. The allocentric stage is multidimensional like formal operations: the individual can construe himself as a dimension in a matrix, including abstract principle and social norms as other dimensions (Biggs, 1976, p. 157).

A further example of a sequence is that of understanding the conservation aspects of physical objects. The child's comprehension moves from that of understanding the conservation of the quantity of substance (the space an object appears to take up) to that of weight of substance and then to that of volume of substance.

These sequences, along with a variety of other more specific ones, can suggest to curriculum developers a psychologically sound order in which to confront children with different learning tasks. In the traditional school curriculum, children are often expected to acquire concepts of mass, weight, volume, space, time, causality, geometry, speed, and movement in a sequence that is at odds with the child's natural pattern of comprehending such concepts (Elkind, 1976, p. 196). A curriculum plan founded on Piagetian theory and empirical studies would seek to correct such incoordination between development and school learning activities.

GRADE PLACEMENT OF TOPICS

Piaget's results also suggest at what general age level each step in a given sequence is likely to occur. For instance, understanding of conservation of substance seems to come around age 7 for most children, of weight around age 9, and of volume around age 11 or 12 (Phillips, 1975, p. 100).

These age points are similar, but not identical, from one child to another and from one ethnic or socioeconomic group to another. Differences among children in the age at which they achieve a particular new level are apparently due to differences in those primary causal factors that Piaget said underlie development: the genetic time schedule for internal maturation, self-directed experience with the world, and instruction or training. Some children are genetically equipped to advance earlier than others. Some have better opportunities to engage in profitable direct experiences and to receive more useful instruction. What these differences in influence mean for curriculum developers is that some flexibility is needed in the grade placement of learning goals founded on Piagetian theory. Not every child will be ready at the same time to accomplish the next step in a cognitive development sequence. However, the general placement of a given objective in the school's grade hierarchy can be estimated. Curriculum developers know whether a particular cognitive skill is more suitable for the preschool years than the primary grades (1 through 3) or for the upper elementary grades (4 through 6). They also know whether a particular understanding is more likely achieved in the junior high (grades 7 through 9) than senior high years (10 through 12).

As already noted, Piaget, besides outlining the stages of development described earlier for general cognitive development, also identified within the general structure a variety of separate sequences, such as one for the understanding of number, another for causality, a third for conservation of physical aspects, a fourth for moral reasoning, and so on. Though the pattern of one such sequence is much like the pattern of another, the timing of steps within different sequences does not always coincide. In other words, there is some unevenness in progress between sequences.

We can illustrate this incoordination between sequences by noting that the logic children use to explain their moral or ethical judgments usually lags a couple of years behind the level of logic they use to explain physical phenomena. It is not yet known whether this lag is due entirely to the greater amount of experience and instruction children have with physical events as compared to moral issues or whether some maturational factor also contributes its influence. As Piaget's most frequent collaborator, Barbel Inhelder, has written:

> The general succession of stages seems to be confirmed by all authors, but the relationship between different tasks and substructures, apparently requiring the same mental structure, is still far from adequately explored; what is more, the experimental findings on this point are difficult to interpret (1968, p. vii).

However, the implications of such a finding for curriculum developers seem clear. It is not sufficient to use only Piaget's *general* developmental stages as guides to the placement of learning activities in the school's grade structure. Rather, it is important to assign activities according to the various types of sequences that are involved. For example, activities to promote a given level of moral judgment would be assigned a grade or two later in the school program than would activities to promote a similar level of mathematics and science knowledge.

It is possible, though, to use the same general topic or problem situation at both a lower and an upper grade level and still fulfill the objectives of Piagetian curriculum. For instance, Peel (1976, p. 181) has recommended that a spiral plan for teaching both physical science and social science can be adopted for adolescents. In such a program, students in an upper secondary grade can return to topics they studied three or four years earlier. The virtue of this approach, from a Piagetian viewpoint, is that the pupils are thereby not simply reviewing or repeating their earlier experience, since during the intervening years the *quality* of the students' intelligence has changed. Whereas a child at the beginning of the secondary school could offer only partial and single explanations of a phenomenon, the youth in high school is able to apply "a greater conceptual repertoire and more mature form of intellectual enquiry" (Peel, 1976, p. 181) to the same phenomenon.

In effect, the second time she studies the topic she does so by means of a new, more complex cognitive lens—in other words, a more complex schema.

THE ASSESSMENT OF
INTELLECTUAL FUNCTIONING

Piagetians are critical of the use of traditional intelligence tests for estimating children's cognitive development and children's readiness for another step in a learning sequence. Their chief complaint is that the typical intelligence test determines whether the child can give a correct answer to questions, but it does not reveal the child's thinking processes. Thus, the test fails to indicate a pupil's current level of cognitive development. As a result, Piagetians prefer to base their judgments of children's cognitive styles on: (1) how children solve the problems posed in the tasks Piaget has used in his research studies and (2) teachers' observations of the level of children's reasoning as they go about the regular activities of the classroom (Elkind, 1976, pp. 171–194).

Dissatisfaction with standard intelligence tests has stimulated a pair of researchers at the University of Montreal, Monique Laurendeau and Adrien Pinard, to devise a new scale of mental development, a test that represents "an attempt to combine the advantages of Piaget's method (thoroughness and flexibility of questioning) with those of traditional psychometric methods (standardization of questioning)" (Phillips, 1975, p. 162). Unlike such tests as the Stanford-Binet or Wechsler Intelligence Scale for Children, the Montreal scale does not involve each child's being asked to answer exactly the same questions. Instead, the way a child responds to one question can influence the nature of the succeeding questions she is asked. Furthermore, the tester is not only interested in the number of right answers the child gives, but is equally interested in "wrong" answers, since they too are valuable in revealing the child's mode of thinking. In sum, the Montreal project represents an extension of Piagetian theory into the realm of formal intelligence testing.

TEACHING METHODOLOGY

A common way to conceive of teaching methodology within a Piagetian-based curriculum is to define the two most basic responsibilities of the teacher as those of:

1. Diagnosing the current stage of a child's development in the various growth sequences which the curriculum is designed to promote, and

2. Offering the child learning activities that challenge her to advance to the next higher step of the particular type of sensorimotor-cognitive development that the sequence involves.

In other words, the teacher is not viewed as being a fount of knowledge from which the pupils are expected to fill their minds. Nor is the teacher's job simply that of a pleasant clerk who displays equipment and materials in the classroom, then stands back while children explore the objects on their own. Instead, the teacher is expected to achieve a proper balance between actively guiding or directing children's thinking patterns and providing opportunities for children to explore by themselves.

Not all educators have come up with exactly the same picture of teacher behavior for achieving this balance between active guidance and passive permission. Furth and Wachs, who describe their experimental Piagetian-type school in their book *Thinking Goes to School* (1975), recommend that the teacher offer a sequence of activities that will enable pupils to achieve their next developmental steps efficiently. The activities give a structure or direction to pupils' work, but each child is free to pursue each activity in her own manner, or she is free not to participate in the activity at all if she so chooses.

> The teacher in our school knows that he can do no more than provide the occasion and leave the child free to use it well. He can coach and facilitate and encourage; but in the final analysis it is the child himself who initiates intellectual growth (Furth and Wachs, 1975, p. 46).

A somewhat different version of the teacher's role within a Piagetian-based curriculum is given by Elkind (1976), who has identified three modes of learning, each featuring a different combination of the assimilation and accommodation processes defined in the Piagetian model of development.

The first mode he calls *operative learning,* which is most prominent when the child's intelligence "is actively engaged by the materials she is interacting with" (Elkind, 1976, p. 113). Working with the materials, the child may face contradictions in the way she supposes they will respond, and the contradictions force her to abstract new understandings from her actions on the materials.

Operative learning, in addition to facilitating the development of mental operations, also gives rise to *practical intelligence.* Practical intelligence consists of the operations and knowledge the child requires to get about in the everyday world. Much of it . . . is unconscious (Elkind, 1976, p. 114).

The second mode is called *figurative learning.* It involves the child acquiring "aspects of reality" that cannot be reconstructed or rediscovered by the child on his own but "must be largely copied" (Elkind, 1976, p. 114). Perhaps the prime example of this mode is the learning of language—the vocabulary, syntax, pronunciation, and gesture that make the speech of one culture different from that of another. For such aspects of reality, the teacher adopts a more active instructional role, more "teaching" in its traditional sense.

The third mode is *connotative learning.* It is the "conscious conceptualization of one's own mental processes, what has been called *reflective intelligence.*" It is most prominent during the years of adolescence (Elkind, 1976, pp. 115–116). "Connotative learning is expressly concerned with the construction of meanings, with establishing connections between concepts and figurative symbols. It is no less than the child's efforts to make sense out of her world" (Elkind, 1976, p. 116).

In promoting operative learning, the teacher may bring objects—a bird, a telescope, a toy boat—to the classroom and may pose questions that stimulate pupils to discover aspects of the item. However, to a great extent the pupils are left on their own to explore the objects. For the figurative mode, the teacher furnishes models and gives demonstrations and explanations, such as showing how to carry out arithmetic computation efficiently or how to use phonics to discover the pronunciation of new words met in a reading passage. With connotative learning the teacher still encourages pupils to make discoveries and use the communication skills they have acquired, but the "teacher's most important role in connotative learning is to help children do work of the quality that they are really capable of doing" (Elkind, 1976, p. 231). In other words, the teacher stimulates them to produce to the best of their ability.

Whether teachers adopt a Furth and Wachs version or an Elkind version of a Piagetian-based instructional style, they need to carry out their teaching in a setting that is conducive to a substantial amount of small-group and individual activities. Tables, desks, and chairs need to be movable. Different interest centers around the classroom need to be available for use by pupils who are at a given developmental level and can most profitably pursue activities and use materials suited to promoting progress to the next level.

In summary, Piaget's theory and his empirical research findings suggest guidelines about how children's sensorimotor-cognitive development can best be nurtured.

PIAGET'S THEORY: AN ASSESSMENT

As in previous chapters, the nine standards of judgment from Chapter 1 provide the framework for evaluating the model of development.

Piaget's theory comes off with rather high marks in all categories. Certainly he has been the single most important stimulator of research studies published in leading child development journals in the past decade or more, so I feel he deserves a top rating on item 8. Hilgard and Bower, in appraising Piaget's work from the viewpoint of learning theory, have written that:

> One of the problems that have beset psychology as a science is that there are so few discoveries of genuinely new phenomena. . . . Consequently, it is worth noting that the facts of conservation, as pointed out by Piaget and his associates, represent one of the genuine "discoveries" within his experimental observations (1975, p. 327).

Furthermore, I can find no fault with the internal consistency (item 5) or economy of explanation (item 6) of the theory.

In terms of reflecting the real world of children (item 1), the theory gains great strength from the host of empirical studies on which the author has based his speculations. The only reservation on this score relates to the matter of individual differences among children. Piaget's great emphasis has been on what the average child does. And though he has given some recognition to individual differences, he has paid only slight attention to the factors that cause such differences. It is true that he has suggested that the social milieu within which a child is reared will affect the rate with which he moves through the developmental stages, but he has not made any careful analysis that I know of of how different factors or agents in the social setting influence the attainment of mental skills. Zigler (1965, pp. 361–362) has charged that "nothing in Piaget allows one to assess the effects of either the state of the

PIAGET'S THEORY

How well do I think the theory meets the standards?

The Standards	Very Well	Moderately Well	Very Poorly
1. Reflects the real world of children	X		
2. Is clearly understandable		X	
3. Explains the past and predicts the future	X		
4. Guides child rearing		X	
5. Is internally consistent	X		
6. Is economical	X		
7. Is falsifiable		X	
8. Stimulates new discoveries	X		
9. Is self-satisfying	X		

organism or of differences in the environment that give rise to individual differences in development."

As for the theory's value in explaining the past and predicting the future (item 3), it does rather well both (1) for the sorts of cognitive behavior on which the model focuses and (2) for the average child. Piaget has claimed that the sequence of the changes plotted in his stages of mental growth is invariant from one child or one society to another. And there have been empirical investigations conducted in many nations that support this claim (Piaget, 1973, p. 7; Sigel and Hooper, 1968). He further notes that the rate of passage through stages may vary as much as two years between the average children of one culture and those of another (Piaget, 1973, pp. 25–27). So he can predict accurately the types and sequence of cognitive behaviors children can be expected to exhibit, but he has not furnished adequate explanations of deviations from the average.

I have found Piaget's works that are in English translation relatively clear (item 2) when studied carefully. Certainly the frequent examples of children's answers to problems posed for them, examples with which Piaget's writings are liberally illustrated, enhance the clarity of his exposition. However, some competent readers have found some of his concepts and explanations quite difficult to grasp. For example, in an early attempt to replicate Piaget's studies of children's ideas of causality, Deutsch (1943, pp. 129–145) was unable to understand the distinctions Piaget proposed among a number of causal explanation categories Piaget included in his description of his own studies of causality. Hence, I have rated the theory between the "very" and "moderately well" designations on clarity.

In terms of guidance for child rearing (item 4), the theory has proven of great interest to educators, who have been making increasing use of Piaget's description of developmental stages to determine the sequence and grade placement of cognitive skills to be learned, particularly skills in mathematics and the physical sciences. Educators are also using Piagetian tasks—the test problems from his clinical method—both for assessing children's developmental status and for providing children opportunities to try the thought processes represented in the developmental stages of the theory (Furth and Wachs, 1975; Tronick and Greenfield, 1973; Piaget, 1970b). Thus the Piagetian model offers a good deal of guidance for child rearing in cognitive areas.

The model does not, however, furnish guidance for a variety of other problems for which parents, teachers, pediatricians, and social workers often seek aid. The problems I refer to are ones reflected in such phrases as *poor self-concept, lack of friends, easily frustrated, too heavily influenced by undesirable peers,* and *lacks significant goals or purpose in life.* For coping with such matters, Piaget is of little help. But, as he has frequently pointed out, his area of concern is that of genetic epistemology; and the above problems are not central to that concern. Nevertheless, I balanced the foregoing positive points against the negative and rated the theory between "very" and "moderately well."

Next, how falsifiable is the theory (item 7)? Many aspects of Piaget's model are in forms that make determining their validity very testable. Such is true of the developmental stages, both their sequence and their age placement. However, several of the concepts at the core of the theory are not, I believe, susceptible to confirmation or disconfirmation. Included are the concepts of schemes, assimilation, and accommodation. Piaget may merely have intended them as one possible set of constructs useful in devising one conception of how physical and mental behavior operates. In this case, people are free to create their own alternatives, and Piaget might then be expected to accept these as readily as the set he proposed. However, he writes as if he is convinced that schemes, assimilation, and accommodation really represent the way things work, and I see no way of testing the validity of such a conviction. Hence, I balanced the many falsifiable aspects of the Piagetian model against the apparently few that must be accepted on faith and marked item 7 somewhat above the center.

Finally, I find the theory to be overall quite satisfying (item 9). Despite the reservations mentioned above, I am convinced that the greater part of what Piaget has to say in his writings is valuable and accurate. After studying his works, I feel that I understand the development of children's thinking processes far better than before. And as a consequence, I believe I can work more effectively with children and youths. I feel the theory rates a high mark.

FOR FURTHER READING

Piaget, Jean and Barbel Inhelder. (1969) *The Psychology of the Child.* New York: Basic Books. Although any of the books listed under Piaget's name in the bibliography at the end of this volume will offer useful insights into his many-sided theorizing, this volume by Piaget and his long-time colleague, Inhelder, is particularly helpful in reviewing not only the principal aspects of basic cognitive development but also the associated social and affective interactions, including moral feelings and judgments.

Battro, Antonio M. (1973) *Piaget: Dictionary of Terms.* New York: Pergamon. People who have had difficulty with the meaning Piaget intends for the specialized terms he uses will find this book useful. Battro has listed Piagetian terms alphabetically, then under each he has given one or more definitions in the form of quotes from Piaget's writings.

Campbell, Sarah F. (1976) *Piaget Sampler*. New York: Wiley. An autobiography by Piaget (1896–1966) appears as Chapter 10 in this potpourri of articles by the theorist.

Many books published in recent years have been designed to offer a condensed version of Piagetian theory, one more readily understood by the uninitiated than are Piaget's original writings. The following two small volumes, one by Phillips and the other by Sigel and Cocking, are among the more readable and up-to-date books of this type.

Phillips, John L., Jr. (1975) *The Origins of Intellect: Piaget's Theory*. 2d ed. San Francisco: W. H. Freeman.

Sigel, Irving E. and Rodney R. Cocking. (1977) *Cognitive Development from Childhood to Adolescence: A Constructivist Perspective*. New York: Holt, Rinehart, and Winston.

CHAPTER 14

VYGOTSKY'S THEORY OF THOUGHT AND LANGUAGE

Lev Semenovich Vygotsky (1896–1934) was a Russian psychologist whose first research as a young scholar between 1915 and 1922 centered on issues of artistic creation (Vygotsky, 1971). In 1924 he began serious work in the areas of developmental psychology, education, and psychopathology, pursuing these interests at a highly productive pace until he died of tuberculosis in 1934 at age 38.

Although his career as a psychologist was brief, Vygotsky earned high regard in the Soviet Union for establishing an acceptable sociopolitical foundation for much psychological investigation. He did this by casting in suitable research form "the Marxist-Leninist thesis that all fundamental human cognitive activities take shape in a matrix of social history and form the products of sociohistorical development" (Luria, 1976, p. v).

In other words, according to his doctrine, the intellectual skills or patterns of thinking that a person displays are not primarily determined by innate factors, that is, inherited intelligence or mental abilities. Instead, patterns and levels of thinking are products of the activities practiced in the social institutions of the culture in which the individual grows up. In keeping with this thesis, as Cole explains:

> It follows that practical thinking will predominate in societies that are characterized by practical manipulations of objects, and more "abstract" forms of "theoretical" activity in technological societies will induce more abstract, theoretical thinking. The parallel between individual and social development produces a strong proclivity to in-

terpret all behavioral differences in developmental terms (Luria, 1976, p. xiv).

From this viewpoint, the history of the society in which a child is reared, and the child's own developmental history in terms of his experiences in that society, are both extremely important in fashioning the ways he will be able to think. Furthermore, advanced modes of thought—conceptual thinking—must be transmitted to the child by means of words, so language becomes a crucial tool for deciding how children learn to think.

It was in an atmosphere of these assumptions that Vygotsky wrote the book *Thought and Language* shortly before his death. In 1936, two years after its publication, the volume was suppressed in the Soviet Union because of disputes within the nation's psychological community. But when the disputes ended, the book was distributed once again. However, not until 1962 was it translated into English, so that only in recent years has Vygotsky's theory become widely understood and discussed in English-speaking countries. Most of Chapter 14 is drawn from *Thought and Language.*

Three characteristics that marked Vygotsky's work were: (1) a thorough acquaintance with the work of leading European and American psychologists of his day and of earlier decades, (2) considerable direct experience with children, and (3) great ingenuity in devising methods for gathering and interpreting data. The results of this ingenuity are summarized in the following sections: (1) the outlines of Vygotsky's theory, (2) the development of speech, and (3) the development of conceptual thought.

THE OUTLINES OF VYGOTSKY'S THEORY

To understand something of the climate for psychological theory in Vygotsky's time, we need to recall two antithetical views of human thought that were prominent in the early twentieth century.

The first was a traditional view of the mind that grew out of the faculty psychology of past centuries. Psychologists in the late nineteenth and early twentieth centuries studied mind and its functions by means of introspection. A person carefully looked into his own mind to analyze the working of perception, thought, memory, feelings, and the like.

The second movement was in direct opposition to the first. It represented an effort to be scientific and objective about the study of man, just as physics, chemistry, and biology were objective sciences. In America this movement became known as behaviorism, for its leaders proposed that the proper study of man was his observable behavior as measured and recorded by scientists outside the man himself. Behaviorists of the early twentieth century rejected the abstract, unobservable items of past speculation, such items as consciousness, feelings, will, and mind itself. But what about thought and thinking? Everybody knows there are such things as thoughts. Behaviorists of the day said that what people for years had been calling "thinking" was really speech behavior, but it was below the hearing threshold, a kind of "silent speech." So the staunchest behaviorists of Vygotsky's day had eliminated mind and its functions in favor of analyzing only man's observable acts.

Vygotsky saw shortcomings in both of these schools of theory. He did not trust introspection as a secure methodological base on which to found scientific psychological theory. And as for behaviorists' rejecting mind, he wrote:

> In that psychology ignores the problem of consciousness, it blocks itself off from access to the investigation of complicated problems of human behavior, and the elimination of consciousness from the sphere of scientific psychology has as its major consequence the retention of all the dualism (mind versus body) and spiritualism of earlier subjective psychology (1962, p. vi).

In his own research Vygotsky set about investigating conscious thought processes, but he did so by means of newly created objective measures that did not depend upon introspection or "spiritualism" for testing.

Vygotsky chose to study, in particular, the relationship between thought and language. Was thought identical with language, as Watsonian behaviorists claimed when they said thinking is just silent speaking? Or was thought independent of language, complete in itself, as many introspectionists seemed to believe, with language simply serving as the tool for communicating thought to others—just as a camera is an instrument for communicating visual images without altering in any way the original scene it depicts? Or, as a third possibility, were thought and language separate functions that could commingle and in so doing modify each other?

To arrive at an answer to these queries, Vygotsky (1) analyzed a host of studies of thought and language conducted by psychologists and anthropologists from numerous countries and (2) devised his own investigations of thought and speech as found among children, adolescents, and adults in the Soviet Union. He cast his interpretations of these findings as three sets of conclusions about child development. The first set concerned the development of conceptual thought, the second the development of speech, and the third the connection between the first two. The nature of these conclusions is the subject of the rest of this chapter. However, we will consider the three sets in reverse order, beginning with Vygotsky's general views on the relationship between the development of thought and the development of language (*language* in this case meaning *speech*).

In general, Vygotsky concluded that the child's thought and speech begin as separate functions with no necessary connection between them. They are like two circles that do not touch. One circle represents nonverbal thought, the other nonconceptual speech. As the child begins to grow up, the circles meet and overlap (Figure 14.1). The juncture of the two represents *verbal thought*, meaning that the child has now begun to acquire concepts that bear word labels. A *concept* here means an abstraction, an idea that does not represent a particular object but rather some common characteristic shared by—or some relationship among—diverse objects.

The two circles never completely overlap. Even though the common portion becomes more prominent as the child develops (particularly in a highly literate cultural setting), there always remains some nonverbal thought and some nonconceptual speech. An example of nonverbal thought in the adult is her skillful use of tools. An example of nonconceptual speech is her singing an old song or reciting a poem or repeating a telephone number she has memorized. These repetitions by rote are "mental activity" but are not of the conceptual variety that Vygotsky identifies as verbal thought.

Figure 14.1 shows Vygotsky's general idea of the thought–language relationship during a child's development, but the actual coordination between the two circles is probably far more complex. Vygotsky admitted that the pattern of their interaction was not yet clear. But he did contend that:

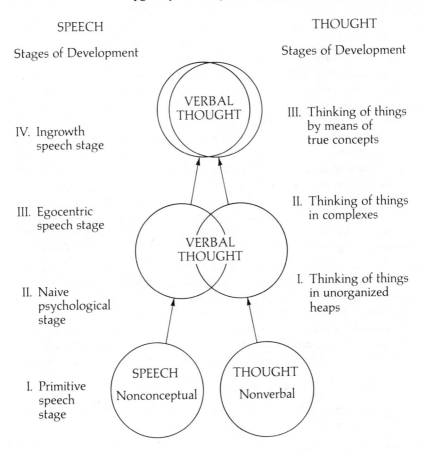

SPEECH

THOUGHT

Stages of Development

Stages of Development

VERBAL
THOUGHT

IV. Ingrowth
speech stage

III. Thinking of things
by means of
true concepts

II. Thinking of things
in complexes

III. Egocentric
speech stage

VERBAL
THOUGHT

I. Thinking of things
in unorganized
heaps

II. Naive
psychological
stage

SPEECH
Nonconceptual

THOUGHT
Nonverbal

I. Primitive
speech
stage

Figure 14.1   Vygotsky's View of Speech and Thought Development

Progress in thought and progress in speech are not parallel. Their two growth curves cross and recross. They may straighten out and run side by side, even merge for a time, but they always diverge again. This applies to both phylogeny and ontogeny (1962, p. 33).

Vygotsky disagreed with theorists who said that the child, as a result of internal maturation, can achieve skill in advanced conceptual thought on his own, distinct from what he is taught. While admitting the necessary role of internal maturation in development, Vygotsky believed that the child's informal and formal education through the medium of language strongly influences the level of conceptual thinking he reaches. If the language climate within which children grow up (direct speech, mass communication media) is dominated by simplistic or "primitive" language, then the children can think only simplistically or primitively. But if the language environment contains varied and complex concepts, then children will learn to think in varied and complex ways, given that their initial biological equipment (sense organs, central nervous system) is not impaired.

In extending the scope of his theorizing beyond the child's development, he suggested that the stages through which a child's thought and language evolve are likely the same as those through which mankind's have evolved over eons of time. Thus, studying the child's ontogenetic development not only helps us understand the child's thought and speech but also serves as the most practical method for estimating the phylogenetic development of the species.

These are the general features of Vygotsky's theory. The model is not a completed theory, with all details filled in and each proposal buttressed with a mass of empirical evidence. Rather, as Bruner (Vygotsky, 1962, p. viii) has written, the book *Thought and Language* "is more programmatic than systematic." It's as if Vygotsky had found only parts of the thought–speech puzzle by the time he wrote the volume, and his theory or "program" represented his assumption that when the rest of the parts eventually were discovered, the final assemblage would take on the general configuration he had outlined in his proposal.

STAGES IN SPEECH DEVELOPMENT

Vygotsky's studies led him to conclude that speech development proceeds through the same four stages and is governed by the same laws as those relating to other mental operations that employ signs, that is, such other operations as counting and memorizing with the aid of mnemonic devices (Vygotsky, 1962, pp. 46–47).

He called the first of these four stages the *primitive or natural stage*. This first period, which represents the time before the circle of language overlaps the circle of conscious thought, lasts from birth until about age 2 in Vygotsky's opinion. The stage is characterized by three nonintellectual speech functions. First are sounds representing *emotional release*—crying with pain or frustration, cooing or babbling with contentment. Next, as early as the second month after birth, these emotional noises are joined by sounds that can be interpreted as *social reactions* to other people's voices or appearance. The noises of social contact include laughter and a variety of inarticulate sounds. The third type of thoughtless speech consists of the child's first words, which are *substitutes for objects and desires*. These are words learned by conditioning, by parents and siblings matching the words frequently to objects, just as some animals can be conditioned to recognize words as labels for things.

Around age 2 the primitive stage ends and the second period begins, that of *naive psychology*. The child discovers that words can have a symbolic function, and she displays this discovery by frequently asking what things are called. She no longer is simply conditioned by others to label objects and actions, but actively seeks this information herself. As a result, her vocabulary increases at a great rate. With the advent of the naive stage, the circles of language and thought begin to merge.

During this second period the child exhibits the beginnings of practical intelligence by recognizing characteristics of her surroundings and by starting to use tools, that is, starting to use objects as means to accomplish desired ends. However, her language is considered naive because she uses grammatical structures properly without recognizing the underlying functions they serve.

The experience she gains using language in relation to the objects of her world subsequently enables her to move to a third level, the stage of *egocentric speech*. This kind of talk makes up a large proportion of the preschool and kindergarten child's speech, particularly that occurring in play situations. It takes the form of a running monologue that accompanies the child's activities, whether she works alone or beside others. It requires no response from anyone, because it is not directed at anyone but the speaker. This commonly observed phenomenon has been interpreted in various ways by different investigators. Some have viewed egocentric speech as a "running accompaniment" or tune that merely parallels the child's thought and activity as she plays. But Vygotsky arrived at a different conclusion. He saw egocentric speech as an important new tool of thought. Not only does the child think to speak, but what she says to herself influences what she then will think, so the two interact to produce together conceptual or verbal thought.

To test this hypothesis, Vygotsky arranged for problems to arise during the play-work activities of young children. For example, a pencil for the drawing task would be missing or the paper would be too small or too large. The investigators then observed that the amount of egocentric talk on these occasions was double that observed when children did not face such problems (Vygotsky, 1962, pp. 16–17). This Vygotsky interpreted as evidence that egocentric speech is not just a release of tension or an expressive accompaniment to activity but is also a significant tool "of thought in the proper sense—in seeking and planning the solution of a problem" (1962, p. 16).

Nor did Vygotsky agree that egocentric speech simply died out after age 7 or so. Rather, he saw the decline of egocentric speech as a signal of the onset of the fourth stage in his developmental hierarchy, the *ingrowth stage*. The child learns to manipulate language in her head in the form of soundless speech, thinking by means of logical memory that employs inner signs for solving problems. Throughout the rest of her life, the individual will use both inner speech and outer speech as tools in conceptual or verbal thought.

In summary, children's speech grows through four stages between the time of birth and the years of the primary school, ages 7 or 8. The process begins with nonintellectual or "thoughtless" speech and develops via naive and egocentric language into inner speech that is inextricably interwoven with conceptual thinking. Now that we have traced development from the vantage point of speech, we will trace the development of verbal thinking from the vantage point of thought.

STAGES IN CONCEPTUAL THOUGHT DEVELOPMENT

Vygotsky's method of studying the development of conceptual thought involved two steps: (1) devising a test that would reveal the process a person follows when faced with the necessity to create a concept, and administering the test to children, adolescents, and adults, then (2) comparing the developmental hierarchy revealed in this testing with reports from other psychologists who had longitudinally followed the conceptual growth of individual children from one year to another. The purpose of this comparison was to determine whether the differences observed in testing cross sections of people of different ages accurately reflected the changes in thought processes that occur in the individual as he matures.

To begin we will briefly look at the testing instrument Vygotsky created (now known as the Vygotsky blocks), for it reveals something of his research ingenuity. One of the sticky problems faced in testing children's concept-formation. process is that of finding concepts for them to generate in the testing situation that you are sure they did not already know. In particular, you want to ensure they have mastered the concept and have not simply memorized a word that suggests they know the concept when they actually do not.

Vygotsky solved this problem by constructing a set of twenty-two wooden blocks of different colors, shapes, heights, and sizes (*size* meaning overall horizontal area). These characteristics vary in such a manner that no two blocks are alike in all ways. On the bottom surface of each block is written one of four nonsense words: *lag, bik, mur, cev.* Irrespective of the blocks' color or shape, *lag* appears on all tall, large blocks; *bik* on all flat, large ones; *mur* on tall, small ones; and *cev* on short, small ones. Each testing session begins with the examiner spreading the blocks before the child in a random mixture, then turning up a sample block and showing the child the name on the bottom. The child is asked to pick out all the blocks he thinks are the same kind, that is, ones that bear the same name. When the child has done so, the examiner turns up one of the selected blocks he knows is wrong and shows the child that it does not bear the correct word. The child is asked to try again. This process is repeated over and over until the child solves the problem. The solution, of course, requires that the child recognize that the word represents a concept composed of two of the dimensions of the blocks—both height and horizontal size. Since there is no single word in normal language representing this combined concept, the child cannot have known or rote memorized it prior to the testing session (Vygotsky, 1962, pp. 56–57).

Throughout the testing session the examiner carefully watches the combinations the child chooses each time, for the nature of each combination reflects the strategy of thought in which the child has engaged. Using the block problem with several hundred subjects of different ages enabled Vygotsky to identify a hierarchy of three major stages children pass through in achieving true conceptual thought between the preschool years and middle adolescence. Within each stage, children also traverse a series of subphases.

Conceptual thinking is really a mode of organizing one's environment by abstracting and labeling a quality shared by two or more phenomena. The major steps in children's intellectually organizing perceived phenomena are (I) clustering things into unorganized heaps, then (II) putting things together in complexes, and (III) as puberty arrives, beginning to think in genuine concepts. But even when the adolescent achieves the ability to think conceptually, he does not entirely abandon the two earlier forms of thought; they merely subside in frequency and reappear on certain occasions.

The subphases of the three major stages, based upon children's and adolescents' solutions to the Vygotsky-block problem, are as follows (Vygotsky, 1962, pp. 58–81):

Stage I. Thinking in *unorganized congeries* or heaps. During this period the child puts things in groups (and may assign the group a label) on the basis of what are only chance links in the child's perception.

> **Subphase I-A.** Trial-and-error grouping. The groups are created at random, blind guess.
>
> **Subphase I-B.** Visual-field organization. The child applies a grouping label to a collection of things that happen to appear together in space and time.
>
> **Subphase I-C.** Reformed heaps. The child first produces groupings on the basis of either guess or visual-field organization, then in dissatisfaction tries to reform his heaps by shifting elements in them around, but the items are still not alike in any inherent way.

Stage II. Thinking in *complexes*. Individual objects are united in the child's mind not only by his subjective impressions but also by bonds that actually exist among the objects. This is a step away from egocentric thinking and in the direction of objectivity. In a complex, the bonds between components to a degree are *concrete* and *factual* rather than abstract and logical. Five types of complexes succeed one another during this stage of thought.

Subphase II-A. *Associative* complexes based on any bond the child notices, such as color, shape, or nearness of objects to each other.

Subphase II-B. *Collection* complexes containing things that complement each other to make up a whole. Items are grouped by contrast rather than by similarity. For example, one block of each color may be put in a group and given a label. (At a dinner table, a knife, fork, spoon, plate, cup, and saucer would make up a set of a collection variety.)

Subphase II-C. *Chain* complexes involving a consecutive joining of individual items with a meaningful bond necessary only between one link and the next (as in the game of dominoes). A *large* green block may be linked to a *large red* block, then a *red* small *round* one followed by a *round* yellow middle-sized one.

Subphase II-D. *Diffuse* complexes—groupings in which there is a fluidity in the attribute that unites the individual elements. The child may put triangles together, then add a trapezoid to the group because the trapezoid's points remind him of a triangle's points.

Subphase II-E. *Pseudoconcept* complexes that at first view appear to be groupings based on true conceptual thinking. But when the label the child has applied is challenged, he shows he is unable to rationalize the grouping condition adequately. If he has put all red blocks together and the experimenter turns two blocks over to show they do not bear the same name (one is *mur* and the other *bik*), the child is unable to give up his first basis for grouping and to seek a different one, a different characteristic that unites the objects. Pseudoconceptual thinking represents a transition from thinking in complexes to thinking in true concepts.

Vygotsky made an important distinction between pseudoconcepts and true concepts: True conceptual thinking requires that the child spontaneously group objects on the basis of abstract characteristics that he perceives and not simply apply ready-made labels that he has been taught to use with other, common groupings. Vygotsky explained this phenomenon, which causes many adults to mistakenly assume that young children think conceptually, in this way:

Pseudoconcepts predominate over all other complexes in the preschool child's thinking for the simple reason that in real life, complexes corresponding to word meanings are not spontaneously developed by the child: The lines along which a complex develops are predetermined by the meaning a given word already has in the language of adults (1962, p. 67).

Stage III. Thinking in *concepts*. On the threshold of this final major stage, we will pause and inspect two paths of thought development—synthesizing and analyzing—that have now converged to make conceptual thinking possible.

The first path was through the sequence of complexes. The main function involved in such complex thinking was the *drawing together* or synthesizing of phenomena that share common aspects. The second path leading to conceptual thinking followed the process of *separating* or analyzing phenomena by singling out or abstracting elements from them. In Vygotsky's opinion these two processes, uniting and separating, arise from different sources in the child's development. We have already traced the path of drawing together or synthesizing. We will now move back to find the beginnings of the other, that of abstracting or analyzing.

In his experiments, Vygotsky located the beginnings of abstracting at the point where children identified ways in which objects were *maximally similar*, that is, alike in as many ways as possible. For example, they pick two blocks that are both tall *and* yellow or both short *and* green. But since such pairs of blocks also differ in shape or horizontal size, the child's abstracting process is somewhat in error. However, at this age the child overlooks the discrepancies and overemphasizes the similarities he first identified.

At the next stage of abstraction, the child identifies a *single characteristic* by which to group objects, selecting only green blocks or only tall ones. Vygotsky called these single-characteristic selections *potential concepts*.

The child then takes the final step into conceptual thinking when he makes a new synthesis of accurately abstracted traits, a synthesis that is stable and convincing in his mind, and this synthesis "becomes the main instrument of thought" (Vygotsky, 1962, p. 78). The child—by now an early adolescent—views things in terms of his synthesized-analyzed concepts. But even among adolescents conceptual thinking is somewhat unstable, being more consistent in concrete situations that have objects present than in solely verbal situations. Furthermore, there is no sharp break between one sort of thought and another. As the child begins to achieve conceptual thought, his thinking in complexes continues, though it diminishes in frequency. A person, even as an adult, is never "purely" a conceptual thinker.

Throughout this process of mental development, language has served as a significant tool or mediator for thinking activity. The intellectual operation of forming concepts, according to Vygotsky (1962, p. 81), "is guided by the use of words as the means of actively centering attention, of abstracting certain traits, synthesizing them, and symbolizing them by a sign."

As noted earlier, after Vygotsky conducted his experiments with the blocks and identified his hierarchy of mental acts leading to true concept formation, he studied the literature on linguistic development of children, on thought processes among primitive peoples, and on the nature of languages as such. The comparison of his own experimental results with those from the professional literature convinced him that the stages he had identified were essentially an accurate description of the development of conceptual thought. He apparently felt that a significant portion of the thought-and-language puzzle had been solved.

VYGOTSKY'S THEORY:
AN ASSESSMENT

As in previous chapters, the nine standards of appraisal from Chapter 1 provide the framework for evaluating Vygotsky's theory.

Vygotsky's theorizing, as described in *Thought and Language*, warrants a rather high mark for how well it reflects the real world of children (item 1). His speculations were founded on results of experiments with children of various ages, and he sought to check his conclusions with other studies from various nations. I would have rated item 1 even higher if his theory had been further supported with data from studies specifically designed to test his hypotheses (1) by experimental methods in addition to those us-

VYGOTSKY'S THEORY

How well do I think the theory meets the standards?

The Standards	Very Well	Moderately Well	Very Poorly
1. Reflects the real world of children		X	
2. Is clearly understandable	X		
3. Explains the past and predicts the future		X	
4. Guides child rearing		X	
5. Is internally consistent	X		
6. Is economical		X	
7. Is falsifiable	X		
8. Stimulates new discoveries	X		
9. Is self-satisfying	X		

ing the Vygotsky blocks and (2) with children from more varied cultural environments.

The theory is clearly described (item 2), particularly in its English-language form, which profits from organizational improvements effected by the translators, Hanfmann and Vakar.

The theory explains the past and predicts the future (item 3) of verbal-thought development for children in general. However, it does not (at least in the form described in *Thought and Language*) provide a means for analyzing the influence of causal factors in a child's life so that the progress toward conceptual thought of the individual child can be explained or predicted. Thus I have given it only a moderate rating on item 3.

Implications for child-rearing practices (item 4) in the form of suggestions for teaching scientific concepts have been included in a portion of Vygotsky's book not reviewed in this chapter. But as in the case of item 3, I feel the theory's usefulness as a guide to child rearing is limited by its failure to specify how causal factors combine in an individual child's life to determine his particular intellectual development. Thus, I have rated the theory as moderate on item 4.

I have not located any internal inconsistencies in Vygotsky's model (item 5), and it appears economical (item 6) in that it does not seem to propose complex theoretical mechanisms to account for phenomena that might be equally well explained by less complex ones. I feel, however, that more elements and a better explanation of their interactions are needed to account for the results he obtained with his block experiments. But, after all, as Bruner observed, the theory as it appears in *Thought and Language* is more programmatic than complete and systematic. At the time of Vygotsky's death it was necessarily still in skeletal form. My mark near the center for item 6, therefore, represents my opinion that the theory was somewhat overly economical, barren in detail.

In terms of falsifiability (item 7), I believe all of Vygotsky's hypotheses and proposals, as well as his actual stages of growth in speech and thought, can be tested experimentally to determine whether they are supportable in fact.

As stimulators of new discoveries (item 8), Vygotsky's theoretical proposals are apparently highly regarded in the Soviet Union (Luria, 1976, pp. v, 11–12; Vygotsky, 1962, pp. ix–x). And since his work has been published in the West, it has set off new speculation and investigation that are showing up in publications of English-reading psychologists. Thus, I have rated it high on item 8.

Overall, despite some qualifications mentioned earlier, I find this theory of thought and speech quite satisfying (item 9).

FOR FURTHER READING

Vygotsky, Lev Semenovich. (1962) *Thought and Language*. Cambridge, Mass.: M.I.T. Press.

For two Soviet psychological investigations utilizing Vygotsky's proposal that cognitive development as reflected in speech is heavily influenced by the child's sociohistorical background, see:

Luria, A. R. (1976) *Cognitive Development: Its Cultural and Social Foundations.* Cambridge, Mass.: Harvard University Press.

Luria, A. R. and F. Yudovich. (1971) *Speech and the Development of Mental Processes in the Child.* Harmondsworth, England: Penguin.

For Piaget's reaction to Vygotsky's criticism of an early version of Piagetian theory, see:

Piaget, J. (1962) *Comments on Vygotsky's Critical Remarks Concerning the Language and Thought of the Child and Judgment and Reasoning in the Child.* Cambridge, Mass.: M.I.T. Press, 16 pages.

CHAPTER 15

BROWN'S IDEAS ON GENERATIVE LANGUAGE ACQUISITION

For centuries people have assumed that the language a person emits, both in speaking and in writing, serves as a useful window through which to view the operation of his mind. Motivated by this same assumption, I have placed in this cognitive development section the theoretical notions of Roger Brown on the matter of how children begin to acquire spoken language.

Brown (born 1924) is a Harvard University social psychologist whose work is included as representative of a highly active movement among scholars of psycholinguistics in recent years. The revolutionary event that so strongly influenced Brown's investigations and those of virtually all modern theorists in language behavior was the publication of *Syntactic Structures* (1957) by Noam Chomsky, a Massachusetts Institute of Technology linguistics professor. Prior to this publication, most analyses of sentence forms had centered on what we think of as traditional grammar—the relationships among such things as subjects and predicates, adjectives and adverbs, conjunctions and prepositions, inflected word endings, and the like. But Chomsky contended that such analysis was not very useful for explaining how people think as they generate sentences to express their meanings. One of the most obvious problems in English is represented by the active and passive voices. Consider the following two sentences:

Active: *Jane poked Dick.*
Passive: *Dick was poked by Jane.*

The meaning is exactly the same, yet the number and position of words are quite different. Chomsky reasoned that underlying these semantically identical but structurally different utterances there must be a single basic structure—a *deep* structure—from which the speaker generates both sentences. In other words, there is a common deep structure which the person transforms into either of the two surface structures to carry the meaning.

By analyzing all sorts of sentences (surface structures), Chomsky created a set of rules by which, he hypothesized, people transform deep structure into the strings of words they utter when expressing their ideas. This set of rules has become known as *transformational grammar.*

Since around 1960 most people who have theorized about and have conducted investigations into language acquisition have assumed that describing the surface characteristics of children's speech is indeed not enough to explain how and why language competency grows as it does. Nearly all theorizing now seeks to account for the nature of a deep structure and for the patterns of rules by which an individual generates his sequence of words. In recent years there have been a great many empirical investigations of children's early speech. These investigations have been done on many languages, and many conflicting theories have been proposed to account for what has been observed. Roger Brown and graduate students who have studied with him have been in the midst of this fray, collecting their own records of children's speech, proposing theories, and critically comparing these theories to those of other investigators. Brown's goals, his style of work, and some of the key generalizations he has derived form the subject matter of this chapter. In considering his work, we will first discuss the focus of his theorizing, then his research methodology, and finally some of the generalizations about language growth that he has derived.

THE FOCUS OF THE THEORY

At the outset it is important to recognize that Brown does not sanctify his proposals by calling them a formal theory. Instead, he refers to them as generalizations that hopefully can contribute in the future to the formulation of a theory of first-language acquisition. The generalizations he draws from the data he analyzes are always tentative, usually accompanied by as-yet-unanswered questions and always subject to alteration on the basis of new data or more reasonable logic. However, from the perspective of the rather loose meaning of the term *theory* that I have used in assembling this book, Brown's cluster of generalizations does qualify as a theory, albeit a theory still in the making.

In regard to the focus of his work, Brown has concerned himself solely with children's ability to generate spoken language rather than their ability to understand speech, to read, or to write. But the limitations of research techniques have forced him to narrow the scope of his generalizations even further. He has restricted his theorizing to speech *production* and has not claimed to describe speech *competence*. In effect, he, like other researchers, has assumed that children have the competence to say a greater variety of things than they actually do say, but as yet there are no adequate ways to measure the portion of speaking ability that remains unsaid, the silent portion of competence that lies between what the child does say and what she could say if she wanted to.

Within this area of speech production Brown has concentrated on issues of syntax and grammar, that is, on how children choose two or more words and string them together. He has not written extensively about either vocabulary generation or phonology in the major publication on which I have based most of the present version of his work (*A First Language: The Early Stages*, 1973).

Key questions he has sought to answer include: (1) Do children reproduce only those sentences they have heard others say frequently, or do children generate novel sentences of their own? (2) Are a child's "errors" in syntax and grammar just random mistakes, or do they reflect a set of individual rules the child has intuitively created? (3) Are there consistent, identifiable steps by which children's syntax and grammar grow? If so, what are the characteristics of the steps, and when do they occur? (4) What are the likenesses and differences in the developmental patterns of speech of children within a single culture and of children in different cultures? (5) Why do children improve or develop beyond the stage of rudimentary language usage, the stage at which they manage to be understood by others? Generalizations Brown has drawn about these questions are described later in the chapter.

For now, we will describe his research methodology and point out what influence such methodology has on the conclusions he is able to draw.

RESEARCH METHODS AND
UNITS OF MEASUREMENT

Like most investigators in the field of psycholinguistics, Brown does not conduct controlled experiments with children. Instead, he records children's speech in their natural habitats, primarily in the home, and analyzes changes that occur in this speech at one-week or two-week intervals over a period between about ages 18 months and 4 years. The most extensive data on which he has based his generalizations were gathered over several years on three children who were assigned the pseudonyms Adam, Eve, and Sarah. All three lived in the vicinity of Cambridge, Massachusetts. Through the years, an hour or two of each child's conversation was recorded each week or so. Since all three were talkative children, this mode of periodic sampling eventually provided a large amount of speech to be analyzed, forming the basis for an important longitudinal study of children's growth in oral language.

In addition to analyzing the speech of Adam, Eve, and Sarah, Brown and his colleagues gathered shorter segments of other children's speech. They also collected the results of other investigators' studies of children learning languages like Finnish, Samoan, Swedish, Spanish, German, Luo, and American English.

To launch his analysis of the growth of children's grammar, Brown had to determine the nature of the scale he would use for judging development. He finally selected *length of utterance* as the unit of measurement for his scale, because the length of what young children say grows by regular, gradual steps from age 2 to 4. The elements that made up Brown's measure were *morphemes*. In the field of linguistics a morpheme is any cluster of letters that make up a basic element of meaning. For instance, a morpheme can be an entire word, such as *talk*. But a single word can be made up of more than one morpheme; that is, more than one element of meaning are combined. So *talked* and *talking* are each composed of two morphemes, since the *ed* and the *ing* add new meaning to the original root word. The *s* at the end of a plural (block*s*) or possessive (Daddy'*s*) also counts as a separate morpheme. The length of an utterance, therefore, is determined by how many morphemes appear in each separate statement or childlike "sentence."

The speech of children between age 9 months and 15 or 20 months is typically composed of one morpheme per utterance. In essence, the child who is just learning to speak expresses each idea

in a single word—*Mommy, eat, dog, ball.* In the field of psycholinguistics, this use of one morpheme to express an entire
phrase is known as *holophrastic* speech (*holo=whole* in Greek, and
phrastic=phrase). Because syntax and grammar are concerned with
the combining of morphemes and words into phrases and sentences, Brown did not concentrate on one-word utterances as the
starting point of his grammar-development scale. Rather, he
moved a bit higher to the point at which children's utterances on
the average include slightly fewer than two words. The base of his
developmental scale, then, was set at 1.5 average morphemes per
utterance (or "mean length of utterance," abbreviated MLU). Obviously no child speaks one-and-one-half utterances at any time;
but if half of what she says is in single words and the other half in
two-word expressions, then the average during an hour of speaking will end up at 1.5. Brown then proceeded up the growth scale
in morphemes to the point at which children exhibit utterances
that average five morphemes in length. This became the upper
boundary of his early childhood speech scale. He then divided
this range into five stages, which had the following mean lengths
of utterance (MLU) as their centers:

Stage	Mean Length of Utterance
I	1.75
II	2.25
III	2.75
IV	3.50
V	4.00

The weekly or biweekly speech records of Adam, Eve, and
Sarah were then plotted on a chart to demonstrate how their performances would appear on such an MLU scale. The pattern
shown in Figure 15.1 was the result.

Three rather obvious conclusions can be drawn from the data
in Figure 15.1. First, MLU appears to be a good unit for measuring
oral-language development in young children, for each child's
MLU grows at a steady pace from month to month. If a child's
MLU takes a temporary jag downward during a given month's

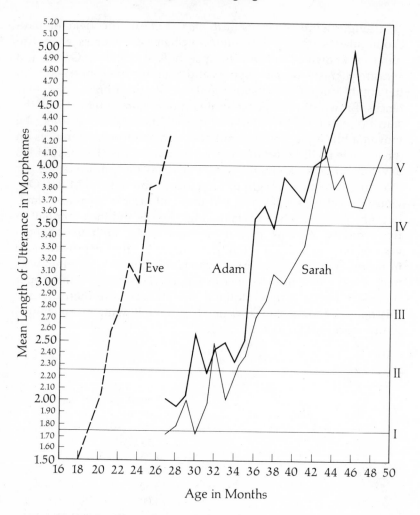

Figure 15.1   Rate of Growth in Mean Length of Utterance for Three Children (Brown, 1973, p. 57)

speech sample, it quickly recovers the upward trend. The tilt of the growth lines (reflecting the rate of development) is not only similar for the three children, but when Brown analyzed the grammatical elements within each of the five steps or stages, he found "a remarkably invariant order in the kinds of things they said" (Brown, 1973, p. 57).

A second conclusion derived from Figure 15.1 is that even though the pattern of language development is similar in the three children, Eve entered and completed each stage far earlier than did either Adam or Sarah. And Adam was slightly ahead of Sarah. Thus, the individual differences among the children in the time they passed through the stages were greater than differences in their performance within a stage.

A third conclusion is that the borderlines between stages have been set rather arbitrarily and do not represent distinctly different levels or breaks in the quantity or quality of speech from one stage to the next. In other words, these are not stages in the Piagetian sense. The stage concept is imposed on continuous growth data by the theorist as an analytical convenience. But even though they merge into each other, every one of the five levels has a cluster of distinguishing characteristics.

Next, let us consider the working style by which Brown arrived at his generalizations. From each of the three children's speech records at each of the imposed five "stages," Brown drew 713 utterances. He then set about analyzing this mass of child talk to discover what sorts of rules or guidelines each child seemed to use within a "stage" to generate speech. These common characteristics or underlying structures that ran through a given child's way of assembling his morphemes were regarded as the child's personal grammar at that stage. In other words, Brown did not accept the idea that children's deviations from adult speech patterns are simply random errors. Instead, he believed, along with all modern psycholinguistic experts, that a child's speech reflects the child's systematic, lawful conception of how words are assembled into strings that express her intentions. A child simply uses a different grammar than does an adult. By poring over the records of Adam, Eve, and Sarah, Brown was able to prepare fifteen different grammars, each about fifty pages long, representing a separate grammar for each of the five stages for every child. These descriptions of the children's apparent systems for producing sensible speech form much of the basis for Brown's theorizing.

Another source of material on which to found or to test generalizations has been the rapidly growing stock of other longitudinal studies of young children in various language cultures. These recent investigations have enabled Brown to broaden the base of his theorizing beyond Adam, Eve, and Sarah and thus draw conclusions about language development among children in other American cultures and in other nations as well.

Brown has carefully inspected the basic speech data collected by other investigators, and has continually weighed their explanations against his own in order to determine which theoretical position best accounts for all facets of the data. He appears to have shown a greater willingness than many theorists to alter his own position in the light of new evidence or more logical explanation, instead of trying to defend his original ideas by rationalizing away apparent discrepancies.

This flexibility of Brown's methodology can be illustrated by describing how his interpretation of children's early telegraphic speech was influenced by the findings of another researcher. The term *telegraphic speech* was coined to describe the fact that when a very young child puts together a few words to express an idea, he leaves out certain words not essential to the gross meaning he is trying to convey. The effect is similar to an adult's composing a telegram and, for the sake of economy, leaving out articles (*a, the*), coupling and "helping" verbs (*is, will*), some pronouns (*my, their*), and the like. The result of an adult's telegram can be: *Trip postponed. See you Thursday New York airport.* The result of a child's telegraphic speech at stage I of Brown's scale can be: *Car go* or *Jimmie ball* or *That dog.*

In writing about telegraphic speech in the early 1960s, Brown concentrated on identifying which classes of words were used by the child (mainly nouns and verbs) and which classes were omitted (articles, prepositions, the final *s* for plurals, coupling verbs, and others). He explained telegraphic speech, then, in terms of kinds of words included and kinds left out. But a study of young German children's speech development by Park in 1970 (Brown, 1973, pp. 79–81) contradicted Brown's assignment of morphemes to classes. For German children, Brown's classes seemed only partially true, so he reanalyzed his position and concluded that whether or not a morpheme is deleted in telegraphic speech depends on several identifiable grammatic and semantic conditions influencing the utterance. It is not simply a matter of separate classes of morphemes used or omitted. Four of these influential conditions or variables are: frequency, perceptual salience, verbal context, and semantic role. We can inspect each of these briefly to see how they might explain, in a more sophisticated way, the nature of telegraphic speech in any culture's language.

Frequency means how often the child has heard the morpheme used by people around her. There is apparently a minimal level of frequency at which a word and its position must be heard by the child in order for the child to command the word for her own use. But once the minimal level has been reached, hearing the word more often will not ensure that it will be used frequently in the child's speech. Children do not simply use those words most that they have heard most often—they hear *a, and,* and *the* many times in adult speech, but young children leave these words out of their own speech.

Perceptual salience means how easily the word stands out from the others in terms of whether it is stressed in the sentence or is the last word in the utterance.

Verbal context refers to the fact that the other words in a sentence string will often determine the particular form a given word takes in that specific environment. For example, if the stem of the surrounding context is *I _____ here yesterday,* then *dug* is the only acceptable form, and *digs, digged,* or *digging* are not proper. Likewise, it is correct to say *She came an hour ago,* but not *She came a hour ago.* There are many other ways in which verbal context influences proper grammatical usage. Brown suggests that some of these contextual determinants are far easier to learn than others. The difficult ones, he proposes, will not be used in early child speech, though the easier ones may appear.

Semantic role refers to how important a morpheme is for conveying the basic meaning of the child's expression. The meaning typically depends heavily on nouns and verbs and in some cases locatives (*here, there*) and adjectives (*two, big*). In contrast, other words only modulate the basic meanings, express nuances, or are really inessential. Articles and state-of-being verbs often play insignificant semantic roles, as in *Dog want cookie* for *The dog wants a cookie* and *Jenny sleepy* for *Jenny is sleepy.*

With these variables of frequency, perceptual salience, verbal context, and semantic role in hand, Brown was now able to explain in a more sophisticated way why certain *functional words* or morphemes (*functors*) appeared in the speech of children on certain occasions during the telegraphic phase of stage I. He no longer had to ignore apparent exceptions to his earlier classes of morphemes. He now was able to propose a set of principles, which he called "a guess," about the way functors are included in child talk. He hypothesized that:

1. A child *will use* a given functor (a functional word or inflection) freely and correctly in stage I if the functor:
   a. Has been heard often (above the minimal frequency level)
   b. Has high perceptual salience

    c. Is not dependent on the verbal context

    d. Plays a necessary semantic role (its inclusion is essential to the basic meaning of the utterance)

2. A child *will occasionally use* a given functor at stage I, but only in prefabricated routines (combinations that sound like a single complete word to the child, such as *gonna* and *piece-of-toast*) if the functor:

    a. Has been heard often (above the minimal frequency level)

    b. Has high perceptual salience

However, it does not matter whether the functor's meaning depends on the verbal context, nor is its semantic role decisive.

3. In stage I a child *will not use* a functor if it:

    a. Has low frequency and low perceptual salience

    b. Depends on the verbal context

    c. Only modulates or slightly varies the basic meaning (adapted from Brown, 1973, p. 88)

Whereas Brown's earlier theory explained how certain classes of words (mainly nouns and verbs) were always included in telegraphic speech while others (articles, conjunctions, and so on) were deleted, his revised principles enabled him to explain the puzzling deviations from the earlier theory as found in English speech and, even more pointedly, the ostensible deviations in the speech of children learning German, Korean, and other languages. In this way, his own research methods and his attention to other theorists' findings bring about a continual revision of his growing list of generalizations, that is, of his theorizing.

SOME GENERALIZATIONS ABOUT SPEECH ACQUISITION

Now, with some background in the nature of Brown's interests and method of working, we are prepared to consider several representative generalizations, or theoretical statements, he has proposed regarding: (1) some characteristics of developmental stages, (2) individual differences among children in language skills, and

(3) the question of what causes children to improve in speaking skill.

SEVERAL CHARACTERISTICS
OF DEVELOPMENTAL STAGES

We noted earlier that Brown produced five "stages" of development between age 18 months and 4 years by imposing borderlines on continuous growth curves on the basis of mean length of utterance in morphemes. Stage I was given a lower border of 1.5 MLU and an upper border of 2.0. Stage II extended from 2.0 to 2.5. And the next three were likewise defined by MLU units. Even though his manner of defining stages is artificial and not based on significant developmental changes that form boundary lines, he still has been able to identify characteristics that tend to distinguish the average performance at one stage from the average performance at another.

For example, during stage I, a child's utterances are pretty well limited to nouns and verbs, the parts of speech most essential to conveying meaning. The child's grammar at this point consists of her putting two or three words into an order that communicates her apparent gross intent. So word order is an important developmental trait at stage I.

During stage II there is a gradual addition of what Brown has called "little words and inflections"—such prepositions as *in* and *on*, some present progressive verb inflections (John's *eating*), some plurals and possessives, and the like. The role of these grammatical morphemes is to modulate or embellish in a simple way the basic content of what the child at stage I said with just a noun and verb.

Brown's data show that children do not suddenly "catch on" to the idea of plurals or possessives, and thus alter their speech radically, after using these new morphemes correctly only once. Rather, the addition of a given morpheme grows over time. Not until stage V may a child get correct over 90 percent of the time some forms initially found in his speech at stage II or III. So it is only through a gradual, complex process that the child gets firm command over forms that make up standard adult speech. During the early years the child gropes to understand the underlying patterns, the grammatical rules, by which his words are best ordered to express his ideas. His sets of rules alter from time to time. They are variable until, as he reaches grammatical maturity in using the standard adult forms of his culture, the rules become categorical and unchanging.

In order to trace the way in which the little words and inflections enter and develop in child speech, Brown selected fourteen morphemes and analyzed their use by Adam, Eve, and Sarah. He also located in other investigators' studies as many of these fourteen English morphemes as he could and traced their acquisition in these other studies as well. From this analysis he discovered that the sequence in which children acquired the fourteen was amazingly the same. The rank order correlations among Adam, Eve, and Sarah were all .87 or above.

After comparing the characteristics of the fourteen morphemes, Brown concluded that the main factors determining the order in which a morpheme enters a child's speech are cumulative grammatic and semantic complexity. He had now established that between stages I and V, three interlinked trends occur. Children's utterances (mean length of utterance) become longer, they express more complicated nuances of meaning, and they do so by arranging morphemes in increasingly complex patterns. By the middle of stage V, however, the length of a child's sentences begins to lose its value as a gauge of developmental progress. At this stage, more complex meanings and grammatical relationships can be generated without necessarily adding more words to an utterance.

Brown's conclusion that the complexity of meaning and of grammar increases as the child's experience increases may seem more like common sense than a scholarly discovery. However, when the details of his work are inspected and compared to alternate theories, his conclusions assume more significance. For example, there have been theorists who have proposed that children learn language by direct conditioning; that is, they copy what they hear most. (This, roughly, is the position held by Skinner, whom we will meet in Chapter 17.) However, when Brown compared the type and frequency of grammatical structures of parents with those of their young children, he decided that frequency of hearing a particular structure or vocabulary has very little to do with how a child's speech patterns evolve (Brown, 1973, p. 368).

In summary, a child's language environment is not as significant in determining the sequence in which different morphemes will enter her speech as the child's own "natural" accumulation of more complex grammatical arrangements and meanings. This increasing-complex factor can account for the great similarity in the sequence of language acquisition between one child and another, both within a given language culture and across cultures.

INDIVIDUAL DIFFERENCES

Though the steps in language development are "approximately invariant across children learning one language and, at a higher level of abstraction, across children learning any language, the rate of progression will vary radically among children" (Brown, 1973, p. 54).

The main difference among children in their acquisition of grammar is the pace at which they move through a common sequence of stages. In seeking to account for these rate differences, Brown has speculated that a substantial part of the cause may be what psychologists have called *general intelligence*. He bases this guess on his conviction that such intelligence can reasonably be conceived as "the rate at which individuals build general systems or theories comprehending sets of data to which they are exposed" (Brown, 1973, pp. 408–409). And since grammars are sets of rules, then the child who moves rapidly through the stages of increasingly complex grammars and semantic relations will logically be one with high intelligence.

By adopting such a view, and by proposing that young children appear little influenced by the frequency of mature grammar heard in their particular environment (beyond the minimal frequency needed to acquire a morpheme at all), Brown seems to be assigning a large role to genetically scheduled maturation in determining the development of language skill. Undoubtedly the child's language environment does influence acquisition, because she cannot devise a particular language's structures by herself in isolation. However, according to Brown's data, both the order and rate of adding more complex morphemes depends heavily on an inborn capacity of the growing child to process language and, in particular, to generate speech in the patterns that psycholinguists have observed.

THE MOTIVE TO IMPROVE

A final question Brown has pondered is: What impels the child to improve at all toward adult standards of usage? Or, what is the motivating force behind speech development? For the child who uses one word, or who advances to stages II or III where he uses two or three morphemes, the answer is that language enables him to communicate his needs more rapidly. Language thus functions to get him what he wants.

Analyses of standard adult grammar, however, show that certain grammatic items are actually not necessary for conveying accurate meanings, particularly when one person is talking directly to another and their conversational setting helps fill in the meaning. Voice stress or inflection often does the trick. A child can point and stress the word *car* in the utterance "That car," and he does not need the full sentence "That is a car." Or he can stress *that* in "That car" and indicate that he is distinguishing a particular car from among several possible ones, so he need not say "That is the car." Why, then, do children continue to improve toward standard adult usage if their less sophisticated grammar suffices after they have reached a particular point? Brown (1973, p. 410) says this remains "something of a mystery."

One possible answer is that people in the environment exert pressures on children to correct their errant speech. In effect, children might be expected to adopt usages that are approved and drop those that are disapproved. But studies by Brown and Hanlon suggest that such is not true, at least not for preschoolers at stages I through V:

> In general, the parents seemed to pay no attention to bad syntax nor did they even seem to be aware of it. . . . I find that what parents generally correct is pronunciation, "naughty" words, and regularized irregular allomorphs like *digged* and *goed*. These facts of the child's speech seem to penetrate parental awareness. But syntax—the child saying, for instance, "Why the dog won't eat?" instead of "Why won't the dog eat?"—seems to be automatically set right in the parent's mind, with the mistake never registering as such (Brown, 1973, p. 412).

Brown proposes, however, that, away from the home, where the child's immature usage is less acceptable or not so readily understood, there may be pressures to select more adequate standard grammar. But at present, in Brown's view, the matter of what motivates language development after a basic level of communication has been attained is still a puzzle. Like many issues in the field of psycholinguistics, it requires more inventive theory and more supporting evidence.

BROWN'S THEORIZING: AN ASSESSMENT

In a sense, it seems not entirely fair to apply all nine appraisal standards to Brown's work since he has not claimed to have con-

BROWN'S THEORIZING

How well do I think the theory meets the standards?

The Standards	Very Well	Moderately Well	Very Poorly
1. Reflects the real world of children		X	
2. Is clearly understandable	X		
3. Explains the past and predicts the future		X	
4. Guides child rearing			X
5. Is internally consistent		?	
6. Is economical		?	
7. Is falsifiable	X		
8. Stimulates new discoveries		X	
9. Is self-satisfying		X	

structed a complete theory of generative language acquisition. However, it may still be useful for purposes of comparing his theory with the others in this volume to try viewing Brown's theorizing from the perspective of the nine criteria.

Brown's speech development principles, being tentative generalizations derived entirely from detailed and carefully analyzed empirical data, appear very falsifiable (item 7). Their validity can readily be checked by observation and experiment. Likewise, Brown's description of how he has produced his principles is quite clear (item 2).

As for reflecting the real world of children (item 1), his generalizations do depict the speech development of at least three real children. In addition, he has adapted data from studies conducted on a number of children in other language environments, so at least some of his generalizations reflect the real speech growth of a number of other children as well. For these reasons, I have rated Brown's work above the center on item 1. He was not rated at the top of the scale because data are needed on additional children who represent more varied language environments, more age levels above the preschool years, and various levels of general intelligence. Evidence about the speech of a more diverse sampling of children can, I believe, effect refinements in Brown's views, just as Park's studies of German children motivated Brown to revise his original interpretation of telegraphic speech.

In their present form, Brown's principles permit predictions of the sequence of syntax and grammar that can be expected for the child between ages 18 months and 4 years. But the rate of progress through these changes cannot be predicted for the individual child. As for explaining the past, Brown's evolving system appears to be still in a very tentative form. He has suggested this by labeling the description of the four factors that apparently influence telegraphic speech as a "guess." And he notes that interpretations of why children's speech improves are still only speculations. Weighing these strengths and weaknesses against each other, I have marked item 3 in the middle.

If parents and teachers of preschoolers are looking for ways to enhance the speech development of young children (item 4), they will find little or no guidance about things to do from Brown's writings (nor was it his probable intention to furnish such guidance). However, two implications that might reasonably be drawn are that parents and teachers should "talk" and should "wait." That is, first, parents and teachers should talk to, with, and around children because the young child cannot use forms of words (morphemes) she has not heard often enough to make an impression on her (minimal frequency). However, just using a word frequently around or with the child will not at all ensure that she will use the word in her own speech. Second, parents and teachers should wait and let nature take her course in carrying the child toward maturity in syntax and grammar, for all children appear to go through the same sequence of stages in syntax and grammar development whatever their language environment.

The great value of Brown and his work as stimulators of research (item 8) is attested by the large numbers of his former students who are in the forefront of modern movements in developmental psycholinguistics and by the frequency with which

Brown is cited in the professional literature. (For examples of former students, see Brown, 1973, pp. x–xi.)

The ratings for the theory's internal consistency (item 5) and economy of explanation (item 6) appear as question marks in the center of the scale. My difficulties in judging Brown's formulations by these two standards have resulted from the fact that as yet his set of generalizations lacks an overall framework linking the parts together to form a general theory of speech development. There is not a clear enough body structure to appraise either the economy or consistency of possible relationships among its intended parts. Hence, I have left these two aspects as open questions.

As already noted, Brown has not called the results of his theorizing a *theory*, but generalizations that may prove useful in constructing a theory of generative language development. Even the generalizations now available in published form are far fewer than what he has available in his notes. His book *A First Language: The Early Stages* offers a detailed treatment of only stages I and II. Another volume or two are promised on Brown's analyses of stages III, IV, and V of his system. Perhaps when he has completed those steps he will be prepared to suggest an overall theory. In the meantime, I feel that his mode of operation as illustrated in *A First Language* and other publications (Brown, 1970) represents a rather satisfying foundation (item 9) on which to erect a theory.

FOR FURTHER READING

Brown, Roger. (1973) *A First Language: The Early Stages*. Cambridge, Mass.: Harvard University Press.

Brown, Roger. (1970) *Psycholinguistics*. New York: Free Press.
This collection of essays pictures some aspects of language development not treated in *A First Language*.

CHAPTER 16

KOHLBERG'S MORAL DEVELOPMENT

So far in this section on cognitive growth and language development we have inspected an overall theory of intellectual growth (Piaget), a theory of the relationship of thought to language (Vygotsky), and a theory in the making concerning children's thinking processes as reflected in their speech development (Brown). To illustrate a different facet of cognitive development, we now consider a theory of how children grow in ways of defending their moral judgments.

The man whose work I have selected to represent theories of moral judgment is Lawrence Kohlberg (born 1927), a Harvard University psychologist and professor of education. Before outlining Kohlberg's theory, it is important that we understand how the word *moral* will be used throughout the chapter, for the word often means different things to different people.

FACTS, VALUES, AND MORALS

To arrive at a clear definition of *moral*, we will first define a more general term, *value*, of which *moral* is a subcategory. We will also recall the definition of the term *facts* given in Chapter 1 and make a distinction between *facts* and *values*.

Earlier we proposed that *facts* are objective information, observations or measurements that are publicly verifiable. In contrast, *values* are opinions about the desirability or propriety or goodness of something. The "something" may be a person, an object, a place, an event, an idea, a kind of behavior, or the like. Statements of fact tell what exists, in what amount, and perhaps in what relation to other facts. Statements of value tell whether something is good or bad, well done or poorly done, suitable or unsuitable. Our focus in the present chapter is on values, not facts, though many of the values discussed will involve the use of facts.

The word *moral* as intended in this chapter is only one subitem under the general term *value*. Many values do not qualify as moral ones. For instance, there are *aesthetic values,* those which involve opinions offered from an artistic viewpoint. Aesthetic values, when applied to a flower garden, a poem, a painting, or a dance performance, are reflected in such phrases as "pleasing to the eye" or "nicely turned metaphor" or "delightfully innovative." Another category is that of *technical values.* These may focus on how efficiently something operates or how well its parts coordinate. There is also the subgroup of *prudential values* which guide a person's social relations and his investment of time and energy so as to yield him the greatest benefits. A girl finds it prudent not to tell her teacher that the teacher's breath smells sour, and a boy finds it imprudent to wander away to play ball after his father has commissioned him to mow the lawn.

At this point you may ask: How are moral-value judgments different from these other sorts? The answer used here is offered by Kohlberg:

> Unlike judgments of prudence or aesthetics, moral judgments tend to be universal, inclusive, consistent, and based on objective, impersonal, or ideal grounds (1968a, p. 490).

According to Kohlberg, it is not a moral judgment when a child says to her companion, "Don't cheat on the math test today, 'cause yesterday she caught Eddie cheating and tore up his paper." This is only a prudential judgment, for it is not universal (does not apply to all test situations), nor is it based on impersonal or ideal grounds. In contrast, it is a moral judgment when a high school youth says, "They should outlaw capital punishment, because no one has a right to take another person's life under any circumstances." This judgment is universal, applies in all situations, and is founded on ideal convictions.

Kohlberg's theory of moral development traces the steps by which children grow toward making truly moral judgments. The steps "represent a progressive disentangling or differentiation of moral values and judgments from other types of values and judgments" (Kohlberg, 1968a, p. 410). If the child is successful in advancing to the highest stage of moral judgment, in adolescence he bases his appraisals of moral issues on concepts of justice. In Kohlberg's view, this means that the youth grounds his opinions on the *right of the individual,* and he judges an act wrong if it violates that right. Kohlberg further contends that a *right* in this sense is founded on *equality* and *reciprocity,* so that people are equal in terms of exchange (or contract) and of reward for merit. Justice implies that the law is impartial and applies to all equally in its maintenance of the rights of the individual (Kohlberg, 1967, pp. 173, 176).

In order to explain how Kohlberg sees children growing toward the position of basing moral judgments on concepts of justice, we will first describe (1) the focus of the theory and (2) its research methodology. Then we will (3) delineate the moral growth stages and aspects, (4) describe how Kohlberg sees children's natures interacting with their environments to determine their stage of moral development, (5) point out several important characteristics of moral growth stages, and (6) note what Kohlberg's beliefs imply for moral education.

THE FOCUS OF THE THEORY

Moral development is usually viewed as one aspect of socialization, with *socialization* meaning the process by which children learn to conform to the expectations of the culture in which they grow up. In the case of moral values, children not only learn to conform, but they also *internalize* these standards and thereby accept the standards as correct and as representing their own personal values. A value is considered to be internalized and not just imposed by outsiders when the child conforms in situations (1) that tempt her to transgress and (2) that afford slight chance of her behavior being discovered, punished, or rewarded.

People who have sought to trace the development of morality in children have typically focused on one or more of three aspects of personality: observed behavior, feelings of guilt, or the basis for a moral judgment.

In the case of *observed behavior,* the question asked by the investigator is: Does the child display greater honesty or integrity or a sense of justice as he grows older? Extensive studies of honesty in children and youths have yielded either inconclusive or negative answers to this question (Hartshorne and May, 1928–1930). Rather than basing their response to temptation only on a growing internal sense of honesty, children and adolescents appear more often to base their actions on prudential judgments (How likely is it that I will be caught?) or on social pressures (Will the group disapprove?). Thus Kohlberg has rejected observed behavior as a profitable criterion for moral development.

A second approach to the study of rule internalization focuses on how the *emotion of guilt* grows as the years advance. This emotion refers to the self-critical and self-punishing acts of anxiety and regret that follow transgression of a rule or cultural standard. Here the assumption is that the child obeys in order to avoid feeling guilty. Kohlberg (1968a, p. 484) says this assumption underlies the concept of conscience in psychoanalysis and in learning theories. He concludes that even though studies of children through projective techniques show a sudden upsurge in such guilt feelings in the years prior to puberty, projective techniques have not been able to predict consistently whether children really will resist temptation. Hence, his own theory is not founded on charting the emotion of guilt over the years of childhood and youth. Instead, his work has centered on a third approach, that of tracing the bases of the child's judgments of moral issues.

In investigating the *judgmental* side of moral development, our question becomes: Has the child internalized a moral standard, and can he justify that standard to himself and to others? Such an approach was used in the early 1930s by Piaget and has since been refined by other scholars, with Kohlberg being the most prominent researcher in the field over the past two decades. In Kohlberg's opinion the issue is not whether the child acts honestly or whether he feels guilty about transgressing the rules. Instead, the moral-development issue is the judgmental basis the child uses for assessing moral behavior.

KOHLBERG'S RESEARCH METHODS

The studies on which Kohlberg's theoretical proposals are founded consist of describing to children a series of incidents, each incident involving a moral dilemma. Each child is then asked which solution would be the best or proper one for each dilemma and why that solution would be better than others. For example, here is a typical Kohlberg incident, the one known as the Heinz problem.

> Mrs. Heinz was near death from a special type of cancer. The doctors thought one kind of drug might save her. The druggist who made the medicine she needed was selling it for ten times the amount that it cost him to make it. The sick woman's husband, Heinz, did not have enough money for the medicine, so he went to borrow the money from everyone he knew, but he could collect only about half of what the druggist was charging. Heinz told the druggist his wife was dying and asked him to sell him the medicine cheaper or to let him pay later, but the druggist refused. The druggist said he discovered the drug and he was going to make money from it. So Heinz got desperate and later broke into the drugstore to steal the drug for his wife. The question then is: Should the husband have tried to steal the drug? Why or why not? (Adapted from Kohlberg, 1971, p. 156)

Responses to such moral dilemmas are then analyzed by Kohlberg and his colleagues to determine which of six developmental stages of moral judgment are reflected in the child's or youth's answers. The task of analyzing and grading children's answers does not involve simply comparing an objective answer sheet to children's responses. Rather, the grading scheme requires training and involves some measure of subjective judgment on the part of the analyst.

Kohlberg began using his moral incidents with a sample of seventy-five young American adolescents in the mid-1950s, and subsequently tested the same subjects as they grew into adulthood in order to discover the pattern of changes in judgments that might have occurred with the passing years. Furthermore, he and his co-workers have tried to discover what influence cultural factors have on the growth of moral judgments. To accomplish this, they have used the test incidents with both middle-class and lower-class adolescents in the United States and with youths in such diverse locations as Mexico, Thailand, kibbutz communities in Israel, a primitive Malaysian village, Turkey, Taiwan, and others. On the basis of these studies, Kohlberg has concluded that the six stages of moral development he identified are universal—found in all cultures—but that the percentage of youths of different age levels who are at a given stage will vary from one society to another. The nature of these variations will be discussed after I explain the characteristics of the stages.

LEVELS AND STAGES
OF MORAL GROWTH

In Kohlberg's system, growing up in moral judgment consists of advancing through three levels of development, from a *premoral* or *preconventional* level to one that involves conforming to *society's conventions* and finally to a top level that transcends convention and is based on personal, *self-accepted moral principles*. This top level is sometimes called *postconventional* or *autonomous*. Each level contains two stages, as defined in Table 16.1.

Besides identifying six steps or stages, Kohlberg has described thirty or more aspects of life about which people make moral judgments. A person will reveal her dominant stage of moral judgment each time she expresses her opinions about any of these aspects. It is Kohlberg's conviction, based on administering his moral-judgment incidents to children and youths, that there is a high correlation between a person's stage in regard to one aspect and his stage in regard to others. For example, a young woman's judgment about the value of *human life*, about telling the *truth*, and about people's *duties* and *obligations* will all tend to reveal the same level of moral development.

The thirty or more aspects of life are divided into three varieties: (1) modes of judgment of obligation and value, (2) elements of obligation and value, and (3) issues or social institutions about which judgments are made. The principal aspects falling within each of these categories are universal, for they are found in all cultures, according to Kohlberg. Here is one version of the aspects (1971, p. 166):

> *Modes of Judgment of Obligation and Value:* Judgments of (a) right, (b) having a right, (c) duty or obligation, (d) responsibility, (e) praise or blame, (f) punishability and reward, and (g) nonmoral value or goodness. Also (h) justification and explanation.
>
> *Elements of Obligation and Value:* (a) prudence (consequences desirable or undesirable to *oneself*), (b) social welfare (consequences desirable or undesirable to *others*), (c) love, (d) respect, (e) justice as liberty, (f) justice as equality, and (g) justice as reciprocity and contract.
>
> *Issues or Institutions:* (a) social norms, (b) personal conscience, (c) roles and issues of affection, (d) roles and issues of authority and democracy (division of labor between roles related to social control), (e) civil liberties (rights to liberty and equality as humans, citizens, or members of groups), (f) justice of actions apart from fixed rights (trust, reciprocity, contract in actions of one person), (g) punitive justice, (h) life, (i) property, (j) truth, and (k) sex.

Table 16.1 Description of Moral-Judgment Stages

I. *Preconventional Level (Premoral Level).* A person follows society's rules of right and wrong but in terms of the physical or hedonistic consequences (punishment, reward, exchange of favors) and in view of the power of the authority who imposes the rules.

> **Stage 1.** *Punishment and obedience orientation.* Whether an action is good or bad depends on whether it results in punishment or reward. If the individual is going to get punished for it, it's bad so he shouldn't do it. If he won't get punished, he can do it, regardless of the human meaning or value of the act.

> **Stage 2.** *Naive instrumental orientation.* Proper action instrumentally satisfies one's own needs and occasionally the needs of others. As in the marketplace, human relations are based on getting a fair return for one's investment. Reciprocity or fairness involves "you scratch my back and I'll scratch yours," but not out of loyalty, gratitude, or justice.

II. *Conventional Level.* A person conforms to the expectations of her family, group, or nation. She actively supports and justifies the existing social order.

> **Stage 3.** *Good-boy, nice-girl orientation.* A person acts in ways that please or help others and are approved by them. For the first time, the individual's intention becomes important ("she means well"). Approval is earned by being "nice."

> **Stage 4.** *Law-and-order orientation.* A person is doing the right thing when she does her duty, shows respect for authority, and maintains the existing social order for its own sake.

III. *Postconventional, Principled, or Autonomous Level.* A person tries to identify universal moral values that are valid, regardless of what authority or group subscribes to the values and despite the individual's own connection or lack of connection with such authorities or groups.

> **Stage 5.** *Social-contract orientation.* This usually involves legalistic and utilitarian overtones. Moral behavior is defined in terms of general individual rights and according to standards that have been critically examined and to which the whole society has given its consent. This is the "official" morality of the American Constitution and the U.S. Government. There is a clear recognition that personal values and opinions are relative, and thus there are procedures for reaching consensus and for changing laws for social-utility reasons (rather than freezing laws because they are inviolate, as under stage 4's law-and-order orientation).

> **Stage 6.** *Universal ethical-principle orientation.* One's moral judgments are based on universal principles of justice, on the reciprocity and equality of human rights, and on respect for the dignity of humans as individual persons. *Right* is defined by one's conscience in accord with self-chosen, general ethical convictions.

Recast and simplified from Kohlberg, 1967, p. 171.

To show how one of these aspects can be interpreted in terms of the stages, we will consider a moral-judgment incident focusing on the issue of life (item *h* in the issues list) and see how three boys reacted to the incident. The event posed to the boys involved a doctor who had to decide whether to "mercy kill" a woman requesting death because she was suffering such intense pain (Kohlberg, 1967, pp. 174–175).

> *13-year-old boy:* "Maybe it would be good to put her out of her pain, she'd be better off that way. But the husband wouldn't want it, it's not like an animal. If a pet dies you can get along without it—it isn't something you really need. Well, you can get a new wife, but it's not really the same." (Scored as stage 2—the value of life is instrumental to satisfying the needs of its possessor or others.)

> *16-year-old boy:* "No, he shouldn't [kill her]. The husband loves her and wants to see her. He couldn't want her to die sooner, he loves her too much." (Scored as stage 3—the value of life is based on empathy and affection of family members toward its possessor.)

> *16-year-old boy:* "The doctor wouldn't have the right to take a life, no human has the right. He can't create life, he shouldn't destroy it." (Scored as stage 4—life is sacred according to a categorical or religious order of rights and duties.)

To summarize, we can note that Kohlberg's six stages represent a movement from lower levels of moral decision, where moral decisions are entangled with other value judgments and the rules are changed as the facts in the case change to higher levels that separate moral values (justice and reciprocity) from other sorts and that utilize universal principles that apply to anyone in any situation. To illustrate this movement from the particular to the universal rule, we can consider three of the stages as they relate to the value of life. At stage 1, only important people's lives are valued, at stage 3 only family members', but at stage 6 all life is to be morally valued equally (Kohlberg, 1971, p. 185).

THE INTERACTION OF NATURE AND NURTURE

In response to the question of which moral stages a given child will pass through and when he will do it, Kohlberg has adopted an interactionist position. He does not believe a child's moral stages are produced entirely by genetic inheritance or by factors in the environment. Rather, he proposes that four principal factors interact to determine how high in the six-stage hierarchy a person will progress and when he will arrive at each stage. The first factor, and the one with the greatest genetic or inherited component, is the individual's *level of logical reasoning* as identified in Piaget's cognitive growth system. The second, a personal factor that probably has both genetic and environmental elements, is the child's desire or *motivation*, sometimes referred to as his *needs*. The remaining two factors are entirely environmental: (1) the child's opportunities to learn *social roles* and (2) the *form of justice* in the social institutions with which the child is familiar. To understand how these factors interact, we need to inspect each in more detail.

LEVEL OF COGNITIVE-LOGICAL DEVELOPMENT

In the realm of children's logical thinking, Kohlberg identifies himself as a disciple of Piaget. First, he is convinced that it is the child's nature to pass through the cognitive development stages identified by Piaget. He further believes that the achievement of a particular cognitive level in Piaget's scheme is a necessary prerequisite to the child's achieving a particular moral-reasoning stage.

To substantiate his belief, Kohlberg administered both Piagetian logical thinking tasks and his own moral-incident tests to the same group of subjects. He discovered that children who did not succeed on a given level of Piaget's tasks almost never showed the moral reasoning level that paralleled the Piagetian tasks. In contrast, children who were in the upper levels of moral reasoning could almost always complete the parallel and the lower-level Piagetian tasks. Consequently, Kohlberg concluded that the sort of logical thinking represented by Piaget's hierarchy forms the necessary foundation for the kinds of moral reasoning measured by his own moral-decision situations. This logical thinking component, then, is the maturational or "natural growth" factor—and perhaps the most powerful of the four factors that Kohlberg believes determine a child's level of moral reasoning.

If the child's cognitive stage were the only component of moral judgment, then as soon as he reached a given cognitive level, his moral judgments would likewise be at the same level. But such is not true. There is often a gap between the two, with moral reasoning lagging behind cognitive skill in various degrees. The cause of this lag, according to Kohlberg, is the condition of the other three factors that interact with mental maturity.

THE FACTOR OF WILL OR DESIRE

While it is always in our own interests to reason at the highest level of which we are capable, it may not be in our best interests to make moral judgments at the highest level. Kohlberg says that some people who are capable of judging morally at stage 6 may not do so because they do not wish to end up as martyrs as did Socrates, Lincoln, and Martin Luther King. So a youth may have the concepts of stages 5 or 6 but not use them habitually because they do not seem worth the trouble or the risk in his particular social setting. Thus, a portion of the slippage between cognitive level and moral stage may be accounted for by the operation of a girl's or boy's emotions, desires, or "will power." However, Kohlberg feels that this factor of *will* plays only a minor part in determining judgment stages. The other three factors in the quartet of influences he feels are far more important (Kohlberg, 1971, pp. 188–190).

SOCIAL ROLE-TAKING

Kohlberg agrees with many social psychologists in proposing that children become socialized by learning to take the roles of people around them. As children interact with others, they learn to imagine themselves in the others' shoes and to see life from others' perspectives. Children also learn to see themselves as others see them. Hence, role-taking or identifying and empathizing with other people enables the child to become an effective social being.

Within the broad sphere of socialization, the development of the more specific area of moral judgment "is based on sympathy for others, as well as on the notion that the moral judge must adopt the perspective of the 'impartial spectator' or the 'generalized other' " (Kohlberg, 1971, p. 190). How well a child learns to adopt others' roles depends to a great extent on the conditions of her social environment. Some environments encourage role-taking and thus hasten children's advance up the moral-judgment hierarchy. Other environments limit opportunities to learn role-taking and thus slow children's advances in moral growth and may prevent them from ever reaching stages 4, 5, or 6.

Kohlberg has suggested that it is this difference in role-taking opportunities between cultures or social-class levels that apparently accounts for the marked differences in moral-judgment development between societies and between middle and lower socioeconomic classes within a society.

> In four different cultures, middle-class children were found to be more advanced in moral judgment than matched lower-class children. This was not because the middle-class children heavily favored a certain type of thought which corresponded to the prevailing middle-class pattern. Instead, middle-class and working-class children seemed to move through the same sequences, but the middle-class children seemed to move faster and farther (1971, p. 190).

Other studies by Kohlberg's group have shown that popular children who participated a great deal with their peers were far more advanced in moral judgment than unpopular or nonparticipating children. At least part of the cause of this difference seems to be differences in role-taking opportunities in the children's families. Greater role adoption seemed to be promoted by families that encouraged sharing in decisions, awarding responsibility to the child, pointing out consequences of action to others, communicating within the family group, and exhibiting emotional warmth.

Some people have assumed that the most crucial of these home elements for furthering moral development is the degree to which the atmosphere is warm, loving, and identification-inducing. However, Kohlberg says this is not so. Apparently some minimum level of warmth in her personal contacts with others is necessary for a child or adolescent to feel she is an accepted participant in the social circle. However, what is far more important is that the environment furnish many role-taking opportunities, not that the child receive maximum affection from the group (Kohlberg, 1971, p. 191).

THE JUSTICE STRUCTURE

The fourth variable that contributes to the growth of moral judgment is the justice structure of the social groups or institutions with which the child interacts. Such social entities include the family, the neighborhood gang or play group, the school, the church, the community, the nation, and those media that provide vicarious opportunities for role-taking—television, radio, books, magazines, and the like.

At all six stages of moral development, the individual has some sort of concern for the welfare of others. But only at stages 5 and 6 is this concern based on what Kohlberg regards as principles of true justice, those of *equality* and *reciprocity*. The principle of equality means that we "treat every man's claim equally, regardless of the man" (Kohlberg, 1967, p. 169). The principle of reciprocity means equality of exchange. It means "punishment for something bad, reward for something good, and contractual exchange" or fulfilling one's bargain.

Within a given society the groups or institutions with which the growing child is intimately involved vary in their justice structures. A public school which the child is forced to attend under compulsory education laws is different from a university which the youth attends voluntarily. A neighborhood play group is different from a reformatory. A Girl Scout troop differs from a family. A family which is dominated by an autocratic father differs from one in which children are encouraged to make decisions, take responsibility, and be rewarded in accordance with how they carry out their self-imposed commitments.

In effect, Kohlberg proposes that children who participate in social groups that operate on a high level of equality and reciprocity will move to higher levels of moral judgment than children whose main participation is in groups that have lower sorts of justice structures.

So we see that in this theory, the dominant level of moral judgment a child or youth uses results from the interaction of four determinants: her level of cognitive-logical maturation, her will or desire, her opportunities for role-taking, and the dominant modes of justice in the main social groups of which she is a part.

THREE CHARACTERISTICS OF STAGES

A large proportion of modern social scientists as well as "culturally enlightened" laymen are what Kohlberg labels *ethical relativists*. They believe that moral principles vary from one culture to another and that there is no logical way to explain or reconcile these differences between cultures. Such a line of thought can easily lead to the conviction that one culture's moral values are as good as another's, since each culture has as much right to its own value system as does any other culture. On the basis of this assumption, we can then conclude that a person is morally developed or well adjusted when he abides by the dominant values of his society. But it is not necessary for an ethical relativist to stop the extension of his line of logic at this societal level. If he chooses, he can carry it on to individuals within a society. In such a case, he can conclude that it is each individual's right to adopt his own code of ethics, and there is no logical way to judge one person's code better than another's. (Of course, it is clear that extending ethical relativism to the individual will have important consequences for the individual's fate, because if he deviates markedly from the group's norms he can be dubbed odd or possibly locked up by the dominant group as a criminal or lunatic.)

However, Kohlberg is not an ethical relativist. He contends that moral development does not depend on the particular society's dominant ideas of justice. Instead, he says that the developmental stages he has identified are universal, integrated, and invariant.

By *universal* he means that the stages are true of all societies. In every culture there are people at all six stages. It is true, however, that the dominant moral stage for the society as a whole, or for a given age level, will differ from one culture to another. One culture may operate mostly on stage 2 reasoning, another on stage 4 reasoning. But this does not mean that the patterns of moral thought are quite different in the two cultures. Rather, the discrepancies result from the children in one society advancing up the six-stage hierarchy at a different rate than do most children in the other society. The differences in rate might be due partially to genetic differences between the two groups but more likely are a result of differences in role-taking opportunities and justice structures in the two cultures. So Kohlberg states that the six stages are universal. The same stages of moral reasoning are found in all societies, though the number at each stage may differ, as illustrated in Figure 16.1. The graphs compare the moral judgments of boys in middle-class U.S. and Mexican communities with those in an isolated village in Turkey. The age levels charted are 10, 13, and 16. As the graphs indicate, by age 16 some boys in each of the cultures were at each of the six levels of moral growth. However, a larger percentage of U.S. and Mexican boys than of Turkish boys were at higher stages at each age level.

By *integrated* Kohlberg means that in various aspects of life a person's moral decisions will reflect a similar level of develop-

Figure 16.1   Boys' Moral Judgments in Three Societies (Kohlberg and Kramer, 1969, p. 104)

ment. It would be rare indeed for a person to operate at stage 1 when judging honesty, at stage 3 when judging freedom, and stage 6 when judging responsibility. Rather, his judgments in all realms will tend to cluster around the same level—around 1 and 2, around 3 and 4, or the like.

By *invariant* he means that a youth cannot skip a stage or two while advancing to a higher level. He must pass through each stage in sequence. A key reason for this invariance, in Kohlberg's opinion, is that each successive stage consists of components of the prior stage plus a new component or two.

These principles of universality, integration, and invariance, when considered in relation to the four proposed determinants of moral growth, have important implications for how Kohlberg's theory can be put to practical use, as we will now see.

FASHIONING A PROGRAM
OF MORAL EDUCATION

If Kohlberg's theory is correct, what then should be the form of moral education? Before applying our foregoing discussion to answering this question, we need to consider one more concept that Kohlberg adopted from Piaget's theory of cognitive development. It is the concept of *equilibration* or of seeking equilibrium. We may recall that in Piaget's system, a child continued to be satisfied with his simplistic, unsophisticated answers to questions of relationships among things until (1) she reached a particular age of internal maturation and (2) she had engaged in enough activities related to the question. At this point she began to feel dissatisfied and a bit disordered, for she felt an incongruence between her existing schemes (or conception of reality) and a newly perceived reality. This dissonance threw her out of cognitive equilibrium and served as a motive to "change her mind" or to accommodate in order to set things right—in order to attain equilibrium once more.

Kohlberg has applied this same principle of equilibration to growth in moral judgment. When the child is cognitively mature enough and when she has had enough role-taking experiences in relation to groups that have suitable justice structures, then she can be stimulated toward upward movement in the moral-judgment stages by being confronted with problems of moral conflict. In other words, moral education properly consists of confronting the child or adolescent with moral dilemmas at the same time that she is maturationally and socially ready to take a step ahead.

With this use of equilibration in mind, let us now review the components of a moral-education system as conceived within Kohlberg's scheme. First, the goal of moral education is not to inculcate a particular set of values that are dominant or at least common in a given society. Instead, the goal is to stimulate the child's growth through the six stages that are considered universally valid for all cultures. The teacher's expectation for where the child or youth should be in moral growth at a particular time is governed by the teacher's recognition of the level of the child's cognitive development (per Piaget) and of the opportunities the child enjoys to adopt roles in social groups. The expectation is also influenced by the sorts of justice found in the groups in which the child participates and by the child's motivation—that is, will it pay the child to think at a higher moral level?

The methodology the teacher adopts consists primarily of posing moral-decision problems for the students, then having various students give their arguments to support their decisions. In this process, some students will argue from the viewpoint of a higher stage than will others. Or the teacher may argue from a higher stage. This conflict of arguments is intended to produce a feeling of disequilibrium in young people who are approaching the threshold of a new stage, so that the basis for their thinking begins to change and they are hoisted to the new level.

In summary, Kohlberg objects to a pair of commonly practiced systems of moral education: (1) the "thoughtless system of moralizing by individual teachers and principals when children deviate from minor administrative regulations" and (2) "the effort to inculcate the majority values, particularly as reflected in vague stereotypes about moral character" (Kohlberg, 1967, p. 169). In place of these he recommends a system that stimulates "the 'natural' development of the individual child's own moral judgment and of the capacities allowing him to use his own moral judgment to control his behavior." The purpose is to aid the child "to take the next step in a direction toward which he is already tending, rather than imposing an alien pattern on him" (Kohlberg, 1967, p. 169).

Such, then, is the practical application of Kohlberg's model to the conduct of education.

KOHLBERG'S THEORY: AN ASSESSMENT

When Kohlberg's model of moral development is appraised according to the standards proposed in Chapter 1, his theory shows up well in several respects.

KOHLBERG'S THEORY _____

How well do I think the theory meets the standards?

The Standards	Very Well	Moderately Well	Very Poorly
1. Reflects the real world of children		X	
2. Is clearly understandable		X	
3. Explains the past and predicts the future	X		
4. Guides child rearing	X		
5. Is internally consistent	X		
6. Is economical	X		
7. Is falsifiable	X		
8. Stimulates new discoveries	X		
9. Is self-satisfying	X		

The theory provides both for explaining past moral-judgment behavior of children and youths and for predicting their future behavior (item 3). Not only does it permit predictions for the average child, but by proposing four interacting determinants of moral-judgment development, it offers the possibility of doing so for individuals as well (if proper measures of the four variables and their interaction are made available).

The moral-education scheme Kohlberg has founded on his theory offers clear guidance for child rearing (item 4). Likewise, the theory appears to be internally consistent (item 5) and economical (item 6). It has also stimulated a variety of new investigations and discoveries, particularly in the way moral judgment develops in different cultures (item 8). Kohlberg has been credited with opening a number of new perspectives on moral growth and for doing "some very hard and very unfashionable thinking on moral thought" along with "producing evidence that should force psychologists to take the cognitive aspects of morality seriously as an important influence on behavior" (Alston, 1971, p. 284).

On the scale of clarity (item 2), the theory deserves a mixed score. On the positive side are the many specific examples Kohlberg cites from children's moral-dilemma responses that clarify terms and differentiate one stage from another. Such phrases as *instrumental relativist orientation* and *social-contract legalistic orientation* are illustrated with examples from respondents' protocols. However, in the opinions of informed scholars in the field, other key terms have not been distinguished clearly. Peters (1971, pp. 246–248) has taken Kohlberg to task for being vague and unsophisticated in comparing *character traits* (honesty, courage, determination) unfavorably with *principles* (a sense of *justice*). A similar criticism has been directed at Kohlberg's distinctions between the *form* and *content* of moral reasoning in a given culture. Kohlberg has said that the content of moral judgments may vary from culture to culture, but the more basic form of judgments does not. Yet, when these two concepts are analyzed in detail, it appears that Kohlberg has failed to produce adequate criteria for differentiating between them.

On item 1, Kohlberg can be credited with basing his model on data drawn from a variety of real children. However, there is a question about how realistic he has been in the scope of moral decisions that he has analyzed. As we have illustrated, the theory is founded on evidence collected from having children and youths offer solutions to moral-dilemma incidents posed for them. Since he wanted to make the respondents think hard so as to test their reasoning, Kohlberg necessarily posed incidents that had no obvious solutions in terms of the dominant standards of a child's culture. However, as Alston (1971, p. 284) has pointed out, these represent only a minor portion of the daily moral decisions a person makes. Thus, according to Alston, Kohlberg's methodology has necessarily caused him to ignore the host of judgments young people make by *habit*. Habitual judgments are easy ones because the reward and punishment system of the culture has fashioned the individual's "character" so that the solution to moral issues is obvious and no alternative solutions can compete successfully with the habitual one. Alston believes that this lack in Kohlberg's research method has distorted the theorist's view of the significance of habit or "character traits" and of emotion in determining moral thought and behavior.

Finally, Kohlberg has been criticized for proclaiming the principle of justice the sole occupant of the highest stage of moral thought without having sufficient cause to label it more worthy than several other virtues that might have been selected—for example, sympathy, compassion, concern for others, courage, integrity, or autonomy. As Peters has written, Kohlberg's findings:

> are of unquestionable importance, but there is a grave danger that they may become exalted into a general theory of moral development. Any such general theory presupposes a general ethical theory, and Kohlberg himself surely would be the first to admit that he has done little to develop the details of such a general ethical theory. Yet without such a theory the notion of "moral development" is pretty unsubstantial (1971, pp. 263–264).

So it is that Kohlberg's theory, like the rest we have considered, has drawn both praise and criticism. But whatever its shortcomings, it remains the most stimulating and potentially fertile model of children's moral growth in current psychological and philosophical circles. For this reason, I have rated it as quite self-satisfying overall (item 9).

FOR FURTHER READING

Kohlberg, Lawrence. (1967) "Moral and Religious Education in the Public Schools: A Developmental View" in Theodore R. Sizer, *Religion and Public Education*. New York: Houghton Mifflin.

Kohlberg, Lawrence and R. Kramer. (1976) "Continuities and Discontinuities in Childhood and Adult Moral Development" in Norman S. Endler et al. (eds.), *Contemporary Issues in Developmental Psychology*. 2d ed. New York: Holt, Rinehart, and Winston.

PART 9

BEHAVIORIST APPROACHES TO DEVELOPMENT

A search for the way principles of learning explain development.

Some psychologists feel very uneasy about theories that propose *mental elements*, such as soul, ego, or conscience. They are also uneasy about proposed *mental functions*—repression, epigenesis, assimilation, and the like. The trouble, they say, is that they are not convinced that these supposed elements and functions really exist, or at least not in the form that various theorists have proposed. It is clear that no one has ever seen or directly measured such things as mind or the unconscious. Another problem is that one theorist who writes about mind or personality often proposes very different elements and functions than other theorists. And if mind is unavailable for inspection, how do we know which theorist is right?

It was this sort of doubting that in 1914 motivated an American psychologist, John B. Watson (1878–1959), to launch the movement known as *behaviorism* (Watson, 1914 and 1919). Watson and his followers felt that it is both misleading and unprofitable to study some speculator's opinions about what the structure of a person's mind or unconscious might be like. They proposed, instead, that it is much more objective and scientific to observe the way people act under different environmental conditions. The observations are organized, analyzed, and then stated as principles that are intended to explain why children develop and behave as they do. In short, proponents of this point of view claim that the proper business of psychology is to identify the observable conditions that influence human behavior.

Since Watson's early advocacy of behaviorism, the movement has attracted many followers and has spawned several subgroups, particularly in the United States. In Part 9 we consider several varieties of behaviorism as they apply to child development. Chapter 17 focuses on B. F. Skinner's operant conditioning and on the Bijou-Baer application of this approach to child development. Chapter 18 describes three variants of social learning theory, those of Bandura, Sears, and the Kendlers.

CHAPTER 17

SKINNER'S OPERANT CONDITIONING

By the 1970s no American research psychologist was better known than B. F. Skinner (born 1904). The public fame of this Harvard professor resulted from his skillful and often controversial application of his learning theory to the solution of practical educational, personal adjustment, and social problems. In the mid-1950s he devised and popularized such learning devices as teaching machines and programmed texts (Skinner, 1972). In the late 1960s the behavior-modification approach to therapy for disturbed people drew heavily on Skinnerian doctrine. In the 1970s his book *Beyond Freedom and Dignity* recommended a plan for social control through operant conditioning that he contended would produce an increasingly peaceful, orderly, cooperative, and efficient society. His theory also has clear implications for the field of child development. In this chapter we first trace the outlines of Skinner's system, then describe the principal ways the system can be applied to the understanding of child growth and behavior. Near the end of the chapter we will discuss the work of Bijou and Baer, who have been leaders among child psychologists in applying Skinnerian behaviorism to the analysis of child development.

THE NATURE OF OPERANT CONDITIONING

The seeds of Skinner's behaviorism can be traced back to Pavlov's dog. In the early twentieth century the Russian physiologist Ivan

Petrovich Pavlov (1849–1936) demonstrated what has become known as *classical conditioning*. He placed meat powder (called an *unconditioned stimulus*) on a dog's tongue, which resulted in the dog automatically salivating (called the *unconditioned response*). Then, on a series of subsequent occasions (called *trials*), he sounded a bell at the same time he gave the food, in the form of meat powder, to the dog. When the food was accompanied by the bell enough times, he found that he could withhold the food and the bell's sound itself would cause the dog to salivate. The bell was now the *conditioned stimulus* that brought about the *conditioned response* of salivating. Classical conditioning, then—which often is called *respondent conditioning*—consists of substituting a new stimulus for an old one by presenting the two at the same time, or nearly the same time, then dropping the old stimulus and allowing the new one to bring about the original response. Pavlov's work inaugurated the era of S-R or stimulus-response psychology.

American behaviorists adopted the S-R concept as the appropriate model for explaining human behavior without having to speculate about what was possibly going on inside an organism's central nervous system. It was no longer necessary to imagine such things as mind or soul to account for the way people acted. By observing what sorts of stimuli elicited what sorts of responses, psychologists could explain what makes people behave as they do.

One problem that early behaviorists met was that they often could not identify accurately what stimulus was bringing about the responses they observed. Hence, they were forced to assume the operation of stimuli they actually could not locate. In the 1930s Skinner suggested a solution to this common problem. He proposed that there was not one kind of conditioning but two. One was the classicial S-R relationship demonstrated by Pavlov. The other, and by far the more frequent in human behavior, Skinner labeled *operant* or *instrumental conditioning*. Instead of the behavior being drawn out or elicited by a stimulus, the behavior (response) was simply *emitted* or expressed without any observable stimulus evoking it.

For example, a pigeon in a cage just naturally does pigeon-like things—walking about and pecking. A baby in a cradle just makes natural baby movements—wiggling its arms and legs in a random way. In Skinner's opinion, it is not important to identify the stimulus that started the pecking and the arm and leg movements. Rather, if we are to understand why behavior occurs, it is far more important to inspect the consequences of these movements, for the consequences are what come to control actions. The term *con-*

sequences here refers to the matter of whether the pigeon's or infant's movements bring satisfaction to the organism. If the pigeon is hungry and he happens to peck a plastic lever that drops food pellets into the cage, then this consequence of the food's satisfying the hunger drive may strengthen the tendency for the pigeon to peck the lever again the next time he is hungry and is in the same cage. After the pigeon has had enough trials at this task, he gradually will become more efficient; that is, he will gradually eliminate the previous random hopping and pecking at other things and will peck the lever directly when hungry. So we say the pigeon has *learned* lever pecking, and this learning has been caused or controlled by the consequences of fulfilling the hunger need.

It is Skinner's contention that all or nearly all behavior is a result of either respondent (classical) or operant conditioning, with by far the larger part of human behavior being operant as the child increases in age. If the consequences are rewarding, the actions will more likely be repeated the next time the individual is in a similar situation. If the consequences are either painful or simply useless, the actions will less likely be repeated in the future. Rewarding consequences strengthen tendencies to act; nonrewarding consequences weaken tendencies to act the same way again, so eventually the nonrewarding acts will be dropped or *extinguished* entirely.

This is the general idea of classical (respondent) and operant conditioning. However, in this introduction the theory has been oversimplified, and we have used terms that Skinner and his followers would find imprecise and perhaps misleading. For instance, Skinnerians do not approve of such terms as *hunger need* if such terms require that we assume something inside a person that we cannot observe. They also object to such words as *reward* when its use assumes a feeling state that cannot readily be identified and that is considered to be the cause of some sort of behavior. However, we used these terms, just as Skinner himself used them, because they are familiar to readers and explain the issues more easily than if I had started off only with behaviorist definitions. However, at this point we will begin using a more standard behaviorist wording in order to delineate the key features of Skinnerian theory.

To begin, we should recognize that Skinner on occasion has denied that he has constructed a theory (Skinner, 1972, pp. 69–71). He claims to be more an empiricist, collecting observable facts of behavior and summarizing them in terms of principles. He proposes that he simply tells it as it is. However, in the broad way that we defined *theory* in Chapter 1, his formulations do indeed qualify as theory, as his own recent writings would attest (Skinner, 1974, pp. 18–20).

He created the concept of *operant* or *instrumental* conditioning to focus prime attention on the importance of consequences in controlling the acts that immediately preceded them. In other words, the act is the operator (operant) or instrument that brings about the consequence.

What most people think of as a reward is called a *reinforcer* by behaviorists. A consequence is a *positive reinforcer* if it causes the act to increase in the future when a similar situation arises. For example, if a hungry infant is fed right after he happens to hit a rattle in his crib, the tendency for him to hit the rattle next time he is hungry is increased. This means that feeding has positively reinforced rattle batting. Likewise, if an affection-hungry school girl picks papers up from around her desk and thus is given a hug by her teacher and told, "You're a great helper, Jenny," then the tendency for Jenny to pick up papers in the future is strengthened. The hug and kind words have positively reinforced the act of tidying up.

Sometimes a child's acts stop an unpleasant condition. For instance, the second-grade teacher is screaming at the children to get into their seats and keep quiet. The unpleasant screaming stops as soon as the children are all in their seats. So the act of sitting down has been instrumental in stopping the unpleasant harangue. The pleasant state of quiet is, for the children, a *negative reinforcer* for sitting down. In effect, a consequence of an action is called a negative reinforcer if the action has caused some unpleasant (*aversive*, in behaviorist terms) condition to stop. Next time the teacher starts ranting at the class, the children can be expected to sit down more promptly because sitting down produced the happy state of quiet the first time.

That is, both positive and negative reinforcement are rewarding. Both increase the likelihood that the child will repeat the same act in similar future circumstances. It is positive reinforcement if it starts a pleasant consequence. It is negative reinforcement if it stops an unpleasant consequence, such as noise or criticism.

A third sort of consequence is *punishment*. Consequences are called punishing or aversive if they reduce the tendency for the child to behave the same way in the future. Punishment, as any parent or teacher knows, is supposed to discourage acts of the same sort on later occasions.

But punishment is not the only way to try eliminating un-desired acts. Another way is simply not to reinforce the acts. If a child crosses his eyes in school to get attention but no one pays any attention to this antic, the eye crossing can be expected to stop, for it has failed to achieve the desired consequences. In brief, *extinction* of the behavior occurs.

Studies by some behaviorists in the past have caused them to conclude that punishment only temporarily suppresses the ex-pression of undesired behaviors but does not eliminate or ex-tinguish them. These investigators have claimed that when the punishing agent is not present, the undesired behaviors occur again. However, more recent analyses of the influence of pun-ishment have caused other learning theorists to disagree that pun-ishment is merely a temporary suppressor. They have concluded instead that punishment can be as effective as nonreinforcement in extinguishing undesired acts (Hilgard and Bower, 1975, pp. 223–225).

The foregoing elements, then, represent the basic framework of operant conditioning. If consequences of acts are reinforcing, then the acts will be learned and will appear again when the child is in similar situations. These reinforced actions become habits and form a pattern of behavior that might be called the child's style of life or personality. Consequences that are unrewarding—either punishing or simply nonreinforcing—result in behaviors being dropped from the child's repertoire of actions.

In our discussion so far we have used the word *learning* to refer to a child's coming to the point of habitually showing a particular behavior when in a given situation. However, there is really a more precise way to view learning from the standpoint of operant conditioning. You may recall that in the operant type of conditioning, the focus is not on how you get the child to display a behavior in the first place, but on what happens to that behavior as the result of the consequences that follow it. From this per-spective, learning is not seen as the process of the child's first displaying the behavior, but rather as the process of his dis-playing it consistently, that is, of his responding at a high rate of frequency when in similar stimulus situations. For example, if a nine-year-old girl comes home from playing with neighborhood friends only one time in ten when her mother calls, "Time to come in, Karin," then we would say that Karin has not learned very well to come when called. Her rate of response is only 10 percent. We do not mean Karin is ignorant of how to return home when her mother calls; her occasional correct response shows that the expected behavior is in her repertoire. But in saying she has not learned very well, we mean she does not respond consistently in this stimulus situation. However, her mother can increase Karin's rate of responding (help her better learn to come when called) by manipulating the consequences. Or, in behaviorist terms, she can rearrange the *reinforcement schedule* to increase her daughter's tendency to come when summoned.

Skinner has made particularly useful contributions to the analysis of the effect on behavior of different kinds of reinforcement schedules. For example, the effects on performance differ when *continuous reinforcement* (rewarding every time the desired act occurs) is used rather than *intermittent reinforcement* (rewarding only certain times the act occurs). Furthermore, different schedules of intermittent reinforcement yield different results. A *fixed-ratio* schedule (such as rewarding every third or every fifth response) has a different effect from a *fixed-interval* schedule (rewarding every two minutes or every five minutes). These sorts of schedules, combined with a variety of others, can produce an array of different behavior results (Hilgard and Bower, 1975, pp. 216–217). For example, when an eight-year-old pupil is in the early stages of learning to raise his hand to speak in class rather than to shout out his opinion, he can profitably be rewarded on each occasion that he raises his hand. But after the habit has been well established, intermittent reward will probably serve to maintain the habit against extinction better than continuous reinforcement.

We can summarize Skinner's viewpoint by saying that from his behaviorist perspective child development is a process of the growing individual's learning increasingly complex and refined ways of acting as a result of the consequences that have followed the behavior he has attempted. The role of parents and teachers is therefore twofold: (1) to get children to try desirable acts and (2) to arrange consequences of children's acts so that the desirable behavior is reinforced and undesirable behavior is extinguished through nonreinforcement or punishment.

CONDITIONED REINFORCEMENT AND CHAINING

One charge frequently aimed at the operant-conditioning model is that the theory is oversimplified. While critics admit that operant conditioning might account for certain simple acts, they claim it cannot explain complex skills or creative thinking. However, Skinner has proposed several mechanisms he believes readily account for any sort of behavior that people exhibit, whether the actions are—as nonbehaviorists might say—mental or physical.

The first mechanism is described in the principle of *conditioned reinforcement:* A consequence (called a *stimulus*) that is not originally a reinforcing one can become reinforcing through repeated association with a consequence that is already reinforcing (Keller and Schoenfeld, 1950, p. 232). In other words, if mother comes to feed her infant son each time he is hungry, and the consequence of the feeding is that it satisfies the hunger, then after enough repetitions of this act the appearance of mother herself—even without food—becomes reinforcing or satisfying. Mother now has the power of being a reinforcer. She has become a *conditioned* or a *secondary* reinforcer. Her appearance and the associated acts that accompanied the original feeding—her smiling and saying, "What a good boy"—can now be used to reinforce or teach other behaviors. For instance, when the growing infant happens to say "mah" during his babblings, the mother's smile and her comment, "What a smart boy—now say Mama," serve to reinforce the utterance of "mah." Consequently, the chance of the child's uttering "mah" again in the mother's presence is increased.

Not only does a growing child soon build up a significant store of conditioned reinforcements that can serve as rewards for actions, but many of these secondary reinforcers become generalized to other actions. That is, the reinforcer not only strengthens its original act, but by being associated with many actions, comes to strengthen any with which it is connected. For adolescents, money is a strong generalized reinforcer and can be used to strengthen or reward all sorts of behavior. For both younger and older children, such phrases as "good girl" and "that's the way to do it" become generalized reinforcers, attached to many behaviors.

Keller and Schoenfeld have summarized in the following way the two principles that govern these examples:

> Once established, a secondary reinforcement is independent and nonspecific; it not only will strengthen the same response which produced the original reinforcement, but will also condition a new and unrelated response. Moreover, it will do so even in the presence of a different motive.

Through generalization, many stimuli besides the one correlated with reinforcement acquire reinforcing value—positive or negative (1950, p. 260).

Two other conditioning functions that help explain complex behavior are *shaping* and *chaining*. Shaping consists of first reinforcing any gross approximation that the child achieves of a desired refined act. Then, after the gross form of the behavior has been well established, you can shape it by gradual steps into the ultimate refined form by requiring better and better approximations before reinforcement is provided. For instance, in teaching a child to bat a ball, we will first offer praise for his swinging the bat, whether or not he hits the ball. As his swing improves, we no longer praise just any swing, but only those that hit the ball. When he can hit the ball nearly every time, we now limit our praise to his hitting the ball into the field in front of him, and we do not praise foul balls that bounce to the side or to the rear. This process of gradually placing more precise limits on the kinds of acts that are reinforced then continues, enabling the child to shape his batting skill till he can hit the ball in more precise directions and to specified distances. In a similar fashion, shaping helps expand and refine children's verbal behavior as their utterances are altered by the positive and negative reactions of people with whom they interact.

Chaining enables a person to hook together a sequence of small, individual conditioned acts to compose a complex skill. The process of chaining begins at the final end of the chain rather than at the beginning. Each preceding link of the chain is hooked on by associating it with the link that has already been established through reinforcement. For instance, consider the complex skill known as "having good table manners." We start with a child who yearns for both food and parental approval. Over a sequence of days the child is permitted to eat and is told, "That's fine" and "You're doing a good job" when she uses a fork rather than her fingers for lifting small pieces of meat to her mouth. When the pattern of using the fork is established, we add a new requirement. The child must use a knife and fork to cut large pieces of meat into smaller pieces before she is permitted to eat or is complimented for her actions. When she has learned these two links— eating with the fork after cutting up the pieces—we impose a new requirement, that of tucking a napkin into her blouse before she cuts up the meat, picks up pieces with the fork, eats, and is complimented. By such a process an extended set of habits or conditioned links can be formed into a complicated skill.

In summary, the simple mechanism of reinforcement not only accounts for specific simple acts, but the processes of secondary reinforcement, stimulus generalization, shaping (response discrimination), and chaining can account for all sorts of complex activities, in the opinion of behaviorists. And, they say, it is not necessary for us to fashion these processes consciously; they occur as natural behavior in everyone.

SCOPE OF SKINNER'S THEORY

In at least three important ways, Skinner's theory can be called broad in scope. First, it is not limited to any cultural setting; it purports to explain development in all societies. Second, its principles apply to all age levels, from the prenatal period to death. Third, it claims to explain all varieties of behavior—physical, mental, social, emotional. Although the first two claims have not attracted much criticism, the third has been the center of an extended debate, so it warrants our close attention.

As noted in Chapter 14, behaviorism was originally a reaction against *mentalism*. It was a reaction against saying that human action was caused by ideas or feelings that arose in an unobservable place called *mind* or *soul*. Furthermore, behaviorism was a reaction against mentalists' research methods, which consisted largely of introspection, of a philosopher pondering about the nature of his own thoughts and emotions and then proposing elements or functions of the mind that he thought produced or controlled the thoughts and emotions.

Early behaviorists like John B. Watson and Max Meyer claimed that if psychology is truly to become a science, it must focus solely on objective, publicly witnessed information. Such things as thoughts, mind, and feelings should have no place in this proposed science of human behavior. However, critics of behaviorism said that it is nonsense to deny the existence of such obvious phenomena as thoughts and feelings simply because these things are not directly seen by people outside the skin of the person who is doing the thinking and feeling. In sum, over the past half century behaviorists, including Skinner, have been charged with proposing a simplistic, mindless psychology. But Skinner, while admitting the charges are valid criticisms of early behaviorists, denies that they apply to him. In order to distinguish himself from the others, he has created two labels: (1) *methodological behaviorism* to identify those who would ignore the existence of thoughts and feelings and (2) *radical behaviorism* to identify his own position, which recognizes thoughts and feelings as normal "covert acts" and accepts introspection as a legitimate mode of inquiry (Skinner, 1974, pp. 13–18).

According to Skinner, the sin of mentalism—as practiced by Puritans, Rousseau, Freud, Piaget, and many others—has been to focus exclusively on mental events. This focus has distracted their attention away from an analysis of the external environment's stimuli and consequences that are the elements, he says, that can really account for why people act as they do. But in censuring the mentalists, Skinner has not uncritically embraced the methodological-behaviorist position of Watson and, more recently, of J. R. Kantor. Rather, Skinner has criticized methodological behaviorism for committing the opposite error:

> By dealing exclusively with external antecedent events, it turned away from self-observation and self-knowledge. Radical behaviorism restores some kind of balance. It does not insist upon truth by agreement and can therefore consider events taking place in the private world within the skin. It does not call these events unobservable, and it does not dismiss them as subjective. It simply questions the nature of the object observed and the reliability of the observations (1974, pp. 16–17).

So Skinner accepts thoughts and feelings, but he believes that people's techniques for investigating them are not well developed or very trustworthy. Consequently, he finds it best to depend heavily on an analysis of environmental conditions and people's observable reactions in order to understand a person's genetic and environmental history. He finds it of no explanatory help to create such words as *mind* or *consciousness* to account for a person's inner life. He contends (1974, p. 17) that "what is felt or introspectively observed is not some nonphysical world of consciousness, mind, or mental life but the observer's own body." In other words, Skinner has not divided the person into the traditional opposing aspects of physical and mental. He considers the individual to be an integrated unit. Some actions are observed by people outside the individual's skin (overt behavior) and others are observed only by the individual himself through introspection (covert behavior).

HEREDITY VERSUS ENVIRONMENT

Behaviorists traditionally have been criticized for underestimating the role of heredity in development. However, Skinner has reacted to such criticism by again distinguishing between the viewpoint of methodological behaviorists and his own. Several decades ago, Watson claimed he could take any healthy infant and raise it to become whatever he chose—doctor, lawyer, artist, beggarman, thief. However, Skinner (1974, p. 221) has dismissed this claim by calling it a "careless remark" and has proposed instead what he considers a more balanced view of the relative contributions of genetic endowment and environmental influences.

To understand Skinner's own position, we should first recognize that he believes the basic drive behind all behavior, human as well as subhuman, is to survive. All actions are designed to promote the survival of both the individual and the species. Humans, like other species, inherit biological potentials that serve in some ways to enhance and in other ways to limit the chance of surviving in different environments. The potentials that a person inherits have been determined over past eons of time by the survival of the fittest, Darwin's natural selection. People with those traits that promoted survival lived on to produce offspring with these same high-survival characteristics. People lacking such traits died early, so their strains were not reproduced.

For purposes of analysis, it is useful to divide inherited characteristics into two types, though in actual practice the two merge into each other. The first type is well suited to stable environments, and the second to variable, unpredictable environments. That is, some environmental conditions—conditions of climate or the nature of predators and diseases, for example—are relatively permanent over time. In these environments that are stable over a period of centuries, a species can directly inherit traits that arm it for survival, traits like a heavy, white fur coat to match the arctic snow color and instincts or reflexes that give ample warning of approaching predators. But frequently, environmental conditions cannot be directly predicted. Conditions change from year to year, even from day to day. In such settings it is not helpful to inherit a specific, limited reflex or instinct. Rather, it is better to inherit the ability to change behavior on the basis of the environment's reaction. In other words, a species can inherit learning capacity, the ability to profit from the consequences of behavior. This is the second sort of inheritance and the one that Skinner considers the most important thing that humans derive from their genetic endowment. Humans' high level of intelligence or adaptability results from an unusually sensitive genetic potential for operant conditioning.

When Skinner has been pressed to tell exactly which behaviors or personality traits he believes people inherit and which he thinks they learn, he has refrained from identifying specific items, for he claims that not enough research has been done to give clear answers. But he has stated that many of the things that other theorists, such as Gesell and Freud, attribute to heredity are actually learned through conditioning. Skinner concludes that:

> Genetic causes sometimes become a kind of dumping ground: any aspect of behavior which at the moment escapes analysis in terms of contingencies of reinforcement is likely to be assigned to genetic endowment, and we are likely to accept the explanation because we are so accustomed to going no further than a stage of the organism (1974, p. 44).

Skinner, then, would not place himself at either extreme in the nature–nurture controversy. And he rejects the methodological behaviorists' contention that human personality is completely malleable, ready to be formed into whatever pattern the controllers of reinforcement desire. In his novel about a utopian community, *Walden Two*, Skinner described a society in which all children have a highly similar environment till age 10, since they are all raised together in communal centers over the first decade of their lives rather than in individual families. Yet even with this common environment, the children living in Walden Two display a range of intelligence "almost as great as in the population at large. This seems to be true of other abilities and skills as well" (Skinner, 1948, p. 104). In effect, Skinner has proposed that genetic endowment accounts for a significant amount of the variation among children. He is not a thoroughgoing environmentalist. Nevertheless, he appears to assign a more important role to environmental forces than do any of the theorists studied so far in this book.

STAGES OF DEVELOPMENT

In several previous chapters, we have seen that theories of development are sometimes divided into *stage* and *nonstage* models. A stage model typically pictures the growth of the child as a series of distinct steps or phases. At around a particular age, the child changes noticeably from being one sort of person into being another sort. Then, for some time, he retains the characteristics of this second sort until once more he makes a noticeable change and reaches a new level or phase of growth.

Contrasting with this conception of sudden change from one phase to another is the nonstage model that pictures growth as a very gradual process. Changes occur in miniscule amounts. It is true that in both stage and nonstage theories the child at age 6 will be obviously different from the way she looked and acted at age 3. But to nonstage theorists she has not arrived at 6 by any sudden leaps or insights. Instead, 6 is just an accumulation of very slight alterations since age 3.

Generally, stage theories have been proposed by investigators who say heredity plays the greater role in development, whereas nonstage models have been devised by those who give more credit to the environment. This linking of stages with hereditarians and gradual growth with environmentalists is not a logical necessity. Gradual growth could reasonably be attributed to a genetic time schedule, and stages might be accounted for by sudden major changes in environmental forces. However, the observed linking has been the dominant trend, and Skinner's theory fits the pattern by being a nonstage model.

Skinner sees development as a continuous, incremental sequence of specific conditioned acts. It is not that he is unable to conceive of behavior being studied in terms of age or the passage of time, "as in the development of a child's verbal behavior or his problem-solving strategies or in the sequence of stages through which a person passes on his way from infancy to maturity" (Skinner, 1972, pp. 567–573). But he feels that (1) it is more accurate to view the developmental steps as very small ones and (2) it is unprofitable to focus only on *what* happens at a particular stage and to ignore the question of *why* it occurs. In other words, he is critical not only of picturing growth as major jumps followed by lengthy plateaus, but also of the developmentalists', or what he refers to as *structuralists'*, failing to explain why these changes occur, other than to state that the cause is an assumed internal maturation whose timing follows a genetic clock. Skinner's interest has been in the management or control of development, not in just describing what it looks like when it takes place.

So in his writings, Skinner makes almost no point of describing the characteristics of children at different age levels. Despite this, he has given some prominent attention to stages, but his stages have been *phases of environmental treatment of the child*, treatment designed to produce optimal development. In short, he prescribes ways to treat children at different age levels to promote their happiness and well being. To explain what these prescriptions are, we will draw upon two of Skinner's publications, which were issued in the middle of his academic career. The first is an article from a 1945 *Ladies Home Journal* describing an air-conditioned, sanitary box in which he and his wife raised their infant daughter (Skinner, 1972, pp. 567–573). The second is the novel *Walden Two* (Skinner, 1948), and particularly the series of chapters detailing child-care methods in the utopian community. We will use child rearing in Walden Two as the focus of our discussion.

In the psychologist's ideal child-rearing system, boys and girls are not raised by their individual families but are brought up in communal care centers till they reach puberty. At around age 13, adolescents, individually or in pairs, set up their own living quarters in the apartment complex that houses the adults in the mythical rural American town called Walden Two.

The first two decades of life in Walden Two are divided into five child-raising stages: (1) a lower-nursery stage for infants from birth to one year, (2) an upper-nursery stage for those ages 1 and 2, (3) a middle-childhood phase for ages 3–6, (4) later childhood for ages 7–13, and (5) adolescence after age 13.

The basic philosophy during this entire two-decade span is that it is important to fulfill children's needs as quickly and as completely as possible in their earliest years. Then, very gradually the demands and annoyances of normal life are introduced at a scientifically controlled rate that ensures that children can master them without acquiring negative feelings. This system of *behavioral engineering* or controlled operant conditioning is designed to encourage "the productive and strengthening emotions—love and joy. . . . But sorrow and hate—and the high-voltage excitements of anger, fear, and rage—are out of proportion with the needs of modern life, and they're wasteful and dangerous." In Walden Two such emotions, along with jealousy and envy, which "breed unhappiness," are almost unknown (Skinner, 1948, p. 83).

This pattern of providing an initially easy environment that becomes more and more difficult as children acquire the ability to adjust is intended to yield the reward of "escape from the petty emotions which eat the heart out of the unprepared." Children raised in Walden Two not only get the satisfaction of pleasant social relations, they also become far more efficient workers, "because they can stick to a job without suffering the aches and pains which soon beset most of us. They get new horizons, for they are spared the emotions characteristic of frustration and failure" (Skinner, 1948, pp. 90–91).

This is the general strategy of child rearing. Over the first five years after birth adults see that no important need goes unsatisfied, so the child begins life practically free of anxiety and frustration. But eventually, through the mastery of gradually increasing frustrations, youths in Walden Two experience "the heartache and the thousand natural shocks that flesh is heir to" (Skinner, 1948, p. 93).

With this overall plan in mind, let us now consider some of the ways Walden Two's adults engineer the environment to produce such admirable results.

Birth to Age 1   Infants in Walden Two do not stay at home with their mothers but are collected together in the "lower nursery," each baby in an air-conditioned, enclosed crib like the "baby box" in which the Skinners raised their second daughter for the first year of her life. The purpose of the box is to furnish the infant with a healthful climate, free from the confinement of clothes and blankets and from dust and germs. The baby, clad only in a diaper, lies or sits or crawls about on an easily cleaned plastic mattress, plays with rattles and toys hung from the ceiling of the box, and gazes at the passersby through the large glass window that forms one side of the enclosed crib. The walls of the box are insulated from noise and temperature changes. A shade lowered over the window when the baby is asleep prevents light from disturbing his naps.

After Skinner's own daughter had been in such a box for eleven months, he reported that because of the box's filtered air:

> The baby's eyes, ears, and nostrils remain fresh and clean. A weekly bath is enough, provided the face and diaper region are frequently washed. . . . She has always enjoyed deep and extended sleep, and her feeding and eliminative habits have been extraordinarily regular. . . . Although there have been colds in the fam-

ily, . . . the baby has completely escaped. She has never had a diaper rash. . . .

One of the commonest objections (of friends) was that we were going to raise a "softie" who would be unprepared for the real world. But instead of becoming hypersensitive, our baby has acquired a surprisingly serene tolerance for annoyances. She is not bothered by the clothes she wears at playtime, she is not frightened by loud or sudden noises, she is not frustrated by toys out of reach. . . . A tolerance for any annoyance can be built up by administering it in controlled dosages, rather than in the usual accidental way. Certainly there is no reason to annoy the child throughout the whole of its infancy, merely to prepare it for later childhood (Skinner, 1972, pp. 570–572).

In Walden Two the parents come each day or so to see the baby, to take it from the box and play with it a while. But this personal attention and display of affection are offered not only by the parents but also by the men and women who are in charge of the nursery. The purpose of sharing the responsibility for infants is to enable a child to imitate numerous desirable models who combine to form "a sort of essential happy adult. He can avoid the idiosyncrasies of a single parent" (Skinner, 1948, p. 119).

Ages 1 and 2 When children are around one year old in Walden Two, they move from their individual cubicles in the lower nursery to the upper nursery. This advanced nursery is composed of several small playrooms furnished with child-size equipment, a dressing room with a locker for each child, and small air-conditioned sleeping rooms. Clad only in diapers, children sleep on easily-cleaned plastic mattresses. At playtime they are either naked or in training pants.

Child-raising practices continue to be guided by the principles followed in the lower nursery. Children's needs are met as soon and as completely as possible, with the result that the young child still knows nothing of frustration, anxiety, or fear. This does not mean, however, that the child has no experiences that might bring about frustration. It means, instead, that the behavioral engineers who schedule the child-raising program introduce potentially discouraging experiences "as carefully as we introduce any other emotional situation beginning at about six months" (Skinner, 1948, p. 100). For example, some of the toys children are given are designed to build perseverance.

The personnel of the nursery is balanced between men and

women so as to "eliminate all the Freudian problems which arise from the asymmetrical relation to the female parent" (Skinner, 1948, p. 120).

Ages 3 to 6, Middle Childhood   From the standpoint of sleeping accommodations, this period is divided into two segments. At ages 3 and 4 each child is given responsibility for her own cot in a dormitory, and she is introduced to wearing regular clothing. At ages 5 and 6 children move into a complex of alcoves, each furnished like a regular room and holding three or four children with their beds and personal belongings. They are expected to gradually assume increased responsibility for the upkeep of their quarters. A careful schedule of conditioning in ethical behavior is conducted so that the foundations of ethical conduct are virtually complete by age 6.

Ages 7 to 13, Later Childhood   At age 7 children move from the alcoves into a complex of small rooms, each room designed for two children. At frequent intervals roommates are changed so children learn to live with different sorts of age-mates. They no longer eat in a dining room for children but use the adults' cafeteria.

It is impossible to distinguish formal from informal education in Walden Two since children are being taught by designed conditioning schedules wherever they are—in their living quarters, on the playground, and in the community's workshops, laboratories, studios, reading rooms, and fields. Early in their lives, children are given work to do, so they come to have a personal stake in contributing to the community.

Walden Two's behavioral engineers claim that their education system is far superior to that of the typical town, because teachers do not waste time duplicating home training or changing the cultural and intellectual habits that children might have acquired outside of school.

From the child's first months after birth, the community depends on his natural curiosity and natural needs to motivate him to learn. The behavioral engineers appeal to humans' "drive to control the environment. . . . We don't need to motivate by creating spurious needs. . . . Promising paradise or threatening hellfire is, we assumed, generally admitted to be unproductive" (Skinner, 1948, pp. 87, 101–102).

The education system has no grade levels, since "everyone knows that talents and abilities don't develop at the same rate in different children" (Skinner, 1948, p. 97). Pupils are encouraged to

progress as rapidly as they like in any field, and they are not
expected to waste time in a classroom being bored by activities
they have outgrown. No subjects like English or social studies or
science are taught. Rather, children are taught techniques of learning and thinking. Then they are provided chances to learn geog-
raphy, literature, the sciences, and the like by themselves, based
on the firm foundation they have received in ways of thinking:
logic, statistics, scientific method, psychology, and mathematics.
Children who do not appear to have an aptitude for learning a
particular skill or type of knowledge are not required to do so. In
other words, Walden Two's educators do not "waste time teaching
the unteachable" (Skinner, 1948, p. 97).

Age 13 and Beyond, Adolescence   As the child passes puberty
and becomes sexually potent, Walden Two does not require that
he or she postpone mature forms of sexual gratification until age
20 or older. Instead, the adolescent finds "an immediate and satisfying expression of his natural impulses . . . very different from
the secrecy and shame which most of us recall in connection with
sex at some time or other" (Skinner, 1948, p. 111). When teenagers
fall in love, they become engaged, at which time they consult
the Manager of Marriages. He examines their interests, school
records, and health status. If there are major discrepancies between the couple in intellectual abilities or temperament, they are
advised not to marry or, at least, to postpone marriage for a while.
But those who do seem well matched are encouraged to marry and
begin having children when they are still age 15 or 16. This early
satisfaction of sexual needs, combined with young people's early
and gradual introduction to the world of work, makes the period
of adolescence "brief and painless."

As for their living accommodations, the young teenagers
move, at least temporarily, into rooms in the adult apartment complex, where they usually live in pairs. At the time of marriage, or
whenever else he or she chooses, the individual can participate in
building a larger room for himself or herself or can refurbish an
existing room that has become available.

In effect, during the latter teens the youth gradually achieves
adult status without the extended period of stress that adolescence
in American society has ostensibly involved.

Next, we consider a different set of growth stages from the
viewpoint of radical behaviorism, a set described by Bijou and
Baer.

BIJOU AND BAER'S ADDITIONS

Perhaps the best known of the child development theorists adhering closely to a Skinnerian behaviorist viewpoint have been Sidney W. Bijou and Donald M. Baer. A significant contribution of these two authors has been their adopting three developmental periods suggested by J. R. Kantor (*Interbehavioral Psychology*, 1959) and their illustrating in detail how traditional behaviorism can account for the changes observed in children at each level of growth. The labels attached to the three successive stages have been *universal*, *basic*, and *societal*.

The universal stage, which extends from the prenatal months until symbolic behavior or language becomes prominent at around age 2, derives its name from the fact that the growth of infants in all societies is much alike during these first years. Although the infant interacts with the environment and thus is influenced by the consequences of his actions, the greater determinant of behavior at this time is the child's maturing biological nature. So environmental stimuli play a very limited role in controlling the infant's "simple but self-preserving respondents" and in guiding the development of other behaviors related to "maintaining the biological necessities of life" (Bijou and Baer, 1965, pp. 2–3). The causes of similarities among children in all societies at this stage are primarily the basic biological similarities of the human species, which are the focus of attention in infancy. But, in addition, the social and physical environments are much the same from one culture to another, "not only because of the similarity in limitations imposed by extreme biological immaturity but also because of the extensive uniformity in infant-caring practices" (Bijou and Baer, 1965, p. 179).

The basic or second stage of development covers the years between about age 2 and ages 5 or 6. By now the child's biological development is sufficiently stable to meet his basic needs so he is more effective in interacting with his environment and can devote more energy to developing psychological behaviors. The patterns of action he acquires during these preschool years depend heavily on the sort of social environment his family provides, although part of the child's characteristics are still determined by his biological structure, which results from his genetic inheritance.

During the basic stage, the personality structure is formed through the kinds of opportunities and contingencies his parents and other family members habitually provide. In these years the child's basic discriminations and forms of behavior are acquired.

The societal stage or third period of development begins around the time the child enters the primary grades, and continues throughout the years of schooling. During this period, a myriad of influences from his culture serve to alter and expand the basic pattern of action or personality structure that was earlier fabricated through biological inheritance and the nurturing practices of his family.

In sum, Bijou and Baer have demonstrated how respondent and operant conditioning principles can account for the similarities and the differences among children at three successive stages of growth.

SKINNER'S OPERANT CONDITIONING: AN ASSESSMENT

I feel that Skinner deserves high scores on nearly all of the criteria proposed in Chapter 1.

Skinner's model is clearly described (item 2), enjoying the advantage over mentalist theories of not including in its elements such nonobservable, internal items as ego or conscience, items whose characteristics are difficult to depict to other people.

As attested by *Walden Two* and the programmed learning and behavior-modification programs that educators and therapists have adopted in recent years, Skinner's theory offers very detailed guidance for child-rearing practices (item 4).

Since the Skinnerian model is founded on empirical studies of overt behavior, and the mechanisms to account for behavior are rather simple, the theory has the qualities of internal consistency (item 5) and falsifiability (item 7). It has also led to a great deal of research and practical application (item 8). It has helped lead to the extensions of behaviorism found in Chapter 18 and to the applications mentioned earlier in the realms of programmed instruction and behavior-modification practices.

However, strong criticisms have been raised about the theory's being overly simple, unrealistically economical (item 6). This ostensible oversimplification has caused critics to question how adequately the theory reflects the real world of children (item 1)

SKINNER'S THEORY

How well do I think the theory meets the standards?

The Standards	Very Well	Moderately Well	Very Poorly
1. Reflects the real world of children		X	
2. Is clearly understandable	X		
3. Explains the past and predicts the future		X	
4. Guides child rearing	X		
5. Is internally consistent	X		
6. Is economical		X	
7. Is falsifiable	X		
8. Stimulates new discoveries	X		
9. Is self-satisfying	X		

and how well it explains the past and predicts the future (item 3). In particular, Skinner has been charged with extending conclusions derived from animal experiments—primarily with pigeons and rats—to humans, without accounting properly for differences of intellectual quality between the species. For example, Noam Chomsky (1967), as a leader in the field of psycholinguistics, has argued that Skinner has been imprecise in analyzing such commonsense terms as *want, like,* and *plan* into operant-conditioning elements. Furthermore, Chomsky has assailed Skinner's assumption that children simply repeat the words or phrases they hear, that is, repeat the ones that have brought reinforcement. Chomsky claims that children formulate for themselves, through unseen mental processes, a deeper grammar that undergirds the meaning of the surface appearance of their sentences. This deep grammar structure enables children to recognize the equivalent meanings of utterances that are dissimilar in their surface structure (*The girl ate the cake* or *The cake was eaten by the girl* or *The cake was gone, for the girl had eaten it*).

Widespread dissatisfaction has also been expressed over Skinner's explanation of creativity. Many psychologists who admit that reinforcement, nonreinforcement, and punishment can affect whether a person retains or drops a given behavior also feel that Skinner avoids the problem of how the behavior got started in the first place. Where does a new or unique behavior come from? Is it proper just to call the pigeon's hopping and pecking about the cage *random behavior* without accounting for why the pigeon hops and pecks rather than skates and coughs? How does a brilliant symphony or novel or scientific theory arise? Any psychologist who gives more credit to unobservable thinking behavior—to cognitive activity—can claim that Skinner's few principles of conditioning fail to offer an adequate explanation of innovative or creative acts.

In addition to the foregoing technical objections to radical behaviorism, other critics have, on humane or religious grounds, reacted against Skinner's views. Such criticism is based on a feeling that "it just doesn't seem right" that life operates on the basis of Skinnerian principles. Stevick, speaking from a Christian perspective, concluded about *Walden Two* that:

> Behavioral engineering rules out the risk and the achievement of freedom, love, self-giving, commitment, self-discipline, loyalty, memory, creativity, and hope. The significance of politics, the integrity of art, the warmth and support of human intimacy—all are lost. . . . The most precious thing about man is his humanity. Walden Two commends its deliberate abandonment (1968, p. 28).

In response to such a charge, Skinner would probably reply that, like it or not, radical behaviorism simply describes the truth about why people act as they do.

Because I believe there is some validity to these criticisms, yet feel the theory still has great virtues, I have marked it slightly above the center on items 1, 3, and 6. And in terms of its overall self-satisfying quality (item 9), I have rated the theory just below the top position.

FOR FURTHER READING

Skinner, B. F. (1974) *About Behaviorism.* New York: Knopf. This is an up-to-date, highly readable overview of radical behaviorism.

Skinner, B. F. (1972) *Cumulative Record: A Selection of Papers.* 3d ed. New York: Appleton-Century-Crofts. Representative articles from various stages of Skinner's career.

For Bijou and Baer's overall scheme, see:

Bijou, Sidney W. and Donald M. Baer. (1961) *Child Development: Vol. I. A Systematic and Empirical Theory.* New York: Appleton-Century-Crofts.

For a detailed analysis of the first stage of development, see:

Bijou, Sidney W. and Donald M. Baer. (1965) *Child Development II: Universal Stage of Infancy.* New York: Appleton-Century-Crofts.

A detailed account of the second stage appears in:

Bijou, Sidney W. (1976) *Child Development: The Basic Stage of Early Childhood.* Englewood Cliffs, N.J.: Prentice-Hall.

CHAPTER 18

SOCIAL LEARNING THEORY: VERSIONS BY BANDURA, SEARS, AND THE KENDLERS

Some writers have found it useful to distinguish between S-R and S-O-R behaviorists (Woodworth, 1929). The S-R designation identifies behaviorists who focus on observable stimuli (S) and responses (R) without proposing what might be happening inside the person between the S and R. In contrast, the S-O-R symbol designates behaviorists who are willing to speculate about what occurs within the organism (O) to transpose a stimulus into a response. Different theorists refer to the O-function in different ways. Some call it *intervening variables,* some call it *thinking,* and others call it *information processing.*

In terms of these distinctions, both John B. Watson and B. F. Skinner belong in the S-R camp. However, most modern behaviorists better qualify as S-O-R adherents, with many of them belonging in the subgroup of social learning theorists.

Social learning theory gets its name from the emphasis it places on social variables as determinants of behavior and personality. It proposes to correct an overdependence of earlier behaviorism on principles derived mostly from studies of animal learning and of human learning in one person experiments. The correction of this earlier bias is attempted by the social learning theorist, who bases many of his principles on studies of the interaction of two or more people.

The social learning movement has sought to offer both (1) a balanced synthesis of mentalism (which is known in respectable circles today as *cognitive psychology*) and principles of behavior modification and (2) an analysis of social influences in human development. Hilgard and Bower (1975, p. 599) have called this movement "a selective distillation of what is probably a 'consensus' position of moderation on many issues of importance to any theory of learning and behavior modification."

In Chapter 18 we include discussions of some important contributions to social learning theory from three different sources—Albert Bandura, Robert R. Sears, and the husband-and-wife team of Howard and Tracy Kendler. The models of development proposed by these theorists are properly considered variants of behaviorism, because each theorist subscribes to many of the basic principles found in the formulations of Skinner and other behaviorists. But each also holds some beliefs that can be considered alterations of, or extensions of, the operant conditioning we considered in Chapter 17. Instead of repeating in the present chapter the aspects of agreement among these investigators—such as the nature of operant conditioning and of reinforcement—we will focus only on the variations to behaviorism that they have contributed.

The chapter begins with the work of Bandura, for his formulation of social learning theory is the most recent and extensively known of the three versions considered here. The discussion turns next to the work of Sears, whose contributions preceded and are related to some of Bandura's. The chapter closes with a brief description of the Kendlers' investigation of children's shifting from perceptual to conceptual thought at the close of early childhood.

CONTRIBUTIONS BY BANDURA

Although Albert Bandura (born 1925), a Stanford University psychologist, shares many basic convictions with nearly all other behaviorists, he disagrees with traditional S-R theorists on the role of imitation in personality development. Among the areas in which Bandura's position differs from that of such radical behaviorists as Skinner, four are of particular importance: (1) the way a child acquires a new behavior that she has never attempted before (an area Skinnerians have difficulty explaining), (2) the key steps involved in the process of learning from models, (3) the way that consequences (reinforcement, punishment) influence future actions, and (4) the development of complex behaviors.

THE ORIGIN OF NEW BEHAVIOR

According to a commonly held S-R view, a child learns such things as language by first babbling a variety of sounds, then having certain of these sounds rewarded by people around her because the sounds approximate words they use. When the child happens to say *dah* or *ee* or *kee*, she is rewarded with smiles and caresses since the sounds have been uttered in the presence of *daddy, eating,* and *kitty*. When such events occur on several occasions, the sounds become conditioned to the objects they represent in the language of that particular culture. Though such a lucky coincidence between sounds and objects might account for children acquiring some simple words, Bandura and other social learning advocates find it inconceivable that this fortuitous process produces the thousands of words and the complex syntax and grammar that the child has mastered by the time she enters school.

In contrast, social learning theorists propose that most of a child's learning comes from her actively *imitating* or *modeling* what she sees and hears other people say and do. Bandura uses the word *modeling*—along with such terms as *observational learning* and *vicarious learning*—to mean that the child adds to her repertoire of actions by seeing or hearing someone else perform the behavior rather than by her overtly carrying out the behavior herself (Bandura, 1969, pp. 118–120). So in the social learning theorist's opinion, children's new actions are not simply spontaneous and random hit-or-miss behaviors, with the hits being learned because they are reinforced. Instead, children seek to reproduce what they observe. In some cases this is *one-trial learning*. The first attempt is perfect. In other cases, the first attempt only approximates the desired action, and so requires *shaping* through more refined attempts before the child achieves a level of behavior considered satisfactory by the reinforcing agents in her environment.

Some theorists agree with the importance of imitation, but they feel that the process only operates when the child's attempts are directly reinforced as he reproduces an observed action. However, Bandura and other social learning investigators have produced evidence to support the belief that a child will also learn when the reinforcement is only vicarious. When six-year-old James observes six-year-old Henry rewarded for saying "please" in order to get something he wants from the teacher, James learns to say "please" in similar circumstances.

People who have spent much time around children are not likely to consider this idea that children imitate others to be a discovery of cosmic dimensions. It seems to be pretty much common sense. Parents, teachers, coaches, and police commonly use principles of modeling to instruct children in how to add a new learning to their array of skills and knowledge. This sort of instruction is reflected in such phrases as "Try it this way" or "Let me show you" or "I'll tell you how to do it" or "Just read the directions." But more controversial and less obvious than these aspects of imitation is the role of *incidental learning.*

The issue of incidental learning has long been a topic of debate among learning theorists. The question at the center of the debate is this: Can a person learn something he sees or hears if this thing does not fulfill a need he is currently seeking to satisfy or if he is not rewarded for learning it? Many theorists say the answer is no. They claim that a person learns only those things that meet a need he is currently seeking to satisfy. Other things in the environment that are not pertinent to fulfilling the present need are passed by and not learned. And many theorists claim that reinforcement or reward is required for learning. Without reinforcement, either direct or vicarious, the child does not acquire a new skill or knowledge. (See the summary of latent-learning studies in Hilgard and Bower, 1975, pp. 134–136.)

However, Bandura and other social learning advocates have conducted experiments that suggest that the answer to the incidental-learning question is yes, at least in some cases. Children who are not seeking to satisfy any apparent need and who are not rewarded by a current happening may actually learn from the experience, storing in memory the results of their incidental observation for use at some later, appropriate time. According to Bandura, the error made by psychologists who do not admit to such incidental learning has been their confusing learning with performance. Since children who were not reinforced for a given act in experiments did not perform that act, it was assumed that without reinforcement, vicarious or direct, there had been no learning. But Bandura's evidence has supported the belief that people do not overtly display many things they have learned from a model if these things do not appear to yield sufficient rewards in the situation at hand. In other words, social learning theorists assume that for a given life situation, each of us has a series of possible reactions we might display. We have several answers we might give to the question being posed. However, in this multiple-choice situation, all answers are not equally plausible. Some seem better than others, and those better answers are the only ones we exhibit publicly, so other people do not realize that we have learned additional possible answers as well.

Bandura, then, contends that children do not just happen to hit on a new sort of behavior which is then reinforced; instead, he says, children acquire new behaviors by observing models in their environment. But what about the child's *creating* a novel behavior that he has not even seen before? How does this come about? Again, radical behaviorists seem to consider such novel acts accidental or built up some way from small links of behaviors already carried out. But the social learning theorist of Bandura's persuasion accounts for novel acts by concluding that:

> When exposed to diverse models, observers rarely pattern their behavior exclusively after a single source, nor do they adopt all the attributes even of preferred models. Rather, observers combine aspects of various models into new amalgams that differ from the individual sources. . . . Different observers adopt different combinations of characteristics (Bandura, 1977, p. 48).

So from the social learning viewpoint, novel behavior results from the child's combining different segments of various behaviors he has observed in other people, with the observation including both direct witnessing of events and such indirect modes of securing examples as reading or hearing about ideas and actions.

THE PROCESS OF LEARNING FROM MODELS

How observational learning takes place is far from completely understood. However, some of the conditions that influence it have been identified. According to Bandura, the main reason a child learns from seeing or hearing a model is that the information he thereby acquires helps him decide how the observed behavior might help or hinder him in fulfilling his needs on some future occasion. This information is stored in the memory in symbolic form, as images or as verbal symbols, for future reference. This process of learning from models consists of five main functions, which we will describe in more detail: paying *attention*, *coding* for memory, *retaining* in memory, and *carrying out motor actions*—and all four of these steps require *motivation* (Bandura, 1977, pp. 22–29).

First, when a child observes a model, he must *attend to the pertinent clues* in the stimulus situation and ignore the aspects of the model and the environment that are incidental and do not affect the performance that the child seeks to learn. The child's failure to perform the behavior properly later, especially if the behavior has been complex, is often due to her misdirecting her attention at the time the model was observed. Teachers frequently try to prevent this error by eliminating as many of the irrelevant stimuli from the setting as possible and by verbally directing the child's attention to those aspects of the model's performance that are most important.

A second requirement for imitative learning is that the child accurately record in memory a *visual image* or *semantic code* for the act she has witnessed. Without an adequate coding system, the child fails to store what she has seen or heard. There are obvious developmental trends in the ability to profit from models. Older children learn more readily from witnessing others' performances than do younger children. This superiority of older children is due in large part to their more advanced ability to use symbols. Bandura points out (1977, p. 30) that the infant's use of modeling is confined mainly to instantaneous imitation. The very young child will imitate the adult's gesture or word immediately instead of reproducing it after a period of time. But as the child grows up and has more experience in associating words or images with objects and events, she can store these symbols in order to recall and reproduce the events after increasingly extended periods of time. In effect, the development of language and of schemes for coding observations enhances the child's ability to profit from models. Not only must the observations be coded for memory (the input portion), but the codes must be suitable for transforming the perceptions into overt actions (the output portion). Otherwise the child ends up with useless knowledge, symbols that have been stored but cannot be retrieved in a form that leads to action.

A third factor influencing whether the knowledge will be available when needed is that of *memory permanence*. Although the operation of memory is still poorly understood by psychologists, one thing is clear—memories fade or disappear with time. Therefore, much that children learn from observing models is forgotten, so that such learning is no longer available when the child needs it to solve some problem in life (Bandura, 1969, p. 202). Such memory-aiding techniques as rehearsal (review or practice) and attaching multiple codes to an event (associating a variety of interlinked words or images with the event) serve to keep the stored information at a level that makes it readily retrieved when needed.

A fourth factor influencing the success of learning from models is that of *reproducing* the observed motor activities accurately. It is not enough that the observer get the *idea* of the actions to perform or that he code and store the idea adequately, it is also necessary for him to get the motor behavior, the muscular, *feel* of the behavior. He usually cannot do this perfectly on the first trial. Thus he needs a number of trials in which he approximates the behavior, then receives feedback from this experience to correct the deviations from the ideal that his early attempts have involved. It should be apparent that developmental trends in learning efficiency are partially a result of the older child's greater muscular strength and control in comparison to that of the younger child. Even if the younger child could attend properly to the cues of the observed performance and could encode the observations mentally as images or verbal symbols, the younger child still would not perform the modeled activities as well because his muscular development is not as advanced as the older child's.

The fifth requirement in the process of learning from models is that the learner be *motivated* to carry through the several steps of the process. In the behaviorist tradition, this motivational function has been embedded in the crucial role of the *consequences of behavior*. Since the interpretation that Bandura and other present-day social learning theorists place on the function of consequences differs from that of radical behaviorists like Skinner, we will give special attention to this aspect of the learning process.

THE ROLE OF CONSEQUENCES

According to Skinner's theory of operant conditioning, in a given stimulus situation a person has a series of likely responses he might give. Which response will actually be given depends upon the comparative strengths of the competing responses in the individual's repertoire of responses. In addition, the strength of a potential response depends on how often that response has been reinforced in the past when the individual has been in a similar situation, that is, when he has faced what he considers a similar problem. In the opinion of radical behaviorists, this strengthening of response tendencies through reinforcement is automatic. When a person's actions are reinforced or rewarded, it is not necessary for him consciously to tell himself, "That worked out well, so I'll try it again in the future." Instead, the strengthening of the response simply comes about without the need for the individual to assess the effect of his behavior. Furthermore, the typical adherent of operant conditioning believes that in order for this automatic strengthening to be most effective, the consequence (reinforcement or reward) must occur as soon as possible after the act so that the two become intimately connected or "conditioned."

However, Bandura disagrees with this interpretation of how consequences influence subsequent behavior.

> Although the issue is not yet completely resolved, there is little evidence that reinforcers function as automatic shapers of human conduct. . . . A vast amount of evidence lends validity to the view that reinforcement serves principally as an informative and motivational operation rather than as a mechanical response strengthener (Bandura, 1977, p. 21).

By *informative* Bandura means that the consequences, rewarding or punishing, tell the child under what circumstances it would seem wise to try a particular behavior in the future. In other words, the consequences improve the child's prediction of whether a given act will likely lead to pleasant or unpleasant outcomes on a later occasion. Bandura does not believe, as radical behaviorists do, that a consequence exerts its influence in reverse chronology, strengthening the behavior that preceded the rewarding consequence. Rather, he contends that the consequence exerts its influence into the future by giving the child information about what effects he can expect if he later acts that same way in a similar stimulus circumstance. By adopting such an interpretation, Bandura feels that he places himself in a better position to account for children learning from models than are the radical behaviorists who propose that consequences automatically reinforce the preceding actions that the individual himself carries out. That is, Bandura points out that the child can learn from observing others as well as from behaving himself, since watching others can give him the same information he gets from his own behavior consequences if he attends to the significant elements of the observed action.

When Bandura speaks of the *motivational* role of consequences, he means that children will more likely try to learn modeled behavior if they value the consequences the behavior seems to produce. If a pupil yearns for the teacher's approval and observes that the teacher gives such approval to children who spell well, then he is motivated to pay attention to the week's spelling words and to rehearse them so they are well stored in memory.

In summary, then, Bandura does not believe that consequences reinforce responses automatically and strengthen the response that immediately precedes the consequences. Instead, he sees consequences as *regulators* of future behavior—they regulate by means of giving the individual information about likely future consequences and by motivating her to act in one way rather than another in order to obtain the results she seeks.

COMPLEX BEHAVIORS

Not only do Bandura's ideas about modeling differ from those of radical or methodological behaviorists, but his beliefs about how complex behaviors are acquired differ as well. Contrary to more traditional behaviorists, he does not believe a child develops complex behaviors by first imitating one small element of the observed pattern, then gradually building up the entire pattern through a step-by-step accrual of successive elements. Rather, he says that:

> Patterns of behavior are typically acquired in large segments or in their entirety rather than through a slow, gradual process based on differential reinforcement. Following demonstrations by a model, or (though to a lesser extent) following verbal descriptions of desired behavior, the learner generally reproduces more or less the entire response pattern, even though he may perform no overt response, and consequently receive no reinforcement, throughout the demonstration period (Bandura and Walters, 1963, p. 106).

However, once the new behavior has been comprehended through observation, the likelihood that it will be displayed in the child's personality is governed chiefly by schedules of reinforcement and punishment.

A final aspect of imitation learning that is important in Bandura's system is the nature of the models. Experimental studies support the commonsense notion of hero worship in the following ways: (1) Children are more likely to model their own behavior after the actions of people they regard as prestigious than after actions of people who are not highly regarded. (2) Children are more likely to adopt behavior patterns from models of their own sex than from the opposite sex. (3) Models who receive rewards, such as money, fame, high socioeconomic status, are more often copied than ones who do not. (4) People who are punished for their behavior tend not to be imitated. (5) Children are more influenced by models they perceive to be similar to themselves, such as in age or social status, than by models they see as being quite different from themselves (Bandura and Walters, 1963, pp. 10–11, 50, 84, 94–100).

In summary, imitation is viewed by Bandura as a major device in children's social development, for through the observation of models, children add new options to their repertoire of possible behaviors. Furthermore, models help children decide under what circumstances they can most profitably put these new options into practice.

From Bandura's social learning perspective we can conceive of child development as a process (1) of the child's gradually expanding his repertoire of answers or possible actions by means of both observing others and trying the actions himself and (2) of the child's using information from the observed consequences to guide future decisions about when one response will be more appropriate than another to fulfill needs and attain rewards. Like Skinner, Bandura does not separate development into a series of stages, but he considers the process of cognitive and social growth to be one of gradual accrual of an ever widening array of response possibilities for increasingly differentiated stimulus situations.

With Bandura's views of the importance of observational learning in mind, let us turn to a currently popular application of social learning theory in the treatment of deviant behavior.

NORMALITY AND DEVIANCE

In putting his model of development to practical use, Bandura has centered attention on psychotherapy and the correction of anti-social behavior. His technique of treating deviance does not take the form of curing mental disorders or of alleviating the underlying causes of mental disease, as has been the case in traditional psychiatric practice. Instead, he has rejected the medical concept of deviance, the concept that the person exhibiting the undesired behavior is sick and that his mental condition must be treated to make him well. In place of this belief about curing illness, Bandura advocates what has been termed *behavior modification*, because he is convinced that an act which "is harmful to the individual or departs widely from accepted social and ethical norms" is not symptomatic of some disease but is simply "a way that the individual has learned to cope with environmental and self-imposed demands. Treatment then becomes mainly a problem in social learning rather than one in the medical domain" (Bandura, 1969, p. 10).

In keeping with this viewpoint, Bandura would treat a child who displays undesirable social behavior by manipulating the consequences of the child's acts so that the child finds it more rewarding to adopt more acceptable behavior than to continue in his currently unacceptable pattern. By extrapolating principles from Bandura's discussion, we can summarize the process of carrying out behavior modification in four basic steps:

1. Identify the specific behavior you wish to have the child substitute for the presently unacceptable behavior.

2. Arrange for the child to try out this new, desirable behavior. There are several ways this can be done: simply wait for it to occur spontaneously, provide a model, verbally explain what the desired behavior is, shape it through gradual approximations, or use several of these techniques.

3. Determine what sorts of consequences will be strongly reinforcing or rewarding to the child and what sorts will be punishing.

4. Manipulate consequences so that the desired behavior, when it appears, will yield greater reinforcement than does the undesirable behavior. In other words, arrange a schedule of reinforcement and/or punishment that will make it profitable for the child to give up the old behavior in favor of the new.

Although this process is easy to outline, it is often difficult to carry out in practice. However, such behavior modification is conceived by social learning theorists to be the most effective means of correcting a child's deviant acts.

Critics of behavior modification have charged that it is a naive, superficial approach to psychotherapy or personality improvement. They claim that seeking to change the child's overt actions directly fails to get at the underlying cause. Such criticism is based on the view that overt behaviors, such as thumb sucking, temper tantrums, or stealing, are just surface symptoms of an underlying disorder that lies deep in the personality, probably in the unconscious. Bandura, in reacting to such charges, says that both psychodynamic and social learning theorists are seeking underlying causes. However, the two camps differ in where they believe these causes lie.

Psychoanalysts propose that the causes are repressed conflicts left over in the unconscious from the child's failing to solve the conflicts faced during earlier psychosexual stages of development. Therefore, the therapist digs into the patient's psyche to identify which events in the past produced the conflicts, and then seeks to help the patient consciously relive these events and put them into a mentally healthy perspective. Such analysis, say the psychodynamic therapists, frees the patient from his symptoms of deviance, and the personality disorder is cured.

In contrast to this psychodynamic view, social learning therapists hunt for "underlying causes" in the child's present environment. For the social learning theorist, the term *cause* refers to the satisfying consequences that the child's deviant behavior continues to bring him. The child's regrettable behavior persists because it pays off or because he does not know any other way to behave that will bring him more satisfactory consequences. The task of the therapist, then, becomes that of carrying out the four steps of behavior modification.

In both psychodynamic and social learning theories it is possible to "simply treat the symptom" without getting at the "real cause." However, the meaning of this phrase is quite different under the two theories. With the typical psychodynamic approach, "simply treating the symptom" usually means punishing or rewarding the child so she will stop sucking her thumb in school or will stop stealing objects from her classmates' desks. Or it could mean giving the child a posthypnotic suggestion to avoid thumb sucking or stealing. However, in the psychodynamic view, such treatment only suppresses the particular symptom on which the treatment has focused. And because the underlying causes—repressed conflicts—have not been touched, other symptoms will arise.

In social learning theory "simply treating the symptom" is a phrase interpreted to mean that the therapist has been too narrow in her perception of the number of different situations in which the child's deviant response is used. For instance, a ten-year-old girl throws temper tantrums at home, around the neighborhood, in the classroom, and on the playground when things do not go her way. According to social learning theorists as well as other behaviorists, this pattern of action is maintained because people ultimately yield to the girl's demands in order to "avoid all that fuss." To solve the problem, her teacher may seek to eliminate the tantrums in class (1) by not reinforcing them, (2) by helping the girl observe models who use such techniques as reasoning or discussion instead of tantrums to get their way, and (3) by rewarding the girl's attempts to use these more mature techniques. Therefore, the undesirable behavior may be reduced in school, but it may persist at home, around the neighborhood, and on the playground, because the consequences in these out-of-class settings have not been altered. Critics of the behaviorists' reinforcement and punishment approach may charge that the classroom treatment of the problem was just getting at the symptoms but not the cause. However, the social learning theorist can reply that if the consequences in all four environments—classroom, home, neighborhood, and playground—were altered, the tantrums would disappear entirely, and the problem would be cured.

However, another difficulty may arise to cause Freudians and their psychodynamic colleagues to continue to criticize the behaviorists' approach. It is possible that the tantrums will disappear in all settings, but the new behavior that is substituted may also be deviant. For example, the girl, when she fails to get her way by tantrums, may withdraw from the classroom group and sit brooding. The psychodynamic therapist can now claim that this is simply *symptom substitution*, that one sort of deviance has replaced another because the real unconscious cause was not unearthed and resolved. The social learning therapist will disagree. He will likely say that for any given stimulus situation the ten-year-old has learned a hierarchy of possible responses. The most powerful of these at the top of her hierarchy of appropriateness has been the temper tantrum. If the consequences are altered so such behavior does not pay off for the child, then she can be expected to turn to the next most promising option in her strata of habits. By *promising* I mean the response she has observed or personally tried out that she estimates will bring the most satisfying results in such stimulus situations. Often this second most likely response is also considered undesirable by the important people in her life. So if withdrawal and brooding is the second choice among her options, the social behavior problem is not solved. She is still labeled an unsatisfactory child.

According to social learning theorists, this is not a problem of symptom substitution, however; it is a problem of the child's having a response hierarchy whose most promising options (that is, promising in the girl's estimation) are all undesirable ones for the society in which she lives. Therapy does not consist of hunting for an unconscious cause. Rather, it consists of helping the girl learn a new, socially approved behavior that is so rewarding that it takes priority over all of the undesirable responses in her repertoire of likely reactions to frustration, both in school and out (Bandura, 1969, pp. 48–52).

As implied, Bandura subscribes to a *reference-group* interpretation of normality and deviance. A child is normal or abnormal only in terms of how his behavior compares to the behavior of other members of a designated group. This reference group might be Catholics, American ten-year-olds, high-income family children, Central Elementary School fifth graders, or any of several score other groups. It should be apparent that a child might be considered normal when compared to one group but deviant when compared to another. Hence, when the question of normality arises, it is important to identify the reference group to be used in answering the question.

This matter of reference groups is important not only for determining normality or deviance in a child's development, but also for understanding why attempts at behavior modification may fail. Consider a junior high school boy who steals money and equipment from his classmates and from the teacher. School authorities consider this behavior undesirable, so they seek to change it by altering its consequences. They punish the boy by keeping him after school, and they offer him special privileges if he will go for a period of one month without stealing anything. But he continues to steal, and this puzzles the teacher and principal, for it is apparently contrary to social learning principles. But, in the eyes of the social learning theorist, they have simply failed to realize that the boy is still being reinforced for stealing. He persists in his deviant act because he continues to be rewarded by his own preferred reference group, by his gang of delinquent peers whose approval he values more than that of school authorities. Consequently, deviant behavior cannot be understood or altered without our recognizing that various groups' norms may be in conflict with each other and that the rewards dispensed by one group are more influential than those dispensed by another because the child values the first group more. This means that we need to identify which reference groups or individuals serve as the most valued ones in the child's life.

Finally, social learning theory discourages the application of such traditional psychiatric labels as *neurosis* and *psychopathic personality* to children exhibiting antisocial behavior. These children are not considered diseased or mentally deranged. The cause of their deviance, whether it appears to be harmful to themselves or to be contrary to social norms, is not to be found by use of special medical terms or principles. Instead, social learning theorists contend that "a single set of social learning principles can account for the development of both prosocial and deviant behavior and for modifications of behavior toward greater conformity or greater deviation" (Bandura and Walters, 1963, p. 221). Thus, treatment of the child consists of altering the consequences the environment provides for the undesired behavior. It does not consist of searching in the depths of the child's psyche for psychosexual or psychosocial conflicts.

CONSCIENCE AND SELF-CONTROL

In social learning theory a child's conscience or moral values are not inborn. The infant arrives in the world amoral. Then, by the same modeling and conditioning principles that produce all of her other beliefs, she gradually acquires her values and a capacity for self-control and self-direction. In other words, her character is learned, not inherited.

Investigations cited by Bandura support his contention that the development of self-control or conscience is heavily influenced by the models children observe and by patterns of direct reinforcement that they encounter, such as disciplinary measures used by parents and teachers. The degree to which a child will resist temptations has been most readily affected in experimental situations by how immediately the model in the situation is rewarded or punished. The characteristics of the model also influence how likely it is that the child will adopt the modeled self-control or lack of it, with the greatest influence exerted by models that are capable, successful, and prestigious.

The timing of reward and punishment is also important. Bandura suggests that many parents mold a child's conscience—meaning her guilt feelings or self-punishing tendencies—more successfully by withholding privileges than by applying aversive stimuli such as a spanking or isolation. He believes that the frequent superiority of withholding or withdrawing positive reinforcers over applying aversive measures is to a great extent the result of timing. Typically, the parent withholds the reinforcer until the child expresses guilt or some self-punishment response. Then the privilege or desired object is restored to the child. In contrast, "parents on most occasions administer aversive stimuli some time after a deviation has occurred and fail to make its termination contingent on the child's expressing self-punitive responses" (Bandura and Walters, 1963, p. 221). As a result of the postponed punishment and the indefiniteness of the time to remove the punishment, the child is less likely to adopt the self-control standards the parent desires. Studies have also suggested that the withholding of privileges serves most effectively to develop the child's self-control if the agents who withhold the rewards and subsequently reinstate them are warm, affectionate people rather than unaffectionate people or people who hold a grudge (Bandura and Walters, 1963, pp. 197–199).

These conclusions about conscience and self-control illustrate the manner in which social learning theorists use concepts of observational learning and operant conditioning to account for the development of personality attributes that Puritans, Rousseau, psychoanalysts, Piaget, and Kohlberg account for in different ways.

Next we consider the work of another neobehaviorist or social learning theorist, Robert Sears, whose studies of imitative behavior preceded those of Bandura.

CONTRIBUTIONS BY SEARS

Between 1945 and 1965, several prominent neobehaviorists displayed an intertheory interest by recasting Freudian ideas into behavioristic terms. John Dollard and Neal E. Miller, two Yale University psychologists, first did this in a 1950 volume entitled *Personality and Psychotherapy*. In their work they explained how neobehaviorist learning theory could account for child-growth patterns that had been postulated in Freud's psychosexual stages.

Later, Robert R. Sears (born 1908), a former Yale professor who moved to the University of Iowa, to Harvard, and then to Stanford, directed several major research projects aimed at investigating the role that various Freudian concepts play in child development. Sears's overall theory is complex and tightly argued within a social learning framework, and its entire structure is worthy of study. (See Maier, 1978, for a summary of the theory.) However, for our present purposes we will consider only an aspect that illustrates the manner in which Sears fits a Freudian proposal into a neobehaviorist model of learning. This aspect is the role that the adjustment mechanism of *identification* assumes in the child's social development.

As Sears has explained, his research has not been aimed at verifying psychoanalytic concepts. Instead, it has been designed as

> a testing of a behavioral theory that was suggested by psychoanalytic observations and was then constructed within the framework of an entirely different theoretical structure. The hypotheses we have proposed . . . are independent of and in some instances irrelevant to psychoanalytic formulations of the theories of identification (Sears, Rau, and Alpert, 1965, p. 242).

Like other behaviorists, Sears believes that the consequences of children's behavior determine which characteristics they will acquire from the environment. However, as Sears and others have observed, many, perhaps most, of the ways that children become like their parents have not been the result of conscious, consistent parental instruction. But if parents do not consciously reinforce and punish behaviors in order to mold children's actions into a pattern acceptable to the culture, how then do children acquire such behaviors and traits? One answer is that children do it spontaneously through identification, that is, through following a model. When identification is interpreted according to an S-O-R paradigm, the assumption can be made that identification is an intermediary process between the S and the R which, "very early in life, enables the child to *learn* without the parents' having to *teach,* and which creates a *self-reinforcing mechanism* that competes effectively in some instances with external sources of reinforcement" (Sears, Rau, and Alpert, 1965, p. 2).

To account for the idea that the child reinforces himself for patterning his behavior after a parent, Sears proposed that the infant initially depends on his mother for nearly all gratification of needs. Later, other needs may be satisfied by the father and other members of the family. In effect, the child acquires a dependency relationship to his parents. But as the child matures, the busy parents have less time for meeting the child's needs. To make up for this loss, the child, by means of some unexplained process, begins to imitate the parent. As a result of thus modeling himself after the person he has depended on for satisfaction, the child finds that his imitative behavior furnishes him some of the same satisfactions or reinforcement earlier supplied by the parent. In this way, identification or imitating the parent enables the child to become self-reinforcing.

Once Sears and his colleagues thus cast Freud's identification into a behavioristic paradigm, they were able to derive a series of hypotheses about how different sorts of parents might affect their children through the models they provided. These hypotheses were then tested through the study of child-rearing practices in several score of American families. At the end of the investigation, Sears concluded that the hypotheses were at least partially supported by the data. However, a number of puzzling questions were still unanswered, leaving the team of psychologists in the typical position of the investigator at the close of any study—the position of concluding that more research is necessary.

THE KENDLERS' DEVELOPMENTAL-MEDIATION THEORY

For more than two decades the husband-and-wife team of Howard H. Kendler (born 1919) and Tracy S. Kendler (born 1918) of the University of California at Santa Barbara have been evolving a theory of how children learn to distinguish likenesses and differences among things in their environment. The work of the Kendlers illustrates the way neobehaviorists employ what they call a *hypothetico-deductive* approach to building theory through formulating hypotheses and then experimentally testing them.

The Kendlers began with some discrimination-learning experiments which other psychologists had conducted, experiments that led to conflicting interpretations about how such learning occurs. Over the years the Kendlers have carried out their own experiments in an attempt to resolve this conflict and other puzzles that have continually arisen in their own and others' studies.

Before describing the Kendlers' main conclusions, we will examine what discrimination experiments involve. A typical, simple experiment requires the subjects (rats, monkeys, children, college students) to figure out which of two choices is the correct one. The problem may involve a white rat having to decide which of two alleys of a maze leads to food, when one alley is marked with a black circle and the other with a white circle. By a succession of tries over a series of days, the rat learns that the white-circle alley leads to food, no matter whether the circle is over the left or right alley.

Discrimination problems can be made more complex if two dimensions are included among the stimuli—for example, both brightness and shape. Now the rat must learn that it is brightness (white) and not shape (a circle contrasted to a square) that discriminates between the food alley and the no-food alley.

The task can be made even more difficult if, after the subjects have learned the correct response fairly well, the experimenter shifts the rule in the middle of the game. The correct answer can be reversed (reversal shift), making black the food alley, or the answer can be shifted to the other dimension (extradimensional shift), making the square figure the correct answer, no matter whether the square is white or black.

The foregoing, then, are typical discrimination-learning situations. Psychologists have exposed many facets of such situations by altering the stimulus characteristics, by shifting the rules, and by using different sorts of subjects (rats, pigeons, monkeys, children, college students). By observing the results of the manipulations, neobehaviorists have been able to create theories to explain what underlies discrimination learning. From their theories, scientists are then able to produce new *hypotheses* and to estimate (*deduce*) what should happen if they conduct another experiment designed to test a particular issue that remains unresolved. The scientist reasons, "If my theory is correct, then I should be able to pose this new sort of discrimination task and the subjects should respond in this predicted way." By carrying out his new experiment, he learns whether his prediction has been accurate and thereby confirms his theory, or whether the results are at odds with his expectation so that he needs to readjust the theory. This is the neobehaviorist's hypothetico-deductive approach to theory construction.

The reason the Kendlers' work deserves a place in a child development book is that their studies have been conducted with children and college students rather than with animals. Children receive rewards for correctly discriminating among pictures of shapes, sizes, and colors or pictures of animals, vehicles, and toys. From their experiments the Kendlers have concluded that very young children learn to discriminate in about the same fashion as infrahumans, that is, rats, pigeons, and monkeys. Young children draw their conclusions directly from the characteristics they see in the stimuli, the size or shape or color. But when they reach kindergarten or the early primary grades, their discriminations begin to be *mediated* by concepts. In general terms this means that the child develops concepts or mental symbols as mediators, which she manipulates in arriving at decisions, instead of reacting directly to the discrimination stimuli. This mediator or "idea" may be either verbal (a label for an object—*circle, green, small*) or nonverbal. The Kendlers have concluded that the skill of discriminating likenesses and differences among things in the world develops through two main stages—an early direct-reaction stage and a later mediation stage. (These findings clearly parallel those of Piaget and Vygotsky.)

Theories like the Kendlers' are never complete. They are always tentative estimates of relationships, estimates that continually undergo refinement and expansion through hypothesis and experiment. They often move in new directions. Recently the Kendlers have been investigating a likely linkage between their results and Feschwind's studies of brain neurology (Kendler and Kendler, 1975, pp. 191–247). Trends of development of the brain from lower species to higher ones (phylogeny) and trends in the maturation of an individual child's brain (ontogeny) parallel the stages of discrimination-learning in the Kendlers' mediation-development model. Thus it appears possible to give a reasonable neurological explanation for the behavioral changes the Kendlers have observed in children's cognitive processes. In such a way neo-behaviorists' theories move ahead.

SOCIAL LEARNING THEORY: AN ASSESSMENT

Since the social learning theorists discussed in this chapter subscribe to many of the same principles considered in Chapter 17, it seems unnecessary here to repeat the entire assessment process used to appraise Skinner's radical behaviorism. Instead, we will first look at the items or scales on which the social learning theorists would receive very similar ratings to those applied to Skinner. Then we will examine those items on which the social learning theorists can be rated somewhat differently than Skinner.

Like Skinner's system, those of the theorists reviewed in the present chapter are clearly described, are falsifiable, lead to suggestions about child-raising practices, and appear to be internally consistent. They also have helped stimulate further discoveries, with Bandura's work perhaps stronger in this respect than that of Sears and the Kendlers.

Compared to Skinner's radical behaviorism, social learning theories are not as subject to the charge of devaluing mental activity. And unlike Skinner, social learning theorists have accorded a prominent place to the function of imitation in personality development. Furthermore, Bandura, Sears, and the Kendlers have conducted their own research on people, particularly on children, rather than on animals, thus avoiding the criticism directed at Skinner that he has drawn simplistic conclusions about human development by founding many of his principles on conditioning experiments with pigeons and rats. For all of these reasons, I would rate the social learning theorists somewhat higher than Skinner on how well they reflect the real world of children and explain the past and predict the future.

I would also give social learning theory a higher rating on economy of explanation, because the versions of the theory that we have inspected in Chapter 18 appear to suffer less from the charge of being overparsimonious than Skinner's behaviorism.

Despite this array of strengths, however, social learning theory has not been universally adopted by people concerned with explaining child development. Parents and teachers who seek information about what children are like at different age levels receive no aid from the social learning model, for it describes *how* children learn rather than *what they are like* at different stages of their lives. This criticism is more true of Bandura's work than that of Sears and the Kendlers, who have indeed included some description of child characteristics at levels of development.

A developmentalist who sees a child's genetic endowment and the influence of internal maturation as prime factors behind child growth may also find fault with social learning theorists' slighting of hereditary influences on development.

Finally, all behaviorist approaches, social learning theory included, have been criticized for giving too little recognition to how a child thinks and feels about himself. A developing child, critics have claimed, is not just an animated mechanism to be programmed to suit the desires of agents that control his environment. Rather, in the opinion of humanistic critics (Chapter 19), a child is a unique personality with hopes and plans and feelings that make up the essence of his or her humanness. Behavioristic approaches appear to overlook this matter.

While social learning theory has not satisfactorily answered all the questions about development posed by other theorists, parents, and teachers, it has come perhaps the closest of any theory to describing how children acquire the learned, rather than the inherited, aspects of their personalities. In comparing it to other learning models, Hilgard and Bower have concluded that:

> social learning theory provides the best integrative summary of what modern learning theory has to contribute to solutions of practical problems. It also provides a compatible framework within which to place information-processing theories of language comprehension, memory, imagery, and problem solving . . . . For such reasons, social learning theory would appear to be the "consensus" theoretical framework within which much of learning research (especially on humans) will evolve in the next decade (1975, p. 605).

In regard to its overall self-satisfying quality, I would rate social learning theory higher than Skinner's radical behaviorism.

FOR FURTHER READING

Bandura, Albert. (1969) *Principles of Behavior Modification.* New York: Holt, Rinehart, and Winston.

Bandura, Albert. (1977) *Social Learning Theory.* Englewood Cliffs, N.J.: Prentice-Hall.

Kendler, Howard H. and Tracy S. Kendler. (1975) "Discrimination and Development" in William K. Estes (ed.), *Handbook of Learning and Cognitive Processes.* New York: Halsted Press. Pp. 191–247.

Maier, Henry William. (1978) *Three Theories of Child Development: Erik H. Erikson, Jean Piaget, and Robert R. Sears.* 3d ed. New York: Harper & Row.

Sears, Robert R., Lucy Rau, and Richard Alpert. (1965) *Identification and Child Rearing.* Stanford, Calif.: Stanford University Press.

FOR FURTHER READING

PART 10

THE HUMANISTIC APPROACH

A search for the way the innermost self develops.

In contrast to the behaviorists' practice of analyzing people from the outside, there have always been theorists who prefer the opposite perspective—analyzing from the inside. Introspection becomes their chief investigative technique, for they believe the essence of an individual is found not in his overt acts but in his thoughts and feelings about his personal experience.

This inward view of personality has appeared over the centuries in numerous versions, each bearing its own name. One variety created in nineteenth-century Europe was *existentialism*, which proposed that the reality of life resides in the individual's interpretation of his own existence. In early twentieth-century Europe another school of thought, *phenomenology*, also placed personal experience at the core of its system. A mid-twentieth-century variant appeared in a book entitled *Individual Behavior* by two U.S. psychologists, Combs and Snygg, who accorded prime attention to the *phenomenal self*, meaning the personally recognized "I" or "me." The most recent popular revival of the inner view appeared in the 1960s under the title *humanistic psychology*. Although advocates of a humanistic model of development may differ among themselves on details of their theory, they share in common a cluster of basic tenets. In Chapter 19 we will examine a series of these tenets as they appear in books by two leaders of the movement, Abraham H. Maslow and Charlotte Buhler. Other versions of the humanistic approach can be found in the writings of Carl Rogers, Gordon W. Allport, and authors who publish in the *Journal of Humanistic Psychology* (Allport, 1961, 1968; Rogers, 1961, 1973).

CHAPTER 19

THE HUMANISTIC PERSPECTIVES OF MASLOW AND BUHLER

The official birth of the humanistic-psychology movement in the United States occurred in 1962 with the formation of the Association of Humanistic Psychology and the initial publication of the *Journal of Humanistic Psychology*. The movement was at the same time a reaction against two current streams of psychological thought and the opening of a third stream. Thus it was dubbed "a third force" in psychology by a Brandeis University professor, Abraham Maslow (1908–1970).

The two theoretical positions that humanistic psychology rejected were behaviorism and psychoanalysis. Behaviorism was accused of reducing humans to a system of observable acts and thereby missing such human aspects as people's values, feelings, hopes for the future, choices, and creativity. Behaviorists were charged with neglecting to picture the human being as a unitary person in pursuit of goals and ideals (Maslow, 1968, 1970).

Freudian psychoanalysis was accused of adopting a negative model of humanity, of espousing a morbid emphasis on neurotic behavior and of failing to define the nature and path of positive, healthy personality development.

Central convictions of the humanistic psychologists were published by the Association in the following form. The humanistic movement is marked by:

1. A centering of attention on the experiencing *person*, and thus a focus on experience as the primary phenomenon in the study of man. Both theoretical explanations and overt behavior are considered secondary to experience itself and to its meaning to the person.

2. An emphasis on such distinctively human qualities as choice, creativity, valuation, and self-realization, as opposed to thinking about human beings in mechanistic and reductionist terms.

3. An allegiance to meaningfulness in the selection of problems for study and of research procedures, and an opposition to a primary emphasis on objectivity at the expense of significance.

4. An ultimate concern with and valuing of the dignity and worth of man and an interest in the development of the potential inherent in every person. Central in this view is the person as he discovers his own being and relates to other persons and to social groups (The Brochure of the AHP).

The ancestry of humanistic psychology has been traced mainly to a pair of somewhat related philosophical traditions, those of humanism and of existentialism. Philosophers of a humanistic persuasion over the past few centuries have stressed a belief in man's possessing a free will that allows him to make choices and display creative powers as an individual. Existentialists have emphasized the importance of a person's fully experiencing each moment of life. They contend that pondering and savoring this experience is the essence of existence. So the "truth" about life is found in this experiencing and not in objective observations of man's behavior as reported in research studies.

With these philosophical beliefs as their foundation, proponents of humanistic psychology: (1) criticize adherence to a rigid scientific methodology modeled after the "objective" sciences of physics and chemistry, (2) propose a positive, optimistic picture of humans, and (3) believe that life "is to be lived subjectively, as it takes place." Even in the moment of observation, humanistic psychologists "do not claim to be 'objective.' They are intent on the discovery of methods within the highly subjective interchange of a relationship which will garner 'personal knowledge' of another human being" (Buhler and Allen, 1972, p. 24).

Ideas arising within the humanistic movement have not been molded into one system, nor do the beliefs of one theorist always agree with those of others. Furthermore, it is not specifically a child development theory, for most of its materials focus on adults or speak about the life span in general without distinguishing very clearly between one age period and another. However, from the writings of humanistic psychologists it is possible to extract theoretical proposals to answer many of the child development questions we posed in Chapter 2. The contents of this chapter have been drawn by such an extraction process from the writings of two leaders of the humanistic movement, Abraham Maslow and a well-known European psychologist, Charlotte Buhler (1893–1974), who made her first contributions to the child development literature in Austria before establishing her home in the United States.

The topics on which the following discussion is centered include (1) the original nature of the child, (2) the importance of needs and goals, (3) the nature of the self, (4) directions and stages of development, (5) healthy growth, disease, and deviance, (6) teaching and learning, (7) nature and nurture, and (8) methods of investigation and validation.

THE ORIGINAL NATURE OF THE CHILD

The biologically determined inner nature of the human consists of basic needs, emotions, and capacities that are either neutral or positively *good*. They certainly are not evil. Such "bad" characteristics as destructiveness, cruelty, and malice are not innate, according to Maslow (1968, pp. 3–4), but are "violent reactions *against* frustration of our intrinsic needs, emotions, and capacities. . . . Since this inner nature is good or neutral rather than bad, it is best to bring it out and to encourage it rather than to suppress it. If it is permitted to guide our life, we grow healthy, fruitful, and happy."

Therefore, the goal of guiding child development is one of fostering the expression of the child's inner nature. This task is a difficult and crucial one because the inner essence of the child's personality is not very hardy. It is delicate and easily damaged by unfavorable experiences. Suppressing or distorting the expression of the inner nature causes some type and degree of sickness, bodily ailments or behavior deviations that sometimes show up immediately but at other times wait to surface months or years after the maltreatment. Nevertheless, even when the inner essence is suppressed, it continues to live in the depths of the unconscious, always striving for expression or, in Maslow's language, for *actualization*.

HUMAN NEEDS AND GOALS

A key concept to which humanistic psychologists subscribe is that human behavior is motivated primarily by the individual's seeking to fulfill a series of needs. To differentiate the humanistic view from the concept of needs in other theories, Maslow distinguished two types.

The first type he labeled *deficiency needs*. Examples of this variety are the needs for food, for drink, for a comfortable temperature, for safety from bodily harm, for close love relationships, for respect, and for prestige. He proposed that deficiency needs can be recognized by five objectively observed characteristics of the person and by two subjectively experienced feelings. Objectively, a need for something exists if (1) its absence breeds illness, (2) its presence prevents illness, (3) its restoration cures illness, (4) under certain free choice situations it is preferred by the deprived person over other satisfactions, and (5) it is found to be inactive, at a low ebb, or functionally absent in the healthy person. Subjectively, a deficiency need is felt as (6) conscious or unconscious yearning and desire and (7) a lack or deficiency (Maslow, 1968, p. 22).

Beyond these deficiency needs, which are also parts of other theories of child development, humanistic psychologists postulate a second cluster called *growth* or *self-actualization* needs. Theorists have had far more trouble in specifying this second group than in identifying deficiencies. Maslow admitted that:

> Growth, individuation, autonomy, self-actualization, self-development, productiveness, self-realization, are all crudely synonymous, designating a vaguely perceived area rather than a sharply defined concept. . . . We just don't know enough about growth yet to be able to define it well (1968, p. 24).

But in an initial attempt at a general definition, Maslow proposed that the self-actualizing need is a striving to realize one's potentials, capacities, and talents; it is a seeking to fulfill a mission or destiny or vocation; it can be a fuller knowledge and acceptance of one's own personality and "an unceasing trend toward unity, integration, or synergy within the person" (Maslow, 1968, p. 26).

The highest stage of growth in humans, then, is the achievement of this self-actualization. Commenting on this highest stage, Buhler and Allen (1972, p. 45) have said, "All humanistic psychologists see the goal of life as that of using it to accomplish something in which one believes."

The human needs in Maslow's system, then, form a hierarchy ranging from the most basic physiological deficiency needs at the foundation to the self-actualization needs at the apex. In descending order from the apex, they can be placed in five clusters (Maslow, 1970, pp. 80–98):

1. Need for self-actualization: doing what one, *individually*, is fitted for: "What a man *can* be, he *must* be. He must be true to his own nature."

2. Esteem needs: for self-respect and self-esteem and for the esteem of others.

3. Belongingness and love needs: for family, friends, lover; affection, rootedness, intimacy.

4. Safety needs: for security and stability, for freedom from fear, anxiety, and chaos. This includes a need for structure, law, and limits.

5. Physiological needs: for air, food, drink, rest, fulfilling the appetites and for achieving balance or homeostasis within the body.

THE NATURE OF THE SELF

The term *self* appears frequently in humanistic-psychology writings, and it is not always described in the same way by different writers or even the same way at all times by a single writer. We can, however, identify several characteristics of the self that most humanistic theorists would agree on.

Both Maslow and Buhler accept the principal agents that Freud defined as composing the personality or mind: id, ego, and superego. They also accept the various Freudian instincts, impulses, and defenses, as well as the primary process (the asocial id demands) and the secondary process (the ego's recognizing the real world and fulfilling id demands in light of the realities). But for the humanistic psychologist these separate and often conflicting agents and tendencies become increasingly integrated into a compatible unity—into the essential self—as the person matures. Thus, the individual who is fulfilling all of her needs, basic as well as the higher self-actualizing ones, is marked by a smooth working together or *synergy* of the composite elements of personality (Buhler and Massarik, 1968, p 19).

Humanistic psychologists accept the levels of consciousness postulated by Freud. They feel that much of human behavior arises from unconscious motives and that "those portions of ourselves that we reject and repress out of fear and shame do not go out of existence" (Maslow, 1971, p. 158) but go underground into the unconscious. However, humanistic writers strongly disagree with Freud's idea that the contents of the unconscious are all antisocial, that is, all selfish and contrary to moral values. The contents also include the roots of creativeness, joy, and goodness.

In humanistic belief, conscience differs somewhat from the punitive Freudian superego whose contents derive exclusively from the rules and expectations imposed by the environment, particularly expectations imposed by parents. Maslow proposed that in addition to values the child ingests from people around him, his conscience also has a genetic source, a kind of intrinsic feeling or knowledge of the right thing to do. This instinctoid, faint voice had its beginnings in the ancient nature of humans and is linked to the instincts of lower forms of life. It is an inner knowledge of one's true self. Maslow said that intrinsic guilt arises when an individual senses he has betrayed his own inner nature and has deviated from the path of self-actualization.

In Maslow's view, intrinsic guilt is a most desirable thing, for it warns the child that she is deviating from her true destiny. On the other hand, guilt based on unreasonable expectations from the environment is frequently nonconstructive and detracts from the pursuit of one's true identity and self-actualization.

DIRECTIONS AND
STAGES OF DEVELOPMENT

As noted, humanistic psychology was not created as a child psychology. It was devised by theorists concerned chiefly with helping adults achieve better personal-social adjustment or, in more positive terms, achieve greater self-actualization. Hence, the attention of most humanistic psychologists has focused on childhood only in incidental ways. Our picture of the directions of development in childhood and of stages of growth must therefore be gleaned from passing comments found in the writings of such people as Maslow, Buhler, Rogers, and the Gestalt-therapy theorist, Fritz Perls. In effect, humanistic psychology, as outlined by its best known proponents, has not been organized as a system of phases of childhood and adolescence correlated with chronological ages.

Despite the fact that the first two decades of life lack a clearly defined set of growth steps, both Maslow and Buhler identified at least two general levels, childhood and adolescence. In discussing these levels, Buhler said that it was important to distinguish between biological and psychological development. From a biological standpoint, she divided the first twenty-five years of life at age 15. During childhood, ages 0–15, there is progressive physical growth without reproductive ability. During adolescence or youth, ages 15–25, there is continued growth following the onset of reproductive ability (Buhler and Massarik, 1968, p. 14).

Psychological development can also be viewed as two general segments, childhood and adolescence, but the distinctions are not nearly as clear as in the biological realm. Psychologically, the child grows toward self-actualization, toward achieving clearer goals in life and better integrating her needs and values. This development of *self* is somewhat correlated with biological growth, in that the very young child is not very self-actualized. It requires time and experience for her to achieve greater self-realization and synergy. But time alone is not enough. Just becoming older does not assure self-actualization. There are many adolescents and adults who still have not achieved psychological maturity. So the passing of childhood and the arrival of adolescence provides opportunities for *becoming* mature, but such maturing is not automatic.

Buhler concluded that the first appearance of a self-conscious ego occurs when the young child is between ages 2 and 4. During this time "I want" behavior is prominent as "the child begins to discover his own self and the possibility of giving himself a direction of his own" (Buhler and Massarik, 1968, pp. 30–31). The way a child expresses this self-consciousness varies greatly from one child to another, providing an individuality that is both genetic and environmental in origin. "The child with creative potential begins his first attempts toward self-realization when he is between 2 and 4 years" (Buhler and Massarik, 1968, p. 32).

Throughout the next eight or ten years the child's personality gradually evolves until the arrival of marked psychological change around age 10 to 12 or so. At this time, according to Buhler, several *motivational trends* appear, trends that extend into the future and mark the child's individuality in rather permanent ways.

One trend concerns a *constructive-destructive* dimension. A person's basic attitude toward life—whether to build up or to tear down and damage—is becoming well set. It is most clearly evidenced in conflicts between the growing child and his parents.

A second trend relates to *achievement motivation*. The extent to which a child will strive to achieve in his adult life and the form this achievement may take show up most clearly after puberty.

Beliefs and values that are based on more than blind acceptance develop in these early adolescent years, along with *love* and other *commitments* to a cause or to other people. Buhler (Buhler and

Massarik, 1968, p. 37) said that the voluntarily chosen bonds of intimacy and commitment in a mutually shared sex and love relationship that can develop in youth may result in "the ecstatic experience of unity . . . one of the most, if not *the* most, essential aims of the maturing person." Maslow called this feeling of unity one of the individual's *peak experiences* (Buhler and Massarik, 1968, p. 37).

But even with the new concern for personally adopted values and immediate ambitions, adolescents usually have only vague and tentative life goals, and they do not often view life as an entirety, as a complete span of years with possibilities of an integration of all its aspects. "It is the exceptional youth who asks what life is all about," according to Buhler (Buhler and Massarik, 1968, p. 42).

Like Buhler, other writers in the humanistic vein consider adolescence to be a time of increased awareness and searching in the realm of values, goals, and commitment to something considered worthwhile. It is a time accompanied by a significant measure of confusion. In this sense, the typical humanistic psychologist would agree with Erikson's view that adolescence is experienced as an identity crisis. Maslow commented that the uncertainty of many adults in the United States about their own values has led many young people to live not by clear adult values but by "adolescent values, which of course are immature, ignorant, and heavily determined by confused adolescent needs" (Maslow, 1968, p. 206).

In summary, while humanistic psychologists recognize at least prepuberal childhood and postpuberal adolescence as separate stages in personality development, they do not define substages within these periods, nor do they discuss even these two broad periods in a systematic way. Instead, they give only incidental attention to any idea of growth stages correlated with age.

Rather than being a *growth-stage* theory, the humanistic model is more accurately described as a *growth-directions* theory— a person grows gradually out of being one kind of person in a direction of becoming a different kind. If we are then to recognize whether a person is indeed growing in a proper direction, we need a definition of the desired end product or the desired goal that development is to pursue. Maslow defined this *direction of healthy growth* in two ways, one general and the other more specific.

As a general definition, he said that people are motivated in their development toward "ongoing actualization of potentials, capacities and talents, as fulfillment of mission—or call it fate, destiny, or vocation—as a fuller knowledge of, and acceptance of, the person's own intrinsic nature, as an unceasing trend toward unity, integration or synergy within the person" (Maslow, 1968, p. 25).

But many of Maslow's audience found the foregoing definition unduly vague, so he provided a more specific description of the end condition of healthy development by specifying a series of traits displayed by a self-actualized person. Such a paragon of excellence exhibits (Maslow, 1968, p. 26):

1. Superior perception of reality
2. Increased acceptance of self, of others, and of nature
3. Increased spontaneity
4. Increase in problem solving
5. Increased autonomy, and resistance to enculturation
6. Increased detachment and desire for privacy
7. Greater freshness of appreciation, and richness of emotional reaction
8. Higher frequency of peak experiences
9. Increased identification with the human species
10. Changed (the clinician would say, improved) interpersonal relations
11. More democratic character structure
12. Greatly increased creativeness
13. Certain changes in the value system

If these symptoms are the marks of the self-actualized person at the apex of development, then their opposites can be considered symptoms of those at the bottom or the beginning end of development. Therefore, we can regard each of these characteristics as the top end of a growth scale. The infant will be at the bottom on each of the thirteen dimensions. Normal growth consists of the child's progressing up the scale as the years pass. The immature or unhealthy adult is one who becomes fixated in progress up one or more of the scales.

In speaking of these growth scales, we have mentioned an apex or top point. However, in the opinion of many humanistic psychologists, there is no ultimate peak that a human being is able to reach. In real life, the scales are open-ended at the top, so no one ever becomes completely self-actualized. There is always room for improvement. But what is important is that the individual is always *becoming* more self-actualized, always moving up to more positive, self-fulfilling levels. However, Maslow did seek to be realistic; he defined a level of development that conceivably could be realized by the most mature among us, though only a few ever make it—by Maslow's criteria, certainly less than 1 percent of the adult population.

HEALTHY GROWTH, DISEASE, AND DEVIANCE

In place of the terms *normal* and *abnormal*, Maslow spoke of *health* and *illness* or of *mature* and *immature* development. For example, he distinguished between two sorts of immaturity, *chronological* and *unhealthy*. Chronological immaturity is found in the child as she grows up; it is expected, even necessary, for it consists of the healthy process of developing from a state of weakness, ignorance, lack of goals and direction to an adult state of self-actualization. But when the same sorts of symptoms are found in the adult, they are considered unhealthy, for by adulthood the individual should have become strong, wise, well integrated, and clear in her values and goals.

Deviance, in the sense of being different from others or not fitting the norms, is not regarded as necessarily unhealthy. Indeed, being deviant in terms of expressing one's own talents and of following the guidance of one's unique inner gyroscope is viewed by Maslow as essential to achieving self-actualization. If a person adopts the typical behavior or norms of a culture that blocks the expression of her essential core or inner nature, then she is not considered to be normal in the sense of developing properly or in a healthy pattern. Instead, she is regarded in Maslow's system as being immature and unhealthy, for "the main source of illness (although not the only one) is seen as frustrations (of the basic needs, . . . of idiosyncratic potentials, of expression of the self, and of the tendency of the person to grow in his own style and at his own pace) especially in the early years of life" (Maslow, 1968, pp. 193–194).

So it is not deviance from the common or typical behavior of a society that is viewed with disapproval in the humanistic model; it is deviance from one's potential and inner nature. A child who does not "fit in" to his culture or who "stands against the crowd" is a psychologically healthy child by humanistic standards if that culture is a bad one. And by *bad* Maslow meant a culture that is growth-inhibiting rather than growth-fostering. "The 'better' culture gratifies all basic human needs and permits self-actualization. The 'poorer' cultures do not" (Maslow, 1968, p. 211).

TEACHING AND LEARNING

Maslow recognized several types of learning that have been investigated by other theorists, such as associative learning and conditioning. He concluded that both of these kinds are necessary and desirable for acquiring all sorts of automatic habits, such as those needed in writing or speaking a language. But since he felt the prime goal of education is that of helping children toward self-actualization, toward their becoming "fully human," he saw the most significant learning experiences as being very different from association and conditioning. He termed this more important type *intrinsic learning* (Maslow, 1971, p. 169).

In contrast to behaviorists like Skinner and Bandura, who specify precisely the teaching methodology of their behavior modification, Maslow did not delineate exactly how parents or teachers should conduct intrinsic education. Apparently he felt he could not give a clear recipe since he believed:

> We know only too well that a parent cannot make his children into anything. Children make themselves into something. The best we can do and frequently the most effect we can have is by serving as something to react against if the child presses too hard (Maslow, 1971, p. 169).

Maslow's faith in the essential correctness of the child's natural inclinations caused him to recommend a *permissive regime,* meaning that parents begin meeting the child's needs directly and with as little frustration as possible in early infancy. But as the child acquires greater strength and experience, adults should gradually cease gratifying his needs directly. They should now arrange his environment so he can gratify his own needs and make his own choices, for "*he* 'knows' better than anyone else what is good for him" (Maslow, 1968, p. 198).

The intention of Maslow's educational scheme is not to prevent the developing child from ever experiencing frustration, pain, or danger. But, with a good foundation in the early years of safety, love, and respect, the child should increasingly be allowed to face difficulties that enable him to acquire frustration tolerance. Part of self-realization comes as the older child and youth learn about their strengths and limitations and learn ways to extend their abilities by overcoming difficulties, "by straining . . . to the utmost, by meeting challenge and hardship, even by failing" (Maslow, 1968, p. 200). Curiously, this general pattern of child raising sounds much like the pattern found in Skinner's *Walden Two*, illustrating the observation that children may be treated in similar ways from quite different theoretical viewpoints.

In addition to offering such general guidelines as the above, Maslow directed his attention to the role of more formal schooling in promoting intrinsic learning. Instead of focusing so heavily on learning subject matter, he felt, "schools should be helping the children to look within themselves, and from this self-knowledge derive a set of values" and "search for spontaneity and for naturalness" (Maslow, 1971, pp. 185–186). He proposed that art, music, and dancing might become the core of the intrinsic learning program, with dancing the first to be introduced, because he considered it the easiest for the preschool child. "Such experiences could very well serve as the model, the means by which perhaps we could rescue the rest of the school curriculum from the value-free, value-neutral, goal-less meaninglessness into which it has fallen" (Maslow, 1971, p. 178).

While emphasizing the importance of the expressive arts in helping a child discover her true identity, Maslow did not discount the importance of academic disciplines in furnishing opportunities for peak experiences and self-discovery. He felt that self-actualization can be promoted as well by studying mathematics, history, anthropology, paleontology, and the physical sciences (Maslow, 1971, pp. 177–178).

NATURE AND NURTURE

As our discussion of Maslow's views has already suggested, he assigned heredity a strong role in personality development. The essence of the sort of person a child should become is established in the genetic structure as a unique self composed of potential talents and interests. It then becomes the role of environment to determine how adequately this idiosyncratic self or identity unfolds or becomes actualized. Curiously, in one way Maslow's concept of the nature–nurture relationship is similar to the Puritans' and in another way is similar to Rousseau's. Like the Puritans, Maslow believed that each person is innately suited to a *calling* in life, a particular role. According to both Puritan and humanistic theory, a key task of later childhood and adolescence is that of discovering what one's calling is to be—or, in Erikson's terms, of discovering one's proper identity. The Puritan youth was to seek this identity through prayer and meditation. Under modern humanistic psychology, a youth discovers this calling by interacting with a growth-supporting, permissive, but realistic social environment and, at the same time, by trusting her intuition to guide her toward her calling.

But like Rousseau, and unlike the Puritans, humanistic theorists have suggested that the natural instincts of the child are good and should be followed. Thus the environment should furnish opportunities for the good nature to flower rather than restrict the child's expression by imposing Biblical prohibitions on her to combat an ostensibly devil-sent evil nature.

METHODS OF INVESTIGATION AND VALIDATION

Humanistic methods of investigating personality development include both observation from outside the individual and introspection from inside. Although Maslow accepted the objective, scientific modes of studying people that have evolved over the past century or so, he criticized the adoption of behaviorism and of logical positivism as the exclusive, or even as the preferred, mode of understanding human development. He claimed that such approaches to studying the growing child result only in verbal, analytic, conceptual rationality and ignore the more significant aspects of personality—the hopes, feelings, fears, and ambitions of the experiencing self. For example, in discussing motivation, Maslow stated that:

The original criterion of motivation and the one that is still used by all human beings except behavioral psychologists is the subjective one, I am motivated when I feel a desire or want or yearning or wish or lack. No objectively observable state has yet been found that correlates decently with these subjective reports, i.e., no behavioral definition of motivation has yet been found.

Now of course we ought to keep on seeking for objective correlates or indicators of subjective states. . . . But until we find (them) we ought not make believe that we have. Nor ought we neglect the subjective data that we do have (1968, p. 22).

Not only does humanistic theory draw upon self-reports, but it accords a key position to nonlogical, or even illogical, intuitive impressions or feelings, which it claims are so often expressions of the true inner self.

If our hope is to describe the world fully, a place is necessary for preverbal, ineffable, metaphorical, primary process, concrete experience, intuitive, and esthetic types of cognition, for there are certain aspects of reality which can be cognized in no other way (Maslow, 1968, p. 208).

This attitude about the proper sources of evidence about personality development also influences the humanistic view of the way the theory is validated. In earlier chapters we noted that behavioristic theories depend upon the experimental or field-study testing of hypotheses as the appropriate way to determine whether the theory or some part of it is true. But humanistic psychologists trust their own feelings and logic more than many sorts of objective data to validate their theory. To most if not all humanistic psychologists, it appears to be enough to contend that "I know that's the way things are because it makes sense and feels right to me." But such a testimonial would less likely satisfy a behaviorist, a Piagetian, or a psychoanalyst.

HUMANISTIC THEORY: AN ASSESSMENT

Three of the greatest strengths of the humanistic approach are its attention to children's feelings and values as part of their real world (item 1), its concern for the individual's hopes and plans for the future (item 3), and its application of a humanistic view to child raising (item 4).

I agree with humanistic psychologists that the world that is most significant to the child or adolescent is the one she feels that she is experiencing at the moment. This attention to the phenomenal self seems to be a proper counterbalance to the heavy dependence on objectively observed actions of behaviorist views. The typical humanistic theory seeks to devise general principles that underlie different facets of growth, not just one aspect such as cognitive development. However, by concerning itself only with general principles, it has failed to trace the specific ways one aspect, such as language usage, develops in comparison to the ways other aspects, such as physical agility, grow. Hence, I have rated humanistic psychology high on item 1 but not at the top.

The humanistic approach has also given attention to the role of hopes, expectations, and plans for the future, facets of development that have been unduly neglected in many other theories. I have sought to recognize this contribution by a high rating on Item 3. But the manner in which humanistic theory explains the past appears to me to be imprecise, so the rating for item 3 is not the highest.

Two general principles of child rearing that humanistic theorists appear to support are (1) the adult seeks to perceive life from the emotional and cognitive perspectives of the child, and through such empathy, to treat the child in ways that show respect for and understanding of the child's phenomenal self and (2) the adult respects the child's right to be an individual with interests, talents, and emotions of her own. These principles are proper ones for child raising, so I have rated humanistic theory high on item 4. But again, the rating is not at the top of the scale, for I believe humanistic theory lacks the specificity that parents and teachers look for in their search for ways to treat the growing child. Of course, such a lack of specific directives to parents is perhaps a necessary part of a theory that emphasizes the unique character of each child.

On other dimensions of the rating sheet, I have judged that humanistic theory fares not so well. One problem is the theory's clarity (item 2). Humanistic writers describe their ideas in terms that can carry quite different meanings for different readers. When you speak of your *peak experiences*, of your *self-realization*, and of your *identity*, how am I to know whether I have experienced the same things that cause you to use these words? Likewise, when I

HUMANISTIC THEORY

How well do I think the theory meets the standards?

The Standards	Very Well	Moderately Well	Very Poorly
1. Reflects the real world of children	X		
2. Is clearly understandable		X	
3. Explains the past and predicts the future	X		
4. Guides child rearing	X		
5. Is internally consistent		?	
6. Is economical		?	
7. Is falsifiable			X
8. Stimulates new discoveries		X	
9. Is self-satisfying		X	

seek inner guidance in making a decision, how do I know which of my impulses represents my true inner self, the one that directs me toward self-actualization, and which impulses represent values I have learned from my environment, values that may conflict with my innate essence or calling?

Further puzzles have arisen from seemingly self-contradictory principles offered by humanistic writers. For example, Maslow wrote that "for self-actualizing people, there is a strong tendency for selfishness and unselfishness to fuse into a higher, superordinate unity" (1968, p. 207).

In addition, Maslow's system proposes that children are immature because they are at lower levels in the needs-fulfillment hierarchy and at lower levels on the scales of maturity. Yet he has stated that "the highest maturity is discovered to include a child-like quality" (Maslow, 1968, p. 207). If such is true, then how it operates requires a clearer explanation than the existing humanistic literature seems to provide.

In effect, one of the very strengths of humanistic theory, its insistence on the importance of unique personal experiences, leads also to one of its serious weaknesses—its imprecision in communicating the essence of one person's experience to another.

The same personal or existential quality of humanistic thought also contributes to the theory's lack of falsifiability (item 7). Ultimate validation depends on the individual's feeling that the theory is right, upon his finding the theory self-satisfying, regardless of any ground rules of objectivity or falsifiability. A theory, or an aspect of it, becomes false only if you feel it is not true to your inner essence or sense of unity.

In terms of the theory's internal consistency (item 5) and economy of explanation (item 6), I have placed question marks in the lower reaches of the appraisal scales. My puzzlement regarding these matters is occasioned by lack of precision in the definition of terms and of the relationships among variables. I find myself unable to make a careful estimate of internal consistency and economy of explanation when I fail to understand the elements of the system adequately. To a considerable extent, humanistic writing appears cast in unscientific, literary language. Rhetoric and obvious enthusiasm do not, I feel, sufficiently make up for what seems to be structural imprecision in the theory.

Over the past two decades or so, humanistic views have gained wide public attention and have influenced the way teachers, parents, social workers, and others perceive children (Brown, 1971, 1976; Fantini and Weinstein, 1968; Leff, 1978). However, this success of humanistic writers in attracting people's interest in perceiving children in ostensibly more "humane" ways has not led to a significant number of new discoveries about children. It is true that such proposals as Maslow's hierarchy of needs have been innovative. But in many instances, the matters of which humanistic writers speak have been matters that people of earlier times had sensed intuitively, and it has been the humanistic theorists' contribution to stimulate the rediscovery of these insights about the *self*, about feelings, and about hopes for the future. If you search through current child development textbooks or inspect journals in the field, you will not likely find many new items of knowledge about child growth contributed by theorists and researchers who have used humanistic approaches. Hence, I have marked the theory in the lower ranges of item 8. My purpose in giving such a rating is not to downgrade the significance of the humanistic persuasion but to note that it has not stimulated, at least not up to the present time, significant amounts of new knowledge about development.

Humanistic theory, then, appeals most to people who place a high degree of trust in their intuitive sense of what is true about the development of one's self. The theory is less convincing to people who require a tightly reasoned, logical model whose elements can be verified through experimental or observational approaches. However, humanistic theorists do not claim to have produced a finished, close-knit theory of child development. Instead, they see their proposals as constituting only a beginning toward a model of human nature "as a total, single, comprehensive system of psychology" (Maslow, 1968, p. 189). However, they also believe that their approach, with its emphasis on the experiencing self, holds more promise for revealing the essence of human personality than do such systems as psychoanalysis and behaviorism. I find it moderately self-satisfying (item 9).

FOR FURTHER READING

Buhler, Charlotte and Melanie Allen. (1972) *Introduction to Humanistic Psychology*. Monterey, Calif.: Brooks/Cole.

Maslow, Abraham H. (1970) *Motivation and Personality*. 2d ed. New York: Harper & Row.

Maslow, Abraham H. (1968) *Toward a Psychology of Being*. Princeton, N.J.: Van Nostrand.

PART 11

THEORIES FOR SPECIFIC EDUCATIONAL APPLICATIONS

A search for theoretical foundations on which to build instructional programs and evaluation practices.

Underlying every educational or therapeutic program for children and youths is a set of assumptions about how children develop. Each such pattern of assumptions, whether specifically described or left unstated, can be considered a theory of development, in the broad sense of the term *theory* as used throughout this book.

The purpose of Part 11 is to illustrate briefly four of the many dozens of theories or theory segments that have been devised to support educational practices. All four appear in Chapter 20.

The first of the sample theories is one constructed by Maria Montessori as the foundation for an early childhood education program she originally created for training children of below average intellectual abilities. Montessori's model is a modern representative of the educational tradition originating with Rousseau and passed down through subsequent years by the Swiss early childhood educator, Pestalozzi, and the German father of the kindergarten, Froebel. (See Chapter 21 for sources of Pestalozzi's and Froebel's own theoretical positions.) Montessori's views, then, illustrate a set of assumptions that undergird instructional practices for children in their preschool and elementary grade years.

A second area of educational practice from which to select a theory is the field of reading instruction. There are today many different curriculum designs and instructional materials for teaching reading, each built according to a particular cluster of assumptions about children's perceptual and cognitive growth. To illustrate one set of such assumptions, Chapter 20 includes a short description of the convictions about children on which Dolores Durkin founded the practices she recommends for teaching beginning reading to children in an English-speaking culture.

Over the past two decades educators specializing in the diagnosis and treatment of learning difficulties among children have given increased attention to what they refer to as perceptual-motor or psychoneurological disorders. This relatively new movement in remediation has spawned a variety of theories or theory segments, along with allied methods for diagnosing and treating learning disorders. The theory selected to represent ones in this cluster is a model described by Newell C. Kephart.

The fourth theory represents the work of psychologists and educators who, over more than half a century, have been tracing the development in children's art skills, particularly their drawing skills, and have been speculating about how these skills are related to such aspects of personality as general intelligence and personal-social adjustment. The version of such assessments of children's drawings included here is one produced by Elizabeth M. Koppitz.

The intention, then, of Chapter 20 is to offer brief samples of four models of development drawn from the great array of theories or partial theories found in the field of specific educational programs, therapeutic plans, and evaluation practices. Since each of the four descriptions is quite brief, none of them forms a sound basis on which to build a fair assessment of the theory involved. Thus, in contrast to the pattern used in previous chapters, I have not rated any of the four on the basis of the nine standards suggested in Chapter 1.

CHAPTER 20

APPLIED THEORIES: MONTESSORI, DURKIN, KEPHART, AND KOPPITZ

THE MONTESSORI METHOD

Maria Montessori (1870–1952) was the first woman to earn a medical degree from the University of Rome (1896). And in one of her first assignments as a physician, she was given charge of a center for mentally deficient children. Her observations of these children and her concern for their fate stimulated her to start a school for the mentally retarded.

On the basis of careful analyses of the behavior of the mentally deficient pupils, Montessori constructed a theory of child development, then created learning materials and activities to maximize the flowering of what she conceived to be the children's nature. Her educational approach, expanded to apply to children of all intellectual levels, has been known for seventy-five years as the Montessori method.

Her convictions about the child's basic nature follow the tradition of Jean Jacques Rousseau (1712–1778), Johann Heinrich Pestalozzi (1746–1827), and Friedrich Froebel (1782–1852). According to Montessori's view, within the child at birth is a predetermined model of psychic development, a sort of "spiritual embryo" embossed with the child's potential and the stages at which this potential can gradually evolve. But the achievement of the potential pattern is not guaranteed. How well it will be attained depends on the quality of the child's environment, particularly the degree to which the environment provides (1) suitable opportunities for interaction with the physical and social world and (2) freedom for the child to follow his natural drives toward self-realization and service to society.

A crucial element in Montessori's scheme is her view of motivation. She was convinced that the child by nature is intensely driven to explore and comprehend his world and to develop to his fullest potential. The problem in child rearing is not one of motivating children to learn. Rather, it is one of recognizing the sensitive periods in the growth sequence and of furnishing the sorts of opportunities and freedom that will take optimum advantage of the development of each such sensitive time in life. If suitable opportunities are not provided at a given period, the chance is lost, and the child's personality development is thereafter distorted.

Montessori identified five crucial stages of sensitivity, the first four of which come during the earliest three or four years of life. Period 1 involves a seeking for *order* in the environment, a seeking that is satisfied by consistent, precise physical and social surroundings that allow the child to readily classify his perceptions and form a clear internal map of his world, a map of the relationships among things. During period 2 the child seeks to *explore* things with tongue and hands, those two body elements that Montessori considered to be the chief tools of the growing intelligence. Such exploration prepares the neurological structures for learning language. If the child is not surrounded by language at this time, he will never master language use. In the third period the child seeks to *walk*, to become a mobile and highly active being. Period 4 is marked by a seeking to *inspect and manipulate* tiny objects. Period 5, which lasts for some years, focuses on observing and actively exploring *social relationships*.

Essential to psychic development throughout these sensitive periods is what Montessori called the *absorbent mind*. By this she meant that the child enters the world with an innate template for future development, but his mind is yet devoid of actual structure and contents. During the first three years he absorbs what he senses about him in a way that is not consciously directed. The absorbent mind during this period is of a type "that the adult cannot approach, that is to say, we cannot exert upon it any direct influence" (Montessori, 1967, p. 19). These first three years, then, form what Montessori regarded as the first significant subphase of growth.

The next subphase, still marked by an unconsciously directed structuring of the psychic processes, lasts from about age 3 to 6. This is actually a subphase of the major growth period of birth to age 6. At the end of this time, the child is ready for directed, consciously recognized instruction, that is, ready for school.

Beginning at age 6 the child enters the second major phase or period; this lasts till about age 12, when the child has mentally achieved "a state of health, strength, and assured ability" (Montessori, 1967, p. 19).

The third major period, divided into two subphases of equal length, extends from ages 12 to 18, when the child reaches maturity. During these years of adolescence, life is less stable and secure than during the prepuberal period that preceded it. The teenager displays indiscipline and rebellion.

For each of the stages of development, Montessori identified a series of principles of growth that were designed to guide proper child-raising practices. Her precisely structured teaching materials and learning activities were fashioned according to these principles to promote optimal natural development during each subphase of growth. These activities and their underlying theory of development distinguish the teaching practices found in Montessori schools today.

DURKIN'S THEORY:
CHARACTERISTICS OF YOUNG READERS

Of all the subjects taught in school, reading is considered the most crucial for academic success because children depend on their ability to read to learn most school subjects. If all children learned to read at the same age and with relative ease, then educators would not bother to create improved programs of instruction. However, this is not the case. Some children can read far earlier than others. Some learn easily, others with great difficulty, and some learn hardly at all, even as teenagers. Consequently, for several decades educators have regularly devised new approaches to reading instruction—with each approach founded on a particular set of convictions about the nature of children. Thus, there is an intimate relationship between a theorist's concept of development and the reading methods she will advocate.

To illustrate the way convictions about development influence a reading program, we will review several characteristics of the approach to early reading instruction recommended by Dolores Durkin. I have chosen her system because she gained attention in the 1970s for advocating that reading be taught to many children before they enter first grade, that is, at ages 3, 4, and 5. Why she adopted this nontraditional position can be explained by the beliefs she expresses about the nature of the preschool and primary grade child.

As a starting point, Durkin has rejected a series of commonly held beliefs that have determined the characteristics of many reading programs of the past. For example, she has disagreed with the convictions that:

1. Prior to entering first grade, children's personalities will be damaged if they face academic learning; therefore, pre-primary experiences for children should focus exclusively on physical and social development.

2. In first grade, most children are ready for the same sorts of reading experiences at about the same time in the school year.

3. Children are not ready to read until they have reached a mental age of 6½ years.

4. Young children have short attention spans, so they cannot be expected to concentrate on academic work, such as reading.

5. Gross visual-motor training, as recommended by such practitioners as Kephart (whose theory we review next), enhances children's reading skill, because reading is simply a higher level of a perceptual-motor hierarchy that has lower-level skills as foundation learnings (such lower-level skills as copying geometric forms and tracing figures embedded in a background of lines).

In contrast to the above beliefs, Durkin is convinced that there are marked individual differences among children in the sorts of reading (academic studies) they are ready for at a given age level. Some children are ready for simple reading, such as recognizing their printed name, at age 3 or 4. Others are not ready till later. Thus a reading program needs to be as individualized as possible. As a consequence, Durkin disagrees with the practice of requiring every kindergarten child to work on particular prereading skills, such as those that often appear in workbook programs. She also disagrees with every child's being forced to wait until first grade to start reading, with every child's being expected only to pursue physical and social activities before that time.

In Durkin's opinion, a mental age of 6½ years on an intelligence test is not a proper guide for determining reading readiness. Instead, she subscribes to Ausubel's definition of readiness as "the adequacy of existing capacity in relation to the demands of a given learning task" (Durkin, 1976, p. 76). With this definition as a guide, Durkin does not speak of reading readiness as a general trait related to all varieties of reading tasks. Rather, she views some reading tasks as being easier than others, and she judges a child's readiness for a specific task by how well he can attack that task. Hence, in her view, reading and readiness move in parallel. While a child is reading at a simple level (recognizing labels on the classroom door, window, and TV), he is getting ready for a more advanced task (learning phonics principles that enable him to sound out new words).

Durkin believes that the length of a child's attention span depends on such conditions as the intensity of his interest in a given activity, his level of success at it, and such physiological conditions as nutritional state and sleepiness. Hence, children can, without harm, focus on academic tasks at preprimary ages if the tasks are well suited to the individual child's interest, ability, and physiological condition.

Her reaction against the purported value of gross visual-motor training for promoting beginning reading is based on research studies that convince her that "learning experiences ought to be closely related to goals," that teachers should use actual letters, not geometrical shapes, to improve children's skills in discriminating among letters. "Use words, not pictures, to help with word discrimination" (Durkin, 1976, p. 87). In effect, she has adopted the belief from studies of transfer of training (something learned in one situation applied to improving performance in a different situation) that the greater the similarity of elements between two sorts of behavior, the more likely the skills in one of the behaviors will enhance skill with the others.

The foregoing examples, then, indicate ways that a recommended program in reading instruction derives its form to a great degree from the child development convictions to which its author subscribes.

PERCEPTUAL-MOTOR THEORIES: KEPHART'S VERSION

Just as Freud's stages of psychosexual development derived from his attempts to explain neurotic behavior, so in a similar way a variety of theories of perceptual-motor development have evolved from clinicians' attempts to explain certain learning disorders.

Prior to the 1950s and 1960s, teachers and clinical psychologists usually blamed children's learning problems on such causes as low intelligence, slow maturation, inadequate prior learning opportunities, or emotional distress. However, it was apparent that some children who were not learning to read or calculate normally did not suffer from any of these causes. A different source of the problem had to be sought. In the course of this search, clinicians identified symptoms commonly displayed by such children, and techniques were devised for helping them learn more adequately. At the same time, theories were proposed to account for both the learning disabilities and the steps taken to ameliorate them.

According to perceptual-motor theories, a child experiences learning difficulties because something is wrong with the circuits of her perceptual-motor system, the system of perceiving or taking in impressions, of interpreting them, and of expressing reactions in motor activities. Such a child does not suffer low "intelligence," which is known as *incapacity*, but seems instead to suffer a disordered circuitry in a nervous system that potentially is of adequate "intelligence." In other words, she suffers a *disability* that, hopefully, can be remedied by special teaching procedures and perhaps by chemotherapy.

Not all children who have been placed in the perceptual-motor disorder category exhibit the same symptoms. However, many of them have been found to display one or more of the following (adapted from Lerner, 1971, chap. 7.):

1. Erratic and inappropriate behavior on mild provocation
2. Hyperactivity and overreacting to stimuli; fidgeting, moving, chattering
3. Poor organization of behavior, both physical and mental
4. Distractibility of more than ordinary degree under ordinary circumstances; difficulty in concentrating on a task
5. Persistent faulty perceptions—seeing or hearing things wrong. When she looks at a picture, the child sees parts instead of wholes, or confuses the background with the foreground. With letters, she may see a capital *A* as three unrelated lines rather than a meaningful whole.
6. Awkwardness and consistently poor motor performance

7. Perseveration—continuing an activity once it has started
and having difficulty changing to another

Each theory of development that has been proposed to explain
such phenomena has certain unique features, but all tend to share
the following three assumptions:

1. Perceptual-motor skills are organized in the form of a developmental ladder or hierarchy, with mastery of the lower
skills on the ladder serving as a foundation for mastering
skills at higher levels.

2. From the time he is born, the child begins acquiring the
simpler skills at the bottom of the hierarchy, such as control of his limbs. As the years pass, he moves from gross-
motor skills to fine-motor skills and more precise perceptions, and by middle and late childhood he is able to succeed with such advanced tasks as reading, calculating, and
writing.

3. Incomplete mastery of any skill on the hierarchy makes it
either impossible or extremely difficult to master the
higher skills. Hence, the source of a child's difficulty in
learning to read may lie in his failure to master one of the
foundation skills earlier in the developmental sequence. To
solve his learning problem, he must return to the earlier
incomplete skill and master it. Then he will be prepared to
attack the higher-level skill with hope for success.

Of the several theories based on these notions, the most carefully formulated is perhaps that of Newell C. Kephart, who for
years headed a clinic for diagnosing and treating learning disabilities at Purdue University. In the developmental hierarchy Kephart
has described, the child passes through three major stages of
growth, each stage consisting of two or more substages.

The first of the child's information-processing stages is the
innate or *stimulus-response reflex* period. The child looks, blinks,
winces, turns, sucks, coughs, cries, and such by means of automatic or inborn responses to stimuli. She does not have to think
about or analyze a sudden light, a loud sound, the touch of a
nipple to her cheek, or the stroking of her foot. She responds to all
of these by *reflex action.*

But gradually over the first months of her life, the child's nervous system and musculature grow, and her original reflex actions

are expanded and modified by *conditioning*. The child now not only salivates in anticipation of food when a nipple touches her cheek, but she learns to anticipate food when she hears her mother's soothing voice close by and is lifted into someone's arms, because the nipple and food have so often been associated with the voice and the lifting.

During this same first period, several perceptual and motor processes have been evolving as a result of the child's inner growth and her experiences with her environment. These processes lead to the mastery of the second major stage of growth, the *perceptual stage*, which is the one on which Kephart has focused most of his attention. In the perceptual period the child progresses through a series of five processes that bring her to mastery of perception.

First, the child achieves *perceptual-motor matching*. She learns that the object she sees or the sound she hears belongs to the same object as the one she is touching. Eventually, after enough visual and tactile experience of this sort, the child will achieve the concept of, say, *table* because she has touched, sat at, crawled under, sat on top of, and bumped into many tables. A table, at a distance, even though it casts a small image on the retina of the eye, eventually will be recognized as the same table that was seen up close, where it cast a large image and from quite a different angle. All such conceptual interpretations, Kephart says, have their beginnings in the perceptual-motor matches that began during the first months of life. The practical implication of this theoretical interpretation is that if a child is to progress through the basic substage of matching, she needs an intact neural-muscular system and also many opportunities to view and manipulate or explore her environment physically.

Second, the child attains *figure–ground identification*. This means she must separate objects of attention from their backgrounds. This function begins during the child's differentiating of motor activities early in life. If she wishes to grasp a small object between the thumb and forefinger, she must build up muscle tension to activate the thumb and forefinger in opposition without activating the rest of the fingers, the arm, or any other part of the body. This is kinesthetic figure–ground control. At a later, more advanced level, the school-age child must achieve visual figure–ground control when she sees a printed page, isolating one word after another from the page in order to read what is printed there. In a classroom in which several groups of children are working at activities, the child must separate from the overall noise the voices of her own group and of the teacher if she is to work successfully in the setting.

A third process is that of attaining *movement control*, a skill that is built on successful perceptual-motor matching and figure–ground discrimination. The child watches her hand write or her foot kick a ball, and she uses the visual feedback information to coordinate the hand and leg movements to her liking. In doing so, she must isolate the appropriate sights and muscle movements from unrelated sights and movements. A school-age child whose feedback system is faulty or underdeveloped moves in bursts. She may have control when she begins her pencil stroke, but she cannot alter the pencil's direction or speed until it has darted to the end of the stroke. As a result, her writing, drawing, lifting, pouring, fitting together, dancing, and the like appear careless and awkward.

A fourth phase consists of *systematic exploration* of the environment. The child no longer gropes at random or explores objects aimlessly. Instead, her search is guided by the eyes, by visual intent. Perceptual information now takes on a continuity it never had before, a continuity that "will be reflected in all future processing of information, for relationships are now more significant to the child than elements. The square is now more important than its four lines" (Kephart, 1971, p. 29).

Finally the child achieves *intersensory integration*. She not only matches sight and movement, but coordinates simultaneous messages from the other senses—the sound, taste, and smell that accompany the sight and movement—as well.

When the child has progressed through all of the foregoing substeps, she is said to have mastered the perceptual stage of development. She has learned relationships among movements, sights, and sounds so that now she can intellectually derive new relationships by manipulating the structures she has experienced.

> Qualities which do not exist per se in the concrete world can be generated through such manipulations. . . . The squareness of a square form does not itself exist as a quality of any perception. It emerges from the manipulation in an orderly fashion of the elements (sides and angles) against each other within the perceptual structure. Once having emerged, it becomes an element in itself, and it is this emergent element, not the concrete elements, upon which we depend for meaningfulness (Kephart, 1971, p. 30).

The child thus passes from the second major stage of perceptual-motor growth into the third and final one, the *conceptual pe-*

riod. A concept may be thought of as a characteristic abstracted from a variety of actual experiences or objects. *Squareness,* for example, is a concept. The child's grasping the idea of "squareness" or "roundness" or "table" moves him into the stage of concept development.

Prior to reaching this level, the child could not compare objects or experiences for their similarities and differences unless the objects were present at the same time. Now, with his memories of concrete experiences in store, he is freed from this space and time limitation. He can now classify recalled experiences into groups in order to compare and contrast them in terms of their abstract characteristics. He recognizes patterns of likenesses and differences and learns to move to an even higher level of abstraction—comparing one pattern with another. Eventually he can grow up to speak meaningfully of the solar system, gravity, nutritional balance, economic supply and demand, the Middle Ages, sportsmanship, romanticism, and holophrasis. It should be apparent that achieving Kephart's conceptual level of development is the same as reaching Piaget's period of formal operations and Vygotsky's higher verbal thought.

Having now described the stages in Kephart's system, we are prepared to consider his answers to several of the traditional questions asked about stage theories.

Question 1: Is growth gradual and continuous, or does it proceed in distinct steps? Kephart says it does both. As the solid line in Figure 20.1 shows, Kephart believes that as the months pass a child accumulates skills and knowledge that carry him gradually toward maturity (the upward sloping segments). But when sufficient experience has been accumulated, the child moves up sharply (the vertical segments) to a new stage. Kephart has applied the term *normative* to the gradual-growth portions and the term *Piaget-type* to the abrupt movement from one substage to another.

> When the [current stage's] structure has been elaborated sufficiently to permit the formation of a pattern, the new quality would emerge as an "aha" idea upon solidification of the pattern (Kephart, 1971, p. 17).

Question 2: If a child does not completely master the skills at a given substage, does her development stop? Does she become fixated at that point? Kephart gives neither an absolute yes or no as an answer. Instead, he says that children who do not master a substage may continue to improve in physical and intellectual skills, but that their progress is distorted. The distortion consists of using lower-level information-processing patterns to deal with problems solved far more readily by higher-level processes. A child might progress in arithmetic computational skills by rote memorizing addition combinations and multiplication tables, but she does not truly understand such concepts as place value, carrying, or even multiplication itself. Hence, she can solve certain problems when they are set up in computational form, but she cannot solve others, such as everyday practical problems requiring such operations.

When a child thus fails to make the stepwise jump to a higher pattern of perceptual-motor processing, she still progresses in a

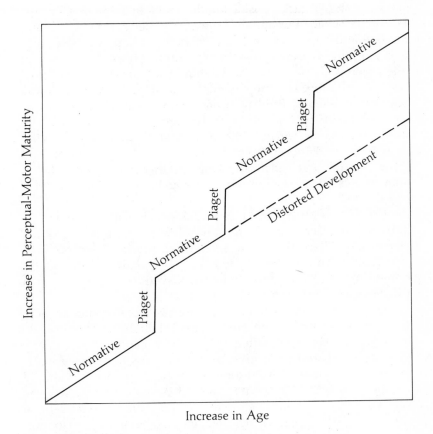

Increase in Age

Figure 20.1   Kephart's Concept of Developmental Stages (Adapted from Kephart, 1971, p. 18)

limited manner—making gains in the *quantity* of development but not the *quality*. Such a child's progress is shown by the broken line in Figure 20.1. According to Kephart's analysis, the child's progress is uneven. Some aspects of thinking and acting move ahead, others do not. The ones that move ahead through special training, such as rote memorization, have been labeled *splinter skills*. Kephart says the fact that a child displays such skills may mislead teachers and parents into believing she is progressing satisfactorily in development and that her areas of deficiency are the result of other factors, such as laziness, obstinacy, or poor attention span. To discover whether a child's problem is indeed that of splinter skills, Kephart has devised a series of tests of perceptual-motor function.

Examples of tasks posed for the child in Kephart's Purdue Perceptual Motor Survey are (1) walking along a narrow beam, forward and backward, to show balance, (2) hopping, skipping, and jumping to show gross body control, (3) touching parts of one's own body on command to show body awareness and posture, (4) imitating arm movements while standing, as in a Simon Says game, to show fluidity of body movement, (5) drawing circles and specified lines on a chalkboard to show accuracy and fluidity of arm movement, (6) ocular pursuit—watching a moving object about 20 inches from the face to show eye control, and (7) with paper and pencil, drawing specified geometric forms to show eye–hand control in producing small figures (Kephart, 1960, pp. 120–155).

Question 3: Must a child go through each major stage and its substeps in order to reach the conceptual level, or can he skip a step or stage? Kephart contends that the sequence he has outlined is invariant. To achieve a truly conceptual mode of information processing, the child must have worked his way through each prior perceptual step in the hierarchy.

However, there are many puzzling cases that do not seem to fit Kephart's system. Some children read skillfully and manipulate mathematical concepts with ease, yet their handwriting is nearly illegible, they are hyperactive, and their gross body movements are jerky and clumsy. According to Kephart's theory this should not be possible. The children should have had to master the eye–hand feedback skills before they could achieve the conceptual skills needed for mature reading and mathematical reasoning. Again, Kephart has labeled such anomalies *splinter skills*, the forced learning of a particular skill in isolation from the general development of the overall perceptual-motor system. However, it would appear that such a facile dismissal of the exceptions to his rule is a weakness in his scheme. A better explanation of what is really occurring in the hierarchy is needed. The hierarchy he has proposed may not be invariant—there may be more than one route of development toward the conceptual-level skills of reading, mathematical reasoning, and the like. In effect, not everyone has been satisfied with the splinter skill explanation.

Question 4: Can children regress to an earlier stage once they have achieved a more advanced level of information processing? Kephart says no, they cannot.

> Development is irreversible. . . . Each stage in the developmental process, once established, becomes compulsive. . . . Earlier methods of processing drop out immediately and data previously processed are reprocessed in terms of the new program. Thus, once development has occurred, it cannot be erased (Kephart, 1971, pp. 40–41).

However, the impression that a child has regressed can occur under two circumstances, according to Kephart. First, when the child faces an unduly complicated problem, he may turn back from conceptual to motoric exploration (for example, he tries fitting the model airplane wing to the fuselage by hand if he cannot judge it adequately by calculations) even though he has reached the higher conceptual stage in his information-processing system (and can interpret the airplane assembly diagram fairly well). Second, emotional disturbances may cause the child to subtract some of the more mature elements of his established behavior patterns, thus causing him to give the appearance of having slipped back to a lower level of perceptual-motor activity. However, in Kephart's opinion, the fact that this is not true regression is proven by the recovery of the more mature behavior when the emotional distress is removed.

To sum up the essence of Kephart's stage theory, we note that he conceives development as a process of both gradual increments and periodic leaps to a new stage. Furthermore, development is unidirectional and irreversible. Deviations from this pattern are explained as instances of either splinter skills or apparent slips backward under vexing circumstances, slips that are temporary and superficial, not instances of true regression.

On the basis of his theory, Kephart has devised his test activities to estimate where in the hierarchy a child's perceptual-motor development may have gone awry. And on the basis of this diagnosis, he provides activities or exercises intended to enable the child to master those lower steps in the sequence that have not yet been achieved and, then, progress through subsequent steps satisfactorily.

ART DEVELOPMENT THEORIES:
KOPPITZ'S VERSION

For a long time, art teachers and child psychologists have recognized that as a child grows older his drawings change in somewhat predictable ways. Over the past half century a variety of schemes have been devised for interpreting the meaning of these changes—meaning in terms of mental development and personal-social adjustment.

The most significant early interpreter of drawings was Florence Goodenough (1886–1940), whose doctoral dissertation at Stanford University laid out a system for scoring children's sketches of the human figure so as to reflect levels of mental growth. In her 1926 book *Measurement of Intelligence by Drawings*, she agreed with views from the newly evolving child-study movement "that the drawings made by young children have an intellectual rather than an aesthetic origin. They are determined by concept development rather than by visual imagery or by manual skill. . . . A child draws what he knows, rather than what he sees" (Goodenough, 1926, pp. 12–13). Goodenough's system of scoring children's figure drawings, revised and brought up to date by Dale B. Harris in 1963, remains today the most popular method for estimating mental growth from drawings.

Over the years clinical psychologists and researchers have proposed that drawings by children "reflect more than sheer developmental or conceptual maturity" (Harris, 1963, p. 38). Drawings also appear to tell something about the child's emotional condition and his personal-social relationships. Perhaps the best known work on this topic has been Machover's *Personality Projection in the Drawing of the Human Figure* (1949). Machover proposed that

> The drawing of a person, in involving a projection of the body image, provides a natural vehicle for the expression of one's body needs and conflicts. Successful drawing interpretation has proceeded on the hypothesis that the figure drawn is related to the individual who is drawing with the same intimacy characterizing that individual's gait, his handwriting, or any other of his expressive movements (1949, p. 5).

Subsequently, Elizabeth Munsterberg Koppitz, a clinical psychologist in Yorktown Heights, New York, began conducting studies to incorporate both the mental-development and personality-analysis aspects into one system for estimating the meaning of children's figure drawings. Her work, as represented in the 1968 volume *Psychological Evaluation of Children's Human Figure Drawings* has been selected to represent theories and evaluation schemes in the realm of art or drawing development.

Some systems for judging drawings cover a rather wide age range, from the scribblings of two-year-olds through the sophisticated sketches of older adolescents. Koppitz's system, however, is restricted to the elementary school ages of 5 through 12. Her study of human drawings by 931 boys and 925 girls in regular elementary school classes, along with drawings by a smaller number of emotionally disturbed and brain-injured children, led her to conclude that such children's figure drawings provide signs of mental development and personal-social adjustment.

The thirty mental-development indicators that she identified consist of the number of elements included in the drawing (such as the head, eyes, nose, legs, clothing) and the manner in which the elements are drawn (for example, arms are drawn in two dimensions rather than in one). The emotional or attitudinal indicators consist of the style in which elements are drawn (such as whether the eyes are crossed) and the omission or inclusion of certain elements at a particular age level (omitting the legs at age 11 or including genital organs at any age).

Koppitz considered the thirty development items valid signs of intellectual growth because they increased regularly with increasing age. In addition, significant correlation was found between scores on these items and scores on traditional intelligence tests. For instance, correlations of drawing scores with the Stanford-Binet test ranged from .55 to .63 at different age levels and with the Wechsler Intelligence Scale for Children from .45 to .80 (Koppitz, 1968, pp. 30–31).

Although Koppitz's interpretation of developmental signs coincides with the traditional interpretation by Goodenough, the interpretation of emotional indicators differs from that adopted by a variety of other theorists. Some writers in the field have proposed that a child's figure drawing reveals the core of his personality, the essence of his permanent *self*. According to this view, a drawing made by a child at one time will lead to the same conclusions about his personality as a drawing made a few weeks or a few months later. Other writers have suggested that the child's drawing is his image of his actual appearance—the way he thinks he looks to others. Koppitz, however, disagrees with both of these interpretations. She believes instead that emotional indicators in

EXAMPLES OF SCORING WITH
DEVELOPMENTAL AND EMOTIONAL ITEMS

For each age level, Koppitz has identified four categories of *developmental items*, that is, elements that children may include in their drawings of a person: (1) *expected items*, elements found in 86 percent to 100 percent of drawings at a given age level; (2) *common items*, those found in 51 percent to 85 percent of drawings; (3) *not-unusual items*, those in 15 percent to 50 percent of drawings; (4) *exceptional items*, elements found in 15 percent or fewer of the drawings. In the scoring scheme she has devised, Koppitz has found it sufficient to use only the first (expected) and fourth (exceptional) items to estimate a developmental or "intelligence" range for a child. Figures 20.2 and 20.3 illustrate drawings scored by Koppitz's system. (Figure 20.2 is 100 percent of original size; Figure 20.3 has been reduced to 65 percent of original size in order to include it here.)

In Figure 20.2, the sketch by nine-year-old Mikie contains all ten expected developmental items for boys age 9—head, eyes, nose, mouth, body, legs, arms, feet, arms in two dimensions, and legs in two dimensions. The drawing also contains a variety of common and not-unusual items, and it displays one exceptional element—the profile view of the face. The single emotional indicator is the small size of the figure (less than 2 inches tall). In Koppitz's system, Mikie's score places him in the average to superior range (I.Q. 90 to 135). His actual

Figure 20.2   Drawing Scored by Koppitz System

Figure 20.3 Drawing Scored by Koppitz System

intelligence quotient as measured on the Stanford-Binet Intelligence Scale is 133, indicating a mental age of 12.

In Figure 20.3, the sketch by twelve-year-old Brenda contains all fifteen expected items for girls age 12—head, eyes, nose, mouth, body, legs, arms, feet, arms in two dimensions, legs in two dimensions, hair, neck, arms hanging down, arms correctly attached at the shoulder, and two items of clothing. The drawing includes a variety of common and not-unusual items (hands, eyebrow, fingers, and others) but no exceptional ones. The one emotional indicator in the sketch is the partially shaded face (apparently intended as freckles). However, according to Koppitz, usually more than one such indicator is required before the child's emotional adjustment is seriously questioned. Brenda's developmental score suggests that she is in the average to high average range of mental ability (I.Q. 85 to 120). Brenda's more specific intelligence quotient, according to the Wechsler Intelligence Scale for Children (WISC) is 112. (Cases from the files of Shirley M. Thomas.)

In sum, Koppitz has used developmental items to compute an estimated broad range within which the child's mental ability seems to fall, but she has not recommended that her scoring method is suitable for deriving a precise intelligence quotient. Furthermore, she has suggested that more than one of the thirty possible emotional indicators must be present before it is usually appropriate to conclude from the drawing that the child may suffer personal-social maladjustment.

---

the drawing reflect the child's interpersonal relationships, that is, his attitudes toward himself and toward "the significant others in his life" (Koppitz, 1968, pp. 3–4). She believes further that a drawing may reveal a child's reactions to life's stresses and the anxieties he feels at the moment. As the conditions of his life change from day to day, his drawings will alter to reflect changes in his attitudes. According to this viewpoint, a single drawing is not a valid indicator of core personality traits over an extended period of time.

As Koppitz sought to identify which properties of children's drawings were more the result of internal maturation than of environmental influences, she investigated the effects of (1) the drawing medium used, (2) school instruction in drawing, (3) special drawing ability as contrasted to general intellectual growth, and

(4) social and cultural experiences. She also compared the drawings of boys and girls (Koppitz, 1968, pp. 21–26, 33–34).

The two drawing media Koppitz compared were pencil and crayon. She discovered that generally the quality of children's drawings was the same whether they used pencil or crayon. When she compared the apparent influence of one year of kindergarten instruction on drawings, she concluded that the improvement in human figure sketches at the kindergarten level, at least, was due primarily to maturation rather than school training. Furthermore, comparisons of drawings of boys and girls suggested that girls' earlier general maturation is revealed in their higher developmental scores at ages 5 and 6 but that by the latter elementary school ages boys have caught up and in some cases have surpassed the girls.

Koppitz's system of rating children's mental development, then, is founded on the assumption that the appearance of the thirty developmental items in drawings of children ages 5 through 12 is governed mainly by genetically controlled maturation rather than environmental influences. Furthermore, scores derived from developmental items correlate significantly with scores children receive on standard general intelligence tests. However, the fact that the correlations are still far from perfect suggests that drawings and such tests do not measure exactly the same things.

In regard to personal-social adjustment, Koppitz first compared features of apparently well-adjusted children's drawings with features of children being treated for adjustment problems. By such a comparison she identified elements that appeared to differentiate the well-adjusted boys and girls from those experiencing personal-social difficulties. Second, she used other information about a child, coupled with psychological theory from a neo-Freudian tradition, to speculate about the likely meaning of other features of a child's drawing. Through this process she found thirty-eight characteristics of figure drawings that she felt would be likely indicators of emotional problems. To check on the validity of the characteristics, she then analyzed drawings of well-adjusted and maladjusted children according to three criteria. In order for an attribute of a drawing to be accepted as a distinguishing sign (adapted from Koppitz, 1968, p. 35):

1. It must be clinically valid; it must differentiate between drawings of children with emotional problems and those without such problems.

2. It must be unusual, that is, occur infrequently on drawings of normal children (on less than 16 percent of drawings at a given age level).

3. It must not be related to maturation, meaning that it should not increase solely on the basis of increase in age.

Of the thirty-eight potential indicators, only thirty met all three standards. They were then placed in three categories: quality signs, special features, and omissions (Koppitz, 1968, p. 37).

The *quality signs* are: transparent features (lines overlap so we seem to see one body part through another), poor integration of the figure's parts, shading (of the face or part of it, of the body, of limbs, of hands, or of neck), gross asymmetry of limbs, figure slanting by 15 degrees or more, tiny figure (less than 2 inches tall), or big figure (more than 9 inches tall on 8½-by-11-inch sheet).

The *special features* are: tiny head (one-tenth of total height of figure), crossed eyes, teeth, short arms, long arms, arms clinging, big hands, hands cut off, legs together, genitals, monster or grotesque figure, three figures, clouds or rain.

The *omissions* are of: eyes, nose, mouth, body, arms, legs, feet, neck.

When Koppitz applied these emotional indicators in the analysis of drawings, she arrived at two generalizations. First, the presence of a single indicator in a child's sketch does not necessarily mean the child is maladjusted or has emotional problems. Some well-adjusted children might have one sign in their drawings. However, "two or more Emotional Indicators . . . are highly suggestive of emotional problems and unsatisfactory interpersonal relations" (Koppitz, 1968, p. 42). Second, it is necessary to know a child's age and to be aware of the developmental signs typical of that age in order to determine whether the omission of an element in a drawing is emotionally significant. For example, omitting the neck is expected (normal) for six-year-olds. But by age 10 and above, such an omission becomes an emotional indicator. In effect, omissions above the age at which they are common "may reflect immaturity or malfunctioning due to retardation and/or emotional disturbances" (Koppitz, 1968, p. 36).

In addition to counting the emotional indicators that appear in a drawing, Koppitz has applied her general clinical intuition to inferring what the pattern of the child's drawing means in his emotional life. And it is at this point that subjective judgment begins to play a larger role in interpreting drawings. It is also at this point that disagreements arise among theorists and among clinicians about whether an interpretation truly reflects the child's personality or whether it unduly reflects the clinician's personal biases or perhaps the clinician's own emotional distress. In short, speculating beyond the objective data involves risk of error. Koppitz has been aware of this risk and has suggested that as a proper safeguard, a child's drawings should not be subjected to blind interpretation. A diagnosis should not be made solely on the basis of a figure drawing. Instead, the drawing should be viewed in the context of other information about the child, information based on observations of the child's behavior, interviews with the child and with people well acquainted with him, records of his health and behavior history, test results, and the like. Within this context of other data, the figure drawings assist the clinician in estimating the state of the child's interpersonal concerns.

By having a system of both developmental signs and emotional indicators, Koppitz has been able to use her scheme to help answer several types of questions about children. First, the developmental items have enabled her to estimate how intellectually mature children are. She proposes that her figure-drawing test is particularly useful in screening children for kindergarten or first-grade admission, since the method does not depend on the child's skills of reading, speaking, or writing. Second, she proposes that the emotional items aid in identifying disturbed children, in deriving hypotheses about why they are disturbed, and in estimating their recovery rate as they draw figures periodically during a series of treatment experiences.

Furthermore, Koppitz has identified both developmental and emotional signs that seem indicative of particular disorders, so that figure drawings might aid in establishing a diagnostic category for a child. For instance, she found eleven developmental items and eight emotional indicators that more often appear on drawings of brain-injured children of normal intelligence than on drawings of non-brain-injured children of normal intelligence (Koppitz, 1968, pp 175–176).

In effect, Koppitz's scheme is not simply intended to shed light on drawing behavior as an aspect of development of interest to theorists. More importantly, it is intended to serve clinicians as a diagnostic instrument for guiding the identification and treatment of children who suffer retardation or disturbed interpersonal relations.

CONCLUSION

In Chapter 20 we have briefly inspected four theories or theory segments designed to aid educators and clinicians in evaluating children's characteristics and devising instructional or therapeutic programs. I selected these four as representatives of different types of theoretical viewpoints. Other examples of types of applied theories are cited in Chapter 21.

FOR FURTHER READING

Lillard, Paula Polk. (1972) *Montessori, A Modern Approach.* New York: Schocken. This is an up-to-date review of Montessori theory and teaching methods.

Montessori, Maria. (1967) *The Absorbent Mind.* New York: Dell. A representative key publication by Montessori herself.

Durkin, Dolores. (1976) *Teaching Young Children to Read.* 2d ed. Boston: Allyn and Bacon. Durkin's reading methods and the theoretical foundations on which the methods are built.

Kephart, Newell C. (1960, 1st ed.; 1971, 2d ed.) *The Slow Learner in the Classroom.* Columbus, Ohio: Charles E. Merrill. The theoretical background presented in the two editions differs in a few respects.

Koppitz, Elizabeth Munsterberg. (1968) *Psychological Evaluation of Children's Human Figure Drawings.* New York: Grune and Stratton.

PART 12

SOURCES OF FURTHER THEORIES

The purpose of Chapter 21 is to suggest sources of additional theories or partial theories in which readers might be interested. The list of items included in the chapter is far from definitive. It is merely a sampling from among the scores of theoretical models in the professional literature. Sources of other theories are the bibliographies in child development textbooks and in journals that publish studies of development.

Of the available textbooks treating theories of development, the following four are perhaps the most useful:

Baldwin, A. L. (1967) *Theories of Child Development.* New York: Wiley.

Langer, J. (1969) *Theories of Development.* New York: Holt, Rinehart, and Winston.

Lerner, R. M. (1976) *Concepts and Theories of Human Development.* Reading, Mass.: Addison-Wesley.

Maier, H. W. (1978) *Three Theories of Child Development: Erik H. Erikson, Jean Piaget, and Robert R. Sears.* 3d ed. New York: Harper & Row.

CHAPTER 21

AN ANNOTATED BIBLIOGRAPHY

Ausubel, D. P. and E. V. Sullivan. (1970) *Theory and Problems of Child Development*. 2d ed. New York: Grune and Stratton. In the words of the authors, this is intended to be "a body of relatively doctrine-free theory dealing exclusively with the major kinds of generalizations that can be made about the nature and regulation of development as a process."

Ayres, A. J. (1972) *Sensory Integration and Learning Disorders.* Los Angeles: Western Psychological Services. Ayres's theory proposes (1) that a child's disordered ability to integrate sensory input (visual, auditory, tactile) accounts for some sorts of learning problems and (2) that special activities that enhance sensory integration as the child develops will make academic learning easier for children.

Baldwin, A. L., C. P. Baldwin, V. Castillo-Vales, and B. Seegmiller. (1971) "Cross-cultural Similarities in the Development of the Concept of Kindness" in W. W. Lambert and R. Weisbrod (eds.), *Comparative Perspectives on Social Psychology.* Boston: Little, Brown. The authors interpret the development of kindness from the viewpoint of attribution theory. For a further treatment of the same perspective, see: C. P. Baldwin and A. L. Baldwin. (1970) "Children's Judgments of Kindness." *Child Development*, Vol. 41, pp. 29–47.

Barsch, R. H. (1967) *Achieving Perceptual-Motor Efficiency.* Vol. 1. and (1968) *Enriching Perception and Cognition.* Vol. 2. Seattle, Wash.: Special Child Publications. Barsch's movigenic model (a theory of movement as it relates to learning) proposes that difficulties in learning are associated with the child's inefficient interaction in space.

Bloom, L. (1970) *Language Development: Form and Function in Emerging Grammars.* Cambridge, Mass.: Massachusetts Institute of Technology. Bloom analyzes three children's early speech by means of Chomsky's theory of generative transformational grammar.

Bloom, L. (1973) *One Word at a Time.* The Hague: Mouton. In Chapter 5 Bloom proposes a theory of two alternative strategies for the way one-year-olds learn syntax as they move from one-word to two-word utterances.

Braine, M. D. S. (1971) "The Acquisition of Language" in C. Reed (ed.), *The Learning of Language.* New York: Appleton. Braine interprets early language development from a pivotal open grammar perspective.

Bridges, K. M. B. (1966) "The Development of Emotions" in R. L. Wrenn (ed.), *Basic Contributions to Psychology: Readings.* Belmont, Calif.: Wadsworth, pp. 36–48. Bridges suggests that original diffuse excitement at birth first differentiates into distress and delight, then into seven more specific emotions by age 2, and subsequently into seventeen emotions by age 5.

Chomsky, Noam. (1968) *Language and Mind.* New York: Harcourt, Brace, Jovanovich. Chomsky proposes that children have an inherent sense of grammatical form.

Connolly, K. and J. Bruner. (1974) *The Growth of Competence.* London: Academic. These authors describe how early competence and its cultivation may affect the later functioning of the "more mature organism."

Delacato, C. H. (1966) *Neurological Organization and Reading.* Springfield, Ill.: Thomas. Believing that ontogeny recapitulates phylogeny, Delcato states that (1) the child's nervous system matures by regular stages from the spinal medula to the cerebral cortex and (2) that different behaviors (from gross body movements to high-level intellectual functions) parallel these functions. Disorders of behavioral development are seen as symptoms of inadequate neurological development.

Froebel, F. W. A. (1889) *The Education of Man* (trans., W. N. Hailmann). New York: Appleton. Froebel (1782–1852), the originator of the kindergarten movement, believed that "the spirit of God . . . lives in nature, produces, fosters, and unfolds everything, as the common life principle. . . . All the child is ever to be and become, lies—however slightly indicated—in the child and can be attained only through development from within outward." He traces development through four main stages.

Frostig, M. and P. Maslow. (1973) *Learning Problems in the Classroom*. New York: Grune and Stratton. This approach to treating learning difficulties is based on a visual-perception theory supplemented by behavior modification, humanistic psychology, psychoanalytic concepts, and cognitive development theory.

Getman, G. N. (1965) "The Visuomotor Complex in the Acquisition of Learning Skills" in J. Hellmuth (ed.), *Learning Disorders, Vol. 1*. Seattle, Wash.: Special Child Publications. Getman, an optometrist, has constructed a model of perceptual-motor development levels stressing the role of visual perception in determining the efficiency of a child's intellectual functioning.

Gibson, E. J. (1969) *Principles of Perceptual Learning and Development*. New York: Appleton-Century-Crofts. Gibson conceives of perceptual learning as an active, self-regulating process enabling the child to become increasingly skilled at extracting and differentiating information that is available in the environment.

Guilford, J. P. (1967) *The Nature of Human Intelligence*. New York: McGraw-Hill. Pp. 413–438. Guilford proposes that the mature intellect is composed of a multitude of separate abilities. He rejects the theory that as the child develops the various abilities differentiate gradually out of an initial general ability. He supports the idea that abilities are genetically differentiated from the earliest years.

Heafford, M. (1967) *Pestalozzi, His Thought and Its Relevance Today*. London: Methuen. Pestalozzi (1746–1827), a Swiss educator, followed Rousseau's lead in claiming that the child is innately good "and seeks the good; his conscience only allows him to feel secure when he does the good; and if he is evil, it is surely because the way has been blocked, along which he wanted to be good." The trick in child rearing is to discover nature's patterns of growth and to present the child with a sequence of experiences suited to each growth step.

Himmelweit, T. and B. Swift. (1969) "A Model for Understanding of School as a Socializing Agent" in P. H. Mussen, J. Langer, and M. Covington (eds.), *Trends and Issues in Developmental*

Psychology. New York: Holt, Rinehart, and Winston, pp. 154–181. A model is created for interpreting longitudinal data on the influence of types of schools on socialization.

Hunt, J. McV. (1961) *Intelligence and Experience*. New York: Ronald. Hunt's theory supports Piaget's view of the nature of intelligence.

Huxley, A. (1932) *Brave New World*. New York: Harper. Huxley pictures child-raising practices at some vague future time in a society that controls life carefully, eliminating much of today's individuality and opportunity for personal decision.

Janov, A. (1973) *The Feeling Child*. New York: Simon and Schuster. The growth of children's emotional reactions is pictured from the viewpoint of the primal theory first described in Janov's *The Primal Scream*.

Lowenfeld, V. (1957) *Creative and Mental Growth*. New York: Macmillan. Lowenfeld describes stages in art productions of children and tells what he believes these productions reflect about mental growth. The 1957 edition is the most authentic statement of Lowenfeld's views before his death; subsequent revisions of the book have been substantially altered by his posthumous co-author.

McNeill, D. (1970) *The Acquisition of Language: The Study of Developmental Psycholinguistics*. New York: Harper & Row. McNeill's description reflects a belief in an innate sense of language structure in children.

Neumann, E. (1973) *The Child*. New York: G. P. Putnam's Sons. A description of development from the viewpoint of Carl Jung. Chapter 5 depicts stages in the child's ego development.

Schlesinger, I. M. (1971) "Production of Utterances and Language Acquisition" in D. I. Slobin (ed.), *The Ontogenesis of Grammar*. New York: Academic, pp. 63–101. A model of sentence production based on a child's intention is proposed to replace the grammatical level of deep structure with semantic intentions. The model forms a generative-semantics approach.

Stemmer, N. (1973) *An Empiricist Theory of Language Acquisition*. The Hague: Mouton. The steps of a child's acquiring an understanding of language are explained chiefly by means of classical conditioning.

Stevenson, H. W. (1972) *Children's Learning*. New York: Appleton-Century-Crofts. Results of hundreds of experiments are summarized as generalizations about how children learn, with most experiments interpreted from one or more of four theoretical positions: associative-mediational, reinforcement, cognitive, and perceptual.

Strauss, A. and L. Lehtinen. (1947) *Psychopathology and Education of the Brain-Injured Child*. Vol. 1. New York: Grune and Stratton. On the basis of their theory that perceptual handicaps cause certain learning disorders, the authors suggest remedial measures composed of visual-perception activities.

Sullivan, H. S. (1953) *The Interpersonal Theory of Psychiatry*. New York: Norton. Sullivan's model shows how children's personalities develop in Western societies by means of the interpersonal relations in which they engage as they pass through six stages of social-psychological growth.

Turiel, E. (1969) "Developmental Processes in the Child's Moral Thinking" in P. H. Mussen, J. Langer, and M. Covington (eds.), *Trends and Issues in Developmental Psychology*. New York: Holt, Rinehart, and Winston, pp. 92–133. The writer compares interpretations of moral development from several viewpoints, including those of Kohlberg and Piaget.

van der Geest, T., R. Gerstel, R. Appel, and B. T. Tervoort. (1973) *The Child's Communicative Competence*. The Hague: Mouton. Studies by the writers are used to support the theory that the language of middle-class and lower-class preschool children is different in content but essentially equivalent in structure.

Vaughn, G. M. (1972) "Concept Formation and the Development of Ethnic Awareness" in A. R. Brown (ed.), *Prejudice in Children*. Springfield, Ill.: Thomas, pp. 17–27. On the basis of his research, the author proposes that "where the concept of race is involved, an identification response (meaning that the child identifies with one or more perceived objects or people) preceded ontogenetically the more usual discrimination response."

Wall, C. (1974) *Predication: A Study of Its Development*. The Hague: Mouton. Wall offers generalizations about what children affirm or assert about the subjects of their sentences.

REFERENCES

Adler, A. (1930) "Individual Psychology" in C. Murchinson (ed.), *Psychologies of 1930*. Worchester, Mass.: Clark University.

Adler, A. (1927) *The Practice and Theory of Individual Psychology*. New York: Harcourt, Brace, and World.

Alexander, R. D. and P. W. Sherman. (1977) "Local Mate Competition and Parental Investment in Social Insects." *Science*, Vol. 196, pp. 494–500.

Allport, G. W. (1961) *Pattern and Growth in Personality*. New York: Holt, Rinehart, and Winston.

Allport, G. W. (1968) *The Person in Psychology: Selected Essays*. Boston: Beacon.

Alston, W. P. (1971) "Comments on Kohlberg's 'From Is to Ought' " in T. Mischel, *Cognitive Development and Epistemology*. New York: Academic.

Anastasi, A. (1958) "Heredity, Environment, and the Question 'How?' " *Psychological Review*, Vol. 65, pp. 197–208.

Aries, P. (1962) *Centuries of Childhood*. New York: Knopf.

Ausubel, D. P. and E. V. Sullivan. (1970) *Theory and Problems of Child Development*. 2d ed. New York: Grune and Stratton.

Baldwin, A. L. (1967) *Theories of Child Development*. New York: Wiley.

Bandura, A. (1969) *Principles of Behavior Modification*. New York: Holt, Rinehart, and Winston.

Bandura, A. (1977) *Social Learning Theory*. Englewood Cliffs, N.J.: Prentice-Hall.

Bandura, A. and R. H. Walters. (1963) *Social Learning and Personality Development*. New York: Holt, Rinehart, and Winston.

Barker, R. G. (1968) *Ecological Psychology*. Stanford, Calif.: Stanford.

Barker, R. G., T. Dembo, and K. Lewin. (1943) "Frustration and Regression" in R. G. Barker, J. S. Kounin, and H. F. Wright, *Child Behavior and Development*. New York: McGraw-Hill.

Barker, R. G. and P. V. Gump. (1964) *Big School, Small School*. Stanford, Calif.: Stanford.

Barker, R. G. et al. (1970) "The Ecological Environment: Student Participation in Non-Class Settings" in M. B. Miles and W. W. Charters, Jr., *Learning in Social Settings*. Boston: Allyn and Bacon.

Bernard, H. W. (1970) *Human Development in Western Culture*. Boston: Allyn and Bacon.

Biggs, J. B. (1976) "Schooling and Moral Development" in V. P. Varma and P. Williams (eds.), *Piaget, Psychology, and Education*. Itasca, Ill.: Peacock.

Bijou, S. W. (1976) *Child Development: The Basic Stage of Early Childhood*. Englewood Cliffs, N.J.: Prentice-Hall.

Bijou, S. W. and D. M. Baer. (1961) *Child Development: Vol. I. A Systematic and Empirical Theory*. New York: Appleton-Century-Crofts.

Bijou, S. W. and D. M. Baer. (1965) *Child Development II: Universal Stage of Infancy*. New York: Appleton-Century-Crofts.

Bijou, S. W. and D. M. Baer. (1967) "Operant Methods in Child Behavior and Development" in S. W. Bijou and D. M. Baer, *Child Development: Readings in Experimental Analysis*. New York: Appleton-Century-Crofts.

Boyd, W. (1963) *The Educational Theory of Jean Jacques Rousseau*. New York: Russell and Russell.

Boyd, W. (ed. and trans.). (1962) *The Minor Educational Writings of Jean Jacques Rousseau*. New York: Teachers College, Columbia.

Brown, G. I. (1971) *Human Teaching for Human Learning: An Introduction to Confluent Education*. New York: Viking.

Brown, G. I. et al. (1976) *The Live Classroom*. New York: Viking-Penguin.

Brown, R. (1973) *A First Language: The Early Stages*. Cambridge, Mass.: Harvard.

Brown, R. (1970) *Psycholinguistics*. New York: Free Press.

Brunk, J. W. (1975) *Child and Adolescent Development*. New York: Wiley. Chapter 2.

Buhler, C. and M. Allen. (1972) *Introduction to Humanistic Psychology*. Monterey, Calif.: Brooks/Cole.

Buhler, C. and F. Massarik (eds.). (1968) *The Course of Human Life*. New York: Springer.

Burks, B. S. (1928) "The Relative Influence of Nature and Nurture upon Mental Development" in *Nature and Nurture. Part I: Their Influence upon Intelligence* (27th Yearbook of the National Society for the Study of Education). Bloomington, Ill.: Public School Publishing Co.

Cairns, R. B. (1977) "Sociobiology: A New Synthesis or an Old Cleavage?" *Contemporary Psychology*, Vol. 22, No. 1, pp. 1–3.

California State Penal Code. (1975) Sacramento, Calif.: State of California, Title I, Section 26.

Chomsky, N. (1967) "Review of Skinner's Verbal Behavior" in L. A. Jakobovits and M. S. Morn (eds.), *Readings in the Philosophy of Language*. Englewood Cliffs, N.J.: Prentice-Hall.

Chomsky, N. (1957) *Syntactic Structures*. The Hague: Mouton.

Coles, R. (1970) *Erik H. Erikson: The Growth of His Work*. New York: Little, Brown.

Davidson, T. (1898) *Rousseau and Education According to Nature*. New York: Scribner's.

Deutsch, J. M. (1943) "The Development of Children's Concepts of Causal Relations" in R. G. Barker, J. S. Kounin, and H. F. Wright, *Child Behavior and Development*. New York: McGraw-Hill, pp. 129–145.

Dollard J. and N. E. Miller. (1950) *Personality and Psychotherapy*. New York: McGraw-Hill.

Durkin, D. (1976) *Teaching Young Children to Read*. 2d ed. Boston: Allyn and Bacon.

Eby, F. (ed.). (1971) *Early Protestant Educators*. New York: AMS.

Eibl-Eibesfeldt, I. (1975) *Ethology. The Biology of Behavior*. 2d ed. New York: Holt, Rinehart, and Winston.

Elkind, D. (1976) *Child Development and Education*. New York: Oxford.

Erikson, E. H. (1963) *Childhood and Society*. 2d ed. New York: Norton.

Erikson, E. H. (1969) *Gandhi's Truth*. New York: Norton.

Erikson, E. H. (1959) *Identity and the Life Cycle* in *Psychological Issues* monograph, Vol. 1, No. 1. New York: International Universities.

Erikson, E. H. (1968) *Identity: Youth and Crisis*. New York: Norton.

Erikson, E. H. (1964) *Insight and Responsibility*. New York: Norton.

Erikson, E. H. (1975) *Life History and the Historical Movement*. New York: Norton.

Erikson, E. H. (1977) *Toys and Reasons*. New York: Norton.

Erikson, E. H. (1958) *Young Man Luther: A Study in Psychoanalysis and History*. New York: Norton.

Fantini, M. and G. Weinstein. (1968) *Toward a Contact Curriculum*. New York: Anti-Defamation League of B'nai B'rith.

Ford, P. L. (1962) *The New England Primer*. New York: Teachers College, Columbia.

Frenkel-Brunswik, E. (1954) *Psychoanalysis and the Unity of Science*. Proceedings of the Academy of Arts and Sciences, Vol. 80.

Freud, A. (1974) *The Writings of Anna Freud*. New York: International Universities. In five volumes.

Freud, S. (1920) "Beyond the Pleasure Principles" in J. Strachey (ed.), *The Standard Edition of the Complete Psychological Works of Sigmund Freud*. Vol. 18. London: Hogarth, 1957.

Freud, S. (1923) *The Ego and the Id*. London: Hogarth, 1974.

Freud, S. (1910) "Five Lectures on Psychoanalysis" in J. Strachey (ed.), *The Standard Edition of the Complete Psychological Works of Sigmund Freud*. Vol. 11. London: Hogarth, 1957.

Freud, S. (1900) "The Interpretation of Dreams" in J. Strachey (ed.), *The Standard Edition of the Complete Psychological Works of Sigmund Freud*. Vol. 4. London: Hogarth, 1953.

Freud, S. (1917) "Introductory Lectures on Psychoanalysis, Part III" in J. Strachey (ed.), *The Standard Edition of the Complete Psychological Works of Sigmund Freud*. Vol. 16. London: Hogarth, 1957.

Freud, S. (1938) *An Outline of Psychoanalysis*. London: Hogarth, 1973.

Froebel, F. (1889) *The Education of Man* (ed. W. N. Hailmann). New York: Appleton.

Furth, H. G. and W. Wachs. (1975) *Thinking Goes to School*. New York: Oxford.

Gesell, A. (1940) *The First Five Years of Life*. New York: Harper.

Gesell, A. and F. L. Ilg. (1949) *Child Development: An Introduction to the Study of Human Growth*. New York: Harper.

Goodenough, F. L. (1926) *Measurement of Intelligence by Drawings*. Yonkers, N.Y.: World Book.

Greven, Philip. (1977) *The Protestant Temperament: Patterns of Child Rearing, Religious Experience, and the Self in Early America*. New York: Knopf.

Guilford, J. P. (1967) *The Nature of Human Intelligence*. New York: McGraw-Hill.

Hall, C. S. (1954) *Primer of Freudian Psychology*. New York: World.

Hall, C. S. and G. Lindzey. (1970) *Theories of Personality*. 2d ed. New York: Wiley.

Hall, G. S. (1904) *Adolescence*. New York: Appleton. In two volumes.

Hall, G. S. (1891) "The Contents of Children's Minds on Entering School." *Pedagogical Seminar*, Vol. 1, pp. 139–173.

Hamilton, W. D. (1964) "The Genetical Evolution of Social Behavior." *Journal of Theoretical Biology*, Vol. 7, pp. 1–52.

Hammer, E. F. (1958) *The Clinical Application of Projective Drawings*. Springfield, Ill.: Thomas.

Harris, D. B. (1963) *Children's Drawings as Measures of Intellectual Maturity*. New York: Harcourt, Brace, and World.

Harris, M. L. and C. H. Harris. (1971) "A Factor Analytic Interpretation Strategy." *Educational and Psychological Measurement*, Vol. 31, pp. 589–606.

Hartmann, H. (1959) "Psychoanalysis as a Scientific Theory" in S. Hook (ed.), *Psychoanalysis, Scientific Method, and Philosophy*. New York: New York University.

Hartshorne, H. and M. A. May (1928–1930) *Studies in the Nature of Character*. New York: Macmillan. In three volumes.

Havighurst, R. J. (1953) *Human Development and Education*. New York: Longmans, Green.

Heafford, M. (1967) *Pestalozzi, His Thought and Its Relevance Today*. London: Methuen.

Hebb, D. O. (1949) *The Organization of Behavior*. New York: Wiley.

Hebb, D. O. (1970) "A Return to Jensen and His Social Critics." *American Psychologist*, Vol. 25, p. 568.

Heider, F. (1958) *The Psychology of Interpersonal Relations*. New York: Wiley.

Hilgard, E. R. (1952) "Experimental Approaches to Psychoanalysis" in E. Pumpian-Mindlin, *Psychoanalysis as Science*. Stanford, Calif.: Stanford.

Hilgard, E. R. and G. H. Bower. (1975) *Theories of Learning*. 4th ed. Englewood Cliffs, N.J.: Prentice-Hall.

Hinde, R. A. (1974) *Biological Bases of Human Social Behavior*. New York: McGraw-Hill.

Hirsch, J. (1970) "Behavior-Genetic Analysis and Its Biosocial Consequences." *Seminars in Psychiatry*, Vol. 2, pp. 89–105.

Hook, S. (1959) "Science and Mythology in Psychoanalysis" in S. Hook (ed.), *Psychoanalysis, Scientific Method, and Philosophy*. New York: New York University.

Hurlock, E. B. (1968) *Developmental Psychology*. 3d ed. New York: McGraw-Hill.

Ilg, F. L. and L. B. Ames. (1955) *The Gesell Institute's Child Behavior*. New York: Dell.

Inhelder, B. (1968) "Foreword" in I. E. Sigel and F. H. Hooper (eds.), *Logical Thinking in Children*. New York: Holt, Rinehart, and Winston.

Inhelder, B. and J. Piaget. (1964) *The Early Growth of Logic in the Child*. London: Routledge and Kegan Paul.

Inhelder, B. and J. Piaget. (1958) *The Growth of Logical Thinking from Childhood to Adolescence*. New York: Basic Books.

Jensen, A. R. (1973) *Educability and Group Differences*. New York: Harper & Row.

Jensen, A. R. (1969) "How Much Can We Boost IQ and Scholastic Achievement?" *Harvard Educational Review*, Vol. 39, pp. 1–123.

Jolles, I. (1952) *A Catalogue for the Qualitative Interpretation of the H-T-P*. Beverly Hills, Calif.: Western Psychological Services.

Jones, E. (1961) *The Life and Works of Sigmund Freud*. New York: Basic Books.

Jones, E. E. and R. E. Nisbett. (1971) *The Actor and the Observer: Divergent Perceptions of the Causes of Behavior*. Morristown, N.J.: General Learning.

Kantor, J. R. (1959) *Interbehavioral Psychology*. 2d rev. ed. Bloomington, Ind.: Principia.

Keller, F. S. and W. N. Schoenfeld. (1950) *Principles of Psychology*. New York: Appleton-Century-Crofts.

Kelley, H. H. (1973) "The Process of Causal Attribution." *American Psychologist*, Vol. 28, pp. 107–128.

Kendler, H. H. and T. S. Kendler. (1975) "Discrimination and Development" in W. K. Estes (ed.), *Handbook of Learning and Cognitive Processes*. New York: Halsted, pp. 191–247.

Kephart, N. C. (1960, 1st ed.; 1971, 2d ed.) *The Slow Learner in the Classroom*. Columbus, Ohio: Merrill.

Kilpatrick, W. H. (1916) *Froebel's Kindergarten Principles Critically Examined*. New York: Macmillan.

Kohlberg, L. (1968b) "The Child as a Moral Philosopher." *Psychology Today*, Vol. 2, No. 4, pp. 25–30.

Kohlberg, L. (1971) "From Is to Ought" in T. Mischel, *Cognitive Development and Epistemology*. New York: Academic.

Kohlberg, L. (1968a) "Moral Development" in *International Encyclopedia of the Social Sciences*. New York: Macmillan.

Kohlberg, L. (1967) "Moral and Religious Education in the Public Schools: A Developmental View" in T. R. Sizer, *Religion and Public Education*. New York: Houghton Mifflin.

Kohlberg, L. and R. Kramer. (1969) "Continuities in Childhood and Adult Moral Development." *Human Development*, Vol. 12, pp. 93–120.

Koppitz, E. M. (1968) *Psychological Evaluation of Children's Human Figure Drawings*. New York: Grune and Stratton.

Kounin, J. S. (1943) "Intellectual Development and Rigidity" in R. G. Barker, J. S. Kounin, and H. F. Wright, *Child Behavior and Development*. New York: McGraw-Hill.

Kris, E. (1947) "The Nature of Psychoanalytic Propositions and Their Validation" in S. Hook and M. R. Konvitz, *Freedom and Experience*. Ithaca, N.Y.: Cornell.

Kuhn, T. S. (1962) *The Structure of Scientific Revolutions*. Chicago: University of Chicago Press.

Langer, J. (1969) *Theories of Development*. New York: Holt, Rinehart, and Winston.

Lashley, K. S. (1960) *The Neuropsychology of Lashley: Selected Papers*. F. A. Beach et al., eds. New York: McGraw-Hill.

Laslett, P. in D. B. Rutman. (1970) *American Puritanism*. Philadelphia: Lippincott.

Layzer, D. (1974) "Heritability Analyses of IQ Scores: Science or Numerology?" *Science*, Vol. 183, pp. 1259–1266.

Leahy, A. M. (1935) "Nature–Nurture and Intelligence." *Genetic Psychology Monographs*, Vol. 17, pp. 236–308.

Leff, H. L. (1978) *Experience, Environment, and Human Potentials*. New York: Oxford.

Lerner, J. (1971) *Children with Learning Disabilities*. New York: Houghton Mifflin.

Lerner, R. M. (1976) *Concepts and Theories of Human Development*. Reading, Mass.: Addison-Wesley.

Lewin, K. (1939) "The Field Theory Approach to Adolescence." *American Journal of Sociology*, Vol. 44, pp. 868–896.

Lewin, K. (1942) "Field Theory and Learning" in *Forty-First Yearbook, National Society for the Study of Education, Part II*. Bloomington, Ill.: Public School Publishing Co.

Lewin, K. (1936) *Principles of Topological Psychology*. New York: McGraw-Hill.

Lorenz, K. (1965) *Evolution and Modification of Behavior*. Chicago: University of Chicago.

Lowenfeld, V. (1957) *Creative and Mental Growth*. New York: Macmillan.

Luria, A. R. (1976) *Cognitive Development: Its Cultural and Social Foundations*. Cambridge, Mass.: Harvard.

Luther, M. (1530) "About Aesop's Fables" in F. Eby (ed.), *Early Protestant Educators*. New York: AMS, 1971.

Luther, M. (1519a) "Duties of Parents in Training Children" in F. Eby (ed.), *Early Protestant Educators*. New York: AMS, 1971.

Luther, M. (1519b) "Evil of Lax Discipline" in F. Eby (ed.), *Early Protestant Educators*. New York: AMS, 1971.

Luther, M. (1523) "Harsh Methods Opposed" in F. Eby (ed.), *Early Protestant Educators*. New York: AMS, 1971.

Luther, M. (1529) "A Short Catechism for the Use of Ordinary Pastors and Preachers" in F. Eby (ed.), *Early Protestant Educators*. New York: AMS, 1971.

MacDougall, W. (1908) *An Introduction to Social Psychology*. London: Methuen.

Machover, K. (1949) *Personality Projection in the Drawing of the Human Figure*. Springfield, Ill.: Thomas.

Maier, H. W. (1978) *Three Theories of Child Development: Erik H. Erikson, Jean Piaget, and Robert R. Sears*. 3d ed. New York: Harper & Row.

Maslow, A. H. (1971) *The Farther Reaches of Human Nature*. New York: Viking.

Maslow, A. H. (1970) *Motivation and Personality*. 2d ed. New York: Harper & Row.

Maslow, A. H. (1968) *Toward a Psychology of Being*. Princeton, N.J.: Van Nostrand.

Miller, P. (1963) *The New England Mind: The Seventeenth Century*. Cambridge, Mass.: Harvard.

Montagu, A. (1959) *Human Heredity*. New York: Harcourt, Brace, and World.

Montessori, M. (1967) *The Absorbent Mind*. New York: Dell.

Morgan, E. S. (1956) *The Puritan Family*. Boston: Trustees of the Public Library.

Morison, S. E. (1936) *The Puritan Pronaos*. New York: New York University.

Mussen, P. H., J. Langer, and M. Covington (eds.). (1969) *Trends and Issues in Developmental Psychology*. New York: Holt, Rinehart, and Winston.

Nagel, E. (1959) "Methodological Issues in Psychoanalytic Theory" in S. Hook (ed.), *Psychoanalysis, Scientific Method, and Philosophy*. New York: New York University.

New England Primer: Or An Easy and Pleasant Guide to the Art of Reading. (1836) Boston: Massachusetts Sabbath School Society.

Norton, J. in P. Miller. (1963) *The New England Mind: The Seventeenth Century*. Cambridge, Mass.: Harvard.

Otto, H. and J. Mann. (1968) *Ways of Growth*. New York: Grossman.

Park, T. Z. (1970) *The Acquisition of German Syntax.* Bern: University of Bern.

Patterson, S. W. (1971) *Rousseau's Emile and Early Children's Literature.* Metuchen, N.Y.: Scarecrow.

Peel, E. A. (1976) "The Thinking and Education of the Adolescent" in V. P. Varma and P. Williams (eds.), *Piaget, Psychology, and Education.* Itasca, Ill.: Peacock.

Pepper, S. C. (1942) *World Hypotheses: A Study in Evidence.* Berkeley, Calif.: University of California Press.

Peters, R. S. (1971) "Moral Development: A Plea for Pluralism" in T. Mischel, *Cognitive Development and Epistemology.* New York: Academic.

Phillips, D. C. and M. E. Kelly. (1975) "Hierarchical Theories of Development in Education and Psychology." *Harvard Educational Review,* Vol. 45, No. 3, pp. 351–375.

Phillips, J. L. (1975) *The Origins of Intellect: Piaget's Theory.* 2d ed. San Francisco: W. H. Freeman.

Piaget, J. (1973) *The Child and Reality.* New York: Viking.

Piaget, J. (1969) *The Child's Conception of Movement and Speed.* New York: Basic Books.

Piaget, J. (1952) *The Child's Conception of Number.* London: Routledge and Kegan Paul.

Piaget, J. (1930) *The Child's Conception of Physical Causality.* London: Routledge and Kegan Paul.

Piaget, J. (1946) *Le Développement de la Notion de Temps chez l'Enfant.* Paris: Presses Universitaires de France.

Piaget, J. (1970a) *Genetic Epistemology.* New York: Columbia.

Piaget, J. (1953) *Logic and Psychology.* Manchester: Manchester University.

Piaget, J. (1948) *The Moral Judgment of the Child.* Glencoe, Ill.: Free Press.

Piaget, J. (1963) *The Origins of Intelligence in Children.* 2d ed. New York: Norton.

Piaget, J. (1951) *Play, Dreams, and Imitation in Childhood.* New York: Norton.

Piaget, J. (1972) *Psychology and Epistemology.* London: Penguin.

Piaget, J. (1950) *The Psychology of Intelligence.* London: Routledge and Kegan Paul.

Piaget, J. (1970b) *Science of Education and the Psychology of the Child*. New York: Viking.

Piaget, J., L. Apostel, and B. Mandelbrot. (1957) *Logique et Equilibre*. Paris: Presses Universitaires de France.

Piaget, J. and B. Inhelder. (1956) *The Child's Conception of Space*. London: Routledge and Kegan Paul.

Piaget, J. and B. Inhelder. (1969) *The Psychology of the Child*. New York: Basic Books.

Piaget, J., A. Jonckheere, and B. Mandelbrot. (1958) *La Lecture de l'Expérience* (Etudes d'Epistémologie Génétique V). Paris: Presses Universitaires de France.

Piaget, J. and A. Szeminska. (1952) *The Child's Conception of Number*. New York: Humanities Press.

Reese, H. W. and W. F. Overton. (1970) "Models of Development and Theories of Development" in L. R. Goulet and Paul B. Baltes, *Life-Span Developmental Psychology*. New York: Academic.

Rogers, C. R. (1973) "My Philosophy of Interpersonal Relationships and How It Grew." *Journal of Humanistic Psychology*, Vol. 13, No. 2, pp. 13–15.

Rogers, C. R. (1961) *On Becoming a Person*. Boston: Houghton Mifflin.

Rousseau, J. J. (1955) *Emile* (trans. B. Foxley). New York: Dutton, Everyman's Library.

Rousseau, J. J. (1773) *Emilius; or, A Treatise of Education*. Edinburgh: W. Coke. In three volumes.

Royce, J. (1959) "Herbert Spencer" in *Encyclopedia Americana*. Vol. 25. New York: Americana.

Rutman, D. B. (1970) *American Puritanism*. Philadelphia: Lippincott.

Scarr-Salapatek, S. (1971a) "Race, Social Class, and IQ." *Science*, Vol. 174, pp. 1285–1295.

Scarr-Salapatek, S. (1971b) "Unknowns in the IQ Equation." *Science*, Vol. 174, pp. 1223–1228.

Schneirla, T. C. in L. R. Aronson, E. Tobach, J. S. Rosenblatt, and D. S. Lehrman. (1972) *Selected Writings of T. C. Schneirla*. San Francisco: W. H. Freeman.

Schneirla, T. C. and J. S. Rosenblatt. (1963) " 'Critical Periods' in Behavioral Development." *Science*, Vol. 139, pp. 1110–1114.

Scott, J. P. (1963) "Critical Periods in Behavioral Development." *Science,* Vol. 138, pp. 949–958.

Scriven, M. (1959) "The Experimental Investigation of Psychoanalysis" in S. Hook (ed.), *Psychoanalysis, Scientific Method, and Philosophy.* New York: New York University.

Sears, R. R. (1943) "Survey of Objective Studies of Psychoanalytic Concepts." *Bulletin: Social Science Research Council,* p. 51.

Sears, R. R., E. E. Maccoby, and H. Levin. (1957) *Patterns of Child Rearing.* Evanston, Ill.: Row, Peterson.

Sears, R. R., L. Rau, and R. Alpert. (1965) *Identification and Child Rearing.* Stanford, Calif.: Stanford.

Sheldon, W. H. (1940) *Varieties of Physique.* New York: Harper.

Sheldon, W. H. (1942) *Varieties of Temperament.* New York: Harper.

Shuttleworth, F. K. (1935) "The Nature versus Nurture Problem: II. The Contributions of Nature and Nurture to Individual Differences in Intelligence." *Journal of Educational Psychology,* Vol. 26, pp. 655–681.

Sidgwick, A. (1959) "Recapitulation" in *The Encyclopedia Americana.* Vol. 23. New York: Americana.

Sigel, I. E. and F. H. Hooper. (1968) *Logical Thinking in Children.* New York: Holt, Rinehart, and Winston.

Simonson, H. P. (ed.). (1970) *Selected Writings of Jonathan Edwards.* New York: Ungar.

Skeels, H. M. (1940) "Some Iowa Studies of the Mental Growth of Children in Relation to Differentials of the Environment: A Summary." *Intelligence: Its Nature and Nurture* (39th Yearbook of the National Society for the Study of Education). Bloomington, Ill.: Public School Publishing Co.

Skinner, B. F. (1974) *About Behaviorism.* New York: Knopf.

Skinner, B. F. (1950) "Are Theories of Learning Necessary?" *Psychological Review,* Vol. 57, pp. 193–216.

Skinner, B. F. (1945) "Baby in a Box" in B. F. Skinner (ed.), *Cumulative Record: A Selection of Papers.* 3d ed. New York: Appleton-Century-Crofts, 1972.

Skinner, B. F. (1948) *Walden Two.* New York: Macmillan.

Skodak, M. (1939) "Children in Foster Homes: A Study of Mental Development." *University of Iowa Studies in Child Welfare,* Vol. 16, No. 1.

Smith, J. E. (1959) *The Works of Jonathan Edwards, Volume 2: Religious Affections.* New Haven: Yale.

Spence, K. W. (1965) in Melvin H. Marx (ed.), *Theories in Contemporary Psychology.* New York: Macmillan.

Stevick, D. B. (1968) *B. F. Skinner's Walden Two.* New York: Seabury.

Stone, L. J. and J. Church. (1973) *Childhood and Adolescence.* 3d ed. New York: Random House.

Suppes, P. C. (1969) *Studies in the Methodology and Foundations of Science.* Dordrecht, Holland: R. Reidel.

Thomas, R. M. and S. M. Thomas. (1965) *Individual Differences in the Classroom.* New York: McKay.

Travers, J. F. (1977) *The Growing Child.* New York: Wiley.

Trivers, R. L. and H. Hare. (1976) "Haplodipoidy and the Evolution of the Social Insects." *Science,* Vol. 191, pp. 249–263.

Tronick, E. and P. M. Greenfield. (1973) *Infant Curriculum: The Bromley-Heath Guide to the Care of Infants in Groups.* New York: Media Projects.

Tryon, C. and J. Lilienthal. (1950) "Developmental Tasks: I. The Concept and Its Importance" in *Fostering Mental Health in Our Schools.* Washington, D.C.: Association for Supervision and Curriculum Development, National Education Association, pp. 77–89.

Vaughn, A. T. (1972) *The Puritan Tradition in America, 1620–1730.* Columbia, S.C.: University of South Carolina.

Vygotsky, L. S. (1971) *Psychology of Art.* Cambridge, Mass.: Massachusetts Institute of Technology.

Vygotsky, L. S. (1962) *Thought and Language.* Cambridge, Mass.: Massachusetts Institute of Technology.

Wadsworth, B. J. (1971) *Piaget's Theory of Cognitive Development.* New York: McKay.

Wapner, S. and H. Werner. (1965) *The Body Percept.* New York: Random House.

Watson, J. B. (1914) *Behavior, an Introduction to Comparative Psychology.* New York: Holt, Rinehart, and Winston.

Watson, J. B. (1919) *Psychology from the Standpoint of a Behaviorist.* Philadelphia: Lippincott.

Weiner, B. (1974) *Achievement Motivation and Attribution Theory.* Morristown, N.J.: General Learning.

Weiner, B. (1972) *Theories of Motivation*. Chicago: Markham.

Werner, H. (1961) *Comparative Psychology of Mental Development*. New York: Science Editions.

Werner, H. and B. Kaplan. (1963) *Symbol Formation—An Organismic-Developmental Approach to Language and the Expression of Thought*. New York: Wiley.

White, B. L. (1971) *Human Infants: Experience and Psychological Development*. Englewood Cliffs, N.J.: Prentice-Hall.

Wilson, E. O. (1975) *Sociobiology: The New Synthesis*. Cambridge, Mass.: Harvard.

Wohlwill, J. R. (1976) "The Age Variable in Psychological Research" in N. S. Endler, L. R. Boulter, and H. Osser, *Contemporary Issues in Developmental Psychology*. New York: Holt, Rinehart, and Winston.

Wolman, B. B. (1968) *The Unconscious Mind*. Englewood Cliffs, N.J.: Prentice-Hall.

Woodworth, R. S. (1929) *Psychology*. New York: Holt, Rinehart, and Winston.

Wright, H. F. (1943) "The Effect of Barriers upon Strength of Motivation" in R. G. Barker, J. S. Kounin, and W. F. Wright, *Child Behavior and Development*. New York: McGraw-Hill.

Zigler, E. (1965) "Metatheoretical Issues in Developmental Psychology" in M. H. Marx (ed.), *Theories in Contemporary Psychology*. New York: Macmillan.

INDEX OF NAMES

This index contains two types of names: (1) those of people whose specific publications are cited in the text and (2) those of people whose ideas are cited but whose specific publications are not.

Kris, E., 257
Kuhn, T. S., 12

Langer, J., 53, 180
Lashley, K. S., 186
Laslett, P., 67
Laurendreau, M., 323
Layzer, D., 39, 211
Leahy, A. M., 33
Leff, H. L., 448
Lerner, J., 458–459
Lerner, R. M., 26, 37–38, 75, 183, 211
Lewin, K., 4, 7–9, 21, 31, 48, 124, 143–168
Lilienthal, J., 126–133, 140
Lindgren, H. C., 53
Lindzey, G., 13, 26, 45, 46, 168
Locke, J., 32, 74
Lorenz, K., 186
Luria, A. R., 331, 345, 346
Luther, M., 55, 59, 64, 67, 69, 284

Machover, K., 466
Magnus, A., 59
Maier, H. W., 424, 429
Mandelbrot, B., 293, 298
Marx, M. H., 27
Maslow, A. H., 25, 41, 44–47, 49, 431–449
Massarik, F., 438–439
Mather, C., 57, 66, 67
May, M. A., 367
Medinnus, G. R., 53
Meyer, M., 393
Miller, N. E., 28, 257, 423
Miller, P., 59, 61–63, 72
Montagu, A., 35
Montessori, M., 49, 56, 83–84, 451, 453–455
Morgan, E. S., 64–67, 69, 72
Morison, S. E., 57
Musinger, H., 53
Mussen, P. H., 53

Nagel, E., 257–259
Norton, J., 62

Overton, W. F., 12, 27

Park, T. Z., 354, 362
Patterson, S. W., 74
Pavlov, I. P., 385–386
Peel, E. A., 322
Pepper, S. C., 12
Perls, F., 437
Pestalozzi, J. H., 83, 451, 453
Peters, R. S., 381–382
Phillips, D. C., 42
Phillips, J. L., 290, 321, 323, 330
Piaget, J., 4–5, 21, 23, 42, 47–48, 287–330, 346, 372, 378, 427, 462
Pinard, A., 323
Plato, 74
Prescott, D., 126

Rau, L., 429
Redl, F., 126
Reese, H. W., 12, 27
Rogers, C. R., 431, 437
Rogers, D., 53
Rosenblatt, J. S., 87
Rousseau, J. J., 18–19, 25, 32–33, 40, 44, 49–51, 55–56, 73–87, 423
Royce, J., 171
Rutman, D. B., 67

Scarr-Salapatek, S., 211
Schneirla, T. C., 87, 186
Schoenfeld, W. N., 391–392
Scott, J. P., 87
Scriven, M., 258
Sears, R. R., 257, 384, 423–425, 429
Sewall, S., 57
Sheldon, W., 119–120
Sherman, P. W., 214
Shuttleworth, F. K., 33
Sidgwick, A., 170
Sigel, I. E., 327, 330
Simonson, H. P., 62–63
Skeels, H. M., 34
Skinner, B. F., 4, 8–10, 12, 27, 31, 40, 48, 50, 358, 384–407, 427–429, 442
Skodak, M., 34

INDEX OF SUBJECTS